With over 1,000,000 copies of our MCSE, MCSD, CompTIA, and Cisco study guides in print, we have come to know many of you personally. By listening, we've learned what you like and dislike about typical computer books. The most requested item has been a web-based service that keeps you current on the topic of the book and related technologies. In response, we have created solutions@syngress.com, a service that includes the following features:

- A one-year warranty against content obsolescence that occurs as the result of vendor product upgrades. We will provide regular web updates for affected chapters.

- Monthly mailings that respond to customer FAQs and provide detailed explanations of the most difficult topics, written by content experts exclusively for solutions@syngress.com.

- Regularly updated links to sites that as our editors have determined offer valuable additional information on key topics.

- Access to "Ask the Author"™ customer query forms that allow readers to post questions to be addressed by our authors and editors.

Once you've purchased this book, browse to

www.syngress.com/solutions.

To register, you will need to have the book handy to verify your purchase.

Thank you for giving us the opportunity to serve you.

SYNGRESS®

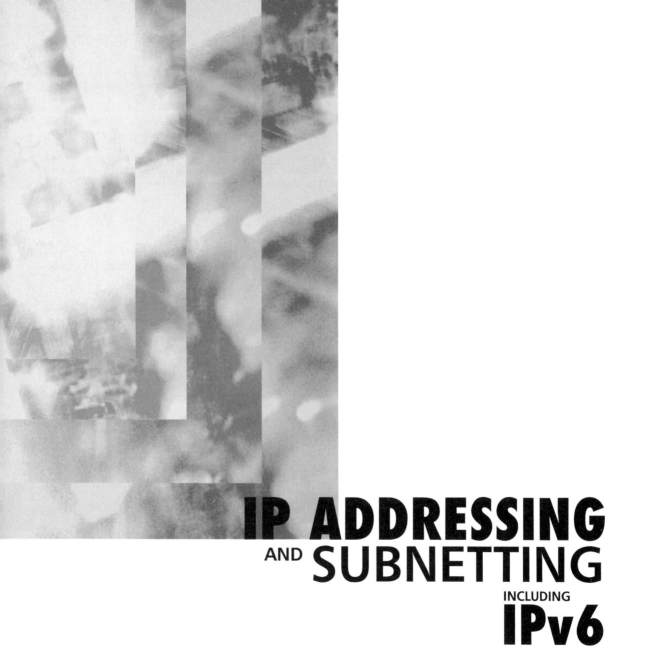

IP ADDRESSING
AND SUBNETTING
INCLUDING
IPv6

SYNGRESS®

KEY	SERIAL NUMBER
001	JF87NBH615
002	KFJB876AAZ
003	LK1AN65498
004	FH766T1NA9
005	JF786B12BV
006	NN7FH419AS
007	FF8AF73198
008	776FNGF67B
009	7683NG5T99
010	WE67822VMA

PUBLISHED BY
Syngress Media, Inc.
800 Hingham Street
Rockland, MA 02370

IP ADDRESSING AND SUBNETTING INCLUDING IPv6

Printed in the United States of America

1 2 3 4 5 6 7 8 9 0

ISBN: 1-928994-01-6

Copy Editor: Adrienne Rebello
Technical Editor: Mark Blanchet
Indexer: Robert Saigh
Product Line Manager: Eva Banaszek

Proofreader: Jim Melkonian
Graphic Artists: Emily Eagar and Vesna Williams
Co-Publisher: Richard Kristof, Global Knowledge

Acknowledgments

We would like to acknowledge the following people for their kindness and support in making this book possible.

Richard Kristof, Duncan Anderson, Jennifer Gould, Robert Woodruff, Kevin Murray, Dale Leatherwood, Shelley Everett, Laurie Hedrick, Rhonda Harmon, Lisa Lavallee, and Robert Sanregret of Global Knowledge, for their generous access to the IT industry's best courses, instructors and training facilities.

Ralph Troupe and the team at Rt. 1 Solutions for their invaluable insight into the challenges of designing, deploying and supporting world-class enterprise networks.

Karen Cross, Kim Wylie, Harry Kirchner, John Hays, Bill Richter, Michael Ruggiero, Kevin Votel, Brittin Clark, Sarah Schaffer, Luke Kreinberg, Ellen Lafferty and Sarah MacLachlan of Publishers Group West for sharing their incredible marketing experience and expertise.

Peter Hoenigsberg, Mary Ging, Caroline Hird, Simon Beale, Julia Oldknow, Kelly Burrows, Jonathan Bunkell, Catherine Anderson, Peet Kruger, Pia Rasmussen, Denelise L'Ecluse, Rosanna Ramacciotti, Marek Lewinson, Marc Appels, Paul Chrystal, Femi Otesanya, and Tracey Alcock of Harcourt International for making certain that our vision remains world-wide in scope.

From Global Knowledge

At Global Knowledge we strive to support the multiplicity of learning styles required by our students to achieve success as technical professionals. As the world's largest IT training company, Global Knowledge is uniquely positioned to offer these books. The expertise gained each year from providing instructor-led training to hundreds of thousands of students worldwide has been captured in book form to enhance your learning experience. We hope that the quality of these books demonstrates our commitment to your lifelong learning success. Whether you choose to learn through the written word, computer based training, Web delivery, or instructor-led training, Global Knowledge is committed to providing you with the very best in each of these categories. For those of you who know Global Knowledge, or those of you who have just found us for the first time, our goal is to be your lifelong competency partner.

Thank your for the opportunity to serve you. We look forward to serving your needs again in the future.

Warmest regards,

Duncan Anderson
President and Chief Executive Officer,
Global Knowledge

Contributors

Cameron Brandon (MCSE, CNE, CNA, MCSE+Internet, A+, Network+) works as a Network Engineer/Administrator in Portland, Oregon, and he specializes in Windows NT with BackOffice Integration. He helped in Intel Corporation's large-scale migration at its Oregon facility to Windows NT. Cameron completed all of his certifications in five months, demonstrating that determination and a strong sense of direction are the key to success in one's career.

Ryan Russell (CCNA, CCNP) has been employed in the networking field for more than 10 years, including more than five years working with Cisco equipment. He has held IT positions ranging from help desk support to network design, providing him with a good perspective on the challenges that face a network manager. Recently, Ryan has been doing mostly information security work involving network security and firewalls. He has completed his CCNP and holds a Bachelor of Science degree in Computer Science.

John Pherson (Microsoft MCSE and MCT, Novell Master CNE and Master CNI, and Certified Cisco Systems Instructor), has more than 18 years of technical-consulting and technical-management experience in the computer industry, specializing in networking technologies and operating systems. He also has a B.S. in Business Administration. John has been a member of several CompTIA (Computer Industry Technology Association) committees responsible for the growth and direction of the A+ Certification. He is also a contributing author to several books, including CCNA Study Guide (Osborne/McGraw-Hill, 1998) and the MCSE: Networking Essentials Study Guide (Osborne/McGraw-Hill, 1998). He is a member of American Mensa, Ltd. John is currently employed as an Instructional Consultant at Global Knowledge in Dallas, TX., and he also provides independent network consulting services.

J.D. Wegner is a founder and director of The Empowerment Group, Inc. He has been working with computers for over 30 years. The last twelve of those, he has been involved with the design, installation and support of data networks. As an instructor and Course Director for Global Knowledge, he has presented topics ranging from Internetworking with TCP/IP to Web Security to IP Address Management to thousands of IT professionals in the U.S. and abroad. His clients include many of the Fortune 500 as well as several government agencies. He lives in Hickory, North Carolina with his wife, Laurie, and their two children, David and Sarah.

Robert Rockell has been at Sprint Internet Services for the past 3 years. He currently works in the Operations Engineering department, where he and his group are responsible for top-level technical escalation of all Internet operation problems. In addition, Rob runs an IPv6 network with over 50 customers attached. If interested, you can join the 6Bone through Rob's network by writing him at rrockell@sprint.net.

Technical Editor

Marc Blanchet (Marc.Blanchet@viagenie.qc.ca) is a network engineer working at Viagenie Inc. as a consultant in network security, network architectures and electronic commerce for companies, organisations and governments. He has been involved in TCP/IP since 1983. Marc wrote a book in French entitled *TCP/IP Simplifii* published at Iditions Logiques. At the Internet Engineering Task Force (IETF), he has been involved in many working groups, especially in IPv6 group, for which he wrote a few standard documents. One of those is about IPv6 address assignments. Marc is also an architect of the IPv6 CA*Net network and the 6tap IPv6 exchange. He is a regular speaker at conferences and gives courses about TCP/IP, Security, IPv6 and other related subjects.

Contents

Preface

Solutions in this chapter:

- Why this Book is Necessary
- Content of this Book
- Editor's Acknowledgments

Why this Book is Necessary

Internet Protocol (IP), the network protocol of the Internet, is seen as the protocol for the convergence of telephony and data. Addressing is an important part of network engineering, either in the telephony world or the Internet world. One of the richest parts of IP is its addressing. Addressing has been so well designed in IP that the Internet has grown from three computers to hundreds of millions of computers, used in day-to-day work and fun, while remaining efficient.

As you will see, this book discusses two versions of IP: IPv4 and IPv6. The current Internet is IPv4 (Internet Protocol version 4), and the new Internet beginning to be deployed is based on IPv6 (Internet Protocol version 6). This book describes addressing for both versions.

Although many books cover TCP/IP, no book really goes into as much depth with all issues related to IP addressing as this one does. The intended audience of this comprehensive, intermediate-level book is someone with a technical or management background, who understands the basics of TCP/IP and wants a complete hand-book related to addressing.

Addressing is so important in any networking world that a mis-understanding can have important consequences. For example, a poorly designed addressing architecture for a large network can cause the organization to renumber the whole network, which can involve a long down-time as well as instability during the renumbering phase. This can cost a lot of money. But, at the same time, a good addressing architecture costs no money, just good planning and good understanding of the issues. This is one reason why this book exists.

Content of this Book

Chapter 1, "Addressing and Subnetting Basics," discusses the IPv4 addressing architecture, which is the basis of this book. Classes and subnetting are key in the IPv4 design. Once you understand IP addresses, Chapter 2, "Creating an Addressing Plan for Fixed-Length Mask Networks," tells you how to make an address plan for your network.

If your network is not connected to the Internet, or if you use any kind of network address translation (NAT) device, you are going to use the private addresses reserved for that purpose. Private addresses are detailed in Chapter 3, "Private Addressing and Subnetting Large Networks." If you use NAT, or simply want to know about it, then you should read Chapter 4, "Network Address Translation," which is a comprehensive chapter on this technology.

Although most networks can have a good address plan using standard subnetting techniques, some networks need variable-length subnet masks (VLSM), mostly because they are not balanced in the ratio of number of networks to number of hosts. VLSM is covered in Chapter 5, "Variable-Length Subnet Masking."

IP addressing is the basis of routing; Chapter 6, "Routing Issues," deals with all the details of routing as they relate to addressing.

IP requires more configuration in comparison with other LAN protocols. These issues have been resolved by BOOTP and DHCP, which are covered in Chapter 7, "Automatic Assignment of IP Addresses with BOOTP and DCHP."

Multicast provides a way to have one-to-many or many-to-many packets by giving the group of destination hosts a specific and special IP address in the class D range. This is a great and innovative way to use IP addressing, and it is covered in Chapter 8, "Multicast Addressing."

Since the growth rate of the Internet is phenomenal, engineers developed a new version of the IP protocol, called IPv6, which brings new schemes of addressing. With addressing, IPv6 enables autoconfiguration, renumbering, efficient routing on the backbone, etc. Chapters 9 and 10, "IPv6 Addressing" and "The IPv6 Header," discuss IPv6 and its header and addressing structure in depth.

The entire book covers the technology of IP addressing. In addition, you need to get a range of addresses for your network. The Annex discusses address assignments and registration.

This book demonstrates that IP addressing is a very important feature of IP, which has evolved over time, as the Internet and other organizations needed change. The new version of IP, IPv6, continues to use addressing as an important tool for network engineering.

Editor's Acknowledgments

I would like to thank Eva Banaszek and Matt Pedersen from Syngress Media for their support; my colleagues of Viagénie (Florent Parent, Régis Desmeules, and Annie Morin) with whom I always have good discussions on technical issues that enrich my own experience; Hélène Richard, our technical writer, who reviewed my own chapters, and finally my wife, for all her patience.

I hope you will enjoy this comprehensive book on IP addressing.

—*Marc Blanchet*

Chapter 1

Addressing and Subnetting Basics

Solutions in this chapter:

- **IP Address Basics**
- **Purpose of Subnetting**
- **The Basic Fixed Length Mask**

IP Address Basics

IPv4 addressing is used to assign a logical address to a physical device. That sounds like a lot to think about, but actually it is very simple. Two devices in an Ethernet network can exchange information because each of them has a network interface card with a unique Ethernet address that exists in the physical Ethernet network. If device A wants to send information to device B, device A will need to know the Ethernet address of device B. Protocols like Microsoft NetBIOS require that each device broadcast its address so that the other devices may learn it. IP uses a process called the Address Resolution Protocol. In either case, the addresses are hardware addresses and can be used on the local physical network.

For IT Professionals

RFC

In this chapter you will see references to the term RFC. An RFC, Request For Comment, is a document created by the Internet community to define processes, procedures, and standards that control how the Internet and associated protocols work. Each RFC is assigned a number and a title that describes the contents. As an example, RFC791 is entitled "Internet Protocol" and is the standard that defines the features, functions, and processes of the IP protocol. RFCs are free and the whole text of any RFC can be downloaded from the Internet. You can find them at the following URL: http://www.isi.edu/in-notes.

As an IT Professional, you may often ask, "Why did they do that?" Since the RFC is the official documentation of the Internet, you can often gain insight into why things are the way they are by reading RFCs related to your question.

What happens if device B, on an Ethernet network, wants to send information to device C on a token-ring network? They cannot communicate directly because they are on different physical networks. To solve the addressing problems of both device A and B, we use a higher layer protocol such as IPv4. IPv4 allows us to assign a logical address to a physical device. No matter what communication method is in use, we can identify a device by a unique logical address that can be translated to a physical address for actual information transfer.

Classful Addressing–Structure and Size of Each Type

The designers of IPv4 faced an addressing dilemma. In the early days of Internet development, networks were small and networking devices were big. Another issue was the future. In the early 1970s, the engineers creating the Internet were not aware of the coming changes in computers and communications. The invention of local area networking and personal computers was to have a momentous impact on future networks. Developers understood their current environment and created a logical addressing strategy based on their understanding of networks at the time.

They knew they needed logical addressing and determined that an address containing 32 bits was sufficient for their needs. As a matter of fact, a 32-bit address is large enough to provide 2^{32} or 4,294,967,296 individual addresses. Since all networks were not going to be the same size, the addresses needed to be grouped together for administrative purposes. Some groups needed to be large, some of moderate size, and some small. These administrative groupings were called address classes.

For IT Professionals

Addressing

From RFC791, page 7:

"A distinction is made between names, addresses, and routes [4]. A name indicates what we seek. An address indicates where it is. A route indicates how to get there. The internet protocol deals primarily with addresses. It is the task of higher level (i.e., host-to-host or application) protocols to make the mapping from names to addresses. The internet module maps internet addresses to local net addresses. It is the task of lower level (i.e., local net or gateways) procedures to make the mapping from local net addresses to routes. Addresses are fixed length of four octets (32 bits). An address begins with a network number, followed by local address (called the "rest" field). There are three formats or classes of internet addresses: in class a, the high order bit is zero, the next 7 bits are the network, and the last 24 bits are the local address; in class b, the high order two bits are one-zero, the next 14 bits are the network and the last 16 bits are the local address; in class c, the high order three bits are one-one-zero, the next 21 bits are the network and the last 8 bits are the local address."

IPv4 addresses are expressed in dotted decimal notation. For example, a 32-bit address may look like this in binary:

01111110100010000000000100101111

To make it easier to read, we take the 32-bit address and group it in blocks of eight bits like this:

01111110 10001000 00000001 00101111

Finally, we convert each eight-bit block to decimal and separate the decimal values with periods or "dots." The converted IPv4 address, expressed as a dotted decimal address, is:

126.136.1.47

It is certainly easier to remember that your IP address is 126.136.1.47 instead of remembering a string of bits such as 01111110100010000000000100101111.

What Is a Network?

When talking about IP addressing, it is important to understand what the word "network" means. A network is a group of computing devices connected together by some telecommunications medium. It may be as small as a workgroup in the accounting department or as large as all of the computers in a large company, such as General Motors. From an addressing perspective, all computers in a network come under the administration of the same organization. If you want to send information to a computer, you can identify the computer by its IP address and know that the IP address is assigned to a company. The IP network can locate the computing resources of the company by locating the network. The network is identified by a network number.

Network numbers are actually IP addresses that identify all of the IP resources within an organization. As you can see in Figure 1.1, some organizations will require very large networks with lots of addresses. Other networks will be smaller, and still other networks will need a limited number of addresses. The design of the IPv4 address space took this factor into account.

Figure 1.1 Networks and the Internet.

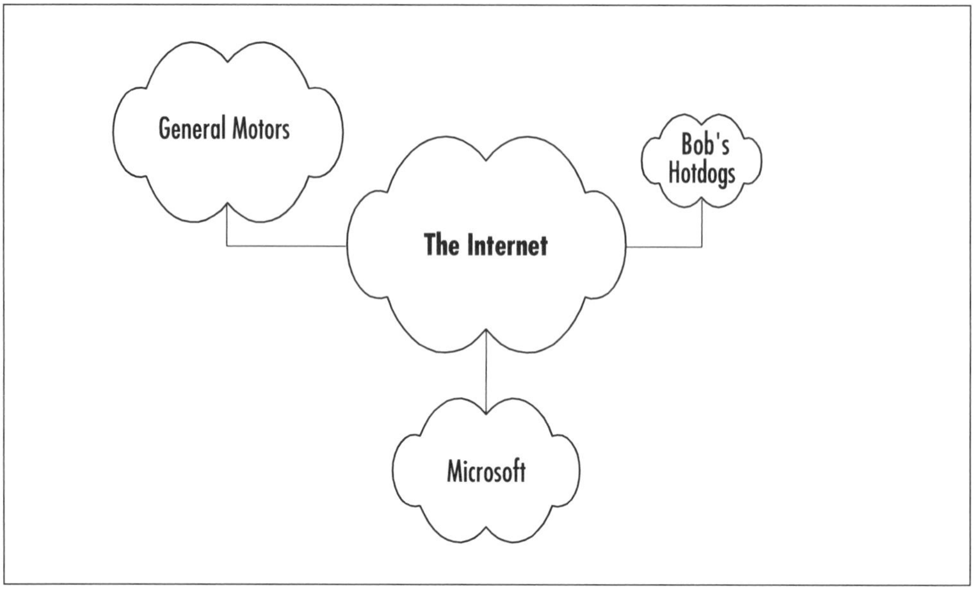

Class A

The largest grouping of addresses is the class A group. Class A network addresses can be identified by a unique bit pattern in the 32-bit address.

    0nnnnnnn 11111111 11111111 11111111

In the preceding group, you will see a 32-bit representation of a class A address. The first 8 bits of a class A address indicate the network number. The remaining 24 bits can be modified by the administrative user of the network address to represent addresses found on their "local" devices. In the representation above, the "n's" indicate the location of the network number bits in the address. The "1's" represent the locally administered portion of the address. As you can see, the first bit of a class A network address is always a zero.

With the first bit of class A address always zero, the class A network numbers begin at 1 and end at 127. With a 24-bit locally administered address space, the total number of addresses in a class A network is 2^{24} or 16,777,216. Each network administrator who receives a class A network can support 16 million hosts. But remember, there are only 127 possible class A addresses in the design, so only 127 large networks are possible.

Here is a list of class A network numbers:

10.0.0.0
44.0.0.0
101.0.0.0
127.0.0.0

Notice that these network numbers range between 1.0.0.0 and 127.0.0.0, the minimum and maximum numbers.

Class B

The next grouping of addresses is the class B group. Class B network addresses can be identified by a unique bit pattern in the 32-bit address.

10nnnnnn nnnnnnnn 11111111 11111111

In the preceding example, you will see a 32-bit representation of a class B address. The first 16 bits of a class B address indicate the network number. The remaining 16 bits can be modified by the administrative user of the network address to represent addresses found on their "local" hosts. A class B address is identified by the 10 in the first 2 bits.

With the first 2 bits of class B address containing 10, the class B network numbers begin at 128 and end at 191. The second dotted decimal in a class B address is also part of the network number. A 16-bit locally administered address space allows each class B network to contain 2^{16} or 65,536 addresses. The number of class B networks available for administration is 16,384.

Here is a list of class B network numbers:

137.55.0.0
129.33.0.0

190.254.0.0
150.0.0.0
168.30.0.0

Notice that these network numbers range between 128.0.0.0 and 191.255.0.0, the minimum and maximum numbers, respectively. And remember that the first two dotted decimal numbers are included in the network number since the network number in a class B address is 16 bits long.

Class C

The next grouping of addresses is the class C group. Class C network addresses can be identified by a unique bit pattern in the 32-bit address.

110nnnnn nnnnnnnn nnnnnnnn 11111111

In the preceding example, you will see a 32-bit representation of a class C address. The first 24 bits of a class C address indicate the network number. The remaining 8 bits can be modified by the administrative user of the network address to represent addresses found on their "local" hosts. A class C address is identified by the 110 in the first 3 bits.

With the first 3 bits of class C address containing 110, the class C network numbers begin at 192 and end at 223. The second and third dotted decimals in a class C address are also part of the network number. An 8-bit locally administered address space allows each class C network to contain 2^8 or 256 addresses. The number of class C networks available for administration is 2,097,152.

Here is a list of class C network numbers:

204.238.7.0
192.153.186.0
199.0.44.0
191.0.0.0
222.222.31.0

Notice that these network numbers range between 192.0.0.0 and 223.255.255.0, the minimum and maximum numbers, respectively. And remember that the first three dotted decimal numbers are included in the network number since the network number in a class C address is 24 bits long.

To summarize, each of the three IP address classes has the characteristics shown in Table 1.1.

Table 1.1 Address Class Characteristics

Class	Network Bits	Host Bits	Total Networks	Total Addresses
A	8	24	127	16,777,216
B	16	16	16,384	65,536
C	24	8	2,097,152	256

For IT Professionals

Mapping Internet Addresses to Local Net Addresses

From RFC791, page 7:

"Care must be taken in mapping internet addresses to local net addresses; a single physical host must be able to act as if it were several distinct hosts to the extent of using several distinct internet addresses. Some hosts will also have several physical interfaces (multi-homing). That is, provision must be made for a host to have several physical interfaces to the network with each having several logical internet addresses."

Address Assignments

One task of address management is address assignment. As you begin the process of address allocation, you must understand how the addresses are used in the network. Some devices will be assigned a single address for a single interface. Other devices will have multiple interfaces, each requiring a single address. Still other devices will have multiple interfaces and some of the interfaces will have multiple addresses.

Single Address per Interface

A device connected to a network may have one or many networking interfaces that require an IP address. A word processing workstation in your network has a single Ethernet interface (see Figure 1.2). It needs only one IP address.

Figure 1.2 Single address per interface.

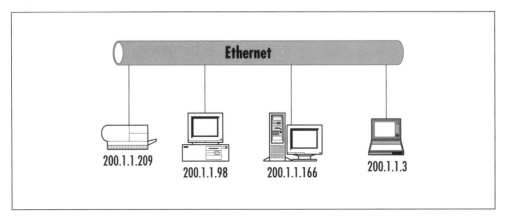

Multihomed Devices

A router is a networking device used to transfer IP datagrams from one physical network to another. The router by its very nature and function will have more than one interface and will require an IP address for each interface. Devices with more than one interface are called *multihomed*, and the process is called *multihoming*.

In Figure 1.3, the router has two interfaces. One interface is attached to the token-ring network and the other interface is attached to the Ethernet network. This is a multihomed device.

Figure 1.3 Multihomed device.

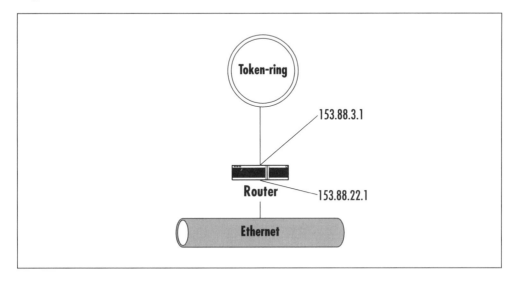

Assigning IP addresses to devices is a simple process (see Figure 1.4). A new device is installed in the network and the address administrator selects an unused address of the group of available addresses. The information is provided to the user of the device and the device is configured. The address given to the user must be from the same address group as all other devices on the same network or the IP data transmission rules will not work. The IP data transmission rules will be discussed in a later chapter.

The actual configuration process for IP addresses varies from operating system to operating system and from device to device, so consult your system documentation for instructions. An important final step requires that a careful notation about assignment of the address be made in the address administrators' documentation so that the address is not assigned to another device.

Figure 1.4 IP address configuration.

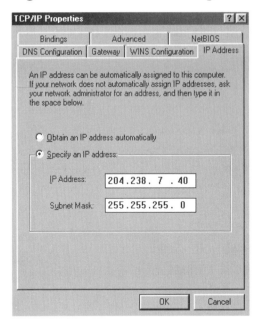

Multinetting—Multiple Addresses per Interface

It is also possible that certain devices will have interfaces with more than one IP address assigned. Here is an example:

A new Internet site is under development for a small corporation. The network administrator knows that the site will grow in the future, but today there is no need for a complex network. A server is installed that will be used as a Web server, ftp server, mail server, and the corporation's DNS server. Later, when the use of the network services grows, new servers will be used for each of the functions.

When the time comes to address the current server, the administrator has a choice. A single IP address can be used on the server and later, when the new servers are needed, new IP addresses can be assigned to them. Another way of assigning addresses can be used. The administrator can assign four IP addresses to the server. Each IP address will match the IP address to be used in the future on new servers. The administrator now knows what addresses will be used and can create DNS entries for the new devices with the correct addresses. The process of providing more than one IP address on an interface is often called *multinetting* or *secondary addressing*.

Examples

Assigning secondary addresses on Cisco routers is done using IOS configuration commands. Here is an example of how to assign a primary IP address and two secondary IP addresses to an Ethernet interface:

```
interface ethernet 0
ip address 183.55.2.77 255.255.255.0
ip address 204.238.7.22 255.255.255.0 secondary
ip address 88.127.6.209 255.255.255.0 secondary
```

The router's Ethernet 0 interface now has addresses in the 183.55.0.0 network, the 204.238.7.0 network, and the 88.0.0.0 network.

Purpose of Subnetting

When the IP protocol was designed, the networks and computers were very different than they are today. With the advent of local area networks (LANS) and personal computers, the architecture of the computer networks changed. Instead of having big computers communicating over low-speed, wide area networks, we had small computers communicating over fast, local area networks.

To illustrate why IP subnetting is necessary, let's take a look at how IP sends datagrams. And to make it easy to understand, let's compare the process to sending mail at the post office. If you have a message to send to a member of your local family, you can deliver it to the family member by writing it down on a piece of paper and giving it directly to him or her. IP networks do the same thing. If an IP datagram is to be sent to a computer on the same physical network, the two devices can communicate directly (see Figure 1.5).

Figure 1.5 IP network with no subnetting.

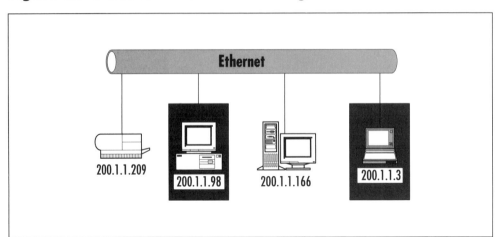

The device 200.1.1.98 wants to communicate with 200.1.1.3. Since they are on the same Ethernet network, they can communicate directly. They are also on the same IP network, so communication can take place without the help of any other devices.

Let's go back to our post office analogy. One of the children has now moved out of the house and has gone to college. To communicate with that child, you will need to have some help. You write a letter, put it in an envelope, and mail it. The post office makes sure that your letter reaches the addressee. Computing devices work according to the same principle. To communicate with devices not in the same physical network, the computing device needs some help. Here is how it is done:

In the illustration in Figure 1.6, James wants to send a message to Sarah. They are all part of the same IP network, 153.88.0.0, but not a part of the same physical network. As a matter of fact, James' computer is on a token-ring network in Los Angeles. Sarah's machine is located on an Ethernet network in Philadelphia. A connection between the two networks is required.

Figure 1.6 Two networks, different locations.

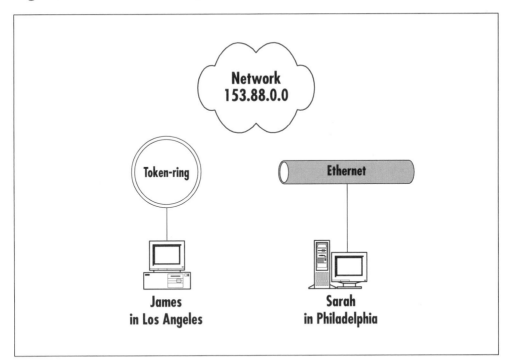

Just like the post office helps to deliver the letter to the student in college, routers help James to send a message to Sarah over the wide area network from Los Angeles to Philadelphia (see Figure 1.7). The IP process must send the message from James to the router. The router will send it to other routers until the message finally reaches the router on Sarah's network. Then the router on Sarah's network will send it to Sarah's machine.

The routers enable IP to send information from one physical network to another. How does IP know that Sarah's machine is not on the same physical network as James's? IP must determine that Sarah's machine is on a different physical network by using the logical IP addressing scheme. In this instance, the address administrator must assist the network managers by breaking the 153.88.0.0 network into smaller components and place a block of addresses on each physical network. Each block of addresses that apply to each physical network is known as a *subnet*.

Figure 1.7 Inter/Intranet connectivity.

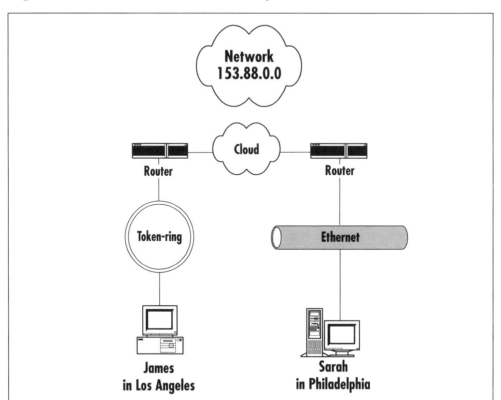

In Figure 1.8, James' machine is now found in the 153.88.240.0 subnet. Sarah's is in the 153.88.3.0 subnet. When James sends a message to Sarah, the IP process determines that Sarah is in a different subnet and sends the message to the router for forwarding.

Let's see how subnets are determined and how IP devices decide to forward datagrams to a router.

Figure 1.8 Two locations, subnetted.

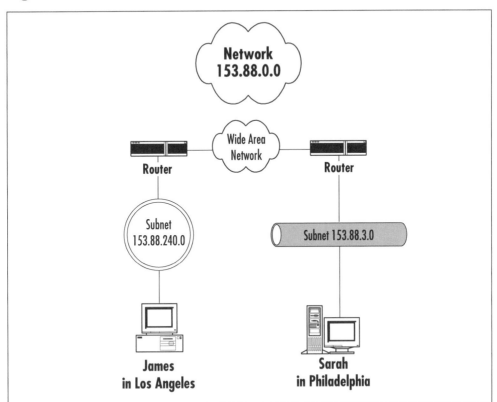

Numbering Systems— Decimal and Binary

Let's quickly review numbering systems before we get into subnetting. Our numbering system is based on 10 digits, the decimal system. Computers work on the binary system with two digits, 0 and 1. To group computer data elements together more efficiently, a 16-digit representation system was developed, the hexadecimal system. There are elements of the decimal system that we understand but may not realize. When you read the number 1245, you say, "one thousand two

Continued

hundred forty five." But how do you know that? Because you use a decimal system that is based on the following information:

Base	10^3	10^2	10^1	10^0
Decimal	1000	100	10	1
	1	2	4	5
1245	1000	200	40	5

So the number 1245 is actually:

```
1000  (1 thousand)
 200  (2 hundreds)
  40  (4 tens)
   5  (5 ones)
1245
```

The binary numbering system is similar, but based on the number 2. We often must convert binary numbers to decimal. In the following chart, you see the breakdown of the binary numbering system and the relative decimal number for each value. Given the binary number 11001011, we can convert it to decimal using the chart.

Base	2^7	2^6	2^5	2^4	2^3	2^2	2^1	2^0
Decimal	128	64	32	16	8	4	2	1
	1	1	0	0	1	0	1	1
11001011	128	64	0	0	8	0	2	1

So the binary number 10010101 converted to decimal is:

```
128
 64
  8
  2
  1
203
```

The Basic Fixed-Length Mask

To help the IP device understand the subnetting used in the network, IP designers described the process of using a subnet mask in RFC950.

For IT Professionals

Utility of "Subnets" of Internet Networks

From RFC950, page 1—Overview:
    This memo discusses the utility of "subnets" of Internet networks, which are logically visible sub-sections of a single Internet network. For administrative or technical reasons, many organizations have chosen to divide one Internet network into several subnets, instead of acquiring a set of Internet network numbers. This memo specifies procedures for the use of subnets. These procedures are for hosts (e.g., workstations). The procedures used in and between subnet gateways are not fully described. Important motivation and background information for a subnetting standard is provided in RFC-940.

What the Mask Does

Simply stated, the mask is used to indicate the location of the subnet field in an IP address. What does that mean? In the previous figures, 153.88.0.0 is the network address. It is a class B address, which means that the first 16 bits of the address is the network number. James' machine is in the 153.88.240.0 subnet. How do we determine that?

James is in the 153.88.0.0 network. The administrator reserved the next 8 bits to hold the subnet number. In the preceding example, James is in the 240 subnet. If James' IP address were 153.88.240.22, James would be in the 153.88.0.0 network, in the

240 subnet of that network, and would have a host address of 22 in that subnet. All devices within the 153.88.0.0 network with a third octet of 240 are assumed to be on the same physical network and in the same subnet, the 240 subnet.

The subnet mask is used to interpret addresses to understand how they are subnetted. The mask is made up of 32 bits, just like the IP address. There are certain masks that are natural or default to the three classes of addresses.

The default or natural mask for the class A address is 255.0.0.0. In this case, the mask indicates that the first 8 bits represent the network number and must be used when evaluating a class A address for subnetting. If a device has a class A address assigned and has a mask of 255.0.0.0, there is no subnetting in that network. If a device has a class A address and has a mask that is not 255.0.0.0, the network has been subnetted and the device is in a subnet of the class A network.

No subnetting   88.0.0.0 255.0.0.0
Subnetting   125.0.0.0 255.255.255.0

In the preceding example, the 125.0.0.0 network has been subnetted. The mask is not the default mask so we know that the network has been subnetted. What does the rest of the mask mean?

As stated earlier, the mask is used to indicate the location of the subnet field in an IP address. Let's look at what makes up a mask.

For IT Professionals

255 Reference

Subnet masks frequently contain a reference to 255. The 255 reference simply indicates that all 8 bits of that portion of the mask contain a 1. For instance, the binary representation of the mask 255.0.0.0 is 11111111000000000000000-000000000. The mask 255.255.0.0 is 1111111111111111-0000000000000000.

Components of a Mask

The mask is a 32-bit binary number that is expressed in dotted decimal notation. By default, the mask contains two fields, the network field and the host field. These correspond to the network number and the locally administered part of the network address. When you subnet, you are adjusting the way you view the IP address. If you are working with a class B network and are using the standard mask, there is no subnetting. For example, in the address and mask in the following example the network is indicated by the first two 255 entries and the host field is indicated by the ending 0.0.

153.88.4.240 255.255.0.0

The network number is 153.88 and the host number is 4.240. In other words, the first 16 bits are the network number and the remaining 16 bits are the host number.

When we subnet a network, we increase the hierarchy from network and host to network, subnet and host. If we were to subnet the 153.88.0.0 network with a subnet mask of 255.255.255.0, we will be adding an additional piece of information. Our view changes in that we will be adding a subnet field. As with the previous example, 153.88 is still the network number. With a mask of 255.255.255.0, the third octet is used to tell us where the subnet number is located. The subnet number is .4 and, finally, the host number is 240.

The locally administered portion of the network address can be subdivided into subnetworks by using the mask to tell us the location of the subnet field. We allocate a certain number of bits to the subnet field and the remainder is then the new host field. In the following example, we took the 16-bit host field that comes with a class B address and broke it down into an 8-bit subnet field and an 8-bit host field.

255.255.255.0 for a class B network

Network	Network	Subnet	Host
255	255	255	0
11111111	11111111	11111111	00000000

Binary Determination of Mask Values

How do you determine which mask to use? On the surface it is a fairly simple process. You first determine how many subnets are required in your network. This may require you to do a lot of research into the network architecture and design. Once you know how many subnets you will need, you can decide how many subnet bits are needed to provide you with a subnet field big enough to hold the number of subnets you need.

When a network is in the design phase, the network administrator discusses the design with the address administrator. They conclude that there will be a total of 73 subnets in the current design and that a class B address will be used. To develop the subnet mask, we need to know how big the subnet field must be. The locally administered portion of a class B address contains 16 bits.

Remember that the subnet field is a portion of these 16 bits. The challenge is to determine how many bits are required to store the decimal number 73. Once we know how many bits are needed to store the decimal number 73, we can determine what the mask should be.

The first step is to convert the decimal number 73 to binary. The number of bits in the binary number is seven.

73 decimal=1001001 binary

So we need to reserve the first 7 bits of the locally administered portion of the subnet mask for the subnet field and the remainder will be the host field. In the example below, we are reserving the first 7 bits for the subnet field, indicated by the 1 bits, and the remainder to the host field, indicated by the 0 bits.

11111110 00000000

If we convert this binary information into decimal for the subnet mask and add it to the portion of the mask for the network number, we will have the entire subnet mask necessary.

```
11111110=254 decimal
00000000=0 decimal
```

255.255.254.0 is the mask

Remember, 255.255.0.0 is the default mask for a class B address. We have replaced the locally administered portion of the mask, the .0.0, with the 254.0 that depicts the subnetting scheme. The 254.0 portion tells the software that the first 7 bits of the locally administered portion of the address is the subnet field and the remainder is the host field. Of course, if the subnet mask numbers change, the interpretation of the subnet field changes.

Decimal Equivalent Mask Values

Tables 1.2, 1.3, and 1.4 show the possible subnet masks that can be used in class A, class B, and class C networks.

Table 1.2 Class A Subnet Table

Subnets	Hosts	Mask	Subnet Bits	Host Bits
2	4,194,302	255.192.0.0	2	22
6	2,097,150	255.224.0.0	3	21
14	1,048,574	255.240.0.0	4	20
30	524,286	255.248.0.0	5	19
62	262,142	255.252.0.0	6	18
126	131,070	255.254.0.0	7	17
254	65,534	255.255.0.0	8	16
510	32,766	255.255.128.0	9	15
1,022	16,382	255.255.192.0	10	14
2,046	8,190	255.255.224.0	11	13
4,094	4,094	255.255.240.0	12	12

Continued

Subnets	Hosts	Mask	Subnet Bits	Host Bits
8,190	2,046	255.255.248.0	13	11
16,382	1,022	255.255.252.0	14	10
32,766	510	255.255.254.0	15	9
65,534	254	255.255.255.0	16	8
131,070	126	255.255.255.128	17	7
262,142	62	255.255.255.192	18	6
524,286	30	255.255.255.224	19	5
1,048,574	14	255.255.255.240	20	4
2,097,150	6	255.255.255.248	21	3
4,194,302	2	255.255.255.252	22	2

Table 1.3 Class B Subnet Table

Subnets	Hosts	Mask	Subnet Bits	Host Bits
2	16,382	255.255.192.0	2	14
6	8,190	255.255.224.0	3	13
14	4,094	255.255.240.0	4	12
30	2,046	255.255.248.0	5	11
62	1,022	255.255.252.0	6	10
126	510	255.255.254.0	7	9
254	254	255.255.255.0	8	8
510	126	255.255.255.128	9	7
1022	62	255.255.255.192	10	6
2046	30	255.255.255.224	11	5
4094	14	255.255.255.240	12	4

Continued

Subnets	Hosts	Mask	Subnet Bits	Host Bits
8,190	6	255.255.255.248	13	3
16,382	2	255.255.255.252	14	2

Table 1.4 Class C Subnet Table

Subnets	Hosts	Mask	Subnet Bits	Host Bits
2	62	255.255.255.192	2	6
6	30	255.255.255.224	3	5
14	14	255.255.255.240	4	4
30	6	255.255.255.248	5	3
62	2	255.255.255.252	6	2

These subnet mask tables can make it easier for you to determine which subnet mask to use for any given situation. Look at the tables for just a minute and notice what happens. As you go down the table, the number of subnets increases and the number of hosts in each subnet then decreases. Why? Look at the right-hand side of each table. As the number of subnet bits increases, the number of host bits decreases. Since we have a fixed number of bits to work with in each class of network address, each bit can be used in only one way—specified by the mask. Each bit must be either a subnet bit or a host bit. An increase in the number of subnet bits causes a reduction in the number of host bits.

Notice too that the tables are different sizes for each class of address. Because of the 24-bit, 16-bit and 8-bit host fields for class A, B, and C networks, respectively, we have three different tables.

Creating Masks for Various Networking Problems

The tables make it easy to locate the correct mask for your networking problem. Consider the following problems:

Bob was given a class A network to administer. He needs to subnet the network into 1,045 subnets with 295 devices in the largest subnet. He looks up the subnet and device numbers in the class A table and finds that the following five entries can be used to solve his problem. Which should he use?

2,046	8,190	255.255.224.0	11	13
4,094	4,094	255.255.240.0	12	12
8,190	2,046	255.255.248.0	13	11
16,382	1,022	255.255.252.0	14	10
32,766	510	255.255.254.0	15	9

Bob must select one mask to use. As he looks at his possible solutions, he also has to understand another factor involved in his decision: the growth of the network. Will his company add more subnets in the future, or will each subnet get bigger, or both?

If the number of subnets will increase without an increase in devices in each subnet, Bob could select 255.255.254.0 as his mask and be comfortable with his decision. If the number of devices in each subnet will increase, he could select 255.255.252.0 as his mask. Depending on the physical protocol in use, there may be practical limits to the number of devices in each subnet. In some networks, having more than 100 physical devices in a network segment or subnet may seriously impact the usability of the network. Using realistic estimates of devices in each subnet is essential to subnetting success.

In another example, Sarah is in charge of a small corporate network with two Ethernet segments and three token-ring segments. They are connected together with one router. Each subnet will contain no more than 15 devices. Sarah has been assigned a class C network address. As Sarah looks at the class C table, she finds that the following entry may be used to solve the problem as described:

6	30	255.255.224	3	5

The only entry that allows five subnets with 15 devices is 255.255.255.224.

If you have a good idea of the number of subnets and the number of hosts in each subnet, you can use these tables to find the proper mask. It is always important to know if the number of subnets will grow in the future or if the number of hosts in the subnets will grow. Once the growth factors have been included in the current need, check the tables to determine your mask.

Addresses and Mask Interaction

Let's review the concept of IP addresses. An IP address identifies a device on a network. IP addresses are assigned from classes that contain different groups of addresses. Each IP network has a network number. Each IP subnet has the network number of its parent network and a subnet number. The subnet number can be found by locating the subnet field in the subnet mask.

If you have an IP address of 153.88.4.240 with a mask of 255.255.255.0, you know that you have an address in the 153.88.0.0 network. You know you are in subnet .4 because the third octet of the mask says that all 8 bits of the address in the third octet make up the subnet number. By the way, all devices with a 153.88 in the first two octets are in the same network and all devices with a 4 in the third octet are in the same subnet. Why is that?

In a class B network, the first 16 bits are the network number. If devices have the identical first 16 bits, they are in the same network with a class B address. When you want to send a datagram from the source address to the target address, IP has to make a routing decision. Look at the following example:

	Network	Network	Subnet	Host
Source 153.88.4.240	10011001	01011000	00000100	11110000
Target 153.89.98.254	10011001	01011001	01100010	11111110

Notice that these are different networks. They are both class B addresses, but the first 16 bits do not match. They are different; therefore, IP "assumes" they are on different physical networks and will send the datagram to the router for forwarding to the target device. IP only looks at subnetting when the network numbers of the two addresses are the same.

We had mentioned earlier that the subnet mask helps us locate the subnet number. Here is another example:

	Network	Network	Subnet	Host
Source 153.88.4.240	10011001	01011000	00000100	11110000
Target 153.88.192.254	10011001	01011000	11000000	11111110
Mask 255.255.255.0	11111111	11111111	11111111	00000000

In this example, you will see that we have modified the target address. We have also added a subnet mask that we can use to determine subnetting. Notice the mask, 255.255.255.0. The first two 255s in the mask point to the network portion of the address since we are using a class B address. The third 255 is the location of the subnet field in the locally administered portion of the addresses. The ones in the mask point to the subnet bits. Are these two devices in the same subnet? Look at the bits in the third octet of each address. The source address has a binary subnet field of 00000100 and the target address has a binary subnet field of 11000000. Since these two binary numbers are not the same, these two devices are in different subnets and the source device will send datagrams to the router for delivery to the target device in the target network.

So far we have been working with the easiest subnetting, the 255.255.255.0 mask. Using a mask of 255.255.255.0 allows us to interpret the address by reading the dotted decimal address. For example, an address of 165.22.129.66 contains the network address 165.22.0.0. The subnet number is 129. The host number is 66. Each portion of the dotted decimal address contains address information that is easy to interpret.

What happens when the mask is not so simple? In the next example, we will work with a class B network, 160.149.0.0. The subnet mask selected by the administrators is 255.255.252.0. This gives the network 62 subnets with 1022 devices in each subnet.

Let's see what happens when we try to determine the subnet identity of two devices:

	Network	Network	Subnet	Host
	Network	**Network**	**Subnet**	**Host**
Source 160.149.115.8	10100000	10010101	01110011	00001000
Target 160.149.117.201	10100000	10010101	01110101	11001001
Mask 255.255.252.0	11111111	11111111	11111100	00000000

The network portion of the two addresses in the example above is identical, so they are in the same network. The subnet portion of the mask contains 6 bits, so the first 6 bits of the third octet contains the subnet number. The first 6 bits of the third octet is 011100 for 115 and 011101 for 117. These devices are in different subnets. Datagrams sent from the source machine would have to be sent to the router to reach the target device.

Why are these two devices in different subnets? First, they are in the same network and are candidates for being in the same subnet. The subnet portion of the mask says that the first 6 bits of the third octet of each address contains the subnet number. In comparing the subnet portion of the two addresses, bit patterns do not match. They are in different subnets. Here is another example:

	Network	Network	Subnet	Host
Source 160.149.115.8	10100000	10010101	01110011	00001000
Target 160.149.114.66	10100000	10010101	01110010	01000010
Mask 255.255.252.0	11111111	11111111	11111100	00000000

In this example 160.149.115.8 and 160.149.114.66 are in the same network and subnet. Look at the third octet. Where the ones bit exist in the mask, the bits in both addresses are identical, indicating that they are in the same subnet. Even though the third octet contains 114 in one address and 115 in the other, they are in the same subnet because the significant bits are the same in both addresses.

For IT Professionals

What is a Host?

IP addresses are assigned to interfaces on devices in an IP network. Often the terms used to indicate this assignment can be confusing. The RFCs dealing with IP often refer to the devices as *hosts*. A host is an entity assigned an IP address. With multinetting and multihoming, it is possible to assign more than one address to a device or to an interface. With the term *host address* we can then relate IP addresses to the host of the IP process, regardless of the actual physical structure of the device or interfaces. So when you see host, hosts, or host address, remember that it is not all that complicated. It is just another way to refer to entities that are assigned IP addresses.

Reserved and Restricted Addresses

When assigning addresses to devices in networks and/or subnets, there are some addresses that cannot be used. We reserve two addresses in any network or subnet to uniquely identify two special functions. The first reserved address is the network or subnet address. The network address is the address that includes the network number and a host field filled with binary zeros. 200.1.1.0, 153.88.0.0, and 10.0.0.0 are network addresses. These addresses identify the network and cannot be assigned to a device.

Another reserved address is the broadcast address. When used, it is meant to attract the attention of all devices in the network. The network broadcast address is the network number followed by a host field of binary ones. The addresses shown in the example below are network broadcast addresses: 200.1.1.255, 153.88.255.255, and 10.255.255.255. Since this address is supposed to attract the attention of every device, it cannot be used on any single device.

We also restrict addresses in subnets. Each subnet has a subnet address and a broadcast address. Like the network address and broadcast address, these addresses cannot be assigned to devices and contain host fields of all zeros and all ones for the subnet address and subnet broadcast.

	Network	Network	Subnet	Host
Subnet Add. 153.88.4.0	10011001	01011000	00000100	00000000
Broadcast 153.88.4.255	10011001	01011000	00000100	11111111
Mask 255.255.255.0	11111111	11111111	11111111	00000000

In this example, the subnet address is shown with all zeros in the host field, and the broadcast address is shown with all ones in the host field. Regardless of the size of the subnet field or host field, the bit structure of all zeros in the host field is the subnet address, and all ones in the host field is the subnet broadcast address.

Determining the Range of Addresses within Subnets

Once you have determined what mask to use and understand the special subnet address and subnet broadcast address, you can begin the process of determining what addresses are going to be assigned to specific devices. To do that, you will need to "calculate" which addresses are in each subnet.

Each subnet will contain a range of addresses with the same network and subnet number. The difference will be in the host numbers. Below is an example of a set of addresses in a subnet of a class C network.

Network Address 200.1.1.0
Subnet Mask 255.255.255.248

Subnet 1 Address

Mask	11111000		
	00001000	200.1.1.8	Subnet Address
	00001001	200.1.1.9	Host 1

00001010	200.1.1.10	Host 2
00001011	200.1.1.11	Host 3
00001100	200.1.1.12	Host 4
00001101	200.1.1.13	Host 5
00001110	200.1.1.14	Host 6
00001111	200.1.1.15	Subnet Broadcast

In the preceding example, we are using the 200.1.1.0 class C network. The subnet mask is 255.255.255.248. Subnetting can only occur in the fourth octet in a class C address. Each subnet can contain six devices using this mask. In creating the addresses for subnet number 1, notice that the subnet field of each address is 00001. The subnet field is indicated by the 11111 portion of the fourth octet of the mask. The subnet field exists in the first five bits of the fourth octet. The remaining 3 bits are used to indicate the host field.

The host field for each address increases from 000 for the subnet address to 111 for the subnet broadcast address. The addresses that can be assigned to specific hosts increase from 001 to 110, the binary equivalent of decimal 1 to decimal 6. So why do the addresses look the way they do? We simply combine the subnet number, 00001, with each host field, 000 through 111, and convert each address from binary to decimal. We begin with 200.1.1.8 (00001000) and end with 200.1.1.15 (00001111). In this case, we don't change the 200.1.1. part of the address because that is the network number.

More information and the processes used to develop an addressing plan will be found in Chapter 2.

Determining Subnet Addresses Given a Single Address and Mask

If you have an IP address and a subnet mask, you can determine the subnet where the device is located. The steps are as follows:

1. Convert the locally administered portion of the address to binary.

2. Convert the locally administered portion of the mask to binary.

3. Locate the host field in the binary address and replace with zeros.

4. Convert the binary address to dotted decimal notation. You now have the subnet address.

5. Locate the host field in the binary address and replace with ones.

6. Convert the binary address to dotted decimal notation. You now have the subnet broadcast address.

Everything between these two numbers represents IP addresses that may be assigned to devices.

The following is an example of how to use this process. The address of the device is 204.238.7.45 and the subnet mask is 255.255.255.224. Since this is a class C address, subnetting occurs in the fourth octet.

Address 200.1.1.45	00**01101**
Mask 255.255.255.224	11**00000**

Convert host to zeros	00100000	.32 Subnet Address
Conver host to ones	00111111	.63 Subnet Broadcast

The host field is located in the last 5 bits of the address. Replacing the host field with zeros and converting the binary number to decimal gives us the subnet address. Replacing the host field with ones results in the subnet broadcast address. The address 200.1.1.45 subnetted with a mask of 255.255.255.224 is in the subnet 200.1.1.32. The addresses that can be assigned in this subnet are 200.1.1.33 through 200.1.1.62.

Interpreting Masks

Dec	Binary
0	00000000
128	10000000
192	11000000
224	11100000
240	11110000
248	11111000
252	11111100
254	11111110
255	11111111

Each subnet mask is made up of binary values and is represented in dotted decimal notation. The allowable decimal values that can be used in the mask are seen in Figure 1.23. In order to use these values, there must be a 255 immediately to the left. The subnet mask bits must be contiguous. For example, a mask of 255.255.0.224 is not appropriate.

We are sometimes asked "How many bits are in the mask?" The question is answered by expressing the number of bits in the mask with relation to the class of address. For instance, if a mask of 255.255.254.0 is used with a class B address, there are 7 bits in the mask. It may look like there are a total of 23 bits, which there are. To clearly express the subnetting, however, we must say that the mask is a 7-bit mask for a class B address. Only 7 bits of the total 23 bits are used for subnetting. The remaining 16 bits come with the class B address.

This may seem like a silly little point but it can lead to a very bad miscommunication. If I tell you I have a 6-bit mask, what does that mean? Without the class of address, the mask could be 255.252.0.0, 255.255.252.0, or 255.255.255.252. Each of these masks is a 6-bit mask, but they apply to different classes of addresses and give us a completely different subnet picture.

Reserved Addresses

Earlier in the chapter we talked about certain reserved addresses. Specifically we said that the network address, network broadcast address, the subnet address, and the subnet broadcast address could not be assigned to any device or host. This is to avoid confusion on the part of the IP software that is responsible for transporting the IP datagrams. These addresses do not uniquely identify any particular device. IP devices may send datagrams using the broadcast address, but the broadcast address means everyone. A single device cannot be everyone, it must have a unique address.

We need to remove the reserved addresses from our address calculation and do so by using a special formula to determine how many hosts are available in a subnet or network. If you know the number of bits in the host field of an address, you can calculate the number of devices in the network or subnet. The formula that we use is:

$$2^n-2$$

In this formula, **n** represents the number of bits in the subnet or host field. We subtract two to remove the two reserved addresses from the calculation. In the following excerpt of the class C subnetting table, you can see the results of using this formula.

Subnets	Hosts	Mask	Subnet Bits	Host Bits
14	14	255.255.255.240	4	4

Using a subnet mask of 255.255.255.240, we have 4 bits in the subnet field. The number of bit patterns that exist in 4 bits is 2^4 or 16. They are as follows:

0000	0100	1000	1100
0001	0101	1001	1101
0010	0110	1010	1110
0011	0111	1011	1111

Removing the two reserved bit patterns, 0000 and 1111, from the possible subnet values leaves us with 14 subnet numbers to use. This same calculation also applies to the bits in the host field.

For IT Professionals

Subnet Zero and Subnet "All Ones"

RFC950 requires that subnet number zero and subnet "all ones" be restricted and not assigned to any subnet. Subnet zero contains all zero bits in the subnet field and subnet "all ones" contains all one bits in the subnet field. Early IP implementations often confused these addresses with broadcast addresses, and the designers of RFC950 decided to restrict these addresses to end the confusion. Today, the use of subnet zero and subnet "all ones" is allowed. The actual use depends on the IP software on the devices in use in those subnets. In certain cases, the use of these restricted subnets must be enabled in the IP devices before they can be used. Check with your vendor documentation to see if these restricted subnets are allowed in your network.

Summary

In this chapter, you have learned about the IPv4 32-bit address structure. You've seen the components of an IPv4 address, learned about the classes of addresses, and found out exactly how many addresses are available in each class.

You then learned why we subnet and how we subnet. You've discovered the contents of the subnet mask and how the subnet mask is created. You were shown the process used to convert decimal number to binary and binary numbers to decimal. The contents of subnet mask tables were made available and the process of selecting a subnet mask for a networking problem was described.

Finally, you were shown how to determine if two addresses were in the same subnet and which addresses were in a subnet. Additionally, you've learned which addresses could not be used on IP devices.

FAQs

Q: Can I use a mask like 255.255.255.139 in a class B network?

A: IP subnetting rules do not restrict you from using any sequence of bits to represent a subnet mask. The subnet field in the preceding mask includes all of the one bits in the last two octets. The bits in the last two octets are not contiguous. They all don't sit side by side.

```
255            139
11111111       10001011
```

This forces the address administrator to calculate each address individually. There is also no continuous range of addresses in each subnet. It is too confusing and too difficult to subnet using strange and wonderful masks like the preceding one. Select your masks from the tables in the chapter.

Q: I confuse my address with my mask. How can I tell the difference?

A: The mask will always have 255 in the first octet. The address will never have 255 in the first octet.

Q: How can I be sure that the mask I select for my network is correct?

A: It is always a good question. The answer is "You cannot!" Even if you did the correct research and created the best possible mask with current information, changes in network design and network administration may force you to modify the addressing structure. That would mean that the mask you selected may not be appropriate. The best suggestion is to make sure there is plenty of room for growth in subnets and hosts in each subnet when you select your mask and create your addressing plan.

Q: Why do I need to know the decimal-to-binary conversion?

A: To understand fully how subnetting works, it is necessary to understand how the bits in the mask and the address are related. To see the relationship, it is often necessary to view the addresses in binary along with the binary representation of the mask. Without decimal-to-binary conversion, it is difficult to view the relationship.

Chapter 2

Creating an Addressing Plan for Fixed-Length Mask Networks

Solutions in this chapter:

- Determining the number of addresses needed

- Obtaining the correct size block of addresses

- Choosing the correct mask to use

- Allocating addresses to devices

- Documenting what you've done

- Using tools to ease the job

Introduction

Many organizations, especially smaller ones, use fixed-mask addressing. Fixed-mask addressing is easier to understand and simpler to implement than variable-mask addressing. In fixed-mask networks, every device uses the same mask and all subnets have the same number of available addresses—they're all the same size.

In Chapter 1 we learned about IP addresses and the basics of mask operation and subnetting. In this chapter, we'll detail the steps you need to take to assign appropriate IP addresses to those devices that need them. We'll also show you some effective and surprisingly simple tools to make the job easier.

Your choice of routing protocols can affect your choice of mask. Of the popular routing protocols, RIP (version 1) and IGRP impose certain requirements on addressing—all devices on all subnets must use the same mask. In other words, you are forced into a fixed–length–mask addressing plan. If you use RIP (version 2), OSPF, or EIGRP, then you can still *choose* to use the same mask for each subnet, but the protocols do not demand it.

Determine Addressing Requirements

When you need to develop an IP addressing plan, whether it is for fixed– or variably–subnetted networks, you have to start by determining exactly what your needs are. As you recall, IP addresses contain information that helps routers deliver datagrams to the proper destination networks or subnets. Since such a close relationship exists between IP addresses and their target network segments, you must be careful to determine the proper range of addresses for each network or subnet.

Review Your Internetwork Design

We start by reviewing our network documentation. If this is a newly designed IP network, you'll need the design specifications. If the network has been in operation for some time, you can use the "as built" documentation. These specifications should include information such as:

- The number and type of devices on each LAN segment
- An indication of which of those devices need an IP address
- The devices connecting the segments, for example: routers, bridges, and switches.

For Managers

Network Design Specifications

You *do* have a complete, updated, and available set of network design specifications and layouts, don't you?

How Many Subnets Do You Need?

As you review your design, identify and list each subnet, noting the number of IP addresses needed in each. Take a look at Figure 2.1.

Figure 2.1 Sample Network Layout.

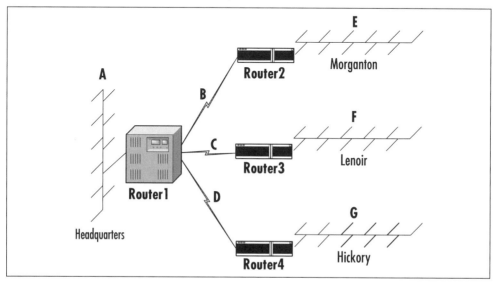

One definition of a router is that it is a device that interconnects networks. Routers and layer–3 switches operate by forwarding packets from one network to another so that the packet gets one step closer to its final destination. Each interface on a router needs a unique IP address. Furthermore, each interface's IP address must belong to a different network or subnet. Put another way, each router interface *defines* a network or subnet. This last statement is the cause of much "weepin' and wailin'" on the part of IP network administrators.

Look again at Figure 2.1 in light of our routers' configuration needs. Router1 has four interfaces—one LAN interface and three WAN interfaces. Therefore Router1 needs four IP addresses, and each of those addresses needs to be in a different network or subnet. Now look at Router2. It has two interfaces—a LAN interface and a WAN interface. Therefore, two addresses are needed, one in each of two networks or subnets. The same can be said for the other two branch office routers.

Let's tally what we have so far. The Headquarters router needs four addresses and each of the branch routers needs two, for a total of ten addresses. Does that mean that there are ten subnets? Look again: Router1 and Router2 are connected to the same subnet (labeled B in Figure 2.1). Router1 shares connections with Router3 and Router4 in the same way.

So we see a total of seven subnets: four are LANs and three are WAN connections. Do you need to allocate IP address ranges for all of them? In general, the answer is yes. As with most topics in the IT industry, the precise answer is more complicated than that.

How Many IP Addresses Are Needed in Each Subnet?

Now that you know how many different subnets (address ranges) you need, it's time to determine, for each subnet, how many devices need addresses. The basic guideline here is that each interface that will be "talking IP" needs an IP address. Here are some examples:

- Routers: one IP address per interface (see the next section for a discussion on *unnumbered interfaces*).

- Workstations: generally one address.

- Servers: generally one address unless the server is *multihomed* (has more than one interface).

- Printers: one address if they are communicating with a print server via IP, or if they have an integrated print server feature (like the HP JetDirect). If the printer is attached to the serial or parallel port of another device, it does not need an IP address.

- Bridges: normally bridges do not communicate using IP, so they do not need an address. However, if the bridge is managed using an SNMP-based network management system, it *will* need an address, because the data collection agent is acting as an IP host.

- Hubs: same as bridges.

- Layer-2 switches: same as bridges.

- Layer-3 switches: same as routers.

In Table 2.1, you can see the number of various devices on each LAN of our sample organization.

Table 2.1 Devices in the Sample Network

LAN	Devices
Headquarters	20 workstations, 2 servers, 1 managed hub, 1 network-attached printer, 1 router
Morganton Branch	11 workstations, 2 network-attached printers, 1 router
Lenoir Branch	12 workstations, 1 router
Hickory Branch	5 workstations, 1 server, 1 router

Is the table complete? No. What's missing? Remember that each router interface needs an IP address, too. Also, what about the WAN links?

Table 2.2 summarizes our actual needs, on a subnet–by–subnet basis.

Table 2.2   Number of IP Addresses Needed

Subnet	IP Addresses
Headquarters	25
Morganton	14
Lenoir	13
Hickory	7
WAN1	2
WAN2	2
WAN3	2

After adding the WAN links and router addresses, we can say that we need 7 subnets, with anywhere from 2 to 25 IP addresses in each.

What about Growth?

Data networks seem to have a life of their own. It is a rare network that does not change and grow. As your users become comfortable with the applications they use via the network, they will start to ask for more features. You will probably find that you will be adding users, applications, servers and internetworking devices throughout the life of your network.

When you design an addressing plan, make sure you allow enough room for growth both in the number of subnets required and the number of addresses required in each subnet. The amount of growth depends almost entirely on your organization. What kind of expansion plans does your organization have? Are you more likely to add users/servers, or new branch offices? Are there any mergers/acquisitions anticipated for your future?

Choose the Proper Mask

The next step in creating your addressing plan is choosing a mask to be used in your network.

Going back to how a mask works, remember that each bit in the mask determines how the corresponding bit in the IP address is interpreted. Where there is a zero–bit in the mask, the corresponding bit of the IP address is part of the interface (host) identifier. Where there is a one–bit in the mask, the corresponding bit of the IP address is part of the network or subnet identifier.

So, the number of zero–bits in the mask determines the number of bits in the host field of an IP address, and thus the number of possible IP addresses for each subnet. Remember the formula 2^n-2 (where n is the number of bits)? Working backwards, you can determine the number of host bits required in the IP address given the number of addresses needed. The idea is to find the smallest value for n where the formula 2^n-2 gives you the number of addresses needed.

For example, if you need 25 addresses in a subnet, there must be at least five host bits in the IP address. That is, there must be at least five zeros in the mask: $2^4-2 = 14$ (not enough); $2^5-2 = 30$ (enough). If you need 1500 addresses, there must be at least 11 zeros in the mask ($2^{11}-2 = 2046$).

Consult the Tables

If you've been given a "classfull" block of addresses to use—that is, an entire class A, B, or C network address—then you can refer to the corresponding subnet tables at the end of the chapter. Those tables can guide you to the proper mask to choose and how to allocate address ranges.

Let's look at our sample network shown in Figure 2.1. After our analysis, Table 2.2 showed that we need to support seven subnets, and the maximum number of addresses needed in any subnet is 25. Let's assume we've been given class C network 192.168.153.0 to use in our organization.

Table 2.3 is a traditional (RFC 950) class C subnetting table. Consulting this table, we can try to find an appropriate mask.

Table 2.3   Class C Subnet Table

# Subnet Bits	# Subnets	# Host Bits	# Hosts	Mask
2	2	6	62	255.255.255.192
3	6	5	30	255.255.255.224
4	14	4	14	255.255.255.240
5	30	3	6	255.255.255.248
6	62	2	2	255.255.255.252

Can you locate a mask that will support seven subnets with 25 hosts each? No; a mask of 255.255.255.224 gives us enough host addresses, but not enough subnets, and 255.255.255.240 supports enough subnets, but not enough host addresses. Now what? In this situation, you have four options:

1. Use unnumbered interfaces.
2. Ask for a bigger block of addresses.
3. Play some tricks with your router.
4. Use "subnet zero."

Use Unnumbered Interfaces

Many popular routers today provide a feature known as *unnumbered interfaces* or *IP unnumbered*. This feature can be used when the interface connects to a point–to–point network, such as a leased 56k or T1 line. When you use this feature, the point–to–point network does not need IP addresses and can be omitted from the total number of subnets. If we took advantage of this feature in our sample network, we would need to provide addresses only for the LAN segments. This can lead to substantial savings in the number of IP addresses needed. We'll look at some examples in the next section.

One disadvantage of using unnumbered interfaces is that you cannot directly access those interfaces for testing or management purposes. So you will have to make a choice for manageability or for address conservation. In most networks, the choice will be clear, based on the needs of the organization. In other networks, you may just have to make a judgement call.

Using unnumbered interfaces in our example eliminates the need for three subnets—the three WAN connections. Now we need only four subnets, and a mask of 255.255.255.224 would be appropriate.

Ask for a Bigger Block of Addresses

If you had two class C addresses, you could use one for the Headquarters LAN, and subnet the other for the branch LANs and WAN links. For example, if you were allocated two class C addresses (192.168.8.0 and 192.168.9.0), you could use 192.168.8.0 with the mask 255.255.255.0 for the Headquarters LAN. For the remaining LANs and WAN links we can subnet 192.168.9.0 with the mask 255.255.255.224. This gives us six subnets with 30 host addresses each—plenty to cover our needs.

Router Tricks

Most routers allow you to assign more than one IP address to an interface. This feature is called *multinetting* or *secondary interfaces*. Thus, you can actually support more than one subnet on a single router interface. In our sample network, you could use the mask 255.255.255.240 (which gives you 14 subnets and 14 host addresses), then assign two addresses on the Headquarters LAN interface of the router.

The choice of the two addresses is important. The first address must be a valid address on one subnet, the second address must be a valid address on *another* subnet.

Now we have 28 addresses available on the Headquarters LAN. Pretty handy, right? Yes, but at a price.

Remember that the Internet Protocol (IP) determines local vs remote delivery using the IP address. If your workstation is communicating with a host on another subnet (as determined by your mask and the target IP address), the datagrams will be delivered to your default gateway (router). Take a look at Figure 2.2.

Figure 2.2 Multiple subnets on a LAN segment.

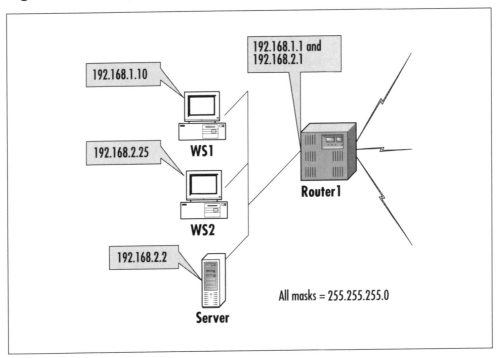

WS1 is on one IP network, and WS2 and the server are on another. They (and the router) are *all* on a single LAN segment (i.e., they are all connected to the same Ethernet hub).

When WS2 wants to communicate with the server, the IP software in WS2 determines that, based on the mask of 255.255.255.0, the server is on the same IP network/subnet. So, WS2 will send a packet directly to the server.

What happens when WS1 wants to talk to the server? Are they on the same IP network? They aren't, so WS1 will send the packets to its default gateway (Router1). Router1 will then forward the packets to the proper network for the server. Thus, each packet transmitted between WS1 and the server will appear on the Ethernet segment *twice*—once from WS1 to the router and again from the router to the server (and vice–versa).

TIP

If you choose to use this trick, you need to be careful about which devices you place in which network/subnet. Try to keep devices that talk to each other on the same subnet.

Use Subnet Zero

To help avoid potential interoperability problems, conservative network managers still follow the original specification and choose not to use the all zeros and all ones subnets. If this is the path you choose to follow, then you must subtract two from the number of subnets shown in each row of the tables at the end of the chapter. In some cases, such as the example we're working on, it may be necessary to go ahead and use the additional subnets.

In our example, you could choose to use 255.255.255.224 as your mask, which gives you enough host addresses. By using subnet zero, you would have enough subnets to cover your needs.

For more practice choosing the correct mask for your network, please refer to the exercises at the end of the chapter.

TIP

In the original subnetting standard (RFC 950), the subnets whose binary subnet ID is all zeros or all ones could not be used (thus the –2 in the subnetting formula 2^n-2). In RFC 1812, this restriction has been lifted. Here is a quote from RFC 1812:

> "Previous versions of this document also noted that subnet numbers must be neither 0 nor –1, and must be at least two bits in length. In a CIDR world, the subnet number is clearly an extension of the network prefix and cannot be interpreted without the remainder of the prefix. This restriction of subnet numbers is therefore meaningless in view of CIDR and may be safely ignored."

Obtain IP Addresses

If you have already been given a block of addresses to use, and that block is sufficient for your needs, you may proceed to the next step (calculating the appropriate address ranges for each subnet).

If you have not been given any addresses, or if you determine that the addresses you've been given are not sufficient, then you will need to obtain one or more blocks of addresses. You should try these three sources in order:

1. Your organization's network manager

2. Your Internet Service Provider

3. The Internet Address Registry

WARNING

Keep in mind one important reality: IP Addresses are a scarce and valuable commodity. No matter who supplies your addresses, they are under pressure to allocate addresses efficiently. It is likely that you will be asked to justify your request. Most often, your request will be honored as long as you can document that you will actually use at least half the addresses you ask for in the near future.

From Your Organization's Network Manager

In most organizations of any size at all, there is, or at least there *should be*, one person (or a small group) responsible for allocating IP addresses to individuals and groups. Your first source of IP addresses would be such a resource.

From Your ISP

If your organization does not have a central allocation resource, or if *you* are that resource, then you may have to go outside your organization to obtain the addresses.

If you plan to connect to the Internet, then you must use either globally-unique addresses, or private addresses and network address translation (refer to Chapters 3 and 4). If you do not plan to connect to the Internet (really?), then technically, you can use any addresses you want. However, RFC 1918 recommends that you use the addresses set aside for such purposes. Again, refer to Chapter 3 for details.

To obtain globally-unique addresses, you should contact your Internet service provider (ISP) and present your request. You will be allocated a block of addresses that is a subset of the block that your ISP has been assigned.

For IT Professionals

Hierarchical Allocation of IP Addresses

This hierarchical allocation of addresses—from Internet registry, to major ISP to minor ISP, to end user—increases the efficiency of the overall Internet by keeping major blocks of IP addresses together, thus reducing the size of the core routing tables.

From Your Internet Registry

The ultimate source for IP addresses is the Internet Registry that has jurisdiction in your country. There are currently three regional registries:

- ARIN: American Registry of Internet Numbers (www.arin.net). ARIN has jurisdiction for North America, South America, sub–Saharan Africa, and the Caribbean.
- RIPE NCC (www.ripe.net). European Registry.
- APNIC (www.apnic.net). Asia Pacific Registry.

RFC 2050 describes in more detail the policies regarding IP address allocation.

NOTE

Addresses obtained directly from an Internet Registry such as ARIN are guaranteed to be unique, but *they are not guaranteed to be globally routable*—in fact, you can almost count on the fact that they won't be. To make them work on the global Internet, you will need to be a "peer" on the Internet, interconnecting with other major ISPs.

Calculate Ranges of IP Addresses for Each Subnet

Let's recap. So far we have

- Determined our addressing requirements
- Chosen the proper mask
- Obtained sufficient IP addresses.

Now it's time to determine the appropriate range of addresses for each subnet.

Doing It the Hard Way

If you find yourself without any tools, you can always fall back to the manual method. There are shortcuts floating around "on the grapevine" that work in certain circumstances, but not in others. The following procedure works with all classes of addresses and all masks. Let's apply the procedure to our sample network.

First, identify the number of locally administered bits in your network address. In our example, we've been assigned a class C network (192.168.153.0). Class C networks have 24 network bits and 8 local bits.

Second, make a place for each of the local bits—eight of them in our example:

_ _ _ _ _ _ _ _

Next, using the mask, we designate the subnet bits and the host bits. In our example, we chose 255.255.255.224 as our mask. Consulting Table 2.3, we see that this mask specifies three subnet bits and five host bits.

Subnet | Host
_ _ _|_ _ _ _ _

Now we can start plugging in various combinations of valid bit patterns as we learned in Chapter 2. Three bits can be combined in 2^3 (8) combinations as listed:

000	100
001	101
010	110
011	111

In our example, we chose to use subnet zero, so we'll start there. Filling in the valid subnet bits into our template, we have

```
Subnet |   Host
0 0 0 | X X X X X
```

Remember, for each subnet there are four meaningful addresses:

- The subnet address (host bits all zero)
- The first assignable IP address
- The last assignable IP address
- The broadcast address (host bits all ones)

So our first subnet looks like this:

```
Subnet |    Host
0 0 0 | 0 0 0 0 0 = 0  (subnet address)
0 0 0 | 0 0 0 0 1 = 1  (subnet + 1)
   ... |
0 0 0 | 1 1 1 1 0 = 30 (broadcast – 1)
0 0 0 | 1 1 1 1 1 = 31 (broadcast address)
```

The first subnet address is 192.168.153.0, the range of addresses assignable to various devices is 192.168.153.1 through 192.168.153.30, and the broadcast address for the subnet is 192.168.153.31.

If we repeat the process for the other subnets, we simply use a different subnet bit pattern for each. The second subnet would be calculated as follows:

```
Subnet |    Host
0  0  1 | 0  0  0  0  0 = 32 (subnet address)
0  0  1 | 0  0  0  0  1 = 33 (subnet + 1)
   ...  |
0  0  1 | 1  1  1  1  0 = 62 (broadcast – 1)
0  0  1 | 1  1  1  1  1 = 63 (broadcast address)
```

Continuing through all eight possible subnets, we can summarize in Table 2.4.

Table 2.4 Summary of Addresses for the Example Network

Subnet Address	First Assignable	Last Assignable	Broadcast Address
192.168.153.0	192.168.153.1	192.168.153.30	192.168.153.31
192.168.153.32	192.168.153.33	192.168.153.62	192.168.153.63
192.168.153.64	192.168.153.65	192.168.153.94	192.168.153.95
192.168.153.96	192.168.153.97	192.168.153.126	192.168.153.127
192.168.153.128	192.168.153.129	192.168.153.158	192.168.153.159
192.168.153.160	192.168.153.161	192.168.153.190	192.168.153.191
192.168.153.192	192.168.153.193	192.168.153.222	192.168.153.223
192.168.153.224	192.168.153.225	192.168.153.254	192.168.153.255

Table 2.4, along with all other possibilities for any network/mask combination, can also be found at the end of this chapter.

Worksheets

"Doing it the hard way" can be intellectually satisfying. However, when you want to get real work done, some simple tools can often save you a lot of time. For example, a series of tabular worksheets can serve the dual purpose of helping you calculate address ranges and tracking the assignment of addresses to devices on your network. Table 2.5 is the beginning few rows of a subnet assignment worksheet. The full worksheet (with addresses from zero to 255) is located at the end of the chapter.

Table 2.5 Subnet Assignment Worksheet

Addr	.128	.192	.224	.240	.248	.252	Assigned To
0							
1							
2							
3							
4							
5							
6							
7							
8							
9							
10							
11							
12							
13							
14							
15							
16							

The worksheet provides a visual reference to the addresses that are valid for each subnet, regardless of the mask used. For example, if we had chosen a mask of 255.255.255.248, the range of addresses available in the first subnet would be 192.168.153.1 through 192.168.153.6. The second subnet would contain

192.168.153.9 through 192.168.153.14. This is the same result that we would have obtained by doing the calculations "the hard way" or by using the subnetting tables.

The second benefit of a worksheet like this is that it is self–documenting. As you assign subnets, you can write in the column (under the appropriate mask) descriptive information about the subnet— where it is located, technical contact, etc. You can also track individual address assignments by filling in information in the Assigned To column.

The worksheet is also *scaleable*. Each worksheet can document a single class C network. If you have to track allocations for a class B network, you can use one worksheet to document each group of 256 addresses, then one more worksheet to show a summary of the groups.

Subnet Calculators

Probably the easiest way to calculate address ranges is to use a subnet calculator. There are many such calculators available on the Internet as freeware or shareware. (See the FAQs for sources.) Using the IP Subnet Calculator from Net3 Group (www.net3group.com), we can calculate the address ranges for the subnets in our sample network.

First, we tell the calculator that we are using network 192.168.153.0 (a class C address), and a mask of 255.255.255.224 as shown in Figure 2.3.

Then, we simply click on the **Subnets/Hosts** tab to reveal the usable address ranges as shown in Figure 2.4.

Again, the results seen here match those obtained manually and from worksheets. By clicking the button above the CIDR tab, the calculator will copy the table shown to the Windows clipboard. You can then paste the table into a spreadsheet or other tools for further manipulation.

Figure 2.3 IP Subnet Calculator.

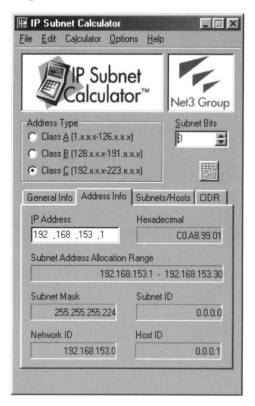

Allocate Addresses to Devices

We've finally arrived at the goal of the exercise—to allocate individual addresses to the IP devices in our network.

Assigning Subnets

The first step is to assign subnets to appropriate network segments. Revisiting our network segments (from Table 2.2) we can now add a third column for the subnets assigned to each segment, as shown in Table 2.6.

Figure 2.4 Assignable address ranges.

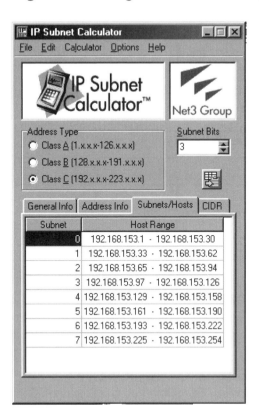

Is this the only way to assign the subnets? Absolutely not: Pick any of the eight subnets and assign them to any of the seven network segments. Technically, it makes no difference at all which subnet is assigned to which segment. The only factor to consider here is ease of use and documentation.

Notice that subnet zero was allocated to one of the WAN links. Since we can't be totally conservative here—we must use subnet zero, we'll allocate it to a network segment that is least likely to have interoperability problems. The idea here is that most routers purchased in the last few years do support the subnet zero feature without any problems.

Table 2.6 Subnet Assignment

Subnet	IP Addresses	Subnet(s)
Headquarters	25	192.168.153.32
Morganton	14	192.168.153.64
Lenoir	13	192.168.153.96
Hickory	7	192.168.153.128
WAN1	2	192.168.153.160
WAN2	2	192.168.153.192
WAN3	2	192.168.153.0

Assigning Device Addresses

Once you've assigned subnets to the various network segments, it's time to assign individual addresses to devices that need them. Here again is where the worksheets come in handy. Let's assign addresses for the Hickory subnet in our sample network. Table 2.7 contains another excerpt from the address assignment worksheet.

Table 2.7 Subnet Assignment Worksheet—Hickory

Add	.128	.192	.224	.240	.248	.252	Assigned To
128							Hickory LAN
129			R				Router
130			S				Server
131			W				WS: John
132			W				WS: Laurie
133			W				WS: David
134			W				WS: Sarah
135			W				WS: Val
136							
137							

Again, there is no *one* correct way to do these assignments—it's up to you. There are basically three schools of thought on the matter: sequential allocation, reserved addresses, and "grow towards the middle."

Sequential Allocation

In Table 2.7, we simply assigned the next available IP address to each device without too much regard to the type or function of the device. The advantages to this approach are flexibility, and no wasted addresses. The disadvantages include no order or scheme of assignment, and no way to determine the function of the device based on its address.

Reserved Addresses

The second approach consists of reserving a range of addresses in each subnet for various functions. For example,

Routers:	first three addresses
Servers:	next five addresses
Misc:	next five addresses (printer, smart hubs, etc.)
Workstations:	all remaining addresses.

The advantage here is that you (and your support staff) can readily determine the kind of device based on its address. Conversely, given a device, you can determine its address. The main disadvantage is that the reserved addresses can go unused, while there may be a need for more addresses in other functional groups.

Grow Towards the Middle

The third technique is to assign the main subnet router the first available address on the subnet, then assign the next higher addresses in sequence to other internetworking and support devices. Workstations are assigned addresses from the top of the address range down, as needed.

This technique allows all available addresses to be used, while preserving some kind of functional consistency.

Use the technique with which you are most comfortable. Many administrators use a combination of the three techniques.

Document Your Work

Congratulations! You've completed the assignment of IP addresses to all the networked devices that need them. Time to relax—almost.

Keeping Track of What You've Done

You've spent quite a bit of time so far working out the details of this project. A small additional investment of time can yield big dividends down the road. Yes, we're talking about documentation—again.

If you've used the worksheet method of allocation addresses, then your work is done. If you used an IP calculator or the back of a napkin, you should probably transfer your work to something more permanent.

Paper

At the very least, write down what you have done:

- Address Blocks obtained
- Mask chosen
- Subnets assigned
- IP addresses assigned (and to whom)

Keep your notes where they can be updated when things change.

Spreadsheets

With a little work, you can create a significant source of information by putting your assignment data into a spreadsheet. Create columns for:

- IP address
- Date assigned
- Assigned to
- Contact information (phone, fax, e–mail)
- Device type

Many spreadsheet applications provide for a simple data entry form to assist in loading the information. Throughout the life of your network you can query, sort, and report on information in the spreadsheet to give you assignments by name, by address, by type, by date, and so on. When the time comes for an upgrade, wouldn't it be nice to have a way to identify quickly the addresses and locations of all your routers?

Databases

Just about anything you can do with a spreadsheet, you can do with a database application as well. Most database software will allow you to create input forms with data validation to help keep errors out, and most provide report–writing capability to produce standard and *ad hoc* reports.

The IP address allocation database does not have to be very sophisticated to be effective. A simple one–table database in Microsoft Access, for example, can provide appropriate information for a very large organization.

Many new Network Management applications now on the market provide asset management functions where networked devices are tracked. Use these facilities to record allocation and contact information as listed earlier.

In Any Case

No network is static. Users come and go; applications just seem to keep coming. Technology changes. Many network designers are replacing routers with layer–2 and layer–3 switches. Keep your documentation up to date! Out of date information is, in some ways, worse than no information at all.

Summary

In this chapter, we have presented the steps required to develop an effective IP addressing plan for networks with fixed masks. First, we determined the number of IP addresses and subnets actually needed, with some hints for squeezing the most out of the addresses you've been given. Using subnetting tables, we determined the proper mask to use. Next came the calculation of appropriate address ranges using manual techniques, worksheets, or subnet calculators. We then assigned IP addresses to those devices that needed them. Finally, we discussed the importance of properly documenting our work.

FAQs

Q: What if my ISP or network administrator won't give me the number of addresses I need?

A: First, be sure your request is realistic. If you're paying $10 per month for dial–up Internet access, don't be surprised if your ISP won't give you 16 class C network prefixes! In fact, if you are simply subscribing to monthly dial–up access, your ISP probably won't want to give you *any* permanent IP addresses. If, however, you are purchasing a T1 line for full–time access, your ISP probably will be more likely to be generous with a block of addresses. In general, if you can document that you will be implementing *at least half* of the addresses requested within six months, your request should be granted. If your ISP is still reluctant to give you enough addresses, you may have to rely on other techniques, such as variable–length subnetting (Chapter 5) or private addresses (Chapter 3).

Q: Where can I get a subnet calculator?

A: URLs:

http://www.net3group.com/download.asp
> Downloadable stand–alone application that runs under Win 95/98/NT.

http://www.cisco.com/techtools/ip_addr.html
> Online calculator.

http://www.ccci.com/subcalc/download.htm
> Java–based calculator.

http://www.ajw.com/ipcalc.htm
> Calculator for the Palm Pilot.

Exercises

1. You've been assigned a "/23" CIDR block. How many traditional class C networks does that represent? What is the equivalent net mask? How many total host addresses does the block cover?

2. What mask would you use if you needed to divide a class B network into 200 subnets with 100 addresses needed in each?

3. Two routers are connected via a leased T1 line. Do these router interfaces need an IP address? Why or why not?

4. Under what circumstances would you use a fixed–length subnetting scheme?

5. Using any method you prefer, calculate the address ranges for all the subnets created in a class B network using the mask 255.255.254.0. Use the all–zeros and all–ones subnets.

6. What size CIDR block would you ask for if you needed 420 subnets with 170 host addresses each?

7. Why can't you use a mask of 255.255.255.254?

8. Why should you bother documenting your address assignments?

Answers

1. 2 class C's; 255.255.254.0; 512 addresses

2. There are two possible masks: 255.255.255.0 and 255.255.255.128. Since we were not given any information about growth, we need to pick the one most likely to meet our future needs. The most common choice would probably be 255.255.255.0 since it is easy to use and allows some growth in the number of subnets and significant growth in the size of each subnet.

3. In general, the answer is yes. However, if the routers support the "IP unnumbered" feature, they do not.

4. You must use a fixed–length subnetting scheme if you are using a routing protocol that does not support variable–length subnetting. Of the common IP routing protocols in use today, RIP (v. 1) and Cisco's IGRP require fixed–length subnetting. RIP2, EIGRP, and OSPF support variable–length subnetting. When using those protocols, you *still* may want to choose fixed–length subnetting for simplicity.

5. 128 subnets as follows:
   N.N.0.0 – N.N.1.255
   N.N.2.0 – N.N.3.255
   N.N.4.0 – N.N.5.255
   ...
   N.N.254.0 – N.N.255.255

6. Based on the 170–address requirement, you would choose a mask of 255.255.255.0. In other words, you need eight bits to cover the host addresses. You need another nine bits to cover the number of subnets for a total need of 17 bits. Since an IP address is 32 bits long, and you need 17 for you own use, you would ask for a (32 – 17) or 15–bit block (/15 in CIDR notation).

7. The host field needs to be at least two bits long. A host field of all zeros denotes the subnet address, and a host field of all ones is the broadcast address for that subnet.

8. To help with future assignments, to assist with troubleshooting activities, to help with upgrades, to prevent duplicate address assignments.

Subnetting Tables

Note that these tables comply with RFC.

Class A Subnetting Table

# Subnet Bits	# Subnets	# Host Bits	# Hosts	Mask
1	2	23	8,388,608	255.128.0.0
2	4	22	4,194,302	255.192.0.0
3	8	21	2,097,150	255.224.0.0
4	16	20	1,048,574	255.240.0.0
5	32	19	524,286	255.248.0.0
6	64	18	262,142	255.252.0.0
7	128	17	131,070	255.254.0.0
8	256	16	65,534	255.255.0.0
9	512	15	32,766	255.255.128.0
10	1,024	14	16,382	255.255.192.0
11	2,048	13	8,190	255.255.224.0
12	4,096	12	4,094	255.255.240.0
13	8,192	11	2,046	255.255.248.0
14	16,384	10	1,022	255.255.252.0
15	32,768	9	510	255.255.254.0
16	65,536	8	254	255.255.255.0
17	131,072	7	126	255.255.255.128
18	262,144	6	62	255.255.255.192
19	524,288	5	30	255.255.255.224
20	1,048,576	4	14	255.255.255.240
21	2,097,152	3	6	255.255.255.248
22	4,194,304	2	2	255.255.255.252

Subnet	First Host	Last Host	Subnet Broadcast
1 Bit (255.128.0.0)			
N.0.0.0	N.0.0.1	N.127.255.254	N.127.255.255
N.128.0.0	N.128.0.1	N.255.255.254	N.255.255.255
2 Bits (255.192.0.0)			
N.0.0.0	N.0.0.1	N.63.255.254	N.63.255.255
N.64.0.0	N.64.0.1	N.127.255.254	N.127.255.255
N.128.0.0	N.128.0.1	N.191.255.254	N.191.255.255
N.192.0.0	N.192.0.1	N.255.255.254	N.255.255.255
3 Bits (255.224.0.0)			
N.0.0.0	N.0.0.1	N.31.255.254	N.31.255.255
N.32.0.0	N.32.0.1	N.63.255.254	N.63.255.255
. . .			
N.192.0.0	N.192.0.1	N.223.255.254	N.223.255.255
N.224.0.0	N.224.0.1	N.255.255.254	N.255.255.255
4 Bits (255.240.0.0)			
N.0.0.0	N.0.0.1	N.15.255.254	N.15.255.255
N.16.0.0	N.16.0.1	N.31.255.254	N.31.255.255
. . .			
N.224.0.0	N.224.0.1	N.239.255.254	N.239.255.255
N.240.0.0	N.240.0.1	N.255.255.254	N.255.255.255
5 Bits (255.248.0.0)			
N.0.0.0	N.0.0.1	N.7.255.254	N.7.255.255
N.8.0.0	N.8.0.1	N.15.255.254	N.15.255.255
. . .			
N.240.0.0	N.240.0.1	N.247.255.254	N.247. 255.255
N.248.0.0	N.248.0.1	N.255.255.254	N.255.255.255
6 Bits (255.252.0.0)			
N.0.0.0	N.0.0.1	N.3.255.254	N.3.255.255
N.4.0.0	N.4.0.1	N.7.255.254	N.7.255.255

. . .

N.248.0.0	N.248.0.1	N.251.255.254	N.251.255.255
N.252.0.0	N.252.0.1	N.255.255.254	N.255.255.255

7 Bits (255.254.0.0)

N.0.0.0	N.0.0.1	N.1.255.254	N.1.255.255
N.2.0.0	N.2.0.1	N.3.255.254	N.3.255.255
. . .			
N.252.0.0	N.252.0.1	N.253.255.254	N.253.255.255
N.254.0.0	N.254.0.1	N.255.255.254	N.255.255.255

8 Bits (255.255.0.0)

N.0.0.0	N.0.0.1	N.0.255.254	N.0.255.255
N.1.0.0	N.1.0.1	N.1.255.254	N.1.255.255
. . .			
N.254.0.0	N.254.0.1	N.254.255.254	N.254.255.255
N.255.0.0	N.255.0.1	N.255.255.254	N.255.255.255

9 Bits (255.255.128.0)

N.0.0.0	N.0.0.1	N.0.127.254	N.0.127.255
N.0.128.0	N.0.128.1	N.0.255.254	N.0.255.255
N.1.0.0	N.1.0.1	N.1.127.254	N.1.127.255
N.1.128.0	N.1.128.1	N.1.255.254	N.1.255.255
. . .			
N.255.0.0	N.255.0.1	N.255.127.254	N.255.127.255
N.255.128.0	N.255.128.1	N.255.255.254	N.255.255.255

10 Bits (255.255.192.0)

N.0.0.0	N.0.0.1	N.0.63.254	N.0.63.255
N.0.64.0	N.0.64.1	N.0.127.254	N.0.127.255
N.0.128.0	N.0.128.1	N.0.191.254	N.0.191.255
N.0.192.0	N.0.192.1	N.0.255.254	N.0.255.255
N.1.0.0	N.1.0.1	N.1.63.254	N.1.63.255
N.1.64.0	N.1.64.1	N.1.127.254	N.1.127.255

. . .

| N.255.128.0 | N.255.128.1 | N.255.191.254 | N.255.191.255 |
| N.255.192.0 | N.255.192.1 | N.255.255.254 | N.255.255.255 |

11 Bits (255.255.224.0)

N.0.0.0	N.0.0.1	N.0.31.254	N.0.31.255
N.0.32.0	N.0.32.1	N.0.63.254	N.0.63.255
N.0.64.0	N.0.64.1	N.0.127.254	N.0.127.255
. . .			
N.255.192.0	N.255.192.1	N.255.223.254	N.255.223.255
N.255.224.0	N.255.224.1	N.255.255.254	N.255.255.255

12 Bits (255.255.240.0)

N.0.0.0	N.0.0.1	N.0.15.254	N.0.15.255
N.0.16.0	N.0.16.1	N.0.31.254	N.0.31.255
N.0.32.0	N.0.32.1	N.0.47.254	N.0.47.255
. . .			
N.255.224.0	N.255.224.1	N.255.239.254	N.255.239.255
N.255.240.0	N.255.240.1	N.255.255.254	N.255.255.255

13 Bits (255.255.248.0)

N.0.0.0	N.0.0.1	N.0.7.254	N.0.7.255
N.0.8.0	N.0.8.1	N.0.15.254	N.0.15.255
N.0.16.0	N.0.16.1	N.0.23.254	N.0.23.255
. . .			
N.255.240.0	N.255.240.1	N.255.247.254	N.255.247.255
N.255.248.0	N.255.248.1	N.255.255.254	N.255.255.255

14 Bits (255.255.252.0)

N.0.0.0	N.0.0.1	N.0.3.254	N.0.3.255
N.0.4.0	N.0.4.1	N.0.7.254	N.0.7.255
N.0.8.0	N.0.8.1	N.0.11.254	N.0.11.255
. . .			
N.255.248.0	N.255.248.1	N.255.251.254	N.255.251.255
N.255.252.0	N.255.252.1	N.255.255.254	N.255.255.255

15 Bits (255.255.254.0)

N.0.0.0	N.0.0.1	N.0.1.254	N.0.1.255
N.0.2.0	N.0.2.1	N.0.3.254	N.0.3.255
N.0.4.0	N.0.4.1	N.0.5.254	N.0.5.255
. . .			
N.255.252.0	N.255.252.1	N.255.253.254	N.255.253.255
N.255.254.0	N.255.254.1	N.255.255.254	N.255.255.255

16 Bits (255.255.255.0)

N.0.0.0	N.0.0.1	N.0.0.254	N.0.0.255
N.0.1.0	N.0.1.1	N.0.1.254	N.0.1.255
N.0.2.0	N.0.2.1	N.0.2.254	N.0.2.255
. . .			
N.255.254.0	N.255.254.1	N.255.254.254	N.255.254.255
N.255.255.0	N.255.255.1	N.255.255.254	N.255.255.255

17 Bits (255.255.255.128)

N.0.0.0	N.0.0.1	N.0.0.126	N.0.0.127
N.0.0.128	N.0.0.129	N.0.0.254	N.0.0.255
N.0.1.0	N.0.1.1	N.0.1.126	N.0.1.127
N.0.1.128	N.0.1.129	N.0.1.254	N.0.1.255
. . .			
N.255.255.0	N.255.255.1	N.255.255.126	N.255.255.127
N.255.255.128	N.255.255.129	N.255.255.254	N.255.255.255

18 Bits (255.255.255.192)

N.0.0.0	N.0.0.1	N.0.0.62	N.0.0.63
N.0.0.64	N.0.0.65	N.0.0.126	N.0.0.127
N.0.0.128	N.0.0.129	N.0.0.190	N.0.1.191
N.0.0.192	N.0.0.193	N.0.0.254	N.0.1.255
N.0.1.0	N.0.1.1	N.0.1.62	N.0.1.63
. . .			
N.255.255.128	N.255.255.129	N.255.255.190	N.255.255.191
N.255.255.192	N.255.255.193	N.255.255.254	N.255.255.255

19 Bits (255.255.255.224)

N.0.0.0	N.0.0.1	N.0.0.30	N.0.0.31
N.0.0.32	N.0.0.33	N.0.0.62	N.0.0.63
N.0.0.64	N.0.0.65	N.0.0.94	N.0.0.95
N.0.0.96	N.0.0.97	N.0.0.126	N.0.0.127

...

N.255.255.192	N.255.255.193	N.255.255.222	N.255.255.223
N.255.255.224	N.255.255.225	N.255.255.254	N.255.255.255

20 Bits (255.255.255.240)

N.0.0.0	N.0.0.1	N.0.0.14	N.0.0.15
N.0.0.16	N.0.0.16	N.0.0.30	N.0.0.31
N.0.0.32	N.0.0.33	N.0.0.46	N.0.0.47

...

N.255.255.224	N.255.255.225	N.255.255.238	N.255.255.239
N.255.255.240	N.255.255.241	N.255.255.254	N.255.255.255

21 Bits (255.255.255.248)

N.0.0.0	N.0.0.1	N.0.0.6	N.0.0.7
N.0.0.8	N.0.0.9	N.0.0.14	N.0.0.15
N.0.0.16	N.0.0.17	N.0.0.22	N.0.0.23

...

N.255.255.240	N.255.255.241	N.255.255.246	N.255.255.247
N.255.255.248	N.255.255.249	N.255.255.254	N.255.255.255

22 Bits (255.255.255.252)

N.0.0.0	N.0.0.1	N.0.0.2	N.0.0.3
N.0.0.4	N.0.0.5	N.0.0.6	N.0.0.7
N.0.0.8	N.0.0.9	N.0.0.10	N.0.0.11

...

N.255.255.248	N.255.255.249	N.255.255.250	N.255.255.251
N.255.255.252	N.255.255.253	N.255.255.254	N.255.255.255

Class B Subnetting Table

# Subnet Bits	# Subnets	# Host Bits	# Hosts	Mask
1	2	15	32,766	255.255.128.0
2	4	14	16,382	255.255.192.0
3	8	13	8,190	255.255.224.0
4	16	12	4,094	255.255.240.0
5	32	11	2,046	255.255.248.0
6	64	10	1,022	255.255.252.0
7	128	9	510	255.255.254.0
8	256	8	254	255.255.255.0
9	512	7	126	255.255.255.128
10	1,024	6	62	255.255.255.192
11	2,048	5	30	255.255.255.224
12	4,096	4	14	255.255.255.240
13	8,192	3	6	255.255.255.248
14	16,384	2	2	255.255.255.252

Subnet	First Host	Last Host	Subnet Broadcast
1 Bit (255.255.128.0)			
N.N.0.0	N.N.0.1	N.N.127.254	N.N.127.255
N.N.128.0	N.N.128.1	N.N.191.254	N.N.191.255
2 Bits (255.255.192.0)			
N.N.0.0	N.N.0.1	N.N.63.254	N.N.63.255
N.N.64.0	N.N.64.1	N.N.127.254	N.N.127.255
N.N.128.0	N.N.128.1	N.N.191.254	N.N.191.255
N.N.192.0	N.N.192.1	N.N.255.254	N.N.255.255

3 Bits (255.255.224.0)

N.N.0.0	N.N.0.1	N.N.31.254	N.N.31.255
N.N 32.0	N.N.32.1	N.N.63.254	N.N.63.255
N.N.64.0	N.N.64.1	N.N.95.254	N.N.95.255
. . .			
N.N.192.0	N.N.192.1	N.N.223.254	N.N.223.255
N.N.224.0	N.N.224.1	N.N.255.254	N.N.255.255

4 Bits (255.255.240.0)

N.N.0.0	N.N.0.1	N.N.15.254	N.N.15.255
N.N 16.0	N.N.16.1	N.N.31.254	N.N.31.255
N.N.32.0	N.N.32.1	N.N.47.254	N.N.47.255
. . .			
N.N.224.0	N.N.224.1	N.N.239.254	N.N.239.255
N.N.240.0	N.N.240.1	N.N.255.254	N.N.255.255

5 Bits (255.255.248.0)

N.N.0.0	N.N.0.1	N.N.7.254	N.N.7.255
N.N 8.0	N.N.8.1	N.N.15.254	N.N.15.255
N.N.16.0	N.N.16.1	N.N.23.254	N.N.23.255
. . .			
N.N.240.0	N.N.240.1	N.N.247.254	N.N.247.255
N.N.248.0	N.N.248.1	N.N.255.254	N.N.255.255

6 Bits (255.255.252.0)

N.N.0.0	N.N.0.1	N.N.3.254	N.N.3.255
N.N 4.0	N.N.4.1	N.N.7.254	N.N.7.255
N.N.8.0	N.N.8.1	N.N.11.254	N.N.11.255
. . .			
N.N.248.0	N.N.248.1	N.N.251.254	N.N.251.255
N.N.252.0	N.N.252.1	N.N.255.254	N.N.255.255

7 Bits (255.255.254.0)

N.N.0.0	N.N.0.1	N.N.1.254	N.N.1.255
N.N 2.0	N.N.2.1	N.N.3.254	N.N.3.255
N.N.4.0	N.N.4.1	N.N.5.254	N.N.5.255
. . .			
N.N.252.0	N.N.252.1	N.N.253.254	N.N.253.255
N.N.254.0	N.N.254.1	N.N.255.254	N.N.255.255

8 Bits (255.255.255.0)

N.N.0.0	N.N.0.1	N.N.0.254	N.N.0.255
N.N 1.0	N.N.1.1	N.N.1.254	N.N.1.255
N.N.2.0	N.N.2.1	N.N.2.254	N.N.2.255
. . .			
N.N.254.0	N.N.254.1	N.N.254.254	N.N.254.255
N.N.255.0	N.N.255.1	N.N.255.254	N.N.255.255

9 Bits (255.255.255.128)

N.N.0.0	N.N.0.1	N.N.0.126	N.N.0.127
N.N 0.128	N.N.0.129	N.N.0.254	N.N.0.255
N.N.1.0	N.N.1.1	N.N.1.126	N.N.1.127
N.N.1.128	N.N.1.129	N.N.1.254	N.N.1.255
. . .			
N.N.255.0	N.N.255.1	N.N.255.126	N.N.255.127
N.N.255.128	N.N.255.129	N.N.255.254	N.N.255.255

10 Bits (255.255.255.192)

N.N.0.0	N.N.0.1	N.N.0.62	N.N.0.63
N.N 0.64	N.N.0.65	N.N.0.126	N.N.0.127
N.N 0.128	N.N.0.129	N.N.0.190	N.N.0.191
N.N.0.192	N.N.0.193	N.N.0.254	N.N.0.255
N.N.1.0	N.N.1.1	N.N.1.62	N.N.1.63
. . .			
N.N.255.128	N.N.255.129	N.N.255.190	N.N.255.191
N.N.255.192	N.N.255.193	N.N.255.254	N.N.255.255

11 Bits (255.255.255.224)

N.N.0.0	N.N.0.1	N.N.0.30	N.N.0.31
N.N 0.32	N.N.0.33	N.N.0.62	N.N.0.63
N.N 0.64	N.N.0.65	N.N.0.94	N.N.0.95
. . .			
N.N.255.192	N.N.255.192	N.N.255.222	N.N.255.223
N.N.255.224	N.N.255.225	N.N.255.254	N.N.255.255

12 Bits (255.255.255.240)

N.N.0.0	N.N.0.1	N.N.0.14	N.N.0.15
N.N 0.16	N.N.0.17	N.N.0.30	N.N.0.31
N.N 0.32	N.N.0.33	N.N.0.46	N.N.0.47
. . .			
N.N.255.224	N.N.255.225	N.N.255.238	N.N.255.239
N.N.255.240	N.N.255.241	N.N.255.254	N.N.255.255

13 Bits (255.255.255.248)

N.N.0.0	N.N.0.1	N.N.0.6	N.N.0.7
N.N 0.8	N.N.0.9	N.N.0.14	N.N.0.15
N.N 0.16	N.N.0.17	N.N.0.22	N.N.0.23
. . .			
N.N.255.240	N.N.255.241	N.N.255.246	N.N.255.247
N.N.255.248	N.N.255.249	N.N.255.254	N.N.255.255

14 Bits (255.255.255.252)

N.N.0.0	N.N.0.1	N.N.0.2	N.N.0.3
N.N 0.4	N.N.0.5	N.N.0.6	N.N.0.7
N.N 0.8	N.N.0.9	N.N.0.10	N.N.0.11
. . .			
N.N.255.248	N.N.255.249	N.N.255.250	N.N.255.251
N.N.255.252	N.N.255.253	N.N.255.254	N.N.255.255

Class C Subnetting Table

# Subnet Bits	# Subnets	# Host Bits	# Hosts	Mask
1	2	7	126	255.255.255.128
2	4	6	62	255.255.255.192
3	8	5	30	255.255.255.224
4	16	4	14	255.255.255.240
5	32	3	6	255.255.255.248
6	64	2	2	255.255.255.252

Subnet	First Host	Last Host	Subnet Broadcast

1 Bit (255.255.255.128)

Subnet	First Host	Last Host	Subnet Broadcast
N.N.N.0	N.N.N.1	N.N.N.126	N.N.N.127
N.N.N.128	N.N.N.129	N.N.N.254	N.N.N.255

2 Bits (255.255.255.192)

Subnet	First Host	Last Host	Subnet Broadcast
N.N.N.0	N.N.N.1	N.N.N.62	N.N.N.63
N.N.N.64	N.N.N.65	N.N.N.126	N.N.N.127
N.N.N.128	N.N.N.129	N.N.N.190	N.N.N.191
N.N.N.192	N.N.N.193	N.N.N.254	N.N.N.255

3 Bits (255.255.255.224)

Subnet	First Host	Last Host	Subnet Broadcast
N.N.N.0	N.N.N.1	N.N.N.30	N.N.N.31
N.N.N.32	N.N.N.33	N.N.N.62	N.N.N.63
N.N.N.64	N.N.N.65	N.N.N.94	N.N.N.95
N.N.N.96	N.N.N.97	N.N.N.126	N.N.N.127
N.N.N.128	N.N.N.129	N.N.N.158	N.N.N.159
N.N.N.160	N.N.N.161	N.N.N.190	N.N.N.191
N.N.N.192	N.N.N.193	N.N.N.222	N.N.N.223
N.N.N.224	N.N.N.225	N.N.N.254	N.N.N.255

4 Bits (255.255.255.240)

N.N.N.0	N.N.N.1	N.N.N.14	N.N.N.15
N.N.N.16	N.N.N.17	N.N.N.30	N.N.N.31
N.N.N.32	N.N.N.33	N.N.N.46	N.N.N.47
. . .			
N.N.N.224	N.N.N.225	N.N.N.238	N.N.N.239
N.N.N.240	N.N.N.241	N.N.N.254	N.N.N.255

5 Bits (255.255.255.248)

N.N.N.0	N.N.N.1	N.N.N.6	N.N.N.7
N.N.N.8	N.N.N.9	N.N.N.14	N.N.N.15
N.N.N.16	N.N.N.17	N.N.N.22	N.N.N.23
. . .			
N.N.N.240	N.N.N.241	N.N.N.246	N.N.N.247
N.N.N.248	N.N.N.249	N.N.N.254	N.N.N.255

6 Bits (255.255.255.252)

N.N.N.0	N.N.N.1	N.N.N.2	N.N.N.3
N.N.N.4	N.N.N.5	N.N.N.6	N.N.N.7
N.N.N.8	N.N.N.9	N.N.N.10	N.N.N.11
. . .			
N.N.N.248	N.N.N.249	N.N.N.250	N.N.N.251
N.N.N.252	N.N.N.253	N.N.N.254	N.N.N.255

Subnet Assignment Worksheet

Addr	.128	.192	.224	.240	.248	.252	Assigned To
0							
1							
2							
3							
4							
5							
6							
7							
8							
9							
10							
11							
12							
13							
14							
15							
16							
17							
18							
19							
20							
21							
22							
23							
24							
25							
26							
27							
28							
29							
30							
31							

Continued

Addr	.128	.192	.224	.240	.248	.252	Assigned To
32							
33							
34							
35							
36							
37							
38							
39							
40							
41							
42							
43							
44							
45							
46							
47							
48							
49							
50							
51							
52							
53							
54							
55							
56							
57							
58							
59							
60							
61							
62							
63							

Continued

Addr	.128	.192	.224	.240	.248	.252	Assigned To
64		░	░	░	░	░	
65							
66							
67						░	
68						░	
69							
70							
71					░	░	
72					░	░	
73							
74							
75						░	
76						░	
77							
78							
79				░	░	░	
80				░	░	░	
81							
82							
83						░	
84						░	
85							
86							
87					░	░	
88					░	░	
89							
90							
91						░	
92						░	
93							
94							
95			░	░	░	░	

Continued

Addr	.128	.192	.224	.240	.248	.252	Assigned To
96			▓	▓	▓	▓	
97							
98							
99						▓	
100						▓	
101							
102							
103					▓	▓	
104					▓	▓	
105							
106							
107						▓	
108						▓	
109							
110							
111				▓	▓	▓	
112				▓	▓	▓	
113							
114							
115						▓	
116						▓	
117							
118							
119					▓	▓	
120					▓	▓	
121							
122							
123						▓	
124						▓	
125							
126							
127	▓	▓	▓	▓	▓	▓	

Continued

Addr	.128	.192	.224	.240	.248	.252	Assigned To
128	▓	▓	▓	▓	▓	▓	
129							
130							
131						▓	
132						▓	
133							
134							
135					▓	▓	
136					▓	▓	
137							
138							
139						▓	
140						▓	
141							
142							
143				▓	▓	▓	
144				▓	▓	▓	
145							
146							
147						▓	
148						▓	
149							
150							
151					▓	▓	
152					▓	▓	
153							
154							
155						▓	
156						▓	
157							
158							
159			▓	▓	▓	▓	

Continued

Addr	.128	.192	.224	.240	.248	.252	Assigned To
160							
161							
162							
163							
164							
165							
166							
167							
168							
169							
170							
171							
172							
173							
174							
175							
176							
177							
178							
179							
180							
181							
182							
183							
184							
185							
186							
187							
188							
189							
190							
191							

Continued

Addr	.128	.192	.224	.240	.248	.252	Assigned To
192							
193							
194							
195							
196							
197							
198							
199							
200							
201							
202							
203							
204							
205							
206							
207							
208							
209							
210							
211							
212							
213							
214							
215							
216							
217							
218							
219							
220							
221							
222							
223							

Continued

Addr	.128	.192	.224	.240	.248	.252	Assigned To
224			▓	▓	▓	▓	
225							
226							
227						▓	
228						▓	
229							
230							
231					▓	▓	
232					▓	▓	
233							
234							
235						▓	
236						▓	
237							
238							
239				▓	▓	▓	
240				▓	▓	▓	
241							
242							
243						▓	
244						▓	
245							
246							
247					▓	▓	
248					▓	▓	
249							
250							
251						▓	
252						▓	
253							
254							
255	▓	▓	▓	▓	▓	▓	

Private Addressing and Subnetting Large Networks

Solutions in this chapter:

- Discover the motivation for using private addresses

- Calculate address allocation efficiency

- Examine RFC 1918 private address ranges

- Develop strategies for subnetting private addresses

Introduction

You've heard it said: "We're running out of IP addresses!" Really? In the IP (version 4) architecture, we use 32-bit address fields. With 32-bits in our addresses, there are 2^{32} unique addresses available. That's over four *billion* addresses! We know that the Internet has experienced exponential growth over the last few years, but even with continued growth, it's unlikely that we'll see anywhere near four billion machines on the Internet any time soon.

So where's the problem? The problem exists in the granularity of address allocation. Prior to Classless Inter-Domain Routing (CIDR), addresses were allocated in classful blocks. That is, if you needed more addresses than a class C network provided, you got a class B network address; if you needed more than a class B provided, you got a class A network address. Those were the only three choices. (Not many organizations actually got class A addresses, of course.)

Although there are indeed over 4 billion unique IP addresses available with the current version of IP, the number of unique *network numbers* is much less. In fact, there are only 126 class A networks, about 16,000 class B networks, and about 2 million class C networks. This design has led to widespread waste of globally-unique IP addresses.

Strategies to Conserve Addresses

In the 1970s, the architects of the Internet envisioned an internetwork with dozens of networks and hundreds of nodes. They developed a design where any node on the internetwork was reachable by any other node. Back then, no one could have guessed the effect new applications like the World Wide Web and vastly increased bandwidth would have on the number of people interested in participating in "the Net." On the Internet today, there are tens of thousands of networks and millions of nodes. Unfortunately, the original design has not scaled well. The increased number of networks joining the Internet has strained router technology, and the sheer number of participants has strained the limits of IP addressing as it was originally designed. Some compromises had to be made to allow the Internet to continue its growth.

Several strategies have been developed and implemented to help the Internet community cope with its growing pains. They help reduce the load on the Internet routers and help us use globally-unique IP addresses more efficiently. These strategies include:

- CIDR
- Variable-Length Subnet Masking (VLSM)
- Private Addressing

CIDR

Classless Inter-Domain Routing (CIDR), specified in RFCs 1517, 1518, and 1519, was introduced in September 1993 as a way to reduce router table growth. As a side effect, it has helped reduce the waste of IP addresses by reducing the granularity of allocation. Now, instead of full class A, B, or C networks, organizations can be allocated any number of addresses. (Normally, addresses are allocated in even powers of two to allow CIDR to realize its maximum benefit, but in reality, any number of addresses can be allocated.)

For example, if you needed 3,000 addresses for your network, a single class C network (256 addresses) would be insufficient. If, however, you were assigned a class B network (65,536 addresses), there would be over 62,000 addresses wasted! With CIDR, you can be allocated a block of 4,096 addresses—equivalent to 16 class C networks (a /20 in CIDR notation). This block of addresses will cover your addressing needs now, allow room for growth, and use global addresses efficiently. CIDR is covered in Chapter 6.

VLSM

Variable-Length Subnet Mask (VLSM) is a technique used to conserve IP addresses by tailoring the mask to each subnet. Subnets that need many addresses will use a mask that provides many addresses. Those that need fewer addresses will use a different mask. The idea is to assign "just the right amount" of addresses to each subnet.

Many organizations have point-to-point WAN links. Normally, these links comprise a subnet with only two addresses required. Our subnetting tables given in Chapter 2 tell us that 255.255.255.252 is the appropriate mask to use for those subnets. But that mask would never do for a typical LAN where there are dozens (if not hundreds) of hosts in a subnet. By using a routing protocol that supports VLSM, we can use a block of addresses much more efficiently. VLSM is explained in more detail in Chapter 5.

Private Addresses

By far, the most effective strategy for conserving globally-unique (public) IP addresses involves not using any at all! If your enterprise network will be using TCP/IP protocols, but will not be communicating with hosts on the global Internet, you don't need to use public IP addresses. The Internet Protocol simply requires that all hosts in the interconnected network have unique addresses. If the internetwork is limited to your organization, then the IP addresses need only be unique within your organization.

Today, many (if not most) organizations want to have at least some ability to communicate over the Internet. Does that mean these organizations must use public addresses? Yes it does—but it does not mean that all of the devices in that network must have public addresses. Such networks can still use private addresses and a technique called Network Address Translation (NAT) to convert those private (inside) addresses to public (outside) addresses. NAT is discussed in Chapter 4.

Addressing Economics

IPv6 is fixing the problem of the limited address space of IPv4. Until IPv6 is fully deployed, we must make use of the IP addressing system we have. Sometimes, the networks we must support are not IP-address friendly. For example, consider the sample network in Figure 3.1.

Figure 3.1 A sample network.

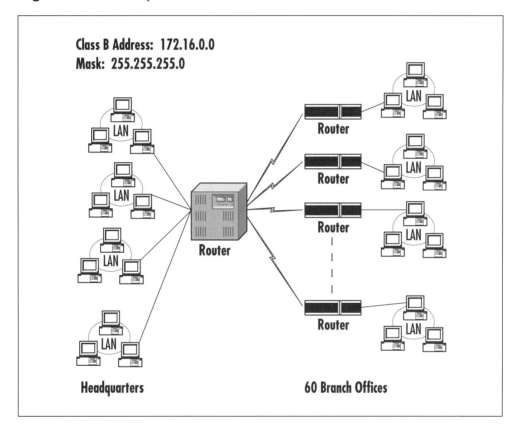

In the network shown in Figure 3.1, we have multiple LANs at the headquarters location and several branch offices that each have one LAN. The headquarters router is acting as a "collapsed backbone," connecting all the headquarters LANs and, via leased lines, the branch office routers. The organization has been assigned class B address 172.16.0.0, which provides 65,536 unique addresses.

As we mentioned in Chapter 2, the serial links connecting routers need their own IP addresses. In a point-to-point network such as the dedicated leased lines shown in Figure 3.1, each of the links is an individual subnet.

For IT Professionals

Using Frame Relay Networks as WAN Technology

When you use Frame Relay networks as your WAN technology, the entire Frame Relay "cloud" is one subnet, and each router interface will have an address appropriate for that subnet.

Table 3.1 lists the various subnets and the addressing requirements for each.

Table 3.1 Sample Network Addressing Needs

Location	# Subnets	# Hosts
Headquarters	1	50
	1	110
	1	190
	1	150
	1	150
Branches	60	30
WAN Links	60	2

In this example, the network is using RIP (version 1) as the routing protocol, so each subnet must use the same mask. Using guidelines discussed in Chapter 2, we identify the largest subnet in our network. One of the subnets at the Headquarters location needs 190 addresses. Consulting the tables in Chapter 2, we see that

255.255.255.0 is the most appropriate mask to use because it provides 254 unique addresses in each subnet. Table 3.2 shows just how inefficient it can be to use a single, fixed mask for all subnets.

Table 3.2 Sample Network Address Analysis

Location	# Subnets	Interfaces	Subnet Unused	Total Unused
Headquarters	1	50	204	204
	1	110	144	144
	1	190	64	64
	1	150	104	104
	1	150	104	104
Branches	60	30	224	13,440
WAN Links	60	2	252	15,120

The Headquarters subnets are sized appropriately, even allowing for some growth. The branch office subnets provide many more addresses than will actually be used. The biggest waste occurs in the WAN links. Since the sample network is using point-to-point links between headquarters and the branches, we will never need more than two addresses in each subnet. If you add up the numbers, there are a total of 2,570 addresses needed, but we are allocating 125 subnets with 254 addresses each for a total of 31,750 addresses. As you can see, we're not using our class B network address very efficiently. The situation is even worse than it first appears. We see there are over 29,000 unused addresses in the subnets we *are* using; we're only using 125 of the possible 256 subnets available. If you include the *other* 131 subnets with 254 possible addresses each, we have a grand total of 62,454 unused addresses. In other words, we're using just under 4 percent of the total addresses provided by our class B network number. This inefficient use of addresses is one of the main causes of IP address exhaustion.

If we could use VLSM, the subnets would be sized more appropriately, but the larger problem remains. We would still be using only about 4 percent of our total class B space.

An Appeal

RFC 1917, published in February 1996, is titled "An Appeal to the Internet Community to Return Unused IP Networks to the IANA." It cites the growing problem of IP address exhaustion and asks administrators to be good "netizens" and return blocks of IP addresses to the Internet Assigned Numbers Authority for reallocation. It suggests three alternatives:

1. If you aren't going to connect to the public Internet, you don't need globally-addresses. Use private addresses instead.

2. If you have a portable block of addresses, return the block to the IANA and use addresses supplied by your upstream Internet Service Provider.

3. If you have a large block of public addresses, but only need a small portion of them, return the large block to IANA and request a smaller block of addresses. This would be the appropriate action for our example network considered earlier.

Public vs Private Address Spaces

The Internet Protocol requires that each interface on a network has a unique address. If the scope of your network is global, then the addresses must be globally-unique. Such is the case with the Internet. Since global uniqueness must be assured, a centralized authority must be responsible for making sure IP address assignments are made correctly and fairly.

For the last few years, this has been the function of the IANA. The Internet has been rapidly expanding in both number of connected networks and number of new applications. The 1990s have seen both the commercialization and the internationalization of the Internet. To meet the demands of a growing Internet community, the IANA is being replaced by the Internet Corporation for Assigned Names and Numbers (ICANN).

NOTE

More information about the ICANN can be found at www.icann.com.

If an organization wants to use IP protocols and applications in its network, but has no intention of connecting its network to the global Internet, the IP addresses it uses need not be globally-unique. A network of this type is called a private network, and the addresses used are called private addresses.

Can I Pick My Own?

If you are deploying IP on a private network, you can use any IP addresses you wish, as long as you adhere to the normal IP addressing rules. Before you go crazy and use an entire class A address for each subnet, consider the following possibilities:

1. Most organizations will eventually choose to implement *some* kind of connection to the Internet—if for no other reason than to exchange e-mail.

2. There may be a merger or acquisition in your future that might require joining your network to one or more other networks.

As an example, suppose you needed a class C address for a small network that will not be connected to the Internet (see Figure 3.2). You chose to use 207.46.130.0 as your network address and configured all your devices accordingly. As soon as you finish getting everything set up, your boss decides to implement Internet e-mail. You consult your friendly neighborhood ISP who tells you not to worry. They can use a trick called Network Address Translation (see Chapter 4) that will allow you to keep using your addresses and give you access to the Internet. Great! Everything works just fine except for one thing—you can't access www.microsoft.com.

Figure 3.2 The danger of picking your own addresses.

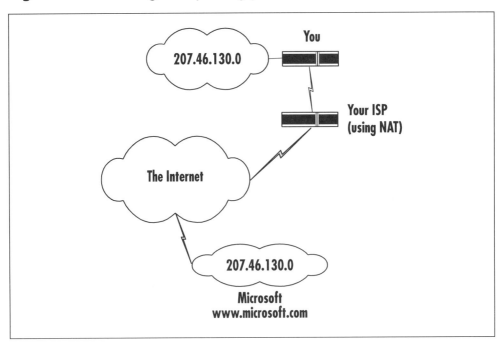

The class C address 207.46.130.0 has been officially assigned to Microsoft, which uses it in its Web server farm. When you try to access the Microsoft Web site, the DNS (Domain Name System) resolves the name to IP address 207.46.130.14. When your browser sends an HTTP request to the target address, the IP software thinks (rightly so) that the address is inside your network and does not forward it to the router.

The lesson here is that there is a risk in dreaming up your own IP addresses—even if you never intend to connect to the global Internet.

RFC 1918—Private Network Addresses

In the midst of the explosive Internet growth in the early 1990s, RFC 1597 suggested a way to help conserve globally-unique IP addresses. The idea was to set aside three blocks of addresses that would never be officially allocated to any organization. These blocks could then be used in any and every private network without fear of duplicating any officially assigned IP addresses in other organizations.

NOTE

Not everyone agreed with this plan. The authors of RFC 1627 (June 1994) complained that an Internet policy decision was made without the normal peer review and public comment process. They also pointed out that the original ideal of the Internet architecture, worked out over decades, was to have every host uniquely addressable. They argued that RFC 1597 violates this ideal. Ultimately, of course, the proponents of private addressing prevailed.

In February 1996, RFC 1597 was updated and made obsolete by RFC 1918, and was assigned the "Best Current Practice" status.

The Three-Address Blocks

RFC 1918 designates three ranges of IP addresses as private:

- 10.0.0.0–10.255.255.255
- 172.16.0.0–172.31.255.255
- 192.168.0.0–192.168.255.255

The first of these address blocks is equivalent to a traditional class A address. In CIDR notation, it would be 10.0.0.0/8. RFC 1918 calls it a 24-bit block of addresses because only 8 of the 32 bits is fixed; the other 24 bits are available for local administration. Either way, the range contains 16,777,216 unique addresses— enough to supply even the largest networks.

The second block is called a 20-bit block and is equivalent to 16 traditional class B networks, or a /12 block in CIDR terminology. This block contains 1,048,576 addresses.

Finally, the third block is known as a 16-bit block and is equivalent to 256 class C networks. This 16-bit prefix supplies 65,536 different IP addresses.

Table 3.3 summarizes the private address blocks defined by RFC 1918.

Table 3.3 Private IP Address Blocks

Address Block	Classful Equivalent	Prefix Length	Number of Addresses
10.0.0.0- 10.255.255.255	1 class A 256 class B 65,536 class C	/8	16,777,216
172.16.0.0- 172.31.255.255	16 class B 4,096 class C	/12	1,048,576
192.168.0.0- 192.168.255.255	1 class B 256 class C	/16	65,536

Considerations

Anyone can use any of the address blocks in Table 3.3 in any network at any time. The main thing to remember is that devices using these addresses will not be able to communicate with other hosts on the Internet without some kind of address translation.

Here are some things to think about when deciding to use private addressing in your network:

Number of addresses. One of the main benefits of using private addresses is that you have plenty to work with. Since you are not using globally-unique addresses (a scare resource), you don't need to be conservative. In the example network shown in Figure 3.1, you could use an entire class B equivalent address block without feeling guilty. Even though you would be using only 4 percent of the available addresses, you are not hoarding a valuable commodity.

Security. Using private addresses can also enhance the security of your network. Even if part of your network is connected to the Internet, no one outside your network will be able to reach your devices. Likewise, no one from inside your network will be able to reach hosts on the Internet. RFC 1918 specifies that:

> "...routing information about private networks shall not be propagated on inter-enterprise links, and packets with private source or destination addresses should not be forwarded across such links. Routers in networks not using private address space, especially those of Internet service providers, are expected to be configured to reject (filter out) routing information about private networks."

For Managers

Security Breaches from Within

Although the preceding information about security and privacy may be comforting, don't let it lull you into complacency. Security experts estimate that anywhere from 50 to 70 percent of all attacks on computer systems come from *inside* the organization. Private network addressing cannot protect against insider attacks.

Limited scope. The reason you have all these addresses available is that your network will not be connected to the global Internet. If, later, you wish to communicate over the Internet, you must obtain official (globally-unique and routable) addresses and either renumber your devices or use NAT.

Renumbering. Anytime you switch to or from private addressing, you will need to renumber (change the IP address of) all your IP devices. Many organizations are setting up their user workstations to obtain IP addresses automatically when booting up rather than assigning a fixed IP address to the workstations.

This facility requires that at least one Dynamic Host Configuration Protocol (DHCP) server be set up for the organization. DHCP is described in RFC 2131 and discussed in more detail in Chapter 7.

Joining Networks. If you join your network with another that has used private addressing, you may find that some devices have conflicting addresses. For example, let's say you chose to use the 24-bit block of private addresses (network 10). You assigned the address 10.0.0.1 to the first router on the first subnet. Now you merge with another organization and must join your networks. Unfortunately, the administrator of the other network chose to assign address 10.0.0.1 to one of its routers. According to IP addressing rules, both devices cannot use the same address. Further, the two routers are probably on different subnets, so not only do you have to assign a different address to the router, you must assign different subnet addresses as well. Again, the solutions include renumbering and NAT.

Which to Use When

According to RFC 1918:

"If a suitable subnetting scheme can be designed and is supported by the equipment concerned, it is advisable to use the 24-bit block (class A network) of private address space and make an addressing plan with a good growth path. If subnetting is a problem, the 16-bit block (class C networks), or the 20-bit block (class B networks) of private address space can be used."

The concept of subnetting was introduced into the IP world in August 1985 (RFC 950). Since most IP software modules in use today were developed after that time, they do understand how to do subnetting. So go ahead and use the 10 network for private addressing unless you have good reasons to do otherwise. By using the 24-bit block, you have 24 bits to play with when designing a private addressing scheme.

Strategy for Subnetting a Class A Private Network

When it comes to developing an addressing plan for a private network, the rules are exactly the same as for any other IP network. Our goals for the addressing plan are as follows:

Simplicity. We want the plan to be as simple as possible so that as many people as possible can understand it. When we look at the IP address of a particular device, we should be able to easily deduce what kind of device it is and where it is in our network without having to refer to volumes of documentation.

Ease of Administration. We want the plan to be easy to implement and maintain. The plan should allow room for anticipated growth and, if possible, make room for unanticipated growth or other changes.

Router Efficiency. As nice as it is for the plan to be understandable by the humans that have to maintain it, the routers have to live with the plan every time a packet needs to be forwarded to another subnet. Therefore, the plan should not place a heavy burden on the resources of our routers. Ideally, the plan should build in addressing hierarchies that allow the routing tables to be kept at a relatively small size.

Documentation. We want to be able to describe the plan in a few short statements without a lot of explanations.

Following the guidelines of Chapter 2, we now present an example of a large organization that has decided to implement private IP addressing in its internetwork. The procedure is the same—choose a mask, allocate the subnet bits, and determine the range of addresses for each subnet.

The Network

The network that we'll study here is relatively stable. There are about 3000 retail stores owned by the company and no store has more than 12 IP devices in it. Reports from management consultants indicate that this number should suffice for the medium term. Each store is connected to its regional distribution center via a leased point-to-point line.

There are currently 18 regional distribution centers, with each center supporting no more than 200 stores. Distribution centers have two physical networks for administration, and one supporting the warehouse. The largest of the admin LANs has 80 IP devices on it, and the warehouse LAN needs 120 addresses. Each distribution center is connected back to headquarters via two parallel T3 links.

The headquarters campus has 14 LANs connected by routers to the corporate backbone network. The largest of the headquarters LANs has 230 IP devices on it.

Figure 3.3 shows a high-level overview of the corporate network. We can summarize the addressing needs of the network in Table 3.4.

Table 3.4   Sample Network Addressing Analysis

Location	# Subnets	Max Addresses
Headquarters LANs	15	230
HQ - DC links	18 x 2 = 36	2
Dist. Ctr. LANs	18 x 3 = 54	120
DC - Store links	18 x 200 = 3,600	2
Store LANs	18 x 200 = 3,600	12
Total Subnets Needed:	7,305	
Max Subnet Size:		230

From the information in Table 3.4 we can obtain the number of subnets needed (7,305) and the number of addresses needed in the largest subnet (230).

Figure 3.3 A large network.

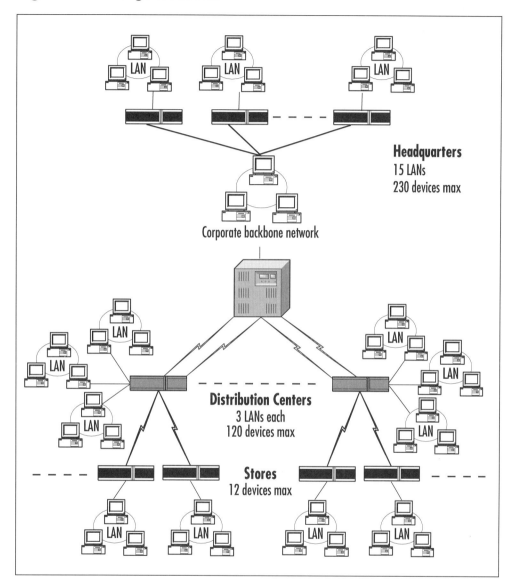

The Strategy

There are many correct solutions to this addressing problem, and arguments can be made for all of them. Since our first goal is simplicity, we'll try to keep the plan as simple as possible. Since all the software we're using understands subnetting, we'll follow the advice given in RFC 1918 and use the 24-bit block—that is, network 10.

Now that we know we have 24 bits to work with, how shall we allocate them? We look for clues in the structure of the network we are studying. There seem to be three levels of hierarchy:

- Headquarters
- Distribution Centers
- Stores

Can we somehow fit that hierarchy into our addressing scheme? Before we delve too deeply into this, we need to decide a couple of things. First, will we use fixed- or variable-length subnet masks? Using the "keep it simple" strategy, let's try using the fixed mask approach, since it is easier to design and maintain.

Our next step is to decide on a mask to use. Looking at our class A subnetting tables in Chapter 2, we decide on 255.255.255.0. Could we have picked another? Sure, but most people would agree that 255.255.255.0 is the easiest mask to work with. The tables tell us we now have 65,535 subnets to work with, each supplying 254 addresses. This should work nicely. Now we have our IP address structure laid out before us:

- Network ID: 8 bits
- Subnet ID: 16 bits
- Host ID: 8 bits

Sixteen bits is represented in dotted decimal notation as two decimal numbers. Perhaps we can reduce the company network hierarchy to two levels: Region and Store. We can do this if we call the headquarters "Region 0." Using this approach, we can try to make our IP addresses look something like this:

10.R.S.H

where R is the region number, S is the store number, and H is the host ID. If we can make this work, the IP addresses will be almost self-documenting—a very desirable feature indeed.

Address Assignment

Let's get down to business. In Table 3.3 we identified five different subnet groups. Looking at each group, we must decide on what the IP addresses should look like.

Table 3.5 Headquarters Subnets

Description	Address Range
Backbone	10.0.0.1–10.0.0.254
LAN 1	10.0.1.1–10.0.1.254
LAN 2	10.0.2.1–10.0.2.254
. . .	. . .
LAN 14	10.0.14.1–10.0.14.254

The Headquarters LANs

We stated that we should call the headquarters "Region 0." There are 15 LANs in this group. Let's use 10.0.L.0 for this group, where L is 0 for the backbone, and 1–14 for the administrative LANs. The LANs at the headquarters location are summarized in Table 3.5.

The WAN Links from Headquarters to the Distribution Centers

Again, there are a number of ways to assign this group of addresses. Let's use 10.100+R.0.0 and 10.200+R.0.0 for the two WAN links to each regional distribution center. Here, R is the region number. Table 3.6 summarizes these assignments.

Table 3.6 Headquarters WAN Links

Description	Addresses
HQ to Region 1	10.101.0.1 & 10.101.0.2 10.201.0.1 & 10.201.0.2
HQ to Region 2	10.102.0.1 & 10.102.0.2 10.202.0.1 & 10.202.0.2
. . .	. . .
HQ to Region 18	10.118.0.1 & 10.118.0.2 10.218.0.1 & 10.218.0.2

The Distribution Center LANs

We don't want to collide with the store LANs here, so we'll start our allocation from the top of the list. The three DC LANs will be addressed using the forms 10.R.255.0, 10.R.254.0, and 10.R.253.0. Table 3.7 shows the plan.

Table 3.7 Distribution Center Subnets

Description	Address Range
Region 1, Admin 1	10.1.255.1-10.1.255.254
Region 1, Admin 2	10.1.254.1-10.1.254.254
Region 1, Warehouse	10.1.253.1-10.1.253.254
Region 2, Admin 1	10.2.255.1-10.2.255.254
Region 2, Admin 2	10.2.254.1-10.2.254.254
Region 2, Warehouse	10.2.253.1-10.2.253.254
. . .	. . .
Region 18, Admin 1	10.18.255.1-10.18.255.254
Region 18, Admin 2	10.18.254.1 - 10.18.254.254
Region 18, Warehouse	10.18.253.1 - 10.18.253.254

The WAN Links from the DC to the Stores

Following the lead of the HQ-DC links, the link from region R to store S will look like 10.100+R.S.0 (Table 3.8).

Table 3.8 Distribution Center WAN Links

Description	Addresses
Region 1 to Store 1	10.101.1.1 & 10.101.1.2
Region 1 to Store 2	10.101.2.1 & 10.101.2.2
. . .	. . .
Region 1 to Store 200	10.101.200.1 & 10.101.200.2
Region 2 to Store 1	10.102.1.1 & 10.102.1.2
Region 2 to Store 2	10.102.2.1 & 10.102.2.2
. . .	. . .
Region 2 to Store 200	10.102.200.1 & 10.102.200.2
. . .	. . .
Region 18 to Store 1	10.118.1.1 & 10.118.1.2
Region 18 to Store 2	10.118.2.1 & 10.118.2.2
. . .	. . .
Region 18 to Store 200	10.118.200.1 & 10.118.200.2

The Store LANs

Finally, we're down to the largest group. Since this is the largest group, we'll make these addresses as straightforward as possible. As we stated earlier, the LAN in store S in region R will have the address 10.R.S.0. Table 3.9 shows some samples of store LAN addresses.

Table 3.9 Store Subnets

Description	Address Range
Region 1, Store 1	10.1.1.1–10.1.1.254
Region 1, Store 2	10.1.2.1–10.1.2.254
Region 1, Store 200	10.1.200.1–10.1.200.254
Region 6, Store 107	10.6.107.1–10.6.107.254
Region 18, Store 5	10.18.5.1–10.18.5.254

Results

The plan seems to work. Here again are the goals we established earlier, and some discussion of how well our plan meets the goals.

Simplicity, ease of administration, and documentation. We're using the same net mask (255.255.255.0) in every subnet. We have a single structure for each of the five types of subnets in our network. Because we are using private addressing, we have plenty of addressing space to work with. We have used this space to give our addresses some intelligence. Some noteworthy features of our plan are:

1. Any address with a zero in the second byte refers to a device at the headquarters location.

2. Any address with a three-digit value in the second byte refers to a WAN link between a distribution center and either a store (third byte > 0) or the headquarters location (third byte = 0).

3. All other addresses refer to devices on LANs either in the DC or in a store.

Router Efficiency. Will each router in the company's internetwork need to list all 7305 subnets? We sure hope not! Our addressing scheme needs to allow for *route summarization*. To take full advantage of route summarization and keep our routing tables down to their absolute minimum size, the structure of our addresses needs to follow exactly the actual hierarchy of physical connections. Unfortunately, this is not the case with the addressing plan we have just developed. Let's look again at the plan in Table 3.10.

Table 3.10 Sample Network Address Structure

Subnet Group	IP Address Structure
Headquarters LANs	10.0.1.0-10.0.15.0
HQ - DC links	10.100+R.0.0
DC LANs	10.R.253.0-10.R.255.0
DC - Store links	10.100+R.S.0
Store LANs	10.R.S.0

In the ideal case, the corporate router would need to have only 19 entries: one for the corporate backbone, and one for each of the regions. To make that happen, all of the addresses associated with a region would have to share a common prefix. That is, they must all have the first several bits in common. This is not the case in our plan. For example, the distribution LAN in region 5 would have the address 10.5.255.0. The link from that distribution center to store 17 would be 10.105.17.0. The only prefix these two addresses have in common is the network ID (10) itself—not very helpful.

Does this mean we have to abandon our plan? No, it doesn't. Although our plan is not *ideal* for route summarization, it well may be good enough. With some careful configuration of the regional routers, we can represent each region with three entries in the corporate router's table. One entry would represent all of the DC and store LANs, and there would be one entry for each of the WAN links between the corporate router and the DC. The central router would then have less than a hundred entries in its routing table—a very reasonable number.

The routers at each distribution center would have an entry for each of the WAN links, store LANs, and DC LANs, totaling a bit over

400 entries. Current router technology is able to handle that number of entries very easily.

Given that the routers will not be overwhelmed by the routing table sizes, and given that the addressing plan presented has some desirable features, we will go ahead and deploy the plan as presented.

Summary

The designers of the Internet Protocol never dreamed that there would be millions of hosts on over 100,000 networks participating in the Internet. At the time, a fixed 32-bit address looked like it would be more than enough to serve the addressing needs of the Internet for years to come. And it has. However, as the Internet continues to grow, more and more pressure is being put on the user community to use globally-unique IP addresses efficiently. This pressure has lead to policy changes at the Internet Registries and to new techniques to conserve addresses.

One of those techniques is to use private addresses, as specified in RFC 1918. There are both benefits and drawbacks to using private addresses.

FAQs

Q: How do I know which one of the private address blocks to use?

A: Unless there is a good reason—such as a specific learning objective, or to force your router into certain behaviors—use "network 10."

Q: Can I use VLSM in private networks?

A: Absolutely! There's no harm in using addresses wisely, even if you have a very large supply.

Q: Why is network 10 included in the private address ranges?

A: Class A network 10 was the address used by the old ARPANET, the precursor of today's Internet. Network 10 was decommissioned in the 1980s and we use it today to honor its auspicious beginnings.

Q: Can I use private addresses and public addresses in my network?

A: Yes. Since the public and private addresses use different network prefixes, they will need to be on separate ports of a router. In other words, they would need to be separate subnets of your network. The devices with public addresses will be able to communicate on the Internet, those with private addresses will not.

Q: I've got a network with private addresses. Now I want to connect to the Internet. Can I?

A: Yes, you have two options. First, you can obtain public addresses and renumber your IP devices. Second, you (or your ISP) can implement Network Address Translation (NAT) to translate your private addresses to public addresses. NAT is covered in Chapter 4.

Exercises

1. In our sample network, we were unable to maximize the benefits of route summarization because of the way we allocated the addresses. Without going to variable masks, design an addressing structure for our sample network that is completely hierarchical.

2. Why should ISPs filter out any references to private address blocks?

3. How does CIDR contribute to address allocation efficiency?

Answers

1. Use five or six of the 16 subnet bits to represent the regions. These bits will be the first bits in the subnet field. The remaining ten or eleven bits will represent the subnets in the region. For example, if we used five bits for the region ID and 11 bits for the subnet within the region, we can allocate 32 regions with 2048 subnets in each region. The addresses would line up like this:

   Headquarters: 10.0.0.0 through 10.7.255.255

   Region 1:10.8.0.0 through 10.15.255.255

   Region 2:10.16.0.0 through 10.23.255.255, etc.

   This plan would be efficient (from the router's point of view), but not very intuitive.

2. Since private address blocks are not, by definition, globally-unique, there may be (and in fact are) many networks using the same addresses. If routing information about those networks or packets containing those addresses were allowed on the Internet, the Internet routers would become confused at best, misrouting packets. At worst, they would become hopelessly congested, causing massive communication failures.

3. By reducing the granularity of address allocation. Prior to CIDR, an organization was allocated 256 addresses (class C), 65,536 addresses (class B), or 16,777,216 addresses (class A). With CIDR, almost any number of addresses can be allocated, reducing the waste associated with the previous scheme.

Chapter 4

Network Address Translation

Solutions in this chapter:

- Learning what NAT is and how it works
- Seeing examples of how to implement NAT
- Learning how NAT interacts with security solutions
- Learning when NAT is appropriate to use

Introduction

This chapter covers Network Address Translation (NAT). In its simplest form, NAT changes network layer (layer 3) addresses as they pass through some device, such as a router or firewall. In theory, other layer 3 protocols can be translated, such as AppleTalk or IPX, as well as other layers (such as layer 2). In practice, it's usually done only with IP addresses at layer 3. Because this is a TCP/IP book, this chapter will focus exclusively on IP.

We will demonstrate, however, that simply changing the layer 3 address is insufficient, and that transport layer (layer 4), and often higher layer, information must also be affected. Therefore, our discussion will also include TCP and UDP, as well as application layer (layer 7) protocols. We will discuss not only what NAT is and how it works, but also what the problems and shortcomings are.

This chapter is not about network security; however, the issues surrounding NAT often intersect with those of security applications. In some cases, particular types of NAT make the most sense in the context of a security application. Many of the commercial NAT implementations are part of a security package. Given that, we will be covering some security information as it relates to NAT, though NAT by itself is not necessarily security technology.

Hiding Behind the Router/Firewall

The ideas behind NAT became popularized in early firewall solutions. These early firewalls were mostly proxy-based. A good example is the FireWall ToolKit (FWTK). A proxy (in the firewall context) is a piece of software that fetches some information on behalf of a client, such as a Web page. The client computer asks the proxy for a particular Web page (it gives it the URL) and awaits reply. The proxy will then fetch the Web page, and return it to the client.

What's the point of that? First, the administrator of the proxy can often program a list of things the client isn't allowed to do. For example, if it's a Web proxy at a company, the proxy administrator may choose to block access to www.playboy.com. Second, the proxy might be able to perform some caching or other optimization. If 50 people visit www.syngress.com every day, the proxy could keep a copy of the Web page, and when a client asks for it, all the proxy has to do is check if there have been any changes. If not, it passes along the copy has stored, and the client typically gets to see the page more quickly.

Usually in this type of proxy configuration, the clients have been blocked from retrieving Web pages from the Internet directly, so they are forced to use the proxy if they want to view Web pages. This is often done with packet filtering on the router. Simply stated, the router is configured only to allow the proxy to pull Web pages from the Internet, and no other machine.

The result of this type of design is that inside clients now talk only to the proxy, and no longer talk directly to other hosts on the Internet. The proxy only needs to accept requests from the "inside" and fulfill them. This means that other machines on the Internet no longer need to speak to inside clients directly, even for replies. Therefore, the firewall administrator can configure their router or firewall to block all communications between the inside and out-side machines. This forces all communications through the proxy. Now, the only machine the outside can talk to (if all is configured correctly) is the proxy. This dramatically reduces the number of machines that outsiders can attack directly. The proxy administra-tor takes particular care to make sure the proxy machine is as secure as possible, of course. Figure 4.1 is a diagram of what it looks like, logically.

This process has been highly simplified for purposes of discus-sion, but the principles are there: a clear division of inside and out-side, and a point between them. This point between the two is sometimes called a *choke point*. In our diagram, the choke point is the proxy and filtering router together.

Figure 4.1 Retrieving a Web page through a proxy.

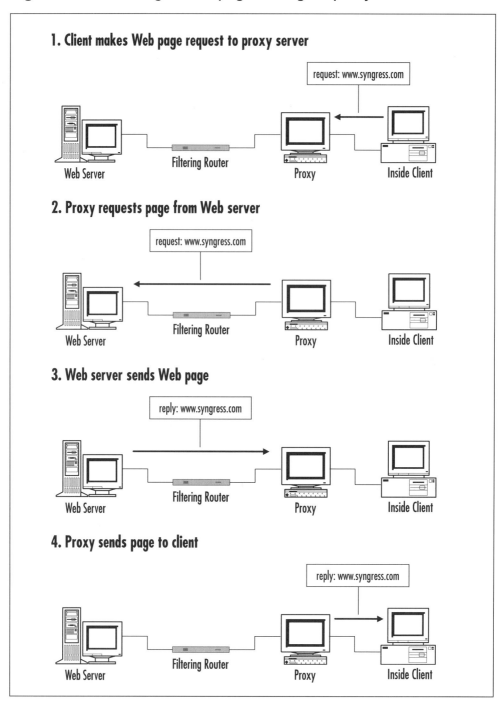

This is a simplified firewall architecture. Issues outside of the scope of this chapter come into play when designing a real firewall, such as:

- Is proxy software available for all needed protocols?

- How is the packet filtering configured on the router?

- How does the Web browser software on the client know to talk to the proxy?

- How does the proxy know which machines are on the inside, and which are outside?

The point of the discussion in this chapter is not what a proxy firewall architecture looks like, but rather, a side effect of it. We already know that all traffic on the Internet from this network originates from the proxy. This means that the Internet only "sees" the IP address of the proxy server. We also know that the Internet can't reach the client machines on the inside.

As far as the Internet is concerned, this means that this site needs *only one IP address*, which is that of the proxy.

Recall from Chapter 3 that address space is considered scarce at present, and that certain IP address ranges, referred to as the private IP address ranges, have been set aside. These ranges are currently listed in the document RFC1918, available at

```
http://www.cis.ohio-state.edu/htbin/rfc/rfc1918.html
```

as well as at a number of other Web sites.

If you happen to read through the RFC, you'll see that it renders RFCs 1627 and 1597 (an older version of RFC1918) obsolete. RFC 1627 attempts to make a case against private IP address ranges. Apparently, RFC1627 lost because it has been declared obsolete by one that explicitly allows private address ranges. The other RFCs can be reached at the previous URL (there are links at the top of that Web page).

Following is a quote from RFC1918, which defines the private address spaces, and when they should be used:

"For security reasons, many enterprises use application layer gateways to connect their internal network to the Internet. The internal network usually does not have direct access to the Internet, thus only one or more gateways are visible from the Internet. In this case, the internal network can use non-unique IP network numbers."

As part of the reason for having private addresses, the RFC recognizes that many companies already have application layer gateways (proxies) in place. Therefore, it would be useful to have a set of addresses that can be reused internally, as long as none of those machines needs to talk to other machines directly.

The RFC also recommends that companies who wish to employ such a proxy obtain address space from Internet Service Providers (ISPs). In recent years, most of the address space has been allocated to ISPs, rather than directly to companies, as it used to be. A big part of the reason for this is to keep routing tables on Internet core routers as small as possible. If a block of addresses is given to an ISP, then the other ISPs can hold a route to that single block, rather than having an entry for each of the separate network ranges in the block, as would be the case if those address ranges were given to various companies. By today's rules, you pretty much have to be an ISP to get address space allocated to you permanently. For more information about how ISPs obtain and assign addresses, please see Chapter 6.

If you run a proxy architecture, it will be fairly easy to get some addresses from your ISP, and you will need relatively few. With this architecture, you are free to use the RFC1918 addresses inside your network, and still have Internet access for your internal client machines.

This type of architecture is in very common use today. Many companies, especially large ones, have some sort of firewall or proxy device that does the direct communication on the Internet. Even companies that have been on the Internet long enough to have their own address space frequently use this type of architecture, though mostly for security reasons.

Now that we have some idea what proxies are, how exactly does that relate to NAT? Well, actually not much—proxies aren't NAT. Towards the end of the chapter, we explain why. However, the discussion is important, because proxies form part of the history of why NAT exists.

What Is NAT?

The idea behind NAT is similar to one of the benefits of proxies: hiding your internal addresses. The usual reason for wanting to hide addresses is the one we mentioned—Internet access for inside client machines. At a high level, the end result is the same. The Internet sees a valid Internet address (a public address), probably assigned by your ISP, and your inside machines are using private addresses.

There is at least one other reason you might want to use NAT if you're using the RFC1918 addresses: What if your company merges with another one? Usually, the two companies will want to link internal networks to facilitate business communications. However, if both companies had previously been using the same RFC1918 address ranges, a conflict arises. Ultimately, a renumbering of some sort will probably have to be done, but as a short-term measure, it's possible to use a type of NAT to translate addresses between the two companies to resolve conflicts. We'll return to this example later.

To understand how NAT differs from proxying, we have to take a detailed look at how NAT works.

How Does NAT Work?

NAT works by modifying individual packets. It modifies (at least) the layer 3 headers to have a new address for the source address, destination address, or both. We'll also see an example where layer 4 headers are modified, as well as the data portion (layer 7).

As we'll see, a few small variations in how the addresses are translated can result in a fairly wide range of behavior and features. We'll also see that for some protocols, it will take a lot more than simply changing the layer 3 addresses for them to function with NAT. There are even protocols that can't function with NAT in place.

The NAT function is usually performed by a router or firewall. It is theoretically possible for a bridge (layer 2) device to do layer 3 address translation, and at least one firewall product on the market functions that way. However, the vast majority of the NAT devices, or software that includes a NAT function, depends on plain IP routing to deliver packets to it. Most NAT devices have an underlying IP routing function.

Network Address Translation (Static)

We'll start with the simplest form of NAT, which is called static, or 1-to-1 translation. This is the most intuitive kind: Simply stated, in static NAT, a particular IP address is changed to another going one way, and changed back going the other way. The change usually is done to the source address for outgoing packets. Figure 4.2 will help clarify this. In the figure, the arrows indicate direction of packet flow (where it's being routed), S indicates source address, and D indicates destination address.

Figure 4.2 Static NAT during the first two packets of the TCP handshake.

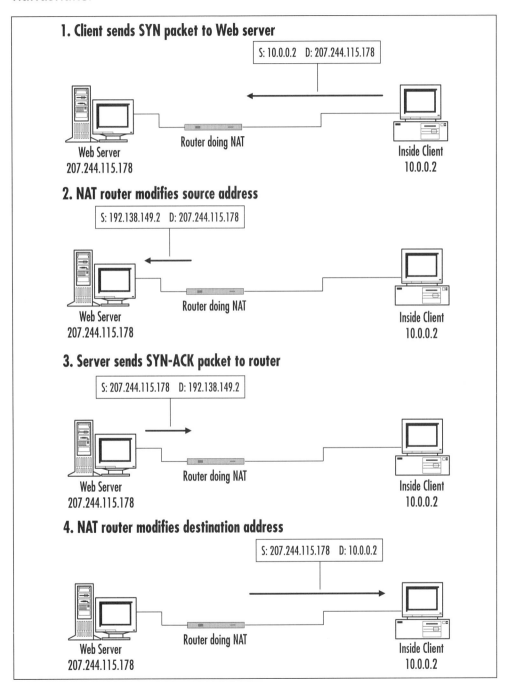

How Does Static NAT Work?

Let's assume for the moment that this is a really simple-minded NAT; that is, all it does is modify the source or destination address when appropriate. What kind of work does the NAT router have to do? First, it has to have some idea of which direction the packet is traveling relative to the NAT configuration. Notice in the example that the router translates the source in one direction, and the destination in the other. It can decide which to do based on particular interfaces being marked as "to" or "from" interfaces. A configuration example, next, will make things more clear. The router also has to decrement the TTL and redo any checksums needed, but routers do that anyway.

The example is also *stateless*, meaning that the router doesn't have to know what went on with previous packets, if anything, in order to modify the current one. All the information it needs to modify the packet is available in the current packet, and in its configuration. Also note that this type of NAT has no security features—all traffic passes regardless, with just an address change in the process. The idea of state information is very important for later NAT examples, and also for firewalls. Keep this in mind for later discussion.

This type of NAT is fairly simple to understand, but it isn't as useful as it might be. Consider our goal of trying to have a few IP addresses represent a group of inside machines. Our example is 1-to-1, meaning there is no address savings! Each inside IP address has to have a matching outside address, so there is no savings of IP addresses. Does this mean that it is useless? No, there are a number of scenarios where we can use a 1-to-1 mapping of IP addresses.

One scenario is that you've got an internal machine with an internal IP address, and you want to make it reachable by the Internet for some reason. One way to do it without having to change anything on the inside machine is to define a static translation for it, like we did in our example. If that's done, you simply have to publish the translated IP address (perhaps by assigning a DNS name to it).

Let's consider another example, which matches the one in Figure 4.2, except that the destination address is changed on the first packet instead of the source address. When would it be useful to change the destination address instead of the source address? There is at least one type of server you generally have to refer to by IP address: DNS servers. Imagine a situation where a DNS server has failed, probably only temporarily, and you would like to have your inside client machines make DNS requests of a new one without having to reconfigure them all, and then put them back when the original DNS server is back up.

Double NAT

The last static NAT example we want to look at is often called "double NAT." Simply put, this is changing both the source and destination addresses of a packet. Many products that support NAT don't support this type of configuration, unless you've got two of them.

Under what circumstances would you want to use double NAT? One possibility is a combination of the previous two examples: You've got inside machines using private IP address, and you need to have them connect to a different DNS server without reconfiguring them. That example is a bit contrived, though, and there's a better one.

Recall that one of the problems with using private IP addresses is the possibility of conflict when you connect to another network that is using the same addresses. Double NAT can help in this situation, though again, you'll probably want to use this only as a temporary measure.

Here's a scenario: You need to connect your network to that of another company, and you just found out that you both are using class C 192.168.1. You have to find a way to enable the two networks to communicate until a renumbering can be completed. This situation is far from impossible, as several firewall/NAT products use this address range by default.

It turns out you've both got routers capable of doing NAT—the same routers you are using to connect to each other. For our example we'll focus on two machines, one on each net, that have the same IP address (see Figure 4.3).

Figure 4.3 Two networks with conflicting RFC1918 addresses.

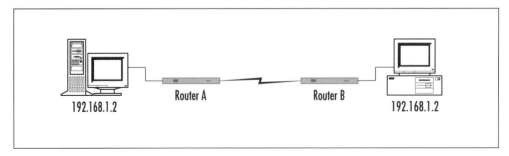

The IP addresses used on the link between the two routers aren't particularly important for this example, as long as they don't create additional conflicts.

The trick is to make each machine believe that the other one is at a different IP address. We accomplish this by making the machine on the left think that the machine on the right is IP address 192.168.2.2, while the machine on the right thinks that the machine on the left is 192.168.3.2.

This is still static NAT: each machine has a 1-to-1 mapping to another IP address. However, in this example, since we're going through two NAT routers, we're going to translate twice. The first router will change the source address on the packet, and the second router will change the destination address on the packet. Double NAT.

Let's walk through an example of the machine on the left sending a packet to the machine on the right (see Figure 4.4).

Since the machine on the left assumes it's simply communicating with another machine at 192.168.2.2, it sends its packet to the local router for forwarding, as it normally would. At this point, router A is going to change the source address on the packet, to hide the fact that it came from a 192.168.1 net (see Figure 4.5).

Figure 4.4 Source address is 192.168.1.2, destination address is 192.168.2.2.

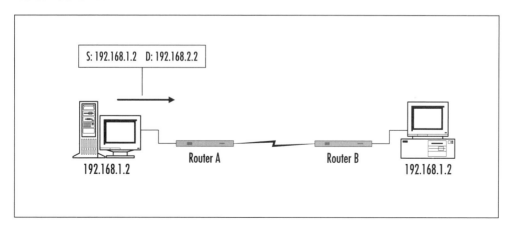

The destination address remains 192.168.2.2 at this point, and router A uses its normal routing tables to determine where the 192.168.2 network is, and forwards the packet. In this case, it forwards the packet to router B. Router B is going to perform its translation next, and it changes the destination address from 192.168.2.2 to 192.168.1.2 (see Figure 4.6).

Figure 4.5 Source address is now 192.168.3.2, destination address is still 192.168.2.2.

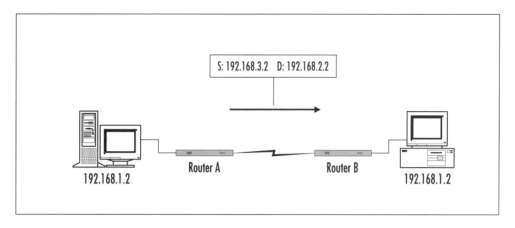

Figure 4.6 Source address is 192.168.3.2, destination address is now 192.168.1.2.

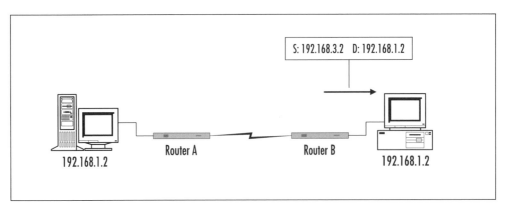

Now the machine on the right receives the packet, and that machine believes it has received a packet from 192.168.3.2. Packets traveling from the machine on the right to the machine on the left will go through a similar, but reversed process.

In this manner, the two machines with the same address, which would normally never be able to communicate with each other, are able to do so. Naturally, to make this type of scenario usable in real life, it will probably require some clever DNS setup as well. The DNS server for the machine on the left would be configured so that the names of the machines on the right resolve to 192.168.3 addresses, and so on.

Problems with Static NAT

So far, we've ignored the problems with NAT, and they are significant. The basic problem is that not all network address information is in the network address headers (IP layer). A fair number of protocols, for various reasons, include address information in the data portion of the packets. We'll look at a few examples.

One of the most problematic protocols for NAT is the File Transfer Protocol (FTP). However, because FTP is so common, most NATs deal with it properly.

What's difficult about FTP? First of all, it passes IP addresses in the data stream, in ASCII. Second, it passes these addresses to inform the other machine on which IP address and port it will be listening for reverse connections. In the default mode, when an FTP client wants to receive a file, it listens on a port number assigned by the operating system, and informs the server of that port number and its IP address. The server then contacts the client and delivers the file. This problem gets worse when security or other types of NAT are considered, which we'll look at later.

This means that the NAT software has to be able to spot the IP addresses when they are being sent, and be able to modify them. FTP also introduces the problem of *state*. Unfortunately for the NAT software designer, the IP address information may be split across more than one packet. This means that the NAT software also has to keep track of what it was doing on the last packet as well as the current one. This is known as maintaining state information; most NAT devices use state tables to maintain this type of information.

Figure 4.7 contains a packet capture of the problem in action.

Figure 4.7 Packet containing the FTP PORT command.

```
IP: - - - - - IP Header - - - - -
     IP:
     IP: Version = 4, header length = 20 bytes
     IP: Type of service = 00
     IP:        000. ....   = routine
     IP:        ...0 .... = normal delay
     IP:        .... 0... = normal throughput
     IP:        .... .0.. = normal reliability
     IP: Total length   = 66 bytes
     IP: Identification  = 3437
     IP: Flags          = 4X
     IP:        .1.. .... = don't fragment
     IP:        ..0. .... = last fragment
     IP: Fragment offset = 0 bytes
     IP: Time to live   = 128 seconds/hops
     IP: Protocol       = 6 (TCP)
     IP: Header checksum = 410F (correct)
     IP: Source address    = [208.25.87.11]
```

Continued

```
       IP: Destination address = [130.212.2.65]
       IP: No options
       IP:
TCP: − − - - - TCP header − − - - -
       TCP:
       TCP: Source port              = 4585
       TCP: Destination port         = 21 (FTP)
       TCP: Sequence number          = 353975087
       TCP: Next expected Seq number= 353975113
       TCP: Acknowledgment number    = 1947234980
       TCP: Data offset              = 20 bytes
       TCP: Flags                    = 18
       TCP:                ..0. .... = (No urgent pointer)
       TCP:                ...1 .... = Acknowledgment
       TCP:                .... 1... = Push
       TCP:                .... .0.. = (No reset)
       TCP:                .... ..0. = (No SYN)
       TCP:                .... ...0 = (No FIN)
       TCP: Window                   = 8030
       TCP: Checksum                 = 1377 (correct)
       TCP: No TCP options
       TCP: [26 Bytes of data]
       TCP:
FTP: − − - - - File Transfer Data Protocol − − - - -
       FTP:
       FTP: Line  1:   PORT 208,25,87,11,17,234
       FTP:
```

Figure 4.7 is a packet from the middle of an FTP session, containing the PORT command. Behind the scenes, FTP is basically a text protocol, with binary transfers added onto it. The command you see at the bottom on the figure, PORT 208,25,87,11,17,234, is the client informing the server what port it will be listening on for receiving data. I had just connected to the server and my client sent an address and port number to which the server could connect in order to send its welcome banner.

Let's take a look at the command. The PORT part is fairly evident: it is telling the server what port it can connect to. The first four numbers, 208,25,87,11, are simply the client's IP address—if you look at the top of the figure (source address), it is 208.25.87.11. The next two numbers are the port number, split into two bytes. Notice that the current source port is 4585. The client in this case is a Windows 98 machine, and like most operating systems, Windows allocates ports sequentially. To convert 17,234 into a single number, follow this conversion routine: Multiply the first number (on the left) by 256, and then add the second number—in this case, 17*256+234=4586. So, our client is telling the server to connect to 208.25.87.11 at port 4586.

Everything worked as expected, and the banner was properly displayed on the FTP client. But had NAT been in use, the NAT software would have to recognize the PORT command, and modify the number for the IP address inside the packet. In this example, all fields were contained in the same packet (as they often are). However, they may be split across more than one packet, so the NAT software must be prepared to handle that possibility.

If the NAT software is able to modify the PORT command correctly, all still works well. The headers are changed, and the PORT command(s) are changed to match, accordingly. Now FTP can work properly across static NAT.

That's only one protocol handled as a special case—there are lots more. Real-world NAT implementations must deal with these in order to be useful to consumers. It's fairly common for NAT vendors to provide a list of protocols for which they do or do not work correctly. The basic problem lies with protocols that pass address and port information as part of the data portion of the packets. When the IP headers are changed, the data portion must also be changed to match. If this is not done, then the protocol most likely will not work properly.

There is at least one other category of protocols that have problems, even with static NAT. Certain protocols exist that can detect when the IP headers have been changed, and will refuse to work when a change is detected. Usually, these are cryptographic protocols. A prime example is the IPSec Authenticate Header (AH) protocol. Without going into too much IPSec detail, the idea behind this protocol is that it is sometimes useful to know for sure that the IP address with which you are communicating is who it claims to be. The two IP addresses communicating using IPSec AH have shared cryptographic keys with which to verify certain types of information. When one of these devices puts together a packet, it includes a large number with it, which is a function of nearly all the information in the packet, as well as the cryptographic key. When the device at the other end sees the packet, it can go through a similar process, and determine if the packet has been tampered with. If it detects any tampering, it discards the packet as invalid.

IPSec AH will see NAT as tampering (unauthorized modification to the headers) and drop the packets as being invalid. Here is a protocol that cannot work with NAT, because of its design. There are not a large number of protocols like this, and they are usually complex enough that network and firewall administrators are often involved in their configuration, so they should be aware of the issues, and be able to work around them. Be aware, though, that some ISPs employ NAT on their networks. Also, some Virtual Private Network (VPN) products use IPSec, and these products often will not work over an ISP that does NAT or any type of firewalling.

Configuration Examples

In this chapter, our configuration examples will be using Cisco's IOS, Windows NT 2000, and Linux. Specifically, we'll be using Cisco IOS 11.3 or higher (on the main Cisco router line), and Red Hat Linux 6.0. Note that some other Cisco devices, such as the 77x ISDN routers, support NAT as well, but they use a different numbering scheme for their software. We use Windows NT 2000 because this is the first version of Windows NT to include built-in NAT capabilities. At the time of this writing, NT2000 is still beta. This feature is expected to be present in the final version, but there is always a possibility it won't be or that it will be slightly changed. The software package we'll be using on Linux is called IP Masquerade, which comes with the most recent versions of all the Linux distributions. The "References and Resources" section at the end of the chapter provides URLs for documents containing information about NAT, including information about which exact versions of the Cisco IOS include NAT features, and where to obtain IP Masquerade if it isn't already included with your distribution. This chapter assumes that the appropriate software is already installed, and that you have a basic familiarity with the operating system.

Windows NT 2000

Windows NT 2000 includes a feature called Internet Connection Sharing (ICS). (ICS is also included in Windows 98 Second Edition.) ICS is intended to allow dial-up users to provide Internet access to other machines attached via a LAN. It does that well, but it's pretty single-minded, so it's not very flexible. The outside interface must be a dial-up connection; that is, if your Internet access method is via a LAN connection (such as a cable modem or most DSL setups) you can't use ICS with it. To accommodate inside machines on the LAN, the NT 2000 box configures its LAN interface to be 192.168.0.1, and turns itself into a DHCP server and DNS proxy. The configuration of the LAN interface might very well cause conflicts if those services already exist, so be careful. We'll assume that NT 2000 is already installed properly, that the LAN interface is functioning properly, and that there is a correctly defined Internet dial-up connection. We'll start with the network control panel, shown in Figure 4.8.

In Figure 4.8, we can see the LAN connection and the Internet dial-up connection. The Internet connection is grayed-out to indicate that it's not up at the moment.

Figure 4.8 Windows 2000 Network connections window.

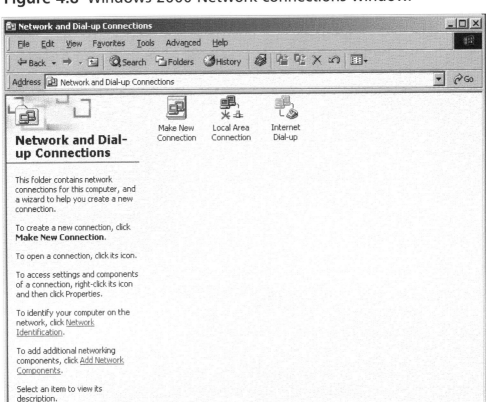

To configure ICS, right-click on the Internet dial-up connection and select Properties. When the Properties window comes up, click on the Internet Connection Sharing tab, shown in Figure 4.9.

Checking on the Enable Internet Connection Sharing box enables ICS. Optionally, you can configure the NT 2000 machine to dial the Internet automatically when an inside machine tries to access the Internet. Checking on this option also enables the DHCP server, so again be sure there isn't already a DHCP server before you check this on.

The short version of this configuration example is that inside machines will now actually be able to access the Internet (after you

Figure 4.9 Dial-up properties window, ICS tab.

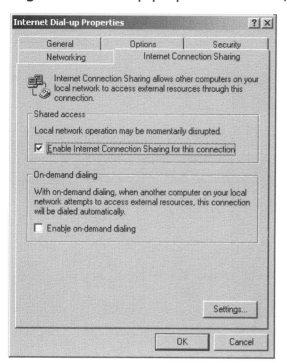

dial-up, of course). However, since we're discussing static NAT, we'll dig a little deeper into what ICS can do. Strictly speaking, ICS doesn't do static NAT (we'll discuss that later in the chapter), but it can perform some of the same behavior.

Notice that there is a Settings button at the bottom of the screen: If you click on that, and then select the Services tab, you will see something like the screen shown in Figure 4.10. In our example, there is already a service defined, called "telnet." By default, this
list is empty. If we click on edit, we will see the screen shown in Figure 4.11.

In the Service port number field, we've got 23 (which is the default port for a Telnet server). The protocol is TCP, and the Name field is portabeast, which is just the name of a machine on our example inside network.

Figure 4.10 ICS Services tab, Telnet service selected.

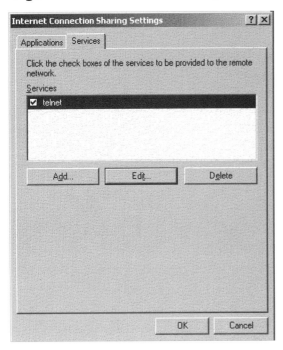

Figure 4.11 Definition of Telnet service.

Since ICS doesn't do real static NAT, inside machines can get out, but outside machines can't get in. The Services feature lets you explicitly allow certain services to be reachable from the outside. In our case, we've made it possible for the outside to Telnet to portabeast. ICS automatically handles FTP properly.

Cisco IOS

Of the three operating systems we're covering, Cisco's IOS has the most flexible NAT software. Using it, we're able to do a true static NAT configuration. This example was done on a 2621 router, which has two Fast Ethernet ports. Here's what the relevant portion of the configuration looks like before we start:

```
Using 827 out of 29688 bytes
!
version 12.0
service timestamps debug uptime
service timestamps log uptime
service password-encryption
!
hostname NAT
!
enable secret 5 xxxxxxxxxxxx
enable password 7 xxxxxxxxxxxxx
!
ip subnet-zero
!
!
interface FastEthernet0/0
 ip address 192.168.0.1 255.255.255.0
 no ip directed-broadcast
!
interface Serial0/0
 no ip address
 no ip directed-broadcast
!
interface FastEthernet0/1
```

```
 ip address 130.214.99.254 255.255.255.0
 no ip directed-broadcast
!
ip classless
ip route 0.0.0.0 0.0.0.0 130.214.99.1
no ip http server
!
!
line con 0
 transport input none
line aux 0
line vty 0 4
 password 7 xxxxxxxxxxx
 login
!
no scheduler allocate
end
```

Interface FastEthernet 0/0 is our inside interface, which uses the 192.168.0 net. 130.214.99 is our outside net, representing the path to the Internet for this example.

There is an inside machine at 192.168.0.2 that we want to be able to get out, so we're going to assign it an outside address:

```
NAT(config) #interface fastethernet 0/0
NAT(config-if) #ip nat inside
NAT(config-if) #int fastethernet 0/1
NAT(config-if) #ip nat outside
NAT(config-if) #exit
NAT(config) #ip nat inside source static 192.168.0.2 130.214.99.250
```

The first step is to mark the inside and outside interfaces, which is done with the ip nat inside and ip nat outside commands. Next, we tell the router to do an IP mapping. The command (global this time, rather than an interface command) is again ip nat. We're mapping an inside address and translating the source address (destination address translation is also possible with IOS). It's a static mapping, and we're translating 192.168.0.2 to 130.214.99.250.

This is a true static mapping, and only the one inside machine is fully reachable from the outside at the 130.214.99.250 address.

As mentioned, the IOS supports destination address mapping as well. It can also do double NAT with just one physical router, if you need it.

Linux IP Masquerade

Our Linux box (Red Hat 6.0) also has two LAN interfaces. IP Masquerade comes standard with Red Hat 6.0, and can be used with other versions and distributions of Linux, although you may have to install it yourself. Instructions are available on how to do so; check the "References and Resources" section at the end of this chapter. Our example begins with the LAN interfaces already configured and working properly. Here is the output from the ifconfig command:

```
eth0      Link encap:Ethernet   HWaddr 00:80:C8:68:C8:44
          inet addr:130.214.99.253  Bcast:130.214.99.255  Mask:255.255.255.0
          UP BROADCAST RUNNING MULTICAST  MTU:1500  Metric:1
          RX packets:547 errors:0 dropped:0 overruns:0 frame:0
          TX packets:10 errors:0 dropped:0 overruns:0 carrier:0
          collisions:0 txqueuelen:100
          Interrupt:11 Base address:0xfc00

eth1      Link encap:Ethernet   HWaddr 00:60:97:8A:9D:30
          inet addr:192.168.0.1  Bcast:192.168.0.255  Mask:255.255.255.0
          UP BROADCAST RUNNING MULTICAST  MTU:1500  Metric:1
          RX packets:35 errors:0 dropped:0 overruns:0 frame:0
          TX packets:3 errors:0 dropped:0 overruns:0 carrier:0
          collisions:0 txqueuelen:100
          Interrupt:3 Base address:0x300

lo        Link encap:Local Loopback
          inet addr:127.0.0.1  Mask:255.0.0.0
          UP LOOPBACK RUNNING  MTU:3924  Metric:1
          RX packets:48 errors:0 dropped:0 overruns:0 frame:0
          TX packets:48 errors:0 dropped:0 overruns:0 carrier:0
          collisions:0 txqueuelen:0
```

The addressing setup is very close to that of the router. Interface eth1 is our inside network, again 192.168.0, and interface eth0 is our outside interface. With IP Masquerade, the address to which the inside is translated is determined by which direction traffic is routed. It will use the IP address of the outside interface. Here's the route table (output from the netstat –rn command):

```
Kernel IP routing table
Destination     Gateway       Genmask          Flag  MSS  Window  irtt  Iface
130.214.99.253  0.0.0.0       255.255.255.255  UH    0    0       0     eth0
192.168.0.0     0.0.0.0       255.255.255.0    U     0    0       0     eth1
130.214.99.0    0.0.0.0       255.255.255.0    U     0    0       0     eth0
127.0.0.0       0.0.0.0       255.0.0.0        U     0    0       0     lo
0.0.0.0         130.214.99.1  0.0.0.0          UG    0    0       0     eth0
```

Since the default route (0.0.0.0) is towards 130.214.99.1, which is reachable via the eth0 interface, all traffic will exit via that interface (unless it's destined for the 192.168.0 net). Therefore, the IP address for the eth0 interface (130.214.99.253) will be used as the translated source address.

IP Masquerade replies on the OS doing routing, so routing must be enabled (it's disabled by default). To turn routing on, issue this command:

```
echo "1" > /proc/sys/net/ipv4/ip_forward
```

This will turn forwarding on, but only until the next reboot (or if it's turned back off manually in a similar manner). To turn it on permanently in Red Hat, you'll want to edit the /etc/sysconfig/network file, and change the line that reads:

```
FORWARD_IPV4=false  to:  FORWARD_IPV4=true
```

That takes care of the forwarding (routing). The next step is to install a masquerade policy that will translate traffic the way we want. IP Masquerade handles FTP properly; in fact, there is a special loadable module that needs to be installed for FTP. Issue this command:

```
/sbin/modprobe ip_masq_ftp
```

From its name, it's pretty obvious what this module is for. There are several modules like this for IP Masquerade, and we'll take a look at more later in the chapter. Next, we'll set some timeout values:

```
/sbin/ipchains -M -S 3600 60 180
```

The first number (3600) specifies how many seconds idle TCP connections will stick around (in this case, an hour). The second number indicates how long after the FIN exchange the connection is tracked, and the last number indicates how long UDP connections will be kept around without any traffic.

Finally, we put in the actual IP Masquerade rules:

```
/sbin/ipchains -P forward deny
/sbin/ipchains -A forward -s 192.168.0.2/32 -j MASQ
```

(192.168.0.2 is still our inside machine for the example.)

At this point, our inside machine will be able to get to the Internet. You won't want to type these commands in every time you reboot, so typically you'll want to put them in a shell script in /etc/rc.d so that they run on startup.

Network Address Translation (Dynamic)

Static NAT is 1-to-1 NAT. Dynamic NAT is many-to-many NAT. Note that 1-to-many NAT is a special case of many-to-many NAT (a subset), and won't really be discussed as a separate issue here. If you can do many-to-many NAT, you can also do 1-to-many NAT.

We've seen how 1-to-1 NAT works, and we've also shown that it doesn't reduce the required number of IP addresses. This is where dynamic NAT comes in. Dynamic NAT works by translating a number of internal IP address to a number (usually a smaller number) of external IP addresses. It does so by dynamically creating 1-to-1 NAT mappings on the fly, as needed. Then, through traffic monitoring and timers, it destroys the mappings as needed, and frees up outside IP addresses for new inside clients. You may have already spotted a problem, but hold that thought for the section on PAT, later in the chapter.

Here's our example scenario: You've got an internal network, 10.0.0.x, with about 50 machines on it. You get an Internet connection, but your ISP can give you only 16 addresses, 192.138.149.0 through 192.138.149.15. Because of standard subnetting issues, 0 and 15 can't be used, 1 is used by the ISP's router, and 2 is your router, leaving only 3 through 14, or 12 addresses. Naturally, you want to provide Internet access for all your inside machines; that's what you got the Internet connection for.

The setup looks like that shown in Figure 4.12. We know from previous discussion that we could do it with only 1 IP address and a proxy server. For this example, to avoid the extra theoretical expense of a new dedicated server, we're going to make use of dynamic NAT.

Figure 4.12 Connecting to the Internet through ISP, 16 addresses assigned.

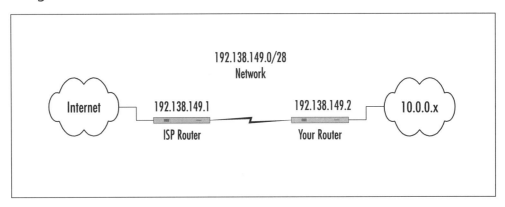

We've already identified the range of available IP addresses, 192.138.149.3 through 192.138.149.14. Our router will be programmed with those addresses as an outside pool and 10.0.0.x as an inside pool. The word "pool" in this context simply refers to a range of IP addresses. To know how to do the dynamic NAT, the router will need to know for which IP addresses it is responsible.

This is more intuitive for the outside IP addresses, because the router needs to be informed of how many of the IP addresses it can use for NAT. The inside pool is a little less intuitive. Why not just NAT any address from the inside? There are a couple of reasons: First, you might want to designate a certain portion of your inside net to go to one outside pool, and another to go to a different outside pool. Second, you might need to do static NAT for certain machines, say a mail server, and you don't want that particular machine being dynamically translated.

How Does Dynamic NAT Work?

What does a router have to do to implement dynamic NAT? We've already discussed briefly all the elements a router needs in order to implement dynamic NAT. It needs a state table, it needs to have an idea of when a connection start and stops, and it needs to have a timer.

We've already seen how static NAT works. For the dynamic NAT discussion, we'll assume that a working static NAT with state tables and protocol specifics is in place, and expand on that. The first major change is that the static NAT mapping will no longer be hardcoded (i.e., manually configured by an administrator), but will be part of another table that the router can change as needed. When we start, the table will be empty, and there will be no 1-to-1 mappings. The table will remain this way until an inside machine tries to connect to the Internet.

Let's take a moment to point out that this is a slight security improvement over static NAT. With static NAT, any machine on the Internet can attempt to connect to the outside IP address in a static NAT mapping at any time, and they will be allowed through to the inside. With dynamic NAT, the default for the outside IP addresses is no mapping. Thus, when the mapping table is empty, any attempts to the outside IP addresses should be futile, as they map to no inside machines at the time. This is not yet sufficient for security purposes, but it is an improvement.

When an inside machine attempts to connect to the Internet, the router will consult its table, and pick an available unused outside IP address. In our example, since the table is currently empty, it will likely pick the first one. It will then create an entry in the mapping table, and create a (temporary) static mapping from the inside machine's IP address to the outside IP address it has chosen. Note that the router's idea of a connection attempt to the Internet may be very simplistic: as soon as it gets any packet from the inside destined for the outside, it may create a mapping. The router will also start a timer at this point.

As long as the inside machine is sending traffic out, or something on the Internet is sending traffic in (via that outside IP address) the mapping will remain. Every time a packet is passed that is part of that mapping, the timer is reset.

There are two ways the mapping will be removed. The first is that the connection is stopped normally. For example, the FTP session is done, and the client has quit. For this to work, the router has to have an idea of what the end of a connection looks like. For TCP connections, this is relatively easy, as there are particular flags that indicate the end of a connection. Of course, for the router to watch for the end of a connection, it would have had to watch for one to start. We'll talk more about how this works in the section on PAT. The second way a mapping is destroyed is that no traffic is sent for the duration of the timer. When the timer runs out, the assumption is that any communications must be finished, and the mapping is removed.

Naturally, while this one inside machine is communicating on the Internet, other inside machines may begin to as well, and they would get their own individual mappings.

Problems with Dynamic NAT

By now, the problems with dynamic NAT may be evident. If we assume the simplistic model, where the router creates a mapping as soon as any packet goes from an inside machine to the Internet, and only gets released when a timer expires, mappings are going to tend to stick around. If we've got 50 inside machines and only 14 outside addresses, there are going to be problems at certain times of the day, like mornings and lunchtime when everyone wants to access the Web.

How can this problem be solved? One way to help alleviate it is to provide more outside IP addresses. In our example, this isn't practical since we got just so many from the ISP. Besides, it seems clear that there is a possibility that all 50 inside machines might want to access the Internet at the same time someday, and we would need 50 outside addresses. At that point, we might as well be back at static NAT, and there would still be no address savings.

Another possibility is to try to reduce the amount of time that a mapping sticks around. This will give inside machines a better chance at getting out at peak times. We could reduce the timer, but that would increase the chances that it might expire while an inside machine is awaiting a response from a slow server on the Internet. This would be effectively broken, and could result in packets reaching the wrong internal client.

The other way to reduce the amount of time is to improve the router's recognition of when connections are complete. However, this adds a fair amount of complexity. Often, a client will have multiple connections open to the Internet at a given time. This is especially true for Web surfing, for example. Each different element on a Web page is retrieved as a separate connection, at least under HTTP 1.0. If you connect to a Web page with 10 pictures, that will result in at least 11 connections—1 for the HTML page, and 10 for the pictures. So, a router can't simply watch for the end of *any* connection, it has to watch for the end of *every* connection. The router has to know how many connections are taking place, which means it has to watch for the beginnings of connections in order to count them.

This is all handled in yet another table. Each time a connection starts, an entry is created in the table. Each of these table entries may have their own timer, rather than using one global time for the whole inside machine. This works pretty well for connection-oriented protocols like TCP, where there is a clear beginning and end to connections, but it doesn't work quite as well for connectionless protocols like UDP and ICMP, so for those we're back to timers.

All in all, dynamic NAT (as stated here) isn't very workable. It seems clear in our example that if 14 people on the inside are actively using the Internet at a given moment, no additional inside people will get to use the Internet.

Clearly, something that can guarantee fair access for an arbitrary number of inside machines simultaneously is needed. That's why dynamic NAT doesn't work exactly the way we said; this is covered in detail in the PAT section.

Configuration Examples

Unfortunately, configuration examples for many-to-many dynamic NAT will be pretty sparse. In fact, out of our three examples, only Cisco IOS supports many-to-many NAT.

Cisco IOS

We're going to look at a many-to-many example using IOS. For this example, we're back to the first config we looked at (no NAT config yet). Here are the commands:

```
NAT(config)#interface fastethernet 0/0
NAT(config-if)#ip nat inside
NAT(config-if)#int fastethernet 0/1
NAT(config-if)#ip nat outside
NAT(config-if)#exit
NAT(config)#ip nat pool dynpool 130.214.99.200 130.214.99.250 netmask 255.255.255.0
NAT(config)#ip nat inside source list 1 pool dynpool overload
NAT(config)#access-list 1 permit 192.168.0.0 0.0.0.255
```

The first five lines are the same as before. The next line defines a pool, named dynpool,. which is a range of IP addresses from 130.214.99.200 through 130.214.99.250. When the router uses them, it will use them as if they had a subnet mask of 255.255.255.0.

Next is the NAT command, which starts with ip nat inside source, like the other. In this case, though, we're going to match against an access list to pick up our source addresses. The translated addresses will be from a pool named dynpool. The overload keyword means that potentially there will be more inside addresses than there are addresses in the pool, and the router is to handle that situation in a particular way (see the next section on PAT). Finally, we define list 1, which we referenced in the previous command. List 1 is simply the inside IP address range.

With this configuration, when an inside machine wants to get out, the router will assign it an IP address from the pool dynamically. When this configuration was tested, IP address .200 was assigned.

Port Address Translation (PAT)

There is a way to address the problems with static and dynamic NAT, to allow more than one inside machine to share one outside IP address. It's called Port Address Translation, or PAT. Some folks may also think of PAT as being dynamic NAT since, as we'll see, PAT is really necessary for dynamic NAT to function properly. In other cases, vendors will refer to PAT simply as "NAT" and you'll have to look at the listed capabilities of the product to determine exactly what type it is. In Firewall-1, which is a very popular firewall product from Checkpoint, PAT is referred to as "hide NAT," making reference to the fact that many inside IP addresses can "hide" behind one IP address.

The reason for the naming confusion is twofold: First, NAT is defined for a given product by the marketing departments of that vendor, so there is bound to be some confusion. Second, PAT is really the dominant form of NAT in use today (though static NAT is sometimes a necessary part of the security architecture). So, many vendors of PAT-capable products oversimplify, and just call the whole collection of features NAT. As with any product evaluation, if you're considering purchasing a product, take a look at the technical documentation to see exactly what the capabilities are.

So what's the problem with two inside machines sharing the same outside IP address anyway? Collisions—not collisions in the Ethernet sense, if you've studied Ethernet at all, but rather colliding port numbers and IP addresses. Let's look at the naïve version of sharing an outside address. Two machines on the inside transmit requests to the Internet. When the replies come back, they both come back to the outside IP address. How can the router decide which of the two IP addresses on the inside the packets should be sent to?

Let's look at a more involved version of a NAT router that is trying to use one outside IP address for more than one inside machine. In the section on dynamic NAT, we discussed a router that is capable of tracking individual connections as they pass through and are translated. Adding this capability would seem to correct the problem of the router not knowing which IP address to send the packet back to. It can simply scan through the table and look for a connection that the current packet seems to match. When the router finds the match, it looks up the inside IP address that connection belongs to, and forwards it to that machine, after proper translation, of course.

Does this work? Not quite yet. Back to the issue of collisions: Imagine that two inside machines, which share the same outside IP address, want to make a query of the ISP's DNS server. Since the DNS server is maintained by the ISP, it's "on the Internet" from the client's point of view. At least, it's on the far side of the NAT router from the client, so there will be a translation on the way out. Let's take a look at what kind of information might be in the connection table we've been talking about. Certainly, there are IP addresses: Internet IP address (the server), inside IP address (real inside machine address), and outside IP address (the address the inside machine is translated to). Another obvious thing to track is the TCP and UDP port numbers for those types of connections, both source and destination ports. For our example, let's assume all of this is tracked.

Back to the clients talking to the DNS server: They will be sending packets to the same server IP address, and the same port number (UDP port 53 for client DNS queries). We already know they share the same outside IP address, so in the connection table for these two separate "connections" (in quotes because UDP is connectionless), the Internet IP address is the same, the outside IP address is the same, and the destination port number is the same. The inside IP addresses are different, and the source port numbers are probably different. The requests go out with no problem.

The problem is, two requests from two separate inside machines look very similar, and probably only differ on the source port and data portion of the packet.

When a reply comes back to the outside IP address, the only differentiating factor at that time (since the router doesn't know which inside IP address to send to; that's what it's trying to figure out) is the source port. More specifically, it looks at what is now the destination port (source and destination port get reversed on replies), decides which of the two inside machines was using that as a source port, and sends it to that one.

There's where the possibility for collision comes in. Most operating systems will start allocating source ports at 1,025, and work their way up sequentially. There's a very good chance that at some point, the two inside machines will happen to be using the same source port at the same moment, trying to talk to the same IP address on the Internet, as the same destination port. Everything matches except for the inside IP address, which is not good since that's the unknown piece of information when the packet arrives at the outside IP address on the router.

The problem lies in the fact that the headers in the two requests are the same, but the data portion differs. The NAT device has to determine which packet goes to which inside machine.

How Does PAT Work?

Statistically, we've got a smaller chance of having a conflict than we did with straight dynamic NAT. Still, we'd like to make the chance of conflict negligible. This is where PAT comes in. If you hadn't already guessed from the name, PAT works by translating port numbers along with IP addresses. Specifically, when it translates the source address on the way out, it also translates the source port.

If the router is careful not to create conflicts when it chooses new source ports, this solution works well and eliminates conflicts, at least for TCP and UDP. Some extra tricks are sometimes needed for ICMP, which had no port numbers per se.

Now, the router has a unique port number to reference when all the other information matches another connection. PAT enables a very large number of inside machines to share even just one outside IP address. How many exactly? It's difficult to give an exact number, since it depends on usage patterns, so let's make some assumptions. Assume that the limit factor will be many inside machines communicating with a single Internet IP address at one time. The worst case will probably be UDP, since we're stuck using timers to emulate connections (to know when they're done). Let's say the timer is set for two minutes. That is, after two minutes of no packets from either side, the connection is declared over. The possible range of port numbers is 0 to 65,535, so the theoretical limit is 65,536 simultaneous connections. This assumes that they are all happening at the same time, either because they all start at the same time and have to wait two minutes, or because the connections are active longer than that, and it builds up to that level. This is for one outside IP address. If a flavor of dynamic IP is being used, multiply that number by the number of IP addresses being used for dynamic NAT with PAT.

Remember, that applies only if all the clients want to talk to the same machine on the Internet. If you consider all the machines on the Internet, the chances for conflict drop to nearly zero. Chances are good that in the real world, you'll exhaust the memory of your NAT device before you start reaching any theoretical limits.

What is the security situation with PAT? It's starting to look a lot better. An outside IP address no longer corresponds to a single inside IP address; it now depends on the connection. This means that if a new connection attempt is made to the outside address, it will not match anything in the connection table, and will therefore not have an internal IP address to connect to. At least, that's the most common behavior when an Internet machine tries to connect to an outside address. It's theoretically possible to design the PAT so that a particular outside IP address maps to a particular inside address (combined static NAT and PAT). For a security application, you would not want that behavior. Another "gotcha" to look out for is that the outside IP address isn't the IP address of the NAT device for that interface. For example, with some routers it's possible to use the router's own outside IP address for PAT. In that case, connection attempts to the outside IP address will connect to the router, which may not be desirable.

Many PAT implementations only allow a particular inside pool to map to a single outside IP address. Presumably, this is because just about any size inside network can map to a single outside IP address.

Let's take a look at what these connection tables we've been discussing might look like. They include inside source IP address, outside source IP address, destination Internet IP address, original source port, translated source port, destination port, transport protocol, FIN flags, and timer. FIN flags would be a couple of simple flags to indicate that a FIN exchange has been done for one of the two directions. TCP connections, if closed properly, close each direction separately, so we need to track each direction. When both flags are set, the whole connection is done. If a RST occurs instead, the flags aren't needed, and the connection is done immediately.

Figure 4.13 contains a diagram of a possible connection, which we can use as an example. In the diagram, the inside machine is 10.0.0.2, the router's outside IP address is 192.138.149.1, and the server we're contacting on the Internet is 207.244.115.178. The line between the Web server and the router represents the Internet between the two.

Figure 4.13 Simple PAT arrangement, using a router's own outside IP address.

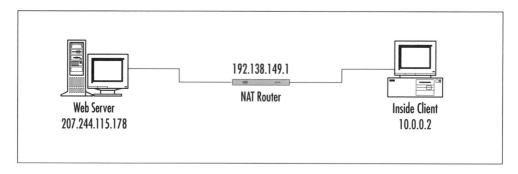

The inside machine sends a SYN packet to port 80 on the Web server, using a source port of 1030. Here's what the table entry might look like:

Source Address	Desti-nation Address	Trans-lated Address	Source Port	Desti-nation Port	Trans-lated Port	Protocol	FIN Source	FIN Desti-nation	Timer
10.0.0.2	207.244. 115.178	192.138. 149.1	1030	80	5309	TCP	Off	Off	2:00

All of the labels that indicate direction are from the point of view of the first packet, the SYN packet, going from the inside to the outside. Many of the items will be reversed for packets going the other way, but the router will keep track of that by noting into which interface the packet arrived.

Here's a rough block diagram of the SYN packet headers just leaving the inside machine:

Destination Address	Source Address	Destination Port	Source Port	Flags
207.244.115.178	10.0.0.2	80	1030	SYN

Here is the same packet after it passes through the router:

Destination Address	Source Address	Destination Port	Source Port	Flags
207.244.115.178	192.138.149.1	80	5309	SYN

Notice that the source address and source port have both been translated. Here's the reply packet from the Web server:

Destination Address	Source Address	Destination Port	Source Port	Flags
192.138.149.1	207.244.115.178	5309	80	SYN-ACK

Source and destination have been reversed, and the flag is now SYN-ACK. This is the packet that will arrive at the outside of the router. The router has to make its decision with these main fields. All the router has to do is match the four leftmost fields to the connection table. If there is a match, it routes the packet and restores the original source address and source port (now destination address and port):

Destination Address	Source Address	Destination Port	Source Port	Flags
10.0.0.2	207.244.115.178	1030	80	SYN-ACK

The address and port the router needs to translate the packet back are simply looked up in the connection table. The connection table entry will remain until one of three conditions are met:

- Both sets of FIN packets are received
- A RST packet is sent by either end
- The timer runs out

The timer is checked periodically to see if time has run out. In addition, each time a packet is routed for this connection, the timer is reset to two minutes, or whatever other value is used.

UDP works much the same, except there are no FIN or RST packets to indicate the end of a connection, so only a timer is relied on to end UDP connections.

Problems with PAT

What kind of problems exist with PAT? PAT has all of the problems of static NAT (i.e., having to translate addresses that appear in the data portion of packets), plus a couple of new ones. Our discussion of PAT was based around the idea of a fully functioning static NAT. So any protocols that pass IP addresses in the data portion of packets, like FTP, should be handled. Well, not quite. The sharing of an outside IP address that gives us the almost-firewall effect of not allowing machines on the Internet to connect inside works against us here.

Again, FTP serves as a good example of the problem. We'll assume the data portion of the packets (the FTP PORT command) is getting modified properly. So what happens when the FTP server tries to connect to the outside IP address at the port supplied? There is no entry in the connection table to permit it, and it will fail.

The solution is obvious. While the NAT software modifies the PORT command (and now it has to change the port passed in the same manner as it does for other connections), it also creates an entry in the connection table.

For this example, refer back to Figure 4.9. This time, the protocol will be FTP instead of HTTP. After the initial connection has been made, the connection table looks like this:

Source Address	Destination Address	Translated Address	Source Port	Destination Port	Translated Port	Protocol	FIN Source	FIN Destination	Timer
10.0.0.2	207.244. 115.178	192.138. 149.1	1042	21	6123	TCP	Off	Off	2:00

At some point during the connection, the FTP client will issue a PORT command. For our example, we'll use PORT 10,0,0,2,4,19. The port number section 4,19 translates to 1043 in decimal, which is what port the OS will hand out next. The router will have to translate this PORT command. If we assume the next translated port the router makes available is 6177, the PORT command becomes PORT 192,138,149,1,24,33. (The PORT command works in bytes: 24*256+33 = 6177.) In addition, the router must add this new port to the connection table. Now the table looks like this:

Source Address	Desti-nation Address	Trans-lated Address	Source Port	Desti-nation Port	Trans-lated Port	Protocol	FIN Source	FIN Desti-nation	Timer
10.0.0.2	207.244. 115.178	192.138. 149.1	1042	21	6123	TCP	Off	Off	2:00
10.0.0.2	207.244. 115.178	192.138. 149.1	1043	20	6177	TCP	Off	Off	2:00

Now, with this addition, PAT properly handles FTP. The data connection will be handled as a separate connection, and will be removed under the same circumstances as any other TCP connection. We have finally achieved our goal of IP address savings, which is the driving factor for wanting to use NAT in the first place.

NOTE

The FTP server will use a source port of 20 when connecting back to clients to deliver data.

With this type of setup, PAT works well. There is one small "gotcha" that comes up on occasion. There really isn't any good reason to do so, but some servers on the Internet will pay special attention to the source port that is used when they are being connected to. This comes up most often with DNS. Traditionally, when two DNS servers communicate using UDP, they will use port 53 as a destination port, as well as their source port. This is a matter of convention rather than a hard and fast rule. If we're translating the source address, though, there could be a problem. There are a few sites on the Internet that have configured their DNS servers to accept connections only *from* port 53.

This has come up in the past with both apple.com and intel.com, but they aren't the only ones. It can be difficult to get others to change to suit you, so if you find yourself having trouble with a particular DNS server, you may have to change the translation for your internal DNS server to static so that the source port of 53 isn't changed on the way out. This applies only if you run your own inside DNS servers. If you use your ISP's DNS servers (which would be outside), then most likely you won't have a problem.

Configuration Examples

In a way, almost all the configuration examples (minus the Cisco static NAT example) have been PAT examples. At their cores, ICS and IP Masquerade are PAT products, even if you're only translating one address to another. IOS can do it or not, depending on how you configure it. Even so, we'll take an opportunity to go into a little more depth, and look at a few more examples.

The reason for the ruse so far is that, practically speaking, NAT (without PAT) doesn't actually work. All of the problems we've discussed so far make plain NAT unusable.

Windows NT 2000

There really isn't a lot more to say about ICS from the first example. It's a PAT product, and all the inside IP addresses are forced to 192.168.0, and are port-translated out using the single dial-up address. There is, however, another option we haven't looked at yet. There was another tab on the window brought up by the Settings button, as shown in Figure 4.14.

Figure 4.14 ICS reverse connection setup.

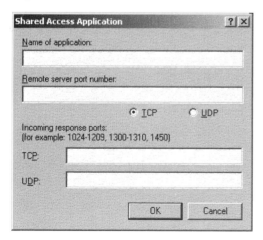

Much like the Services screen, special application handling can be defined here. This is intended to cover behavior like FTP exhibits, where a reverse connection needs to be made. Unlike the FTP handlers we've seen though, this is a little less flexible. With the FTP handlers, just the one port needed is opened long enough for the connection to be made. In this case, we're being invited to leave a range of ports open back to the inside for as long as the service is in use. This also tends to invite more conflicts, since having a port on the outside open gives us all the problems of many-to-one NAT. Even so, using this may make it possible to get an application working that otherwise wouldn't. It's better to have the option than not.

Since the product is still beta, documentation is scarce. I know passive FTP works with no special configuration because I tried it. It's likely that other protocols are handled in a special way, too, but Microsoft hasn't told us which ones yet.

Probably the biggest issue with ICS is that it works only with dial-up, and that it forces DHCP on you. This means it won't work with cable modems, DSL, or any technology that wants to connect via a LAN interface. Microsoft sells a much higher end product called Microsoft Proxy Server (MSP). It's much more flexible, but it retails for $1000 US.

There are other commercial solutions that fill in the price gaps between free and $1000. To find a list of commercial NAT products for NT, consult the "References and Resources" section, later. I've personally had very good luck with Sygate, of which the most expensive version (unlimited inside users) costs only about $300 US.

Linux IP Masquerade

IP Masquerade is also doing PAT, even when working on just one inside IP address. Changing our static NAT to many-to-1 PAT is very simple. Change the line:

```
/sbin/ipchains -A forward -s 192.168.0.2/32 -j MASQ
```

to:

```
/sbin/ipchains -A forward -s 192.168.0.0/24 -j MASQ
```

which will take care of the whole inside subnet.

There is a good set of documents on how to use IP Masquerade; links to them can be found in the "References and Resources" section. If you plan to deploy IP Masquerade in production, you owe it to yourself to read them. You will also need to read the IP Chains documentation (notice the ipchains command we're using to configure IP Masquerade). IP Chains is the built-in firewall for Linux kernel 2.2.x. IP Masquerade is not sufficient to keep your system secure.

Let's take a look at some other aspects of IP Masquerade. We know there's a module that specifically handles FTP. What other modules are there? If you recall, the command that installed the FTP handler was modprobe. The command modprobe –l will list all modules available for install. In that list, these stick out:

```
/lib/modules/2.2.5-15/ipv4/ip_masq_vdolive.o
/lib/modules/2.2.5-15/ipv4/ip_masq_user.o
/lib/modules/2.2.5-15/ipv4/ip_masq_raudio.o
/lib/modules/2.2.5-15/ipv4/ip_masq_quake.o
/lib/modules/2.2.5-15/ipv4/ip_masq_portfw.o
```

```
/lib/modules/2.2.5-15/ipv4/ip_masq_mfw.o
/lib/modules/2.2.5-15/ipv4/ip_masq_irc.o
/lib/modules/2.2.5-15/ipv4/ip_masq_ftp.o
/lib/modules/2.2.5-15/ipv4/ip_masq_cuseeme.o
/lib/modules/2.2.5-15/ipv4/ip_masq_autofw.o
```

Our FTP module is in the list, and judging by the names, there are obviously IP Masquerade modules. Several of those are immediately recognizable, and are known to cause difficulty when used with firewalls or NAT. These include FTP, Real Audio, Quake, IRC (specifically, DCC send), CUSeeMe, and VDOLive.

There is a place where IP Masquerade handlers can be obtained, and ones that don't exist can even be requested. Please take a look at the "References and Resources" section of this chapter for details.

Cisco IOS

We've already seen the Cisco PAT, too—that's what the "overload" configuration was. This variation gets all inside machines to go out using the router's own IP address:

```
NAT(config)#ip nat inside source list 1 interface fastethernet 0/1 overload
NAT(config)#access-list 1 permit 192.168.0.0 0.0.0.255
```

This tells the router to use access list 1 (match all 192.168.0 addresses) and to translate using the router's own IP address for fastethernet 0/1 as the source address.

Here's a full working config for this:

```
!
version 12.0
service timestamps debug uptime
service timestamps log uptime
service password-encryption
!
hostname NAT
!
enable secret 5 xxxxxxxx
```

```
enable password 7 xxxxxxxx
!
ip subnet-zero
!
!
interface FastEthernet0/0
 ip address 192.168.0.1 255.255.255.0
 no ip directed-broadcast
 ip nat inside
!
interface Serial0/0
 no ip address
 no ip directed-broadcast
!
interface FastEthernet0/1
 ip address 130.214.99.254 255.255.255.0
 no ip directed-broadcast
 ip nat outside
!
ip nat inside source list 1 interface fastethernet 0/1 overload
ip classless
ip route 0.0.0.0 0.0.0.0 130.214.99.1
no ip http server
!
access-list 1 permit 192.168.0.0 0.0.0.255
!
line con 0
 transport input none
line aux 0
line vty 0 4
 password 7 xxxxxxx
 login
!
no scheduler allocate
end
```

Naturally, if you want to use this config, you'll have to correct IP
addresses and interface names. Also, the passwords have been

crossed out, so put those in manually. It's always a good idea to sanitize your router configuration files before you let anyone else see them.

This type of configuration (having all inside machines translate to 1 outside IP) is often useful when connecting to an ISP.

The Cisco has another interesting feature that we haven't looked at yet. The IOS lets you examine the connection tables! We looked at some theoretical examples before, and now we can look at some real ones.

Here's an example from the static NAT configuration on IOS:

```
NAT#sho ip nat trans
Pro Inside global        Inside local      Outside local      Outside global
tcp 130.214.99.250:1055   192.168.0.2:1055   130.214.250.9:23   130.214.250.9:23
```

Cisco doesn't expose the FIN flag or timers. Also, notice that there are four address:port pairs. That's because the IOS can do double NAT inside one box.

In this case, inside machine 192.168.0.2 had Telnetted (port 23) to 130.214.250.9. The source address was translated to 130.214.99.250. On the left, you can see that the transport protocol is TCP.

Here's an example from the dynamic NAT config (using a pool of outside addresses):

```
NAT#sho ip nat trans
Pro Inside global        Inside local      Outside local      Outside global
udp 130.214.99.200:1063 192.168.0.2:1063 130.214.250.43:53 130.214.250.43:53
tcp 130.214.99.200:1068 192.168.0.2:1068 130.214.250.9:23   130.214.250.9:23
tcp 130.214.99.200:1066 192.168.0.2:1066 130.214.250.9:23   130.214.250.9:23
udp 130.214.99.200:1067 192.168.0.2:1067 130.214.250.43:53 130.214.250.43:53
tcp 130.214.99.200:1064 192.168.0.2:1064 130.214.250.9:23   130.214.250.9:23
udp 130.214.99.200:1065 192.168.0.2:1065 130.214.250.43:53 130.214.250.43:53
```

The address pool starts at 130.214.99.200, and that address was picked for the same machine for all connections. Here, we see more Telnet connections, and a few DNS connections (UDP port 53).

Here's the state table during our PAT example, when all inside machines are going out as the router's IP address:

```
Pro Inside global       Inside local     Outside local     Outside global
icmp 130.214.99.254:256 192.168.0.2:256   130.214.250.9:256 130.214.250.9:256
udp 130.214.99.254:1069 192.168.0.2:1069  130.214.250.43:53 130.214.250.43:53
tcp 130.214.99.254:1070 192.168.0.2:1070  130.214.250.9:23  130.214.250.9:23
```

Here, we've got TCP, UDP, and ICMP. Notice that the ICMP connections have what appears to be a port number next to them. Some NAT devices will impose state information on ICMP in order to be able to distinguish it. It's unclear if that's what's happening here, but it's possible that the router has replaced part of the ping stream with 256, or some representation of it, and this is how it's tracking that.

Here is what the table looks like during an FTP session, using the PAT config:

```
NAT#sho ip nat trans
Pro Inside global       Inside local     Outside local     Outside global
tcp 130.214.99.254:1080 192.168.0.2:1080 192.138.151.73:21 192.138.151.73:21
tcp 130.214.99.254:1081 192.168.0.2:1081 192.138.151.73:20 192.138.151.73:20

NAT#sho ip nat trans
Pro Inside global       Inside local     Outside local     Outside global
tcp 130.214.99.254:1082 192.168.0.2:1082 192.138.151.73:20 192.138.151.73:20
tcp 130.214.99.254:1080 192.168.0.2:1080 192.138.151.73:21 192.138.151.73:21
```

The first listing is just after an ls command was issued in the FTP client. We can see our connection out to port 21, and the reverse connection back from port 20. The second list is after another ls command. Notice the previous reverse-connection entry is gone. Finally, if need to, it's possible to empty the translation table manually:

```
NAT#clear ip nat trans *
NAT#show ip nat trans
```

IETF WORK

What Are the Advantages?

If you've read the previous sections in this chapter, you probably already have a pretty good idea of the advantages of using NAT. Primarily, it allows you to use a relatively small number of public IP addresses to connect a large number of inside machines to the Internet. It also buys you some flexibility in how you connect to other networks.

For Managers

How Many IP Addresses Do You Really Need?

There are many more Internet connectivity options available today than there were just a short while ago. These include modems, ISDN, traditional leased-line, DSL, cable, wireless, and more. Prices, performance, reliability, and availability vary widely, but they all have one feature in common: The more IP addresses you want, the more expensive it will be. From a financial perspective, it makes sense to get by with as few as possible. NAT can go a long way towards reducing the number of IP addresses needed. PAT can be used in most cases to let all your internal machines access the Internet as if they were one IP address. This can be crucial if the access technology only allows for one IP address, such as dial-up access (modem, ISDN). If you plan to host any publicly accessible services on your premise, such as a Web server or DNS server, you'll need a few more IP addresses. This usually isn't too much of a problem, since dial-up access isn't appropriate for hosting public servers anyway. You can still use PAT to keep the inside Internet access down to one IP address, and get enough other addresses to cover however many servers you want to run. If you do have public servers, however, don't fool yourself into thinking that NAT is a complete security solution. It's not. You must still implement a full security solution, probably including a firewall.

The goal of using a small number of IP addresses on your NAT device for many inside machines is usually the motivating factor behind wanting to use NAT. This goal is achieved in the real world through a particular type of NAT, called PAT. PAT allows many inside machines to use a small number of IP addresses (often as few as one) to connect to the Internet.

NAT also gives you some flexibility in how you handle changes or outages. Sometimes a machine goes down or moves, and rather than reconfigure many client machines, you'd like to translate addresses on the router to point to the new server, or to an existing server at a new address. This can also be useful for temporarily dealing with address conflicts.

What Are the Performance Issues?

What is the cost in performance for all of these NAT features? Not many hard numbers are available. For NT's ICS, performance is probably a moot point, since it has to involve a dial-up interface. Certainly ICS will function fast enough to max out a dial-up connection. IP Masquerade could have some meaningful testing done to it, but I'm not aware of any performance testing that has been done. In addition, Linux is very much a moving target. Changes come quickly, and they may include performance enhancements. Linux also runs on a wide variety of platforms, so if you run into a performance bottleneck while using IP Masquerade, you'll probably be able to scale it up with better hardware. Cisco has provided some rough numbers here:

```
http://www.cisco.com/warp/public/458/41.html#Q6
```

Cisco gives numbers for three of their router platforms: 4500, 4700, and 7500. The 4500 is able to run at about 7.5–8.0 Mbps on 10Mb Ethernet for all packet sizes. The 4700 is able to run at 10 Mbps on 10Mb Ethernet for all packet sizes. The 7500 throughput ranges from 24 Mbps for 64-byte packets, to 96 Mbps for 1500-byte packets on Fast Ethernet.

Of course, for all three NAT packages we've been looking at, this depends on what else these platforms are doing. If the NT ICS server is running a CPU-intensive game at the time, performance may dip. If the Cisco router is also performing an encryption on the traffic, performance will drop there, too.

It's not surprising that there should be some delay when performing NAT versus just plain routing. At a high level, the routing function is relatively simple:

1. Receive the packet.
2. Verify checksums.
3. Consult the routing table.
4. Decrement the TTL field.
5. Recalculate the checksums.
6. Transmit.

Compare this with the functions needed for NAT:

1. Receive the packet.
2. Verify checksums.
3. If entered outside the interface, check if there is a matching connection table entry.
4. Consult the routing table.
5. Check if the outbound interface is marked for NAT.
6. Determine portions of the packet to be modified.
7. If it is the first packet in a new connection, create a table entry.
8. If it is a PORT command or similar, rewrite the data portion and create a new table entry.
9. If it is a FIN packet, remove the table entry.
10. Modify the packet as needed.
11. Recalculate checksums.
12. Transmit.

Even if there is enough CPU speed, there will still have to be a small latency increase, as these steps will require numbers memory lookup and writes. The good news is that under most circumstances, performance won't be an issue. Usually NAT will be a problem only when routers are already under a heavy load.

For IT Professionals

Which Product Are You Going to Pick?

Chances are it's going to depend on which operating system you know best, and possibly what equipment you already have. If you are comfortable with UNIX, then IP Masquerade or something similar would probably be your preference. If you're an NT person, then you'll want something on NT. To be realistic, it probably won't be ICS. ICS is really only good enough for a home LAN, which isn't too surprising, since it was designed for that. In some cases, it isn't even suitable for that, since it might be a cable modem you want to share. If you're a network person, or maybe if you just already have a Cisco router in place, you may want to implement your NAT there. Cisco routers aren't the only ones that do NAT, either, in case you have a different brand. It's doubly important to pick a solution that runs on your platform of choice, because chances are that it's not just a NAT architecture, but also a security architecture. Like it or not, as soon as you hook up to the Internet, you've got a security problem to worry about. You'll have to configure whatever platform you want to run on to be as secure as possible, so it should be whatever operating system you know best.

Proxies and Firewall Capabilities

Now that we've covered in depth what NAT is and how it works, let's discuss security. So far, we've only covered firewalls indirectly, mentioning them here and there while discussing NAT. Let's begin with some basic definitions, and later get to how firewalls are similar to, and different from, NAT packages.

What is a firewall? That's a bit of a religious issue, as firewall means different things to different people. The original meaning of firewall was a barrier, often in a structure, designed to take a certain amount of time to burn through during a fire. For example, a building may have some walls or portions of walls that are firewalls, designed to compartmentalize a fire for a certain amount of time, to limit damage. Some people liken firewalls in the electronic security sense to these barriers, saying they are designed to deter intruders for a period of time, and to compartmentalize parts of the network. So, if there is a breach in one portion of a network, the others aren't instantly affected, too.

Other folks will argue that a firewall is features X, Y, and Z, with X, Y, and Z being whatever features they desire in a firewall. Some say that the firewall is the portion of a security architecture that stops traffic. Others say it includes the pieces that allow certain types of traffic.

The folks who participate in these discussions are the philosophers of firewalls. These discussions often take place on mailing lists dedicated to firewalls. What's a little disturbing is that these folks, some of whom invented firewalls, can't agree on terminology.

Realistically, firewalls are defined by companies who sell products called firewalls. It turns out that the situation isn't as bad as it might seem, because nearly all of these products have a number of features in common. We'll be taking that road, so we'll be discussing features.

Packet Filters

Networks, by their nature, are designed to pass as much as possible, as quickly as possible. The original routers had no need of intentionally blocking things, except perhaps for corrupt packets. That is, corrupt in the sense that the appropriate checksums don't match. Supposedly, in the early days of the Internet, security wasn't much of a concern.

I've heard at least a few stories that indicate that people wanted to start filtering certain kinds of traffic due to errors. Someone, somewhere, made a configuration error, and traffic starts flying that causes someone somewhere else some trouble. Thus were born packet filters.

Packet filters are what they sound like—devices that filter packets. Very commonly they are routers, but they can also be general-purpose hosts, such as Windows NT or Linux. The earliest packet filters would have been able to block packets based on the IP addresses contained within. Later, they would be able to block packets based on port numbers. Modern packet filters can filter on a variety of criteria. These include IP addresses, port numbers, transport type, certain flags in TCP headers, and more.

These packet filters have long been used as part of a traditional proxy/screening router firewall architecture (see the "Proxies" section, next). Typically, they will be used to block types of traffic that aren't allowed by policy. They can also be used reactively to block attacks after they have been detected (i.e., block all traffic from a particular address range).

Traditional packet filters (PF) have the characteristic that they don't change packets, and they don't have state. In other words, a PF can only pass or not pass a packet, and it can only make that decision based on information in the current packet. In addition, PFs are statically configured, meaning that they can't change the filter rules based on traffic.

Many packet filters have a way to filter on "established," which would seem to indicate that they are able to track conversations in progress. In fact, to a PF, "established" simply means that the ACK bit is set in the TCP header.

PFs have some serious limitations as firewalls. Let's go back to the problem of how to handle FTP. Say you have an inside machine that you want to allow FTP access out. The control channel connection is easy. The filter rule says inside IP can go to any IP outside at port 21. Next, you can turn on the allowed established rule to allow established packets from any outside IP to the inside IP. At this point, the control connection will work, and you're relatively protected. The problem becomes how to handle the reverse connections. The first packet back has only the ACK bit on, so the established rule will not help there. You don't know what port the inside IP will be waiting on, only that it's probably above 1023.

With a PF, though, all you can do is add a rule that says to allow packets from any IP, TCP port 20, to any IP at TCP port >1023. This opens up a massive security hole, as machine operating systems run services at ports above 1023. Many of these services have known security holes. Anyone who figures out that you allow access to all inside IP addresses at all ports above 1023, if the source port happens to be 20, can attack you. For the clever attacker, the firewall might as well not be there.

FTP is simply a familiar example. If you take a look at the handlers that are available for IP Masquerade, you'll see many more examples of protocols that would have to be handled in the same way.

However, if you had a special machine that didn't have any vulnerable services running above 1023, and had otherwise been specially secured and locked down, it would probably be acceptable to configure the PF to allow traffic only to it in this manner, depending on the local security policy. Such a machine is often called a *bastion host*. The problem is, these machines tend to be less useful to everyday users, so they really can't be put on everyone's desk to act as their main productivity machine. So, what can the machine be used for? It can act as a proxy.

Proxies

Proxies were discussed somewhat at the beginning of this chapter. A proxy is a machine, often a bastion host, that is configured to fulfill requests on behalf of other machines, usually inside machines. We'll get into the details of how the proxy actually works in a moment.

Imagine now that we've configured our PF to allow traffic only from the Internet to the proxy. Since we've configured it well, the fact that the Internet can get to ports above 1023 is not a major concern. Additionally, another PF between the proxy and the inside would be useful to help keep malicious inside users from attacking the proxy. Our architecture looks like that shown in Figure 4.15.

Figure 4.15 Protected proxy server.

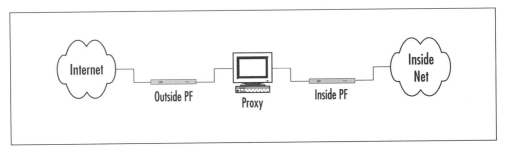

It's important to note that Figure 4.15 is more a logical diagram than a physical one. Although we could implement all of the pieces shown to achieve the desired effect, it may not be necessary. For example, the diagram would seem to indicate that the proxy has two interfaces—it could, but usually doesn't. Traffic may enter and leave the same interface without causing difficulty if addresses are managed properly on the filtering routers. Also, with a flexible enough router acting as PF, this design can be done with one 3-interface router rather than two 2-interface routers. However, this diagram makes it much easier to visualize data flow.

The inside PF has another function besides protecting the proxy from inside users. Should the proxy be compromised in some way, it may help protect the inside against the proxy itself. This concept is important, and it's called a DMZ (Demilitarized Zone). The term

DMZ has a couple of different meanings to the firewall philosophers as well. Some purists call it the network just outside the outside interface of a firewall (or in our case, outside the outside PF). The definition we'll be using is "a network segment that trusts neither the inside nor the outside, and is not trusted by the inside." The word trust in this case implies unfettered network access. For example, the Internet at large trusts everyone, as everyone gets access. The inside network trusts no one, and no one gets direct access to the inside. Practically speaking, most folks consider a DMZ to be a third interface on the firewall (the first and second interfaces being the inside and outside).

So how exactly does a proxy work? We'll start with traditional proxies. Basically, the proxy acts as a server to inside machines, and as a client to the Internet. Inside machines have to use either modified software, or a procedural change to make use of the proxy. Traditional proxies are not routers, and in fact the routing code should be turned off or compiled out of a bastion host that is to be a traditional proxy. If you send a packet towards a proxy, and its destination IP address isn't the proxy's address, the proxy will just throw the packet away. In all of our NAT examples, the destination address of packets always remained (except for the double NAT examples) that of its ultimate destination, some host on the Internet. Proxies work differently, and clients have to change their behavior accordingly.

The first requirement is that the destination IP address must be that of the proxy server, not the server the user actually wants on the Internet. Let's look at a simple (contrived) example: Telnet.

With a NAT-type solution, you would simply Telnet to the name or address you wanted. Let's design an imaginary proxy to handle Telnet. First, we write our program to listen for network connections, and pick a port on the proxy on which to run it. The port could be 23, replacing the regular Telnet mechanism (if any) on the proxy machine, or we could run it on its own port. For our example, we'll pick port 2000. Our program will accept TCP connections, and then prompt for a name or IP address. Once it gets the name, it attempts to connect to that name at port 23. Once the connection is made and output from port 23 on the outside machine is sent to the inside machine, any subsequent output from the inside machine (i.e., the user typing) is sent to the outside machine.

So, an inside user who wants to Telnet out must now Telnet to the proxy at port 2000, and enter the name of the machine to which they really want to Telnet. If it connects, they will see the output from it, and will be able to type input for it.

Of course in the real world, the Telnet protocol isn't that simple, and our example isn't quite sufficient. However, it illustrates the basic idea: have the inside client inform the proxy of what it wants. The proxy makes the connection on behalf of the client, retrieves some data, and passes it back to the client. Pass any input from the client to the server.

How is FTP looking? The problem remains the same: the reverse connections. The proxy does the same trick as a PAT device, but in a slightly different manner. The control channel connection (to port 21) works more or less like the Telnet proxy example just given, until the PORT command. Upon identifying the PORT command in the data stream, it changes it in the same manner that a PAT device would, and substitutes its own address. The proxy also asks the OS for an available port, begins listening on that port, and sends that port number. It has to keep a copy of the original PORT command for later reference. When the outside server connects back to the proxy, the proxy opens a connection to the inside machine in the original PORT command and sends the data.

So what does a user on the inside who wants to use FTP have to do differently? That presents a problem. With our Telnet example, it's pretty easy to see how to get extra input from the user. The problem with FTP is that there are many, many different types of FTP client programs. These range from command-line text clients where users have lots of opportunity to enter input, to fully GUI FTP clients, where nearly everything is point-and-click.

One strategy is to have the inside user put in a special user-name. For example, instead of entering anonymous, they would enter anonymous@ftp.example.com. This would instruct the proxy to use the username anonymous, and connect to the FTP server ftp.example.com. The password would be supplied unchanged.

This works for any FTP client where the user is prompted for a username and password. Problem is, when Web browsers follow an FTP link, they automatically use anonymous and whatever e-mail address you've got programmed into your browser. They don't stop to prompt.

Web browsers are a problem in general. How is the user using a browser supposed to get the browser to connect to the proxy, and how are they to supply the URL of the real site to the proxy? There are tricks that can be tried, such as putting in special URLs and treating the proxy as a Web server. These work theoretically, though with problems, but these mechanisms aren't very practical. Users will tire of them quickly and complain.

There is a separate tactic that can be used for proxy access: special client software. Basically, this means that the client software is modified to access a proxy server, so that the user does the same thing as they might if they were directly connected to the Internet, and the software takes care of using the proxy. So, when the user runs the special Telnet program, it handles contacting the proxy and informing the proxy about which server is desired, transparently. All the user has to do is Telnet to the server they want, using the special Telnet client. Theoretically, this can be done to any client program, so that users don't have to be bothered with the details.

The problem is, there are many, many client programs, most of which don't have publicly available source code for modification. Also, there are potentially many, many proxy protocols, if each site created their own proxy software. Obviously, some standards would be useful.

The currently used proxy protocol standards are SOCKS and CERN proxy, but we won't get into the details. The CERN proxy protocol grew out of a proxy feature of the CERN HTTP server, and as you might guess it's an HTTP proxy. It was important because there was support for the protocol starting with the early Web browsers.

SOCKS enjoyed similar early browser support, with the advantage that it can proxy arbitrary port numbers. Of course, your SOCKS proxy server must still be able to handle the protocol that matches the port number.

SOCKS also came with a few rewritten client programs, like rtelnet and rftp. These were "SOCKSified" versions of the Telnet and FTP programs. They are UNIX source code, so chances are you could compile versions for most UNIX platforms. Later, third-party Windows applications starting appearing with SOCKS support. Nowadays, if a client program supports the use of a proxy, it usually has SOCKS support. More information about SOCKS can be found in the section "References and Resources."

The idea of SOCKS being able to support arbitrary ports begs the question: Is there such a thing as a generic proxy? Indeed, there is. It's possible to proxy a stream of data assuming that there are no reverse connections, and so forth. That is, assume it looks rather like a Telnet connection.

Such a proxy is often called a circuit-level proxy, or a *plug gateway* (after the plug-gw feature in Gauntlet, a popular proxy-based commercial firewall). SOCKS proxies typically can support such an arrangement, if desired.

Yet another way to handle getting the client request to the proxy is to modify the IP stack on the client to do so. This software is typically called a *shim*. The Microsoft Proxy Server works this way; it supplies a shim for Microsoft Windows clients. MSP also supports the SOCKS protocol, for non-Windows clients. In this manner, MSP is able to support arbitrary client programs on the Windows platform, as long as the protocols are simple, or a handler has already been designed.

Finally, before we leave the topic of proxies, some proxies now have a transparency option, which changes the model of how proxies used to work. As discussed, traditional proxies require the clients to behave differently. Transparent proxies can act as routers and proxy connections automatically, much like a PAT device. These proxies have the important advantage that they do not require any special software or configuration of the client. So what's the difference between PAT and a transparent proxy? This is discussed in detail later in this chapter, in "Why a Proxy Server Is Really Not a NAT."

Stateful Packet Filters

During the time that proxies were evolving, so were PFs. The ability to keep simple state information was added to PFs, and thus were born Stateful Packet Filters (SPFs). An SPF could, for example, watch a PORT command go by, and only allow back the port that was mentioned, rather than having to let through everything above 1023. Rather than just let in every TCP packet that had the ACK bit set, it could let in just the ones that corresponded to outgoing packets. The small addition of being able to track what went on before adds an amazing amount of power to the simple PF.

Very few plain SPFs actually exist. That's because they almost all add yet another ability, which will be discussed shortly. An example of an SPF as described is a Cisco router using reflexive access lists. These access lists have the ability to modify themselves somewhat, based on other access list lines being matched.

Stateful Packet Filter with Rewrite

The preceding definition of SPF is not a widely accepted one. Despite its use of the word filter in the middle, when most people discuss SPFs, they mean a device that can also modify packets as they pass through. Adding this capability theoretically gives the SPF complete control over packets.

The packet rewrite also puts one feature into the SPF engine in particular—NAT. Recall that the requirements for NAT are: the ability to rewrite packets, and the ability to track that information. As it turns out, the connection tables needed to do PAT are basically the same as those needed to do SPF. So, if you can do SPF, it's pretty easy to add PAT, and vice versa.

There are many commercial examples of SPF-based firewalls, even if they use a different term for the underlying technology. The market-share leader, Checkpoint's Firewall-1, is based on SPF, which they call Stateful Multi-Layer Inspection (SMLI). Another popular example is Cisco's PIX firewall.

We won't go into a lot of detail about how SPF works—if you understand the details behind PAT, you understand SPF. The tables that need to be maintained to perform an SPF function are the same as those needed to do PAT. An SPF firewall needs to do at least the same amount of work as a PAT device, and should ideally add on a fair amount more, to allow for better data validation and content filtering.

Why a Proxy Server Is Really Not a NAT

At this point, it's appropriate to discuss the differences between proxies and NAT. For purposes of this discussion, all flavors of NAT, PFs, and SPFs are equivalent. Transparent proxies are a little bit of a special case, but they will be treated as traditional proxies for this discussion.

At a very high level, proxies and NAT appear to be the same; they both let you hide many machines behind an IP address. They both modify the data stream as it goes by to account for the change of address. They both keep state about more complicated protocols, in order to handle them correctly.

It turns out that the ends might be the same, but the means are very different. At a low level, the internals of the device (a proxy or NAT device) handle the packet in completely different ways. The basic difference boils down to this: For NAT, the basic unit being worked on is the packet; for a proxy, all of its work is done on a data stream. Let's discuss what that means, starting with the proxy.

When a packet is received by a server, the server first determines if the packet is intended for it (i.e., if the destination address is one of its addresses). In the case of a traditional proxy, it will be. The packet then undergoes a process of being passed up the IP stack of the server. If the packet belongs to an existing connection, the data portion of the packet is extracted, and placed into a buffer for the proxy program to read. If it's a new connection, a new buffer is created and the proxy program is notified that there is a new connection to service, but the process is otherwise the same.

When the proxy needs to send something, a reverse process happens. The information the proxy needs to send is placed into an output buffer. The TCP/IP software on the server will then pull information out of the buffer, put it into packets, and send it.

Under the IP protocol, packets can be a wide range of sizes. Large packets may be split up into fragments in order to cross networks that can handle only frames up to a particular size. For example, a 2000-byte packet would have to be split into at least two parts to cross an Ethernet segment with an MTU of 1500 bytes. On a proxy server, the IP stack will put the fragments together before it places the data into the buffer. Ideally, fragments won't happen. When possible, hosts will not transmit packets that will have to be fragmented. A host doesn't always have a way to determine whether or not a fragment will need to be made along the way across a network, so often the best the host can do is to not transmit packets bigger than its local network.

The goal of the fragment discussion is to illustrate a point: The number of packets that enter a proxy server don't necessarily equal the number of packets that come out. For an overly simplified example, a proxy server may receive a single packet that contains "Hello World!" However, when it transmits it back out, it may be as two packets: "Hello" and "World!" The reverse may happen as well. In fact, the proxy inputs only the string of characters, and outputs them to a different buffer, possibly making changes to them. It doesn't concern itself with how the packet gets divided. When it sees an FTP PORT command, it reads it in, decides on how it should be changed, and outputs the changed version. It doesn't need to do anything special if the command ends up being longer or shorter.

Contrast this with a NAT device. When the IP stack of a NAT device gets a packet that is not addressed to it, which is normally what will happen, it will try to route the packet. During the routing process is when the NAT device has an opportunity to operate on the packet. Except for fragments and a couple of special cases, NAT is one packet in, one packet out. The packet will be basically the same size as well. When a PORT command starts through, the NAT device has to keep the packets as intact as possible. This means there may have to be a special piece of code to expand or shrink a packet to accommodate a longer or shorter address. When fragments arrive, the NAT device typically will have to perform reassembly as well. Although fragments are packets in their own right, they are also pieces of a larger packet. Taken as a whole piece, the packets in and packets out count still holds.

What are the security implications for the two methods? There are pros and cons for each. There exist types of attacks that rely on the exact structure of a packet. With a proxy, since the packets are torn apart, there is little chance of this type of attack succeeding against inside hosts. However, since the proxy has to process the packet itself, it may fall prey to the attack rather than the inside host. A NAT device would likely not fall victim to the same type of attack, but it might pass it along to the inside host, and have it succeed there. Fortunately, these types of attacks are almost always Denial of Service (DoS) attacks, which mean they tend to crash things, but don't result in a violation of information integrity. In one case, the firewall crashes. In another case, the firewall stays functional, but the inside host goes down. Neither is an absolutely better choice, and it depends on the preference of the firewall administrator. No one wants their firewall going down, but on the other hand, its job is to protect the inside.

The other big difference between NAT and proxy is data validation and modification. There are a number of proxy packages out there that take a more conservative security stance. That is, they contain proxies for protocols that the designers were reasonably sure they could validate well. They had an idea of what allowable values are, and designed their proxy to watch for those, and make corrections if needed. In some cases, if it looks like a protocol has some inherent problems, they would not produce a proxy for it, thereby discouraging customers from using that protocol.

Many NAT packages seem to take a different tact. They will do the bare minimum necessary to get a protocol to pass, and they often try to pass as many protocols as possible. They also tend to be more open by default; that is, if a connection attempt is made from the inside and the protocol is unknown, it will try to pass it anyway.

Now, this isn't a fair comparison. I've compared the best proxies against the worst NAT implementations. Naturally, there are products from both camps that meet in the middle, and a good firewall administrator can make a NAT/SPF secure, and a bad one can misconfigure a good proxy. Still, the tendencies are there: NAT devices typically only go above layer 4 when it's needed to make the protocol work (like the FTP example). Proxies always work above layer 4, and even the simplest ones (circuit-level proxies) operate at layer 5. The assumption is, of course, that the higher up the stack they go, the more secure.

All of this is a religious argument though, because you don't buy a conceptual firewall, you buy an actual product. Each product must be evaluated on its own merit.

The other point that makes a lot of the arguing pointless is that the lines between SPF and proxy are blurring. The latest versions of most of the commercial firewalls include features both from the proxy world and the SPF world, regardless of which background they came from. For example, in Firewall-1, there are a number of "security servers" included that optionally can be activated in place of a NAT-style packet passing. These typically include extra capabilities, such as extra authentication, stripping out of undesirable content (such as Java or ActiveX) and blocking of particular sites by name or URL. Many of the proxy firewalls have gone transparent. In order for a proxy to be transparent, it has to change its behavior somewhat. The short explanation is that they have to perform a SPF-type function to deliver the packets to the proxy software, when they weren't addressed to the proxy in the first place.

Shortcomings of SPF

There are plenty of SPF shortcomings to discuss, but only in a security context. In terms of functionality, all the products work well. There are performance differences and administration differences, but if the product claims to pass a particular protocol, it usually does.

Proxies are generally slower, simply because they do more to the information as it goes through. They strip headers off, put them on, allocate sockets, and do a lot of buffering and copying of data. SPFs skip a lot of this work. For protocols without a lot of work to do, this is an advantage. For protocols that should be handled carefully, this is bad. There seems to be a consensus that handling complicated protocols is easier with proxy-style software than with NAT style. It seems that the idea of being able to toss the unit of the packet makes the process easier, at least for TCP protocols. Being able to pick between the two in a single package is one advantage to having the lines between SPF and proxy blur. The firewall designer can pick the best tool for the protocol.

The transparency option for proxies is a very good feature. Not having to change the software on all the inside machines, and not having to support those changes, can be a huge advantage. A subtle bit of information is lost with this option, though.

With traditional proxies, especially with architectures where there is a separate program for each protocol, there is never any question about which protocol was desired. For example, if the user contacted the Telnet proxy, you could be sure they wanted to use the Telnet protocol. If they contacted the HTTP proxy, clearly they want HTTP. If you've spent any time surfing the Web, you've probably noticed that some URLs specify a different port number. For example, instead of:

```
http://www.example.com
```

you see:

```
http://www.example.com:8080
```

In this case, rather than contacting the Web server at port 80 (which is the default for HTTP), we've explicitly told it to contact a Web server via port 8080. For a traditional proxy, this is not a problem. It knows you want HTTP, and it knows you want to do it over port 8080.

This works because the proxy is forcing the client to specify both protocol and port explicitly. Let's look at the same situation with a transparent proxy. The client isn't configured in any special way. The user might not even realize there is a firewall there. Now, the client isn't specifying the protocol to the proxy, because it doesn't know a proxy is there. So, when it contacts port 80, the proxy has to make an assumption—it will assume (almost always correctly) that this is HTTP, and will handle it as such. What about when the browser specifies port 8080? The proxy has to make another assumption. Port 8080 is pretty commonly used as a nonstandard HTTP port, but not always. The proxy must either pick HTTP or a circuit-level proxy. This is commonly configurable.

What happens in this situation?

```
http://www.example.com:21
```

Some joker on the Internet has run his Web server on port 21, and your user has clicked on a link to it. The proxy has to make an assumption—it's going to assume this is the FTP protocol. Chances are, this connection won't work very well.

So, we've lost some information by going transparent. We've forced transparent proxies to make assumptions about protocols based on port numbers. This will work well most of the time, but there is always a weird exception somewhere. SPFs suffer from the same problem as well.

Some folks have argued that an SPF-type architecture makes it too easy for a firewall administrator to do something risky. In other words, SPFs may be more flexible in the range of things they can be made to allow, and that may be too tempting. This is largely untrue now anyway, since most proxies include similar capabilities.

Most firewalls come with some sort of GUI for configuring the rules of what is allowed and what isn't. These can be very convenient for maintaining large rule sets. Some more-experienced firewall administrators have complained that this can be a hindrance to understanding exactly what the firewall is up to. They complain that by putting simplicity on top of a complex product, it gives the illusion to the novice administrator that they comprehend everything that is going on. In other words, it provides a false sense of security.

Summary

Network Address Translation (NAT) changes a packet's layer 3 address as it passes through a NAT device. Other protocols like IPX could also be translated, but the vast majority of the commercial NAT implementations perform NAT on IP addresses. Often, simply changing layer 3 protocols is insufficient, and higher layer information must be modified as well. NAT and security are often used together.

The ideas behind NAT probably came from early proxy-based firewall solutions. Proxy servers allow administrators to filter traffic for content, and to make it appear to outside networks that everything is coming from one IP address.

The proxy administrator usually configures a filtering router (i.e., a packet filter) to block direct access from inside-out, and outside-in. The configuration allows only inside machines to communicate directly with the proxy. This forces inside clients to use the proxy if they want access to the outside net. This single point in the network where all traffic is forced to pass through (on the way to the Internet, at least) is called a choke point. Care is taken to configure the proxy server to be as secure as possible.

A side-effect of a proxy firewall is that the outside needs to see only one IP address. This can reduce the needed publicly routable IP addresses to one. RFC1918 recognizes this, and makes a number of IP address ranges available for private use, behind proxy servers or NAT firewalls. A NAT device usually acts as a router.

There are several types of NAT. The first type is static NAT, a 1-to-1 mapping between two IP addresses. In one direction, either the source or destination address is translated; in the other direction, the reverse happens. Typically, the source address is the one that is translated, but there are uses for translating the destination address as well. One possible use for translating the destination address is redirecting client machines to a different server without having to reconfigure them.

A NAT router has to differentiate between interfaces, typically by marking one "inside" and the other "outside" in order to know when to translate, and whether to translate source or destination addresses. Because of the 1-to-1 mapping, static NAT saves no address space.

Another interesting variation of static NAT is called double NAT, which changes both the source and destination addresses at the same time. This can be useful for connecting two networks that use the same addresses.

A static NAT implementation that simply translates layer 3 addresses and doesn't change the data stream at all may have problems with certain protocols. A classic example of a protocol that passes IP addresses in the data stream is the FTP protocol. In order for a static NAT (or any NAT for that matter) implementation to work with FTP, it must modify the FTP PORT command as it goes by. This must also work if the PORT command is split across more than one packet.

Another flavor of NAT is dynamic NAT. Dynamic NAT is similar to static NAT, except that it is many-to-many, or many-to-1, and the static mappings are done on the fly out of a pool of addresses. Problems for address contention may arise, however, if there are more inside addresses than outside addresses. To help with this problem, the NAT device will attempt to detect when a mapping is no longer needed. Strategies for this may include timers, and watching for packets that indicate the end of connections.

To track these items, dynamic NAT must maintain a connection table to track IP addresses, port number, FIN bits, and timers. Even with these mechanisms, dynamic NAT can still easily result in resource contention, and in inside machines not being able to get out. A further refinement is needed.

Port Address Translation is a type of NAT that allows more than one inside machine to share a single outside IP address simultaneously. This is accomplished by translating ports as well as IP addresses. When an inside machine makes a connection out, its source port and address may be translated. The NAT router will track which source ports are in use, and will avoid conflicts when picking new source ports. PAT finally achieves the address savings desired, and also achieves some level of security.

PAT keeps a connection table similar to that of dynamic NAT. In addition, PAT has to dynamically open ports as needed to handle protocols with reverse connections, like FTP. Most existing NAT solutions are PAT-based, and have the ability to do static NAT as needed.

NAT's major feature is address savings. In addition, it can be used to temporarily work around certain types of network problems. NAT typically carries some small performance cost, but it's usually negligible except under the heaviest network loads.

Proxies and firewalls have a somewhat different mission than NAT, though they often are used together. Firewalls are about security—security in this context means controlling network connections. Historically, there are several types of firewalls: Proxies, Packet Filters (PFs), and Static Packet Filters (SPFs).

Proxies work by having clients connect to them instead of to the final intended server. The proxy will then retrieve the desired content, and return it to the inside client. Like NAT, proxies must understand some of the protocols they pass in order to handle them properly.

PFs are often used in conjunction with proxies to achieve the protection needed, and to create the choke point to force all traffic through the proxy. Packet filters don't maintain state, and must often leave large port ranges open to accommodate protocols like FTP. Like NAT, PFs are usually routers.

SPFs are PFs with state. In addition, almost all SPFs can rewrite packets as needed. If an SPF is able to rewrite packets, it can theoretically do anything to packets as needed, including implementing NAT if desired. The connection tables needed for PAT are about the same as those needed for SPF.

NAT (and SPF) differs substantially from a proxy in terms of how it implements its features. For NAT, the basic unit worked on is a whole packet. For a proxy, it's a data stream. The major practical difference is that a proxy will tear a packet all the way apart, and may reassemble it as more or fewer packets. A NAT device will always keep the same number of packets in and out.

Most firewalls on the market at present are a hybrid of proxy and SPF technology. The main advantage to this is that they are able to be transparent, requiring no special software or configuration on the inside client machines.

FAQs

Q: Why doesn't program X work?

A: If you find yourself administering a firewall, NAT device, proxy, or something similar, invariably you will get questions like this: "I just downloaded a beta of a new streaming media protocol called "foo" and it doesn't seem to work. Can you fix it?" For whatever reason, streaming media protocols have a strong tendency to use reverse connections. Here's what you can do to try to get it to work:

- Visit the Web site for the vendor that produces the program. Often, they maintain a FAQ about how to get their protocol to cooperate with firewalls. In some cases, it may be a simple option that is setable on the client program. In other cases, there will be instruction on how to configure your firewall to make it work.

- Check with your firewall vendor to see if there is an update to handle the protocol. Most firewall vendors maintain a Web site with searchable content, and you can search for the protocol in question.

- Check the firewall logs to see if there are reverse connections that are coming back and being denied. Possibly, you might have to use a protocol analyzer to try to determine what the protocol is up to.

- Don't forget to consider that you may not want to pass this protocol. If you're very security-conscious, you may realize that there may be bugs in the new program that may pose a serious threat to your network. Client-side holes have become very common recently.

Q: Why can't I connect to anything?

A: This relates to when you are first setting up your NAT/firewall/proxy. There can be a large number of reasons why you can't connect, any one of which will break things. Here are some special things to pay attention to:

- Make sure all of your routing is correct. If possible, you might turn off any NAT or security features temporarily in order to see if packets seem to flow. If not, you may have a routing issue. If they do, then you probably need to check your security configuration.

- Make sure you've allowed the traffic you're trying to send. This sounds obvious, but it happens often enough. Probably the easiest place to see this is the logs. If you show up as having been dropped, then you haven't allowed the traffic you're trying to send.

- Make sure any ARP settings needed are in place. For some solutions that require virtual IP addresses, you may have to publish ARP addresses manually. A quick way to check if this is working or not is to look at the ARP table on the router.

- Make sure your client configuration is correct. This applies especially if you're using proxies. Make sure the client program is set to use the proxy, and look for typos or other misconfigurations that might be easy to miss.

- When all else fails, you may have to use a protocol analyzer to see what's actually happening on the wire. Unfortunately, you may have to use it in several places to get the full picture (inside the firewall, outside, etc.).

Q: How do I verify that my address is being translated properly?

A: This one is usually pretty easy. The simplest way is to connect to something that tells you what your IP address is. If it's your network, the router immediately outside your NAT device may tell you. For example, if you log on to a Cisco router and issue the "show users" command, it will tell you the DNS name or IP address from which you're connecting.

If you're an end-user, and you suspect you're being translated and want to find out, it may be slightly harder. If you've got an account on a router or UNIX box somewhere on the Internet, you can usually find out that way. Another choice is a Web page that informs you what IP address you're coming from. An example of such a page is:

```
http://www.anonymizer.com/3.0/snoop.cgi
```

Q: What does a good firewall architecture look like?

A: This is a religious question (i.e., you'll get many people preaching their favorite gospel). However, there are a few generally accepted best practices. We'll use a medium-sized company as our example. They have a full-time Internet link, and have their own Web and e-mail servers on the premises. Let's assume they didn't previously have a firewall, and now they want to install one.

The Web server and e-mail server have to be reachable by the Internet—that's their purpose. They also must be reachable by the inside. They want them to be protected from the Internet as much as possible. The typical setup is a firewall with a DMZ, sometimes called a three-legged or 3-interface firewall. The diagram looks like Figure 4.16.

Figure 4.16 Transparent firewall with DMZ.

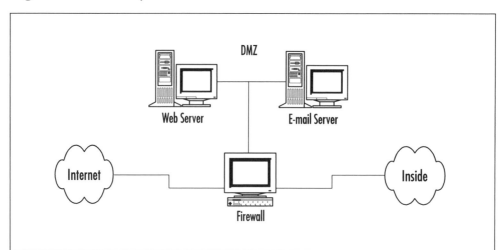

In this example, the firewall does routing. It can be an SPF firewall, or transparent proxy—it doesn't really matter. When an inside user wants to get out, they must traverse the firewall. When either the inside or outside wants to get to the public servers, they must traverse the firewall. It's not depicted on the diagram, but the rules on this type of firewall would prevent the Internet from connecting to the inside. Typically, the inside would be using RFC1918 addresses, and the firewall would be doing PAT for the inside machines.

Most likely, the rules on the firewall are set up for at least a few inside machines to have a somewhat higher level of access to the public servers, for administration purposes.

An important result of this type of architecture is that the inside doesn't fully trust the DMZ. That is, the DMZ machines can't get back inside, at least not for all ports. This means that if the DMZ machines are compromised, the inside may still be protected.

References & Resources

It's impossible to cover every detail of NAT, proxies, and firewalls in a chapter, so we have provided a number of resources to which you may refer. Some of them are general, like the RFCs, and some are very specific, such as Web pages at Cisco about their NAT software. Most likely, you will want to scan through the list and look for topics that are of interest to you. In addition, if you are planning to implement one of the technologies mentioned here, you will need to read the relevant documentation, also referenced here.

RFCs

```
http://www.cis.ohio-state.edu/htbin/rfc/rfc1918.html
```

RFC1918 is the current RFC covering private address space and NAT. The official documentation for the private address ranges (10.x.x.x, 172.16.x.x-172.31.x.x, 192.168.x.x) is located here. In addition, the top of the document contains links to related and obsolete RFCs.

A related RFC that isn't referenced in RFC1918,

```
http://www.cis.ohio-state.edu/htbin/rfc/rfc1631.html
```

is aimed at NAT developers and implementers.

IP Masquerade/Linux

```
http://ipmasq.cjb.net/
```

This is the main place to start looking for IP Masquerade documentation. On this page, you'll find a changelog, a link to the HOWTO:

```
http://members.home.net/ipmasq/ipmasq-HOWTO.html
```

which links to pages on how to join a IP Masquerade mailing list, and links to locations to get IP Masquerade handlers. The links on the page at the time of this writing were broken (may be fixed by the time you check the main page), but this one works:

```
http://www.tsmservices.com/masq/
```

```
http://www.rustcorp.com/linux/ipchains/
```

This is information about IPChains, which is needed to work with IP Masquerade.

Cisco

Cisco has several documents regarding their NAT implementation in their routers. If you plan to use this, you owe it to yourself to at least familiarize yourself with them.

```
http://www.cisco.com/warp/public/458/41.html
```

This is the Cisco NAT FAQ.

```
http://www.cisco.com/warp/public/701/60.html
```

This is Cisco's NAT technical tips, where Cisco documents what protocols are and are not covered, among other things.

```
http://www.cisco.com/warp/public/cc/sol/mkt/ent/ndsgn/nat1_wp.htm
```

This is a Cisco NAT white paper. It's at a similar technical level to this chapter, but obviously with a Cisco focus. They cover configuration examples, and a few features that weren't touched on here, like TCP load balancing.

Windows

```
http://www.uq.net.au/~zzdmacka/the-nat-page/nat_windows.html
```

Here is an excellent list of Windows-based NAT products. In fact, there are several sections on NAT that are worth checking out there.

My favorite low-cost Windows NAT product is SyGate from Sybergen Networks. It's inexpensive, and easy to set up. You can even get a trial version to evaluate. Look for it here:

`http://www.sygate.com/`

Microsoft Proxy Server was mentioned a couple of times; information about it can be found here:

`http://www.microsoft.com/proxy/default.asp`

If you're thinking about running it, you have to check out the MSProxy FAQ:

`http://proxyfaq.networkgods.com/`

NAT Whitepapers

Here are a couple of independent NAT white papers/resources:

`http://www.alumni.caltech.edu/~dank/peer-nat.html`

This one has a focus on peer-to-peer networking and NAT.

`http://www.kfu.com/~dwh/nat-wp.html`

This one reiterates some of the driving issues behind RFC1918. @Work maintains a NAT FAQ. It's geared towards their users, but contains some useful information and definitions:

`http://work.home.net/whitepapers/natfaq.html`

Firewalls

There are several firewall FAQs:

`http://www.clark.net/pub/mjr/pubs/fwfaq/`

This one is particularly good. It's very complete, and covers the basics well.

```
http://www.waterw.com/~manowar/vendor.html
```

This is a good collection of firewall information, in the form of a comparison sheet.

```
ftp://ftp.greatcircle.com/pub/firewalls/Welcome.html
```

This contains the firewalls' mailing list and archive.

```
http://www.nfr.net/firewall-wizards/
```

There are a few Firewall-1 FAQs:

```
http://www.phoneboy.com/fw1/
```

The Phoneboy FAQ; Dameon knows Firewall-1 well.

```
http://www.dreamwvr.com/bastions/FW1_faq.html
```

Here's a second FW-1 FAQ. You might like the organization better.

```
http://www2.checkpoint.com/~joe/
```

Chapter 5

Variable-Length Subnet Masking

Solutions in this chapter:

- Why variable-length subnet masks (VLSM) are necessary

- When to deploy VLSM

- How to plan for creating VLSM-administered networks

- Address management in a VLSM-administered network

- Which routing protocols support VLSM

- Creating an address plan using VLSM

Introduction

Variable-length subnet masks (VLSM) allow network administrators to "right size" each subnet. With fixed-length subnet masks, however, each subnet in the network is the same size because each device has the same subnet mask, regardless of the need for addresses in each subnet. If we select a class mask of 255.255.254.0, each subnet is allocated 510 addresses. Most LANs have an upper limit of less than 150 devices due to traffic patterns and capacity of the physical LAN media.

In actual fact, each network, WAN or LAN, has a different number of devices. With VLSM, the address administrator can more closely match the addressing needs of each subnet and use the address space more efficiently.

Why Are Variable-Length Masks Necessary?

Here is a parallel example of why VLSM is important. When restaurants sell pie, each piece of the pie is the same size. Each restaurant patron gets the same size pie slice regardless of "the need" (see Figure 5.1).

Figure 5.1 Uniform pie slices.

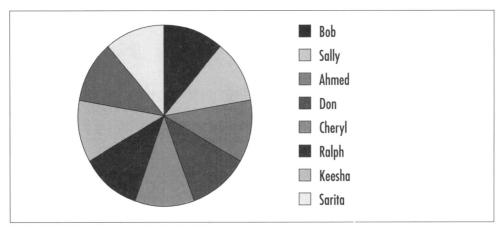

Ah, yes, the pie chart! If these people were subnets, they would all get the same size subnet regardless of how many addresses they really needed. Let's look at another possibility in Figure 5.2. Each person has a different appetite; they all need a different size slice of the pie.

Figure 5.2 Variable-size pie slices.

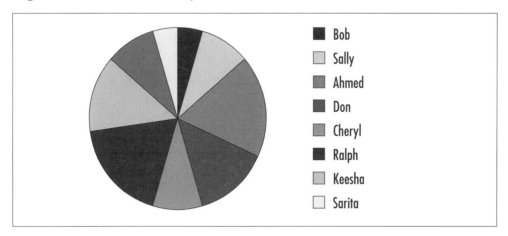

For IT Professionals

VLSM Addressing Plan

Devleoping an addressing plan based on VLSM requires complete knowledge of the network being subnetted. During the design phase of a new network, applying VLSM is complex but a lot easier than applying VLSM to an existing network. In an existing network, moving from fixed-length subnet masks to variable-length subnet masks will require a complete readdressing of the entire network. If you are considering readdressing, it may be simpler to use a private address, like 10.0.0.0, with a fixed-ength mask instead of trying to use VLSM. The private address gives you a lot of flexibility without the complexity of developing a VLSM addressing plan.

When subnetting, it may be necessary to give each subnet an appropriate slice of the pie based on the actual number of addresses needed, rather than assume that all subnets need the same number of addresses. VLSM is the answer to this problem.

Right-sizing Your Subnets

What do we mean by right-sizing subnets? Simply put, it is providing the right number of addresses for each subnet so that we don't end up wasting addresses. Figure 5.3 shows a simple network diagram.

Figure 5.3 The 153.90.0.0 network.

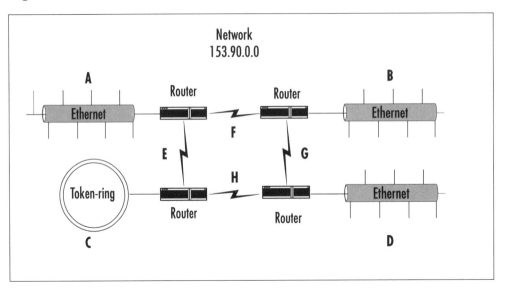

In this diagram there are three Ethernet networks, one token-ring network, and four point-to-point WAN connections. Each of these is a subnet within the total corporate network. The actual number of host addresses for each subnet is in Table 5.1.

If we were to assign a subnet mask of 255.255.255.0 for this class B addressed network, all subnets would be allocated 254 host addresses. This results in a lot of unused addresses, as shown in Table 5.2.

Table 5.1 Subnet Needs

Subnet	Hosts
A	150
B	24
C	90
D	53
E	2
F	2
G	2
H	2

Table 5.2 Addresses Wasted

Subnet	Hosts	Allocated	Unused
A	150	254	104
B	24	254	230
C	90	254	164
D	53	254	201
E	2	254	252
F	2	254	252
G	2	254	252
H	2	254	252
Total		2032	1707

What if we choose a subnet mask for each subnet that allocates a more appropriate number of addresses in each subnet? Using the subnet masking tables from Chapter 1, we determine that the masks in Table 5.3 should be used in each of the subnets.

How did we determine which mask to use? In the subnet mask table for class B networks, we located the mask that allowed the number of hosts required for each subnet.

Table 5.3 Using Needs Appropriate Masks

Subnet	Hosts	Mask Assigned	Allocated	Unused
A	150	255.255.255.0	254	104
B	24	255.255.255.224	30	6
C	90	255.255.255.128	126	36
D	53	255.255.255.192	62	9
E	2	255.255.255.252	2	0
F	2	255.255.255.252	2	0
G	2	255.255.255.252	2	0
H	2	255.255.255.252	2	0
Total			480	155

Subnet A needed 150 hosts. In the class B subnet mask table we found that 255.255.255.0 allocates 254 addresses. We looked at some alternatives: The mask 255.255.255.192 allocates 62 addresses and cannot be used because the number of hosts is too small; on the other hand, the mask 255.255.254.0 allocates 510 hosts. This is far too many for our needs and should not be used. The mask 255.255.255.0 was selected for the best fit.

The rest of the subnets were evaluated using the same process. When it came to subnets E through H, the process was very simple. These subnets are actually point-to-point WAN links, and will have no more than two host addresses. Selecting the mask was easy because 255.255.255.252 allocates two addresses to each subnet and is an exact match for our needs.

More Addresses or More Useful Addresses?

You have probably noticed that we have saved addresses in the VLSM process. That is, we have not placed addresses in subnets that are not being used. That's not quite true—with VLSM we have a much closer match in addresses allocated to addresses needed. We do assign addresses to subnets that are not used, but we do not have as many unused addresses as we do with fixed-length subnetting. Table 5.4 gives the results of the VLSM process for our simple network.

Table 5.4 Address Savings

	Allocated	Allocated
Fixed-Length Mask	2032	1707
Variable-Length Masks	480	155

Did we get more addresses? No, we still have a class B address. Are we using the addresses we have better than before? Yes; as a matter of fact, because we use the addresses more efficiently, VLSM allows us to implement more subnets with the same class of address. We didn't get more addresses, but we do have more useful addresses.

For IT Professionals

Use an IP Address Only Once in a Network

Regardless of the subnetting method, variable or fixed length, you must make sure that an IP address is used only once in any network. A common mistake is to think that addresses can exist in different subnets, but that is not the case. As you develop an addressing plan using a VLSM structure, make sure you keep track of all address ranges that are allocated and those that are available for allocation. Tools presented later in this chapter will help you.

The Importance of Proper Planning

The process of creating a VLSM subnetting structure requires a lot of advanced planning. A survey of the network is required. The survey must include the number of required subnets, the number of planned but not deployed subnets, the number of devices currently in each subnet and the number of planned but not deployed devices in each subnet. That seems like a lot of work but is necessary. You want to develop a plan that covers what you currently have and what you will probably have in the future.

Deciding to convert from fixed-length masks to VLSM requires a large commitment on the part of the address planner, network managers, and users. If an existing network is changed from fixed-length masks to VLSM, the entire network addressing structure will be affected. Every subnet will be assigned new address ranges and the administrative burden necessary to complete the process will be immense. Each and every device in the network will probably have to be readdressed. Do not underestimate the amount of work required to convert an existing network to VLSM.

If you fail to understand your network and subnet requirements adequately, you may develop a plan that cannot be deployed successfully. For existing networks, you may have done a lot of work planning and implementing only to find that your work must be discarded. You or other administrators and users may have readdressed thousands of devices only to find that they must be readdressed again due to a bad address plan. The following steps will help you make sure your address plan is successful the first time.

Creating and Managing Variable-Length Subnets

Creating a variable-length subnet mask addressing design requires the completion of four separate phases. Each of the phases must be completed before moving to the next phase.

1. Analyze subnet needs.

2. Enumerate each subnet and number of required nodes.

3. Determine which mask to use in each subnet.

4. Allocate addresses based on need for each subnet.

The details of each phase follow.

Analyze Subnet Needs

As we mentioned earlier, you need to know exactly what you have today and what you will need tomorrow for each subnet. A simple spreadsheet or matrix detailing each subnet will help you determine your needs. Remember to locate and list **all** networks.

For Managers

How Many Subnets?

The examples used in this chapter contain a limited number of subnets. In the large networks, there may be more than 500 subnets using VLSM allocations. The procedures we show you here will work with small networks with few subnets or large networks with many subnets.

Enumerate Each Subnet and Number of Required Nodes

When the detailed needs survey is completed, the matrix you develop will contain all of the LANs and WANs with the number of hosts in each subnet (see Table 5.5). The matrix in Table 5.6 contains the survey information but has been sorted in descending sequence by the total number of hosts in each subnet in the future. The purpose of sorting the matrix is to group subnets together based on the number of hosts in the subnets. Subnets with similar numbers of host addresses will have the same subnet mask.

Table 5.5 Network Survey

Network	Location	Type	Status	Hosts Today	Hosts Future
Accounting	Building 3, 4th floor	LAN-Ethernet	Operational	131	140
Accounting Link to Building 4	Building 3-4	WAN-PPP	Operational	2	2
Personnel	Building 4, 1st floor	LAN-Ethernet	Operational	72	83
Personnel Expansion	Building 4, 2nd floor	LAN-100MB Ethernet	Planned-Spring 2000		29
Logistics	Warehouse	LAN-Token-ring	Operational	81	89
Shipping	Warehouse	LAN-Ethernet	Operational	18	25
Warehouse to Building 4 link	Warehouse -Building 4, 1st floor	WAN-PPP	Operational	2	2
Loading Dock to Warehouse link	Loading Dock-Warehouse	WAN-PPP	Operational	2	2
Receiving	Loading Dock	LAN-Ethernet	Operational	14	17

Determine Which Mask to Use in Each Subnet

Using class B subnetting table, we select the subnet mask that allocates the necessary addresses for each subnet in Table 5.7.

When working with a real networking problem, make sure you leave enough room for growth in each subnet you specify. If you need 150 devices in a subnet, leave room for 200. If you need 40 devices, leave room for 60. Select a mask that gives you the allocation you need today and may need tomorrow.

Table 5.6 Subnet Address Requirements

Network	Location	Type	Status	Hosts Today	Hosts Future
Accounting	Building 3, 4th floor	LAN-Ethernet	Operational	131	140
Logistics	Warehouse	LAN-Token-ring	Operational	81	89
Personnel	Building 4, 1st floor	LAN-Ethernet	Operational	72	83
Personnel Expansion	Building 4, 2nd floor	LAN-100MB Ethernet	Planned-Spring 2000		29
Shipping	Warehouse	LAN-Ethernet	Operational	18	25
Receiving	Loading Dock	LAN-Ethernet	Operational	14	17
Accounting Link to Building 4	Building 3-4	WAN-PPP	Operational	2	2
Warehouse to Building 4 link	Warehouse-Building 4, 1st floor	WAN-PPP	Operational	2	2
Loading Dock to Warehouse link	Loading Dock-Warehouse	WAN-PPP	Operational	2	2

Allocate Addresses Based on Need For Each Subnet

Now it is time to determine which range of addresses will be assigned in each subnet. With fixed-length subnetting, the ranges of addresses are uniform and easily determined; with variable-length mask subnetting, the address ranges are just as important but more difficult to assign. A tool can be used to help determine which addresses to use.

Table 5.7 Subnet Mask Selection

Network	Location	Type	Status	Hosts Today	Hosts Future	Subnet Mask	Max Hosts/ Subnet
Accounting	Building 3, 4th floor	LAN-Ethernet	Operational	131	140	255.255.255.0	254
Logistics	Warehouse	LAN-Token-ring	Operational	81	89	255.255.255.128	126
Personnel	Building 4, 1st floor	LAN-Ethernet	Operational	72	83	255.255.255.128	126
Personnel Expansion	Building 4, 2nd floor	LAN-100MB Ethernet	Planned-Spring 2000		29	255.255.255.192	62
Shipping	Warehouse	LAN-Ethernet	Operational	18	25	255.255.255.224	30
Receiving	Loading Dock	LAN-Ethernet	Operational	14	17	255.255.255.224	30
Accounting Link to Building 4	Building 3-4	WAN-PPP	Operational	2	2	255.255.255.252	2
Warehouse to Building 4 link	Warehouse Building 4, 1st floor	WAN-PPP	Operational	2	2	255.255.255.252	2
Loading Dock to Warehouse link	Loading Dock-Warehouse	WAN-PPP	Operational	2	2	255.255.255.252	2

For the purposes of this example, we will be subnetting the 172.38.0.0 class B network. The actual range of addresses that can be assigned in this network is 172.38.0.1 through 172.38.255.254. The addresses 172.38.0.0 and 172.38.255.255 are excluded as the network address and the network broadcast address. To simplify allocation, divide the network addresses into 256 groups based on the third octet of the address. In this case, the 256 blocks are given in Table 5.8.

Table 5.8 Address Block Matrix

0	16	32	48	64	80	196	112	128	144	160	176	192	208	224	240
1	17	33	49	65	81	197	113	129	145	161	177	193	209	225	241
2	18	34	50	66	82	198	114	130	146	162	178	194	210	226	242
3	19	35	51	67	83	199	115	131	147	163	179	195	211	227	243
4	20	36	52	68	84	100	116	132	148	164	180	196	212	228	244
5	21	37	53	69	85	101	117	133	149	165	181	197	213	229	245
6	22	38	54	70	86	102	118	134	150	166	182	198	214	230	246
7	23	39	55	71	87	103	119	135	151	167	183	199	215	231	247
8	24	40	56	72	88	104	120	136	152	168	184	200	216	232	248
9	25	41	57	73	89	105	121	137	153	169	185	201	217	233	249
10	26	42	58	74	90	106	122	138	154	170	186	202	218	234	250
11	27	43	59	75	91	107	123	139	155	171	187	203	219	235	251
12	28	44	60	76	92	108	124	140	156	172	188	204	220	236	252
13	29	45	61	77	93	109	125	141	157	173	189	205	221	237	253
14	30	46	62	78	94	110	126	142	158	174	190	206	222	238	254
15	31	47	63	79	95	111	127	143	159	175	191	207	223	239	255

The third octet contains the number of each possible block of 254 addresses that can be assigned if a subnet mask of 255.255.255.0 is used. If a subnet requires 300 addresses, you could use 172.38.1.0 and 172.38.2.0 to allocate a total of 510 addresses for the subnet. You would then strike through the two numbers 1 and 2 in Table 5.8 to show that the two complete 254 address blocks have been used and subsequently cannot be subdivided. Prepare a chart similar to this to keep track of the large address blocks that you have used.

For variable-length masks with allocations less than 254 addresses, each of these blocks may be subdivided. Here is how we will address the example problem.

The first subnet we are going to allocate uses a subnet mask of 255.255.255.0. One address block in Table 5.8 will allocate 254 addresses. This is the number of hosts available in an address block when the mask is 255.255.255.0. We will use 172.38.1.0 for the first subnet. The range of addresses used in that subnet is 172.38.1.0 through 172.38.1.255. In case we need additional subnets requiring a mask of 255.255.255.0, we are reserving the blocks 172.38.2.0 through 172.38.31.0 for that purpose.

For Managers

Keep Blocks of Addresses Assigned by the Same Mask Together

It is good practice to keep blocks of addresses assigned by the same mask together. In this example, we are saving 32 blocks of addresses for mask 255.255.255.0. An additional 32 blocks will be saved for 255.255.255.128. Since other masks result in more subnets, an appropriate number of blocks should be saved and allocated together. Why? A uniform assignment of addresses results in a good distribution of addresses without "stranding" small address ranges that cannot be assigned because they contain a number of addresses that cannot be allocated in any subnet.

The second and third subnets use a mask of 255.255.255.128. This mask allocated one-half of a block of 256 addresses. There are 128 addresses in one allocation and 128 addresses in the other. In Table 5.9 we have allocated one-half of the 172.38.32.0 block to the second subnet and the other half to the second subnet. The 172.38.32.0 block is fully allocated and cannot be used for other subnets. In case we need additional subnets requiring a mask of

255.255.255.128, we are reserving blocks 172.38.33.0 through 172.38.63.0, which will allow us to allocate an additional 62 subnets of 126 addresses.

Table 5.9 Address Assignments

Network	Location	Subnet Mask	Max Hosts/ Subnet	Addresses Allocated
Accounting	Building 3, 4th floor	255.255.255.0	254	172.38.1.0- 172.38.1.255
Logistics	Warehouse	255.255.255.128	126	172.38.32.0- 172.38.32.127
Personnel	Building 4, 1st floor	255.255.255.128	126	172.38.32.128- 172.38.32.255
Personnel Expansion	Building 4, 2nd floor	255.255.255.192	62	172.38.64.64- 172.38.64.127
Shipping	Warehouse	255.255.255.224	30	172.38.128.32- 172.38.128.63
Receiving	Loading Dock	255.255.255.224	30	172.38.128.64- 172.38.128.95
Accounting Link to Building 4	Building 3-4	255.255.255.252	2	172.38.254.4- 172.38.254.7
Warehouse to Building 4 link	Warehouse- Building 4, 1st floor	255.255.255.252	2	172.38.254.8- 172.38.254.11
Loading Dock to Warehouse link	Loading Dock- Warehouse	255.255.255.252	2	172.38.254.12- 172.38.254.15

In completing this table, we assigned addresses from different blocks. To determine which addresses to use with different masks, use the address assignment templates found at the end of this chapter.

Routing Protocols and VLSM

Before you start a major VLSM implementation, there are a few particulars that must be understood. First, VLSM is difficult to implement. In our previous example we looked at a very small number of subnets. Creating a plan for a large number of subnets is time-consuming and requires accurate information. Making mistakes in a VLSM plan can cause a lot of extra administrative problems. Managers just don't appreciate renumbering the network over and over again because the address administrator made a small mistake or two.

The second major issue is that the network routers must be using a routing protocol that supports VLSM—the Routing Information Protocol Version 2 (RIP2), the Open Shortest Path First protocol (OSPF), and Ciscos' EIGRP. If your network does not use these protocols, don't use VLSM.

The protocols support VLSM because they share subnet mask information among all of the routers so the routers can make proper routing decisions. Without the subnet mask information provided by these protocols, routers assume that all subnets have the same mask. With VLSM they don't and routing will fail.

Class C VLSM Problem

You may also need to use VLSM to conserve addresses in a class C network. Some experts say that using VLSM in a class C network is too difficult because of the problems implementing the required routing protocols in a small network. If you are running out of addresses, you may not have a choice and VLSM may be your only solution.

In this example, the organization has four operational locations in the greater Chicago area. They have received a public class C address and wish to subnet it using VLSM. Since the network is small, the administrators have decided to implement the RIP2 routing protocol.

The choice to use VLSM was necessary due to the mix of subnets and sizes. There are seven subnets, and the largest subnet will eventually contain 95 devices; using a normal fixed-length mask will not work. A mask of 255.255.255.224 will accommodate 15 subnets but will allow only 14 devices in each subnet. A mask of 255.255.255.128 will allow 126 devices in each subnet but will allow only two subnets. VLSM is a must for this implementation.

Table 5.10 Class C VLSM Problem

Network	Location	Type	Status	Hosts Today	Hosts Future
Accounting	Chicago	LAN-Ethernet	Operational	92	95
Logistics	Schaumburg	LAN-Ethernet	Operational	37	45
Personnel	Oak Park	LAN-Ethernet	Operational	11	13
Executive	Oak Brook	LAN-Ethernet	Operational	7	9
To Chicago	Schaumburg to Chicago	WAN-PPP	Operational	2	2
To Oak Park	Schaumburg to Oak Park	WAN-PPP	Operational	2	2
To Oak Brook	Schaumburg to Oak Brook	WAN-PPP	Operational	2	2

After reviewing the networking requirements survey, the administrators developed Table 5.10. Each subnet is described and the number of hosts required is also included in the table. The next step is to determine which masks to use for each subnet.

Table 5.11 shows the subnet masks that the administrators determined were required for each of the subnets. The next part of the task is to determine which address ranges to apply to each subnet. Unlike the class B problem, where we selected large blocks of addresses to subdivide based on mask sizes, the class C problem requires a special technique. Class C networks contain 254 usable addresses. In the class C subnetting problem, we use addresses all from the same 254 address block but select ranges based on the mask in use.

Table 5.11 Class C VLSM Subnet Masks

Network	Location	Type	Status	Hosts Today	Hosts Future	Subnet Mask	Max Hosts/Subnet
Accounting	Chicago	LAN-Ethernet	Operational	92	95	255.255.255.128	126
Logistics	Schaumburg	LAN-Ethernet	Operational	37	45	255.255.255.192	62
Personnel	Oak Park	LAN-Ethernet	Operational	11	13	255.255.255.240	14
Executive	Oak Brook	LAN-Ethernet	Operational	7	9	255.255.255.240	14
To Chicago	Schaumburg to Chicago	WAN-PPP	Operational	2	2	255.255.255.252	2
To Oak Park	Schaumburg to Oak Park	WAN-PPP	Operational	2	2	255.255.255.252	2
To Oak Brook	Schaumburg to Oak Brook	WAN-PPP	Operational	2	2	255.255.255.252	2

The subnetting tables in Figures 5.4, 5.5, and 5.6 show an easy way to select addresses for each range. At the top of the tables you will find labels for each of the possible fourth octet of the subnet mask. Each table has been assigned a label from A through H for each grouping of 32 available addresses. To assign addresses based on a given mask, select a column for the mask and follow the column down until the column ends. The addresses on the right-hand side table are included in the range.

Figure 5.4 VLSM table addresses 0 through 95.

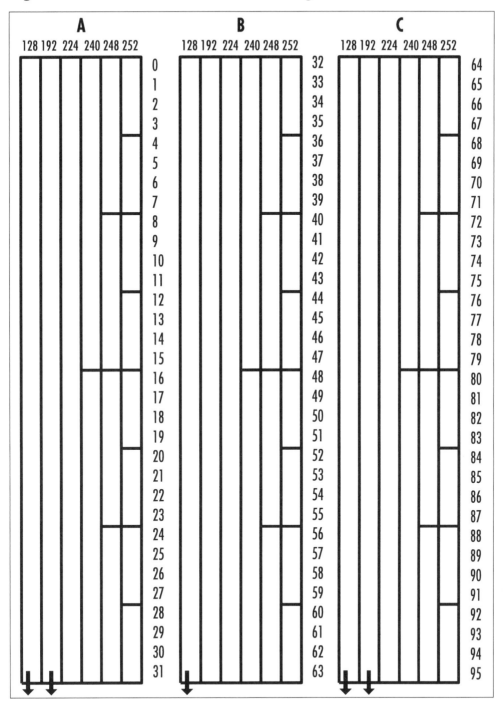

For example, look at Figure 5.4, table A. To assign an address range based on the subnet mask 255.255.255.248, find the column marked 248. The first range of addresses for the .248 mask is from 0 through 7. The second range of addresses for the .248 mask is from 8 through 15, etc. The third range of addresses for mask .252 is 8 through 11. For each mask number, the tables indicate the range of addresses. Referring again to table A of Figure 5.4, look at the bottom of the 128 and 192 columns. You will see a down arrow indicating that you need to go to the same column in the next table to continue the process of locating addresses. As a matter of fact, to assign addresses using the .128 mask, you will need to view tables A, B, and C of Figure 5.4 and table D of Figure 5.5 to determine all of the possible addresses. The end of the 128 segment on table D of Figure 5.5 does not contain an arrow. The address assignment stops when the arrow is missing. To assign the .128 addresses, you will use 0 through 31 from table A, 32 through 63 from table B, 64 through 95 from table C, and 96 through 127 from table D.

Completing the Class C Problem

Table 5.12 shows the completed address assignment matrix for the class C VLSM problem.

Here is how the administrator decided on which address to assign. The first location required a mask of 255.255.255.128. The administrator looked at the VLSM tables, located the 128 column in table A, and followed the column down until the arrow at the end of the column was missing. Remember, the arrow says look at the next table and at the location associated with address 127, and the arrow was missing (see table D). The range of addresses is 0 through 127.

The next location required a mask of 255.255.255.192. Since all of the addresses from the first four tables were already assigned, the administrator then turned to the remaining tables E, F, G, and H. Looking at table E, the administrator found the 192 column and followed it down to the bottom of the table, found an arrow, and looked to table F. The end of the 192 column on table F did not contain an arrow so the administrator knew that the addresses for the second subnet started with 128, the first address in table E, and ended with 191, the last address in table F. The range of addresses for the second subnet is 128 through 191.

Figure 5.5 VLSM table addresses 96 through 191.

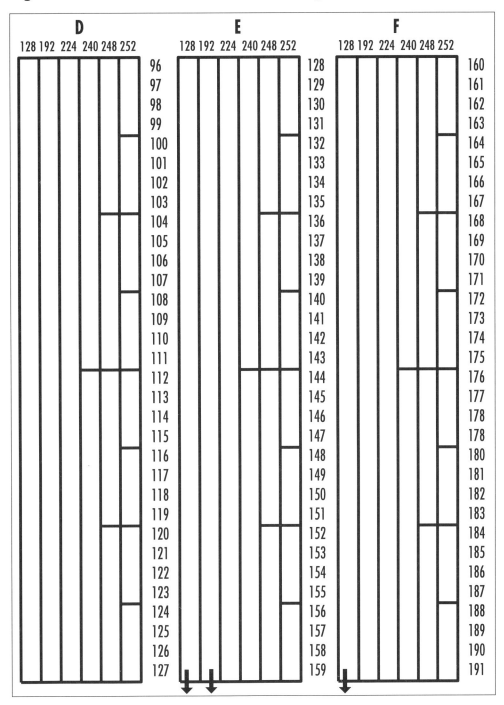

Figure 5.6 VLSM table addresses 192 through 255.

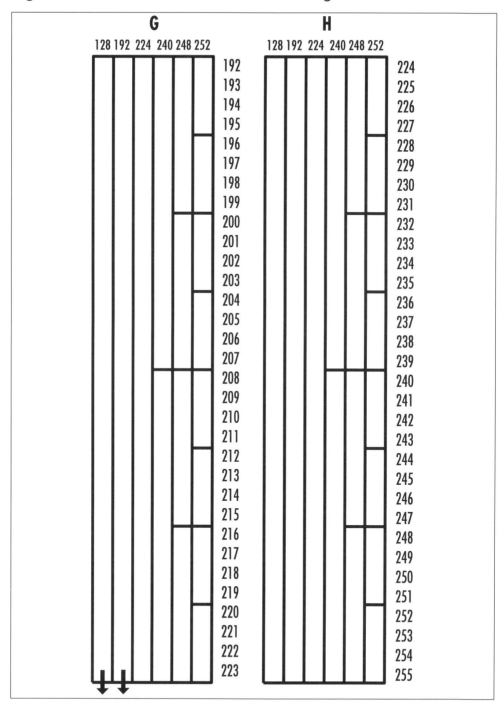

Table 5.12 Class C Address Assignments

Network	Location	Subnet Mask	Max Hosts/ Subnet	Subnet Table Column	Assigned Addresses
Accounting	Chicago	255.255.255.128	126	A,B,C,D	0-127
Logistics	Schaumburg	255.255.255.192	62	E,F	128-191
Personnel	Oak Park	255.255.255.240	14	G	192-207
Executive	Oak Brook	255.255.255.240	14	G	208-223
To Chicago	Schaumburg to Chicago	255.255.255.252	2	H	252-255
To Oak Park	Schaumburg to Oak Park	255.255.255.252	2	H	248-251
To Oak Brook	Schaumburg to Oak Brook	255.255.255.252	2	H	244-247

The next two subnets required a mask of 255.255.255.240. Since all of the addresses had been assigned from tables A, B, C, D, E, and F, the administrator started with table G. In table G, the administrator located the 240 column. The first subnet was assigned the range from 192 to 207, the first grouping in the 240 column, and the second subnet was assigned the range from 208 to 223, the second grouping in the 240 column.

The last three subnets required a mask of 255.255.255.252. The only assignable addresses are found in table H, so looking to the 252 column in table H, the administrator assigned the three subnets ranges 252–255, 248–251, and 244–247. The administrator started at the bottom of the allocation to leave room in case a larger allocation is needed from the top of column H at a later time.

   Using the subnet tables found in Figures 5.4, 5.5, and 5.6 simplifies the procedures for VLSM. You might want to make copies of these pages or create a similar spreadsheet or form to keep track of address you have assigned. It is simple to cross out addresses as you assign them to various subnets. You have a hardcopy record of what you have assigned as well as a graphic representation of the address you have used and the addresses you have available.

Template-based Address Assignment

The following templates can be used in variable-length subnetting when the last octet of the mask contains the given value. For example, with a mask of 255.255.255.252, you would look in the template labeled .252–64 subnets. In that template, select a range of addresses for use in the subnet you wish to allocate. Once the range of addresses has been allocated from a block of addresses, it cannot be assigned to another subnet. Each of these templates represents a way to subnet the fourth octet of any network address.

.128-2 subnets	.0	.127
	.128	.255

.192-4 subnets	.0	.63
	.64	.127
	.128	.191
	.192	.255

.224-8 subnets	.0	.31
	.32	.63
	.64	.95
	.96	.127
	.128	.159
	.160	.191
	.192	.223
	.224	.255

.240-16 subnets	.0	.15
	.16	.31
	.32	.47
	.48	.63
	.64	.79
	.80	.95
	.96	.111
	.112	.127
	.128	.143
	.144	.159
	.160	.175
	.176	.191
	.192	.207
	.208	.223
	.224	.239
	.240	.255

.248-32 subnets	.0	.7
	.8	.15
	.16	.23
	.24	.31
	.32	.39
	.40	.47
	.48	.55
	.56	.63
	.64	.71
	.72	.79
	.80	.87
	.88	.95
	.96	.103
	.104	.111

Continued

.248-32 subnets (continued)	.112	.119
	.120	.127
	.128	.135
	.136	.143
	.144	.151
	.152	.159
	.160	.167
	.168	.175
	.176	.183
	.184	.191
	.192	.199
	.200	.207
	.208	.215
	.216	.223
	.224	.231
	.232	.239
	.240	.247
	.248	.255

.252-64 subnets	.0	.3
	.4	.7
	.8	.11
	.12	.15
	.16	.19
	.20	.23
	.24	.27
	.28	.31
	.32	.35
	.36	.39
	.40	.43
	.44	.47

Continued

.252-64 subnets (continued)	.48	.51
	.52	.55
	.56	.59
	.60	.63
	.64	.67
	.68	.71
	.72	.75
	.76	.79
	.80	.83
	.84	.87
	.88	.91
	.92	.95
	.96	.99
	.100	.103
	.104	.107
	.108	.111
	.112	.115
	.116	.119
	.120	.123
	.124	.127
	.128	.131
	.132	.135
	.136	.139
	.140	.143
	.144	.147
	.148	.151
	.152	.155
	.156	.159
	.160	.163
	.164	.167
	.168	.171

Continued

.252-64 subnets (continued)	.172	.175
	.176	.179
	.180	.183
	.184	.187
	.188	.191
	.192	.195
	.196	.199
	.200	.203
	.204	.207
	.208	.211
	.212	.215
	.216	.219
	.220	.223
	.224	.227
	.228	.231
	.232	.235
	.236	.239
	.240	.243
	.244	.247
	.248	.251
	.248	.251
	.252	.255

Summary

Variable-length subnet masking (VLSM) is often necessary when addresses are scarce and you need to use the addresses you have effectively. With legacy IP networks, implementing VLSM often requires a complete renumbering of the entire network, so the decision to use VLSM must be made with full knowledge of the required administrative processes.

Regardless of the reason why VLSM is implemented, it requires the use of certain routing protocols to be successful. RIP2, OSPF, and EIGRP must be used on your network routers to ensure that VLSM works correctly.

The process of creating a VLSM address plan includes the following steps:

1. Analyze subnet needs.

2. Enumerate each subnet and number of required nodes.

3. Determine which mask to use in each subnet.

4. Allocate addresses based on need for each subnet.

Survey your network to determine the number of subnets present. Determine the type of network and the current and future number of devices in each subnet. Create a list of the subnets you have, and group subnets together by size. With like-size subnets together, determine the appropriate mask for each subnet. Use subnetting tables A through H to help assign addresses where the fourth octet of the mask contains .128, .192, .224, .240, .248, or .252.

Once addresses are allocated to a subnet, they cannot be allocated to other subnets. You must keep track of addresses carefully when you are creating the VLSM address plan to make sure that the subnet allocations for one subnet do not overlap other subnets. This often happens when an address is applied twice because it occurs in one size subnet and in another size subnet. No address ranges are allowed to overlap.

VLSM does save address, but if you have the ability to use a private address space with network or port address translation process, it may be just as useful to implement a fixed-length subnet mask with a private address space. The administration is easier and address planning is simpler.

FAQs

Q: My coworker told me that VLSM gives me a lot more addresses than I had in the past. Is this true?

A: Not really. If you have been assigned a class B address, you have 65,534 addresses. Using VLSM does not increase the number of addresses, but it can allow to you have more useful addresses by allocating addresses based on subnet needs.

Q: We are running RIP in our network because it is an easy routing protocol to administer and because our network is small. Can we use VLSM?

A: RIP version 1 does not allow for the implementation of VLSM, but RIP version 2 does. Check to determine which version of RIP you are using before you commit to VLSM.

Q: Why do I have to understand all about my network to do VLSM? When we did our original subnetting we just started assigning our addresses using a mask and it was very simple.

A: Using fixed-length masks to create your addressing plan is much easier than using VLSM. With fixed-length masks, each subnet is the same size and the number of addresses in each subnet is the same. A very simple process can be used to assign addresses. With VLSM, everything is more complex because all subnets are not all the same size and there is no simple process for allocating addresses. Using the tables found in this chapter is about the easiest manual process available.

Q: Why should I group subnets of similar sizes together before I start allocating addresses?

A: So that you assign uniform blocks of addresses from similar ranges. If you choose arbitrary ranges of addresses, you might create small address blocks in your plan that cannot be used because they are too small for your current requirements. You might actually need some subnets that have 30 addresses, but because you did not plan appropriately, you might be left with lots of 16 address blocks that are not contiguous and cannot be used.

Chapter 6

Routing Issues

Solutions in this chapter:

- **Introduction to routing protocols**

- **Supernetting with Classless Interdomain Routing (CIDR)**

- **Internal Routing with Interior Gateway Routing Protocol (IGRP) and Enhanced Interior Gateway Routing Protocol (EIGRP)**

- **Understanding the history of the Routing Information Protocol (RIP) and RIP-2**

- **Implementing the Open Shortest Path First (OSPF) routing protocol**

- **External network routing with Exterior Gateway Protocol (EGP) and Border Gateway Protocol (BGP)**

Introduction

This chapter will discuss the purpose of routing and the many issues that arise from routing in various network environments, from smaller networks to very large, complicated, dynamic networks such as the Internet. We will introduce the many routing protocols, such as the Routing Information Protocol (RIP), Open Shortest Path First (OSPF), and Border Gateway Protocol (BGP), and discuss the characteristics and issues involved with each. Each routing protocol has its own set of strengths and weaknesses that you will need to assess in order to understand how to implement this protocol. You will also see how these routing protocols are addressing the issue of the exhaustion of available IP addresses, the introduction of the IPv6 protocol, and the concern for growing routing tables on major routers on the Internet.

As most people know, the rate of growth on the Internet is phenomenal, and usage has increased nearly exponentially. Networks and hosts are being added to the Internet, which threatens to eat up every available IP address unless something is done. Not only is the exhaustion of available IP addresses an important issue, we also have to deal with the tremendous amount of routing that takes place on the Internet. Routers are network devices used to route packets to different networks on the Internet. The Internet is composed of hundreds of thousands of different networks. Routers use a *routing table*, which is an internal table that contains routes to networks and other routers. In most routers found on the Internet, these routes are learned dynamically by the use of a dynamic routing protocol such as RIP, IGRP, OSPF, and BGP, to name a few. Routers share information with each other concerning the availability of paths and the shortest distance to a destination. In the past, the routing tables have been growing as fast as the Internet; however, technology has not been able to keep pace. The number of routes advertised has doubled every 10 months. It was estimated that there were around 2000 routes on the Internet in 1990, and two years later there were 8500 routes. In 1995 there were over 29,000 routes, which required around 10MB of memory for the router. A router requires a significant amount of RAM and CPU in order to add, modify, delete, and advertise these routing tables with other routers. The routing tables have been growing at a slower rate, and we now have about 65,000 routes.

With the advent of Classless Interdomain Routing, we have been able to limit significantly the growth of these routing tables, making them more manageable and efficient.

Classless Interdomain Routing

Classless Interdomain Routing (CIDR, pronounced as apple "cider") was developed when the world was faced with the exhaustion of class B address space and the explosion of routing between tons of class C addresses. CIDR allows for a more efficient allocation of IP addresses than the old class A, B, and C address scheme. This old scheme is often referred to as "classful" addressing, whereas CIDR is referred to as "classless" addressing, as illustrated in Figure 6.1.

Figure 6.1 The prefix length of a classless address.

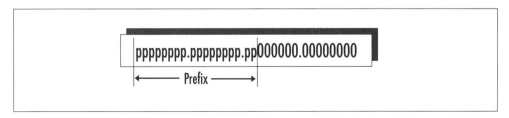

Another term for CIDR supernetting is *prefix-based addressing.* As you can see in Figure 6.1, it looks very similar to custom subnet masking, where the boundary between the network ID and host ID is not fixed.

You will learn later in this section just how this supernetting is possible. If you are familiar with TCP/IP subnet masking, you will have no problems understanding the concept of supernetting and classless addressing. Both concepts involve "masking" a portion of the IP address to reveal a network address. CIDR extended the successful ideas of TCP/IP subnetting.

Some say that if it weren't for the advent of CIDR, the Internet would not be functioning today. That is a testament to the power of CIDR, and the need of CIDR for networking supernetting. CIDR is the best hope we have for smoothing the transition from IPv4 to IPv6.

The IETF wrote the standard for CIDR in the early 1990s, and it is described in RFC1517 through RFC1520. CIDR has a primary requirement for using a routing protocol, such as RIP version 2, OSPF version 2, and BGP version 4.

CIDR helps the Internet reduce the routing overload by minimizing routing tables and making sure the most important routes are carried by most routers, making the path to sites much quicker. These routing tables are global, and contain information for routes across the planet, so you can begin to see how large these routing tables can get. The routing tables are dangerously close to a level where current software, hardware, and people can no longer effectively manage them.

CIDR is very similar to subnetting, but actually is a more advanced method of subnetting that can combine networks into *supernets*; subnetting, on the other hand, involves breaking networks into smaller, more manageable *subnets*. This is accomplished through the use of the subnet mask, which masks a portion of the IP address to differentiate the network ID from the host ID. With CIDR, you basically eliminate the concept of class a, b, and c networks, and replace them with a generalized IP prefix consisting of an IP address and the mask length. For example, a single class C address would appear as 195.129.1.0/24, in which /24 refers to the number of bits of the network portion of the IP address.

With the traditional class A, B, and C addressing scheme, the addresses were identified by converting the first eight bits of the address to their decimal equivalent. Table 6.1 shows the breakdown of the three address classes, and how many bits appear in the host ID and the network ID.

Table 6.1 The Familiar Delineations of the IP Address Classes

Address Class	# Network Bits	# Hosts Bits	Decimal Address Range
Class A	8 bits	24 bits	1-126
Class B	16 bits	16 bits	128-191
Class C	24 bits	8 bits	192-223

Using the old class A, B, and C addressing scheme, the Internet could support the following:

- 126 class A networks that could include up to 16,777,214 hosts each

- 65,000 class B networks that could include up to 65,534 hosts each

- Over 2 million class C networks that could include up to 254 hosts each

As you can see, there are only three classes; every company or organization will have to choose the class that best supports their needs. Since it is nearly impossible to receive a class A or B address, you would be stuck with a class C address, which may or may not be suitable for your needs. If you were assigned one class C address, and you only needed 10 addresses, you would be wasting 244 addresses. This results in what appears to be a condition of running out of addresses; however, the problem stems more from the inefficient use of the addresses. CIDR was developed to be a much more efficient method of assigning addresses.

A CIDR supernet consists of numerous contiguous IP addresses. An ISP can assign their customers blocks of contiguous addresses to define the supernets. Each supernet has a unique supernet address that consists of the upper bits that are shared between all IP addresses in the supernet. For example, the following group of addresses are all contiguous (198.113.0.0 through 198.113.7.0 in decimal notation).

```
11000110 01110001 00000 000 00000000
11000110 01110001 00000 001 00000000
11000110 01110001 00000 010 00000000
11000110 01110001 00000 011 00000000
11000110 01110001 00000 100 00000000
11000110 01110001 00000 101 00000000
11000110 01110001 00000 111 00000000
```

The supernet address for the block is 11000110 01110001 00000 (the 21 upper bits) because every address in the supernet has this in common. The complete supernet address consists of the address and the mask.

- The address is the first 32-bit address in the contiguous address block. In our case this would be 11000110 01110001 00000000 00000000 (198.113.0.0 in decimal notation).

- The mask is a 32-bit string, similar to the subnet mask, which contains a set bit in the supernet portion of the address. In our case this would be 11111111 11111111 11111000 00000000 (255.255.248.0 in decimal notation). The masked portion, however, contains the number of bits that are in the on position; in our case this would be 21.

The complete supernet address would be 198.113.0.0/21. The /21 indicates that the first 21 bits are used to identify the unique network, leaving the remaining bits to identify the specific host.

You can compare this to an office phone system where every phone number starts with a prefix such as 288 and ends with a unique four-digit combination. For example, your phone number is 288-1301, and Doug Fortune, the Human Resources supervisor, has a phone number of 288-2904. Most companies are set up so that you can dial the unique portion of the user's phone number as a means of internal dialing. To contact Doug, you would just dial 2904, which is the unique portion of his full phone number. Continuing the example, 288, the prefix of the phone number, would be the supernet address. Isn't it much easier to dial the person's four-digit extension rather than the entire seven-digit extension? Imagine if you had to dial the area code every time you made a local call. Also continuing the comparison, the area code resembles a supernet address for an area.

CIDR can then be used to employ a supernet address to represent multiple IP destinations. Rather than advertise a separate route for each of the members of the contiguous address space, the router can now advertise the supernet address as a single route, called an *aggregate* route. This aggregate route will represent all the destinations within the supernet address, thereby reducing the amount of information that needs to be contained in the routing tables of the routers. This may not seem like much of a reduction in the routing table, but multiply this by hundreds of routers on the Internet, and you can see the effect CIDR can have on the number of entries in the routing tables.

Table 6.2 shows how the CIDR block prefix is used to increase the number of groups of addresses that can be used, thereby offering a more efficient use of addressing than the class A, B, or C method.

Table 6.2 Characteristics of Each CIDR Block Prefix

CIDR Block Prefix	# Equivalent Class C	# of Host Addresses
/27	1/8th of a Class C	32 hosts
/26	1/4th of a Class C	64 hosts
/25	1/2 of a Class C	128 hosts
/24	1 Class C	256 hosts
/23	2 Class C	512 hosts
/22	4 Class C	1,024 hosts
/21	8 Class C	2,048 hosts
/20	16 Class C	4,096 hosts
/19	32 Class C	8,192 hosts
/18	64 Class C	16,384 hosts
/17	128 Class C	32,768 hosts
/16	256 Class C	65,536 hosts
	(= 1 Class B)	
/15	512 Class C	131,072 hosts
/14	1,024 Class C	262,144 hosts
/13	2,048 Class C	524,288 hosts

For IT Professionals

Upgrading the Routing Protocols on your Network

If you are a network engineer or administrator for a company or organization with a fairly large network, you may be faced with a dilemma—migrating your routers to another routing protocol. Chances are you are still using RIP, as most networks are. However, this routing protocol, as you will see in this chapter, is not the most capable protocol of the many routing protocols in existence. However, RIP may still function perfectly in your network, so you must determine whether you actually need to upgrade the routing protocol. As an IT professional in charge of your network, or contracting for another company's network, you will have to know when, if ever, to make a network protocol migration. You will have to ask yourself several questions in order to gather enough information to make an informed decision:

- How long has this routing protocol been in use in our network?
- Has our network grown significantly in the past few years?
- Has the network been suffering from degradation when communicating with remote networks?
- Do we have goals for the network that may not be met with this current routing protocol?
- Are we eventually going to segment our network into logical areas?

These questions will help you determine whether you need to investigate the possibility of migrating your routing protocols to a more modern, robust routing protocol. Do not make an important decision such as choosing a routing protocol in haste. You can severely hinder your network if you do not implement the routing protocol correctly. Spend the time, research all the available protocols, and do your homework.

At this time, the Internet is not completely CIDR-capable. Some older routers and other network devices must be upgraded to support CIDR, and compatible protocols must also be used. Non-CIDR-capable portions of the Internet can still function fine, but may be required to default towards the CIDR-capable parts of the Internet for routes that have been aggregated for nonnetwork boundaries. CIDR-capable forwarding is described as the ability of a router to maintain its forwarding table and to perform correct forwarding of IP packets without making any assumptions about the class of IP addresses.

The CIDR Applicability Statement composed in September of 1993 required Internet domains providing backbone and/or transit service to fully implement CIDR in order to ensure that the growth of the resources required by routers will provide Internet-wide connectivity. The Applicability Statement also recommended that all other nonbackbone and/or transit Internet domains also implement CIDR because it will reduce the amount of routing between these domains. At this time, individual domains are not required to implement CIDR. Individual domains are also not prohibited from using an addressing scheme that is not compliant with CIDR.

It is very important to note that CIDR does not attempt to solve the problem of eventual exhaustion of the 32-bit IP address space. CIDR can address the short- to midterm difficulties to allow the Internet time to continue functioning effectively while progress is made on the longer term solution of IP address exhaustion. With the development of CIDR around 1993, it was given at least three years as a viable solution until the deployment of the long-term solution, IPv6 (otherwise known as IPng). The next generation of IP is a little behind schedule, but vendors are now making their devices compliant, and the buzz is starting to spread in the Internet community.

From Millions to Thousands of Networks

For engineers, the biggest push on the Internet today is to devise a plan to limit the huge growth in available networks on the Internet. We have learned in the previous section that the addition of so many networks on the Internet has severely hindered the ability to

maintain effective routing tables for all the new networks that have
been added. It was becoming more difficult to route packets to their
destinations because the route to the destination was sometimes
not included in the large routing tables maintained by these routing
domains. This threat, much like a tornado warning, was due to
touch down on the Internet before the dreaded exhaustion of IP
addresses.

Now that CIDR has come to the rescue, the problem is to implement CIDR fast enough to consolidate these networks to minimize the
number of entries in the routing tables. From the millions of networks
out there, CIDR is able to consolidate contiguous IP addresses, known
as *supernetting,* into fewer numbers of networks that contain more
hosts. The only caveat with CIDR is that these must be contiguous class
C addresses. The authority for assigning IP addresses has assigned large
contiguous blocks of IP addresses to large Internet Service Providers.
These large ISPs assign a smaller subset of contiguous addresses from
their block to other ISPs or large network customers, as illustrated in
Figure 6.2.

The bottom line is that the large ISP maintains a large block of contiguous addresses that it can report to a higher authority for CIDR
address aggregation. With CIDR, the large ISP does not have to report
every class C address that it owns; it has to report the prefix that every
class C address has in common. These addresses are aggregated into a
single supernetted address for routing purposes. In our example, the
prefix is 198.113.201, which is what all IP addresses have in common.
Instead of advertising six routes, we are advertising only one. That is a
decrease of 83 percent. Imagine if every ISP were able to decrease the
routes they advertise by this much. This can literally bring the number
of networks from millions down to thousands. Not only does this
decrease the number of networks, but it is a significant reduction in the
number of routing table entries. By March of 1998, the number of global
routing table entries was around 50,000. Without CIDR, it is speculated
that the number of global routes would have been nearly twice that
number. You can always count on the standards committees behind the
scenes of the Internet to deliver effective solutions when adversity stares
them in the face.

Figure 6.2 Maintaining contiguous CIDR blocks while assigning addresses.

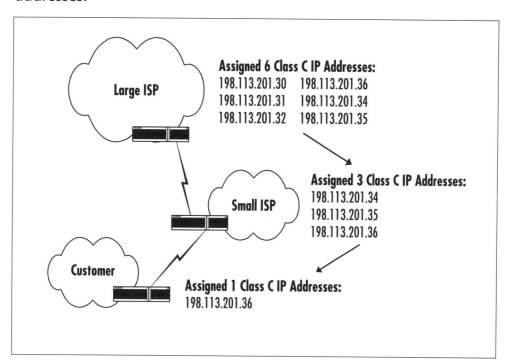

ISP Address Assignment

In the near future, organizations are likely to undergo changes that will affect their IP addresses. This can result from a variety of reasons, such as a change in Internet Service Provider, structural reorganization, physically moving equipment, and new strategic relationships. An IP address renumbering plan can result in easier future IP address management.

When moving from one ISP to another, and CIDR is being used, it will be required to return the addresses that were allocated to the organization from the ISP's original CIDR block. These addresses belong to a single large block of address space allocated to their current ISP, which acts like an aggregator for these addresses. If your address is aggregated into your ISP's larger address block, you can then be routed under their network address.

What if you leave Internet Service Providers and choose to take your IP addresses with you? This is a predicament for the original ISP who can no longer advertise the addresses as part of an aggregated CIDR block, because there is now a hole in the CIDR block (resulting from the loss of the IP addresses you took with you). CIDR can address this issue by requiring routers to accept multiple matches. When a duplicate routing match is found, the router will search for the route with the longest mask, which should be the most recent route. This is referred to as an *exception* to a CIDR block, and is used when a block of contiguous addresses cannot be used, like the example in which we defected from one ISP to another and took our addresses with us.

To contain the growth of this routing information, an organization should change these addresses, which involves renumbering their subnets and hosts. If the organization does not renumber, the consequences may include limited Internet-wide IP connectivity issues. ISPs sometimes have to change to a new and larger block of addresses, and this may affect the organization that currently has addresses that were allocated to them from the original CIDR block.

The easiest form of renumbering is with the use of dynamic addressing, such as Dynamic Host Configuration Protocol (DHCP). However, many servers and network devices such as routers have static addresses, which will hamper the renumbering process.

The most important aspect of the renumbering plan is centered around routing. Routing issues have become very important, due to the large growth of the Internet and the maintenance of large routing tables that accompany this growth. Since routers are a key component to connectivity, they are a large focus of the renumbering plan.

If you are not aggregated into your ISP's larger address block, and you are a smaller organization, you are risking being dropped from the global routing tables. There is no governing force that has control over what addresses are added to the global routing tables; any ISP can manage their routing tables as they see fit. If you are a smaller network, you can still be included in global routing tables if your address is part of a larger CIDR address block.

Using CIDR Addresses Inside Your Network

The interior (intradomain) routing protocols that support CIDR are OSPF, RIP II, Integrated IS-IS, and EIGRP. If you are running one of these routing protocols in your internal network, you have the ability to use CIDR addresses inside your network. Most companies and organizations do not have internal networks large enough to require CIDR addressing. However, CIDR does provide more than just efficient addressing.

When implementing CIDR addressing in your internal network, you have the ability to create smaller subnets than those available with the current classful subnetting schemes. For example, in order to subnet your network using TCP/IP subnet with a custom subnet mask, the smallest subnet you have would still have 254 available hosts. With CIDR you can implement *fractional aggregates*, the ability to take a class C address and assign fractions of it to customers or your internal subnets on your own network. ISPs are now using this technology to assign 64 and 32 block addresses to customers with small networks. This makes efficient use of available class C addresses, because without CIDR, you would be wasting the remaining IP address in the class C address that was not used. This is how you can combat IP address exhaustion within your own network, just like many people are trying to do on the Internet. Table 6.3 shows the fractional aggregates of a single class C address.

Table 6.3 Fractions of a Class C Address Made Possible by CIDR

CIDR Block Prefix	# Equivalent Class C	# of Host Addresses
/27	1/8th of a Class C	32 hosts
/26	1/4th of a Class C	64 hosts
/25	1/2 of a Class C	128 hosts
/24	1 Class C	256 hosts

With CIDR we now have the ability not only to use a full Class C address, but also to assign fractions of the Class C, such as ?th, ?th, or 1/8th the number of available addresses.

NOTE

Two of the addresses in the class C block are reserved for broadcasts, so our theoretical limit is 254 hosts.

As we mentioned earlier, you can also use this fractional class C address for your internal network. The advantages of this are subnetting networks into logical groupings of computers and devices, isolating traffic, and therefore increasing network performance. You will have to use a CIDR-capable routing protocol, such as OSPF or RIP-2 on your network. This will make your network more complex and difficult to manage, but it will help you reap the benefits of subnetting that we described earlier.

Contiguous Subnets

The most important rule to remember with CIDR classless addressing is that subnets must be contiguous. A router cannot process subnet routes for networks to which it is not directly connected. The example in Figure 6.3 illustrates this rule more clearly.

If a router is to take part in the same classful network in order to interpret the prefix length, it must be connected directly to the network.

In Figure 6.3, the router is not a part of the contiguous network, so it has no way of knowing the prefix length that is being used. More specifically, Router1 and Router2 cannot advertise their routes to Router3 because Router3 is not a part of the 201.35.88 network. The only route that can be advertised to Router3 is 201.35.88. This poses a problem because Router3 has no indication of which direction to send a packet with the prefix of 201.35.88; it will undoubtedly send packets to the wrong network.

The problem with the network configuration shown in Figure 6.3 is that the 198.113.201 networks are not contiguous. If we configured a direction connection between Router1 and Router2, we would have a contiguous network, and could benefit from CIDR addressing. The addition of Router3 injects another classful network between the 198.113.201 networks, thus making it discontiguous.

Figure 6.3 An illegal CIDR configuration with disconnected networks.

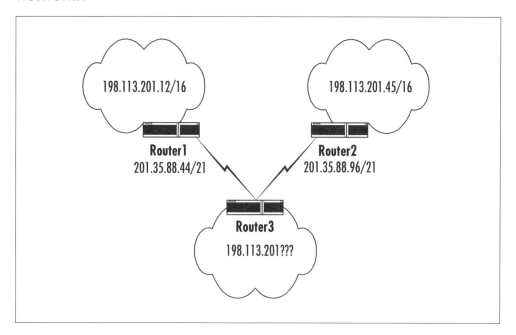

IGRP

The networking community began to realize the limitations of the RIP protocol (which we will see later in the chapter), and something had to be done. Many years ago, the Internet Engineering Task Force (IETF) had not yet formalized the specifications for OSPF, so Cisco had the option of waiting for the specifications, or continuing to develop their own protocol. They chose to implement their own protocol, which turned out to be Interior Gateway Routing Protocol (IGRP).

IGRP is a protocol that is designed to coordinate routing between a number of routers. There are a number of routing goals with Cisco's IGRP protocol:

- Stable routing, even in a very large or complex network
- No routing loops should occur
- Fast response to changing network topology
- Low overhead, meaning IGRP should not use more bandwidth than it needs for its own use
- Splitting traffic among parallel routes when they are of equal desirability
- Taking into account error rates and levels of traffic on different paths
- The ability to handle multiple "types of services" with a single set of information.

IGRP is intended for use within internal networks, under the management of one organization. IGRP is also commonly referred to as IGP (Interior Gateway Protocol). IGRP is intended for maintaining a very accurate representation of the internal network topology. Convergence is very important within internal networks, because the paths to networks must be quickly rerouted in the event a network link were to go down. This is not as important as external networks, because most change in network topology occurs within networks, such as the addition or removal of a broken link. External network links must be stable and consistent to avoid major disturbances from misconfigured or down links. EGRP (Exterior Gateway Routing Protocol) is more important for providing reasonable routes, rather than optimal routes. However, IGRP is very concerned with providing the optimal route when packets are being routed.

IGRP is a distance-vector protocol in which routers (often called gateways) exchange routing information only with adjacent routers. When the adjacent router receives the update, it will compare the information with its own routing table. Any new paths or destinations will be added. Paths in the adjacent router's update will also be compared with existing paths to determine if the new route is more efficient than the route that currently exists in the routing table. If the new path is better, it will replace the existing one. This is the general procedure used in all distance-vector protocols.

The alternative to distance-vector routing is Shortest Path First (SPF) routing, which we will discuss in great detail in the section on Open Shortest Path First (OSPF). This is a link-state technology in which each router contains an identical database.

The routing information exchange contains a summary of information concerning the rest of the network. A collection of routers using IGRP completes the entire network topology, resulting in a distributed algorithm in which each router solves only a portion of the routing. Working together and exchanging routing information with only their adjacent routers, these routers can determine the best route a packet can take. In other words, no one router needs to maintain the information for the entire network.

IGRP goes beyond RIP when it comes to metrics. The added information in IGRP allows the router to make more intelligent choices with regards to the metric cost of one route over another. RIP had no way of choosing the route with the highest bandwidth when both routes had the same metric hop count. The new metrics introduced with IGRP include:

Topological delay time. The amount of time it would take a packet to reach its destination if the network was not busy. You can incur additional delays if there is network traffic on the network.

Bandwidth of the narrowest bandwidth segment of the path. The bandwidth in bits per second.

Channel occupancy of the path. Indicates how much of the bandwidth is currently in use. This number will change often as the network traffic increases and decreases.

Reliability of the path. Indicates the reliability of the path based on the number of packets that actually arrive at the destination, based on the number of packets that were originally sent.

IGRP calculates these factors with a complicated algorithm and determines the best route to take, indicated by the smallest metric value.

IGRP also has substantial stability features, such as Hold-downs, Split horizons, and Poison-reverse updates, which are described as follows:

Hold-downs. Used to prevent a regular update message from reinstating a route that may have gone bad in the past. When a network link goes down, the neighboring routers will detect the lack of regularly scheduled updates, and determine that this link is not functioning. Update messages will then begin to permeate the network regarding the fact this router is not functioning. If this convergence takes too long, it is possible that another router on the network will advertise that this router is still functioning normally. This device potentially is advertising incorrect routing information. A hold-down will tell the routers on the network to hold down any of the changes that may affect the routes for a period of time. The hold-down period is calculated to be just slightly greater than the period of time necessary to update the entire network with a routing change.

Split horizons. Used to avoid routing loops between two routers. It is never useful to send information about the route back in the direction from which the packet was sent. In Figure 6.4, Router1 will advertise a route to Network A, which it is directly connected. Router2 should never advertise this route back to Router1 because Router1 is closer to Network A. This will prevent routing loops between the two routers. For example, if the interface to Network A went down, Router2 may continue to inform Router1 that it can reach Network A through Router1 (which is itself). Router1 may be fooled into believing this route is correct, and a routing loop would then occur. (Remember that split horizons avoid only loops between *two* routers.)

Poison-reverse updates. Used to minimize loops between more than two routers. When the metric is increasing significantly, this may indicate a routing loop. A poison-reverse update is then sent to the router to place it into hold-down.

Figure 6.4 Avoiding routing loops with split horizons.

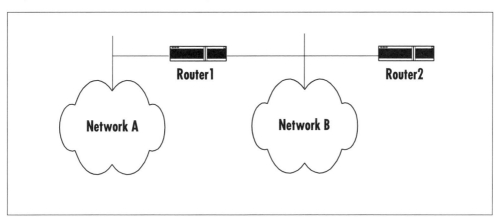

Another feature of IGRP stability is the use of timers and variables that contain time intervals. The timers include an update timer, an invalid timer, a hold-time period, a flush timer, and a sleep timer.

- The update timer will specify how frequently the update messages will be sent. The IGRP update timer default is every 90 seconds.

- The invalid timer will specify how long a router will wait if it is not receiving routing update messages before the route will be declared invalid. The IGRP invalid timer default is three times the update timer.

- The hold-time period (sometimes referred to as the hold-down period) will specify the amount of time for the hold-down period. The IGRP hold-time default is three times the update timer plus ten seconds.

- The flush timer will specify how much time should pass before a route is flushed from a routing table. The IGRP flush timer default is seven times the update period.

- The sleep timer is the amount of time that update messages will be postponed. The sleep value should be less than the update timer because the routing tables will never be synchronized if the sleep value is higher than the update timer.

EIGRP

EIGRP is an enhanced version of the IGRP routing protocol, and is continually evolving. EIGRP uses the same distance-vector-based routing that IGRP uses. What has improved is the convergence and operating efficiency. The main enhancement with EIGRP is the sophisticated Diffusing Update Algorithm (DUAL). This algorithm is significantly more advanced than the distance-vector algorithm used by RIP and previous versions of IGRP. The new algorithm was enhanced to decrease routing loops drastically.

Convergence is improved by implementing a new algorithm that enables all routers involved in a topology change to synchronize their internal routing tables at the same time.

EIGRP is now Network Layer protocol-independent, which means it can support other protocol suites. One of the downfalls of EIGRP is the fact that it is seen as a competitor to OSPF.

EIGRP can be implemented seamlessly within a network or IGRP routers. This makes it possible to benefit from the features of both protocols simultaneously, also providing an upgrade path for continual migration from IGRP to EIGRP. Another benefit of this coexistence is that you can strategically implement EIGRP in specific portions of your network.

Cisco defines the four basic components of EIGRP as follows:

Neighbor Discovery/Recovery. The process of dynamically learning the status of other routers on their directly attached networks. Routers must also continually poll their neighbors to determine if they are still functioning or reachable. This is achieved by sending Hello packets on a regular basis. Once these Hello packets are received, the routers can then continue to exchange route information.

Reliable Transport Protocol. Responsible for the guaranteed delivery of packets in the correct order. For efficiency, reliability is only provided when needed. This is accomplished by sending a multicast Hello packet to the neighbors that states the packet does not have to be acknowledged. As you know, the process of responding to acknowledgment requests is what consumes valuable bandwidth on a network, especially on an Ethernet network with a very broadcast-intensive protocol. Every packet must be captured and analyzed by the network adapters to determine if the packet is destined for them. This can be very CPU-intensive as well.

DUAL Finite State Machine. The decision process for route computations. It is responsible for tracking routes that are advertised by all neighbors. The metric hop count is the distance information used to create loop-free paths. The routes are selected based on feasible successors. A feasible successor will be discussed later in this section.

Protocol Dependent Modules. Responsible for sending and receiving EIGRP packets that are encapsulated in a protocol, such as IP. This module has support for more protocols.

EIGRP Concepts

This section describes the concepts for Cisco's EIGRP implementation.

Neighbor table. A table in which each router keeps track of neighboring (adjacent) routers. When a new neighbor is learned, the address and interface is recorded into the routing database.

Topology table. A table that is populated with protocol-dependant modules containing all destinations advertised by the neighboring routers. Each entry also contains the destination address and list of neighbors that have advertised this particular destination. The table also contains the metric associated with this destination. This is the best metric the router uses and places in the routing table, which is then used for routing and for advertising this route to other routers.

Feasible successors. An entry that is moved from the topology table to the neighbor table when there is a feasible successor. The neighbors that have an advertised metric route that is less than the current routing table metric are considered feasible successors. Feasible successors are routers that are downstream neighbors to the neighboring router, not this particular router. It is the neighbor's neighbor. When a neighbor has changed its metric, or a topology change occurs on the network, the list of feasible successors will have to be recomputed.

Route states. The route can be only one of two states: passive or active. A route is considered passive when the router is not performing a route recomputation. The route is considered active when a router is performing route computation.

RIP-1 Requirements

Routing Information Protocol (RIP), the distance-vector Interior Gateway Routing Protocol that we discussed in the previous section, is used by routers to route packets to remote networks. There are a few differences between RIP and IGRP that we will discuss later in this section.

The RIP protocol is an interior routing protocol, and the most popular of the interior routing protocols. The RIP protocol is based on a 1970s design, and emerged for TCP/IP in the early 1980s. With the rapid advancements in technology, you can see how technology has exceeded the capabilities of the RIP protocol. RIP has changed very little since its emergence, and therefore has some limitations in larger, more complex networks. Some of these limitations have been addressed by the newer RIP-2 protocol specification. Limitations of RIP-1 include the following:

- RIP cannot support an internal network with more than 15 hops within the same network. A router counts the hops a packet makes as it crosses other routers on the way to its destination.

- RIP cannot support variable-length subnet masking. Subnetting is very popular in TCP/IP-based networks, and the RIP protocol is subject to restrictions in this type of network. Another term for this is Variable-Length Subnet Masks (VLSM), which RIP does not support.

- RIP will broadcast updates about every 30 seconds. Bandwidth can be consumed if the router has a large routing table, or the network is very large with slow links.

- RIP has limited security. It is possible to obtain an unauthorized list of routes from other neighboring routers, and it may be possible for a hacker to inject false routes on the network.

- Routing problems are difficult to diagnose in RIP.

- RIP has a slower convergence time than OSPF. RIP routers have a period of hold-down, garbage collection, and will slowly time-out information during the convergence process. This is not acceptable in some large networks and could possibly cause routing inconsistencies.

- RIP has no concept of slow links or network delays. Routing decisions are only made by metrics hop counts. The path with the lowest hop count is the most efficient, which may not be the best method because this does not take into account the speed of some of these network links.

- RIP networks are not hierarchical, and have no concept of areas, domains, and autonomous systems.

- RIP does not support classless routing, which has become increasingly popular and necessary on large networks and on the Internet.

Routers periodically will exchange routing tables with neighboring routers. Routers using the RIP protocol exchange their entire routing table, which can be inefficient. For this reason, routers are using more efficient routing protocols such as Open Shortest Path First (OSPF). Figure 6.5 is an example of a typical routing table.

Not everything about the RIP protocol is negative. Since it is one of the most widespread interior routing protocols, RIP can be supported almost anywhere. As many network technicians and engineers know, any protocol that is almost universal is a welcome addition because of the compatibility. Also, RIP is very easy to configure, which makes it very attractive because of the minimal amount of configuration required.

Figure 6.5 A sample RIP routing table.

Destination	Next Hop	Distance	Timers	Flags
Network A	Router1	5	11,12,13	x,y
Network B	Router2	3	11,12,13	x,y
Network C	Router1	2	11,12,13	x,y

RIP classifies routers as passive and active. An active router will advertise its routes to other routers. Passive routers will receive these routes, but they do not have the ability to advertise their own routes. Typically, a router will run in active mode, and hosts will run in passive mode. The update will consist of an IP network address and the integer distance to that network. RIP uses a hop count, which, as we described earlier, is the number of routers the packet will have to cross to reach the destination network. Each pass over a router increases the hop count by one hop. RIP has a maximum of 15 hops when routing packets to a remote network. These metric counts of hops to the destination determine the most efficient route; that is, the quickest path to the destination network. In other words, a route with 5 hops is more efficient than a route with 8 hops. However, the route with the least number of hops may not be the fastest route to a destination. The hops do not take into account the speed of the route. For example, a route with 5 hops may cross slower serial links in order to reach a destination, rather than another route with 7 hops that crosses an Ethernet network. For this reason, a router can advertise a higher hop count for a slow link to compensate for the slower link. This will deter the use of this slower link.

Comparison with IGRP

The comparison between RIP and IGRP is useful because RIP is used for purposes that are similar to IGRP. However, RIP was designed with smaller networks in mind, and was never meant to be used in large, complex networks.

The most basic difference between the two protocols is the use of metrics. RIP uses a simple hop count, which we discussed in the previous section. RIP has a hop count of 15 when routing packets to a remote network. The hop count, expressed in a decimal from 1 to 15, describes the number of routers the packet will have to pass before arriving at its destination. Since the maximum hop count is 15, it may be difficult to reach a slower network represented with a large hop count. To accommodate the full range of network links, such as serial and asynchronous WAN links, the metric should be increased to a higher number, such as 24. This 24-bit metric could allow for most reliable routing on large, complex networks, or networks with various slow links. Some networks today are so large that RIP cannot pass packets from one end of the network to the other without exhausting the maximum of 15 hops. RIP is just not possible on these large networks.

Since you cannot just increase the hop count with RIP, you must find an alternative. IGRP not only provides a larger metric hop count, but also includes a few more features that make it more robust than RIP. IGRP can express the metric hop count to include factors such as delay, bandwidth, and reliability. RIP can express two different routes as the same hop count, but cannot take into account the fact that these routes may travel slower routes, or consume more bandwidth than desired.

IGRP can also split traffic among several equal routes, which is not very easy to implement with RIP. Instead of implementing a configuration where RIP supports traffic splitting, it may be more effective to update the network to use a routing protocol other than RIP.

RIP updates also contain little information, such as the destinations and the hop counts (metric values). IGRP can support an Autonomous System Number (ASN), which is a number used to describe an area, or domain. We will learn more about the ASN in the section on Border Gateway Protocol (BGP).

And finally, RIP uses the concept of a "default route," a route that will get a packet to a destination that is not specified in the router's internal routing table. This can be compared to the default router in TCP/IP, which is used to send a packet that is destined for a remote network that this host is unable to find. The phrase, "I don't know where this packet is destined for, so you do something with it." is used to describe the concept of the default gateway. RIP and some other routing protocols distribute the default route as if it were a path to a real network, which in most cases it is not. IGRP uses a different approach to the default route. Rather than distribute the default route as a fake route, IGRP can flag real networks (more than one) as candidates for the default route. IGRP can scan all of the default routes to determine which route is the best candidate with the lowest metric. This candidate can then become the actual default route.

Routing Update Impact

As we discussed earlier, one of the disadvantages of RIP routing is the extensive use of broadcasts. A router updates its own routing table with information received from neighboring routers. When a router that is configured to respond hears this request, it will respond with a packet that contains information on routes from its very own routing database. This response packet contains destination network information and metrics (hops) for reaching these destination networks. When the host or router receives this routing information it will rebuild its database by adding new routes and modifying existing routes. To modify an existing route, the host or router will determine if the new route has a better path to the destination, which is a lower hop count. RIP will also delete a route that contains more than 15 hops to the destination. Routes will also be removed from the router's database if no updates are received within a certain period of time. This is a dynamic means of purging routes in the database that have not been used recently. As we have already discussed, routes are usually broadcast every 30 seconds, and routes are deleted from the route database if they are not updated within 180 seconds. To understand the cost of routes, examine Figure 6.6.

Figure 6.6 An illustration of hop count with RIP.

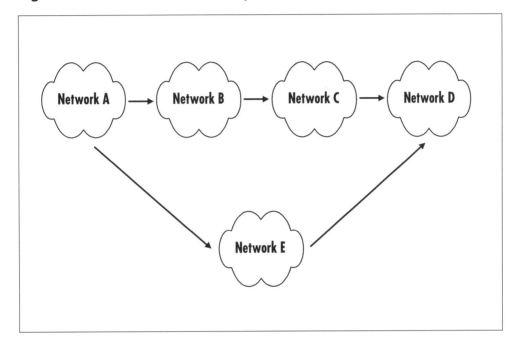

Network A is connected to Network D through Network B and Network C. Once Network E is up and running, packets from Network A destined for Network D can now be sent through Network E, at a hop count of 1. This hop count is less, and will therefore be the route of choice when Network A needs to communicate with Network D. If Network E were to go down, Network A would have to know about it. Since RIP requires a router to send updates every 30 seconds, a broken link will be learned quickly by the rest of the routers on the network. Remember, if RIP does not receive an update from another router in 180 seconds, that route is removed from the routing database because the router believes this route is no longer available.

RIP routing updates are very dynamic, and changes to the network can be updated very quickly and accurately. For example, a change in network topology can easily be reflected in the updated RIP routing updates. These will update the current entries in a router's routing table (if they are present). If the routes are not in the routing database, they will be added. If a router detects a failure for another router on the network, the router can recalculate its routes and send the updated information to other neighboring routers, informing them of the new route. Each router that receives this route update can now update its own database and propagate the changes to the remaining routers on the network.

RIP-2 Requirements

RIP version 2 was developed to address some of the limitations with the original version of RIP. The purpose of RIP-2 is to increase the amount of information in the packet itself, and to increase security, which was lacking in RIP version 1. Since RIP is still in widespread use, it was decided to increase the capabilities of RIP so organizations would not have to implement a brand new routing protocol. RIP is also easier to implement compared to the rest of the interior gateway protocols.

The following is a list of features with the new RIP-2 protocol:

Optional authentication. Most implementations use a simple password authentication.

Routing Domain field. Enables you to ignore logical domains on the same physical network. The default routing domain is assigned the value 0.

Route Tag field. Exists to support Exterior Gateway Protocols (EGP). This field will carry autonomous system numbers for EGP and Border Gateway Protocol (BGP). The Internet is divided into domains, or autonomous systems. Interior Gateway Protocols (IGPs) are the protocols used within a domain for the exchange of routing information. Basically, this route tag will separate internal RIP routes from external ones.

Subnet Mask field. Contains a subnet mask that is applied to the IP address to determine the host network on which the destination is located.

Next Hop. Forwards packets to the immediate next hop. This is useful in networks where the routers can be using routing protocols other than RIP.

Multicasting. Sends broadcast packets out on the network. The RIP-2 multicast address is 224.0.0.9.

The most important aspect of RIP-2 is that it is completely backwards-compatible with RIP-1, and can also run in RIP-1 emulation mode or RIP-1 compatible mode, in addition to full RIP-2 mode.

RIP-2 also keeps the features that made RIP-1 so popular, such as its small size, easy implementation, and the ability to run on embedded systems that cannot afford the memory space consumed by more efficient routing protocols. RIP has also been redefined to support IPv6, which is very similar to RIP-2. Basically all that has changed is the header information contained within the RIP packet. This makes RIP easier to implement in IPv6 networks; however, RIP is still not the most ideal choice for modern networks. Newer routing protocols such as OSPF and IS-IS are hoping to make RIP obsolete, but RIP still is implemented in more networks than OSPF and IS-IS combined; therefore, the push by some to make RIP-2 successful is very strong in the networking community.

OSPF

Open Shortest Path First (OSPF), like RIP, is another Interior Gateway Protocol (IGP).

NOTE

Interior Gateway Protocols (IGP) are often described as Interior Gateway Routing Protocols (IGRP), but they are used interchangeably. IGP and IGRP are the same thing.

OSPF was specifically designed for the Internet, which uses the IP protocol, and is designed with the following features:

- Authentication of routing updates
- TOS-based routing
- Tagging of externally-derived routes
- Fast response to topology changes with low overhead
- Load sharing over meshed links.

OSPF will attempt to open the shortest path to a destination first. This link-state technology is called Shortest Path First (SPF), in which each router contains an identical database. Inside this routing database is a description of a particular router and its current state, which also includes the state of interfaces that this router is connecting. This is much different from RIP routers, which can each have differing entries in their routing databases. SPF-based routers contain the database for the Autonomous System (AS) topology. As you learned earlier, the Internet is divided into domains, or autonomous systems.

NOTE

The term domain is frequently used interchangeably with the term AS, or autonomous system. Try not to confuse domain with an Internet domain name, such as microsoft.com. Also, do not confuse domain with the Windows NT domain, which is a logical grouping of computers. You must know in what context the term is being used to be completely sure of the domain being used.

Another feature of OSPF that is not available with RIP-1 is the ability to support subnet masking. Each route that is distributed by OSPF has a destination address and a subnet mask. When packets are being routed, the routes with the longest match are given a higher priority than routes with a shorter subnet mask.

OSPF is also capable of supporting four types of physical networks: point-to-point, broadcast, nonbroadcast, and point-to-multipoint.

Point-to-point networks. Consist of two routers in which the point-to-point interfaces can be set up as numbered or unnumbered interfaces. A network of synchronous lines is an example of a point-to-point network.

Broadcast networks. For networks with potentially more than two routers, but the OSPF has the ability to send the same broadcast to all of the routers. An Ethernet network is an example of a broadcast-based network.

Nonbroadcast networks. Networks also with potentially more than two routers; however, OSPF does not have the ability to send a broadcast to all of the routers. An example of this type of network is X.25 or ATM.

Point-to-multipoint networks. Resemble a bicycle wheel, with the main router as the hub and the other routers branching off in spokes from the central hub. This appears very similar in theory to the Ethernet star topology.

One concept of OSPF that is very different from RIP is that networks can be split into many *areas*. These areas are described as entirely within an area (intra-area routing) or in another area (inter-area routing). To remember the differences, think of the inter-area as the Internet as opposed to an internal intranet for an organization. When OSPF needs to link together areas, they use the concept of a backbone, which is similar to the use of a backbone in an Ethernet network. This backbone is made up of routers and networks that link together different areas. This backbone must be contiguous, which is also similar to the backbone of an Ethernet bus network. Interfaces can extend from this backbone to other networks. This type of routing is called external routing because the source and destination are located on different networks.

Since an area can be defined in such a way that the backbone is not contiguous, there needs to be a way to continue the backbone connectivity. This is made possible by a *virtual link*. This virtual link is configured between any backbone routers that share a link to this nonbackbone area and function as if they were direct links to the backbone. A virtual link also enables us to patch in the backbone in case discontinuity occurs, such as when a link is down.

When packets need to be sent from one area to another, they will be sent along this backbone. This makes use of an Area Border Router (ABR), a router that is connected to the originating area and then connected to the backbone area. The packet is then sent across the backbone where it is received by another router, which is also another area border router. This router then sends the packet on to its destination.

There are four types of routers associated with OSPF: Internal routers, Area Border routers, Backbone routers, and Autonomous System (AS) boundary routers.

Internal routers. Responsible for routing packets within a single area. They flood the internal area with routing information that occurs within its specific area. This internal router can also be a backbone router if it has no physical interfaces to another area.

Area Border routers. Are responsible for routing packets between multiple areas on which this router has interfaces.

Backbone routers. Have a physical interface to the backbone. These are often called border routers.

Autonomous System (AS) boundary routers. Exchange information with other autonomous systems using EGP protocols like BGP.

Backbone routers, sometimes referred to as border routers, can treat certain areas as stubs. This means the border routers will not forward any information about external routes to these stub areas. These border routers can also be configured not to forward any internal information about internal OSPF routes.

These four types of routers make it possible for OSPF to divide an autonomous system into areas.

Configuring OSPF

To configure OSPF on your Cisco router, you need to enter the router in config mode and enter the following information. First, enable the OSPF process:

```
router ospf <process-id>
```

Then you must assign areas to the interfaces:

```
network <network or IP address> <mask> <area-id>
```

The following is an example of both completed steps:

```
router ospf 5
network 203.11.87.156 255.255.255.0 100
```

The **network** command in the second step is how we assign a router to an area. We must specify the network or IP address to this router, which includes the subnet mask, in order to use TCP/IP to connect to this router. The **area-id** must correspond with the area in which this router will be placed. If you recall, an area is another name for an autonomous system (AS).

To use passwords with OSPF routers, which is one feature we were not able to take advantage of with RIPv1 routers, you must also enter the router in config mode. The passwords should be configured the same for every OSPF router in your area. To enable password authentication, enter config mode on the router and enter the following information:

```
IP ospf authentication-key <key> (this goes under the specific interface
portion)
area <area-id> authentication (this goes under "router ospf <process-id>"
portion)
```

The following is an example of both completed portions:

```
interface Ethernet1
IP address 197.13.55.110 255.255.255.0
IP ospf authentication-key february


router ospf 100
network 45.113.22.188 255.0.0.0 area 200
area 200 authentication
```

From the preceding example you can see that our password is february. Unfortunately, anyone with a link analyzer can obtain this password as it passes over the network.

To implement a more secure means of authentication, we can use OSPF Message Digest Authentication. You must configure the **key** (password) and a **key-id** for each OSPF router that will participate in password authentication. A link analyzer cannot obtain the password because the password (key) is not passed over the network. To enable Message Digest Authentication, enter config mode on the router and enter the following information:

```
IP ospf message-digest-key <key-id> md5 <key> (this goes under the specific
interface portion)
area <area-id> authentication message-digest (this goes under "router ospf
<process-id>" portion)
```

The following is an example of both completed portions:

```
interface Ethernet1
IP address 197.13.55.110 255.255.255.0
IP ospf message-digest-key 10 md5 february
router ospf 100
network 45.113.22.188 255.0.0.0 area 200
area 200 authentication message-digest
```

From the preceding example you can see that our password is still february. Our **message-digest-key** is 10 and our area is still 200.

We have learned about the backbone, which is a contiguous area of physical links. This backbone is called "area 0" and has to be the center of all other areas. We can use a virtual link to provide a logical connection to the backbone from an area that is disconnected, as illustrated in Figure 6.7.

Figure 6.7 Creating a virtual link between two noncontiguous sites.

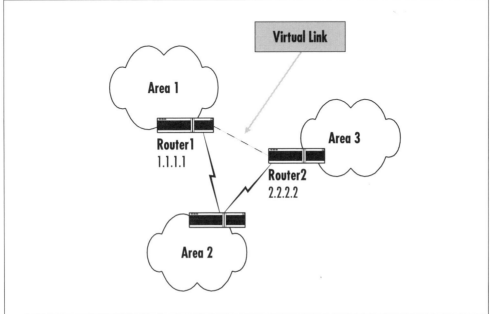

In Figure 6.7, Area 1 does not have a physical, contiguous connection to Area 3. A virtual link has been created between Router1 and Router2. Area 2 is now a transit area and Router2 is now the entry point into Area 3.

In order for this virtual link to work, we need to enter the OSPF router in config mode and enter some information concerning the link:

```
area <area-id> virtual-link <RID>
```

The following is an example of the completed portions on both routers:

```
Router 1#
router ospf 100
area 2 virtual-link 2.2.2.2

Router 2#
router ospf 100
area 2 virtual-link 1.1.1.1
```

The **area-id** in the preceding example is the transit area, which we determined was Area 2. The **RID** is the router ID, in which we entered the IP address of the router.

Routing Update Impact

The RIP protocol is more suited to smaller networks because of the large amount of broadcasts used to update routers about paths to remote networks. The OSPF protocol is well-suited to larger, dynamic, more complicated networks. RIP updates occur every 30 seconds, whereas OSPF updates occur every 30 minutes. RIP routers send the entire routing table to neighboring routers, whereas OSPF sends very small update files to routers whenever they detect a change in the network, such as a failed link or new link. When routers exchange information, it is called *convergence,* where the routers "converge" on the new representation of the network very quickly.

A network of OSPF and RIP routers can possibly coexist. OSPF is slowly replacing RIP as the interior gateway routing protocol of choice. These OSPF routers can simultaneously RIP for router-to-end station communications, and OSPF for router-to-router communications. For example, you can configure a Windows NT computer to participate as a RIP router in a RIP-routing environment, but you cannot configure this same Windows NT computer to participate as an OSPF router in an OSPF-routing environment. This coexistance between RIP and OSPF makes gradual migrations from RIP to OSPF feasible. In fact, RIP and OSPF routers cannot only coexist in the same network, they can actually share routing information. Figure 6.8 shows the enabling of RIP routing on Windows NT.

Figure 6.8 Configuring a Windows NT computer as a RIP router.

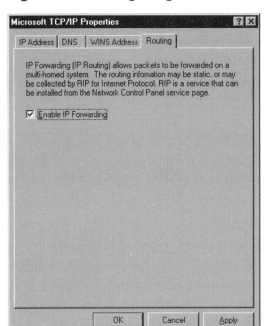

To configure your Windows NT computer to participate in sharing routing updates with other computers on the network, you need to enable IP forwarding. This is done in the Network applet of the Control Panel, by selecting the TCP/IP protocol and viewing the properties. The Routing tab is illustrated in Figure 6.8. You also need to enable RIP in the Services applet in the Control Panel.

In OSPF, a neighbor is another router running OSPF that has an interface on the same network. When discovering and configuring OSPF neighbors, the router will use the Hello protocol to discover their neighbors and maintain this relationship. On two of the types of OSPF networks, point-to-point and broadcast, the Hello protocol will dynamically discover the neighbors. On a nonbroadcast network, you will have to configure the neighbors manually, because OSPF will not have a means of contacting and establishing relationships with its neighbors.

This Hello protocol ensures that the relationships between the routers are bidirectional. This will guarantee that every OSPF router will send as well as receive updated route information to and from each of its neighbors. The communication is bidirectional when the router sees itself in the Hello packet from another router. Included in the Hello protocol packet is the following:

- The router's priority
- The router's Hello timer and Dead timer value
- A list of routers that has sent the router Hello packets on this interface
- This router's choice of designated router and backup designated router.

However, this does not mean OSPF is a perfect routing protocol as far as routing updates are concerned. In really large network configurations, OSPF can produce a large number of router updates that flow between routers. If a network consists of hundreds of routers in a network topology that is designed to be fault tolerant, the number of link-state messages that traverse the network can be in the thousands. These thousands of link-state messages can be propagated from router to router across the network, consuming valuable bandwidth, especially on slower WAN links. The routers then have to recalculate their routing tables, which can consume valuable RAM and CPU cycles if these routing tables are a significant size. Fortunately for OSPF, no routing protocol available today is capable of minimizing routing updates in a very large network with many routers. OSPF is, however, much more capable than RIP at minimizing these bandwidth intensive routing updates. By the way, by "link-state" we mean the state, or condition of a link that is a description of the router's relationship to its neighboring routers. We think of the link as being an interface on the router. An interface, for example, would be the IP address of the physical interface, the subnet mask, the type of network to which it is connected, or the routers connected to the network. The collection of all these link-states would comprise a link-state database.

The link-state algorithm states (in much more complex terms than described here) a few steps of building and calculating these paths:

- Upon initialization or upon a change in routing information, a router will generate a link-state advertisement that will represent the collection of all the link-states currently on the router.

- In an event called flooding, all routers will exchange this link-state information. This flood of routing information will be propagated to all routers in the area.

- After each router has finished compiling the link-state information, they will begin to calculate a Shortest Path Tree to all destinations. This is very CPU-intensive, as there can be hundreds of paths that need to be processed. These paths will include the associated cost and next hop information to reach those destinations.

- If there are no changes in the network topology, OSPF will not be very active. OSPF will not need to exchange link-state information, and the routers will therefore not need to calculate Shortest Path Trees, because they will already have the information processed.

There are also different types of link-state packets, as follows:

Router links. Describe the state and cost of the router's links to the area. These router links are the indication of the interfaces on a router belonging to a certain area.

Network links. Describe all routers that are attached to a specific segment. These are generated by the Designated Router (DR).

Summary links. Describe networks in the autonomous system (AS), but outside of an area. These summary links also describe the location of the ABSR. They are also generated by the ABRs.

External links. Describe destinations that are external to the AS, or a default route from outside the AS. The ASBR is responsible for injecting the external link information into the autonomous system.

Another feature of OSPF is that routing updates are not passed across areas. Remember that areas are separated by the types of routers that we listed before, such as area border routers. If a network link were to fail, only the routers inside that area would exchange routing update information. Area border routers filter the routing updates from separate areas and the backbone. Area border routers can communicate with each other and exchange routing update information, but they use special link-state messages that are a brief summarization of the LAN or WAN topology for their areas.

Figure 6.9 illustrates the use of dividing areas that represent physical regions with area border routers attached to the backbone.

Figure 6.9 Dividing physical regions into areas separated by area border routers.

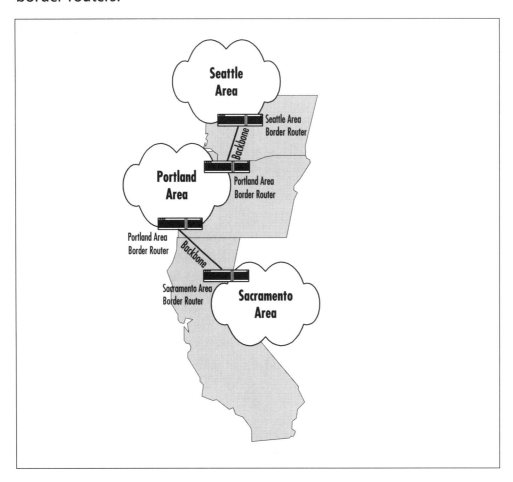

Each city does not want to receive the routing updates from the other cities; therefore, these areas are separated by area border routers, which can and do exchange information between each other, but in a smaller link-state update.

You can also fine-tune OSPF routers to minimize the amount of updates that are unleashed on the network, and therefore minimize the reduction in network bandwidth. You can also fine-tune the rate of convergence, which is the time between the routers receiving the new routing information and the time the network routers have made the necessary adjustments in their routing tables.

Table 6.4 illustrates an example of the OSPF database. This output is from the following command:

```
show IP ospf database
```

OSPF Router with ID (211.231.15.67) (Process ID 10)

Table 6.4 The Complete OSPF Database Taken from an Area Border Router (ABR)

	Router Link States (Area 1)	
Link ID	ADV Router	Link Count
211.231.15.67	211.231.15.67	2
211.231.16.130	211.231.16.130	2
	Summary Net Link States (Area 1)	
Link ID	ADV Router	
211.231.13.41	211.231.15.67	
211.231.15.64	211.231.15.67	
211.231.15.192	211.231.15.67	
	Router Link States (Area 0)	
Link ID	ADV Router	Link Count
211.231.13.41	211.231.13.41	3
211.231.15.67	211.231.15.67	1

Continued

	Net Link States (Area 0)	
Link ID	ADV Router	
211.231.15.68	211.231.13.41	
	Summary Net Link States (Area 0)	
Link ID	ADV Router	
211.231.15.0	211.231.15.67	
	Summary ASB Link States (Area 0)	
Link ID	ADV Router	
211.231.16.130	211.231.15.67	
	AS External Link States	
Link ID	ADV Router	Tag
0.0.0.0	211.231.16.130	10
211.231.16.128	211.231.16.130	0

We can begin analyzing the results, first starting with the Router Link States section of Area 1, shown in Table 6.5.

Table 6.5 The Router Link States Section of Area 1 in the OSPF Database

Link ID	ADV Router	Link Count
211.231.15.67	211.231.15.67	2
211.231.16.130	211.231.16.130	2

The two entries represent two routers in this area. Both routers have two links to Area 1, as represented by the Link Count column.

We continue, skipping past the Summary Net Link States section, and on to the next Router Link States section, which is for Area 0, shown in Table 6.6.

Table 6.6 he Router Link States Section of Area 0 in the OSPF Database

Link ID	ADV Router	Age	Link Count
211.231.13.41	211.231.13.41	179	3
211.231.15.67	211.231.15.67	675	1

Once again, there are two routers in this area. The first router has three links to Area 0, and the second router has one link to Area 0.

The Summary ASB Link States of Area 1 are listed in Table 6.7.

Table 6.7 The Summary ASB Link States of Area 1 in the OSPF Database

Link ID	ADV Router	Age
211.231.16.130	211.231.15.67	468

This gives you an indication of who the ASBR for the area is. The ASBR is a router with the address of 211.231.16.130.

The AS External Link States information contains information about destinations outside of our area, shown in Table 6.8.

Table 6.8 The AS External Link States in the OSPF Database

Link ID	ADV Router	Age	Tag
0.0.0.0	211.231.16.130	1683	10
211.231.16.128	211.231.16.130	65	0

Both of the two external links that are listed have been injected into our area from the OSPF.

OSPF Implementation Recommendations

Consider the following list of suggestions from Nortel Networks when implementing OSPF on your network (see http://support.baynetworks.com).

- Keep the same password within an area, if possible.

- Use the default timers.

- Use the address range if your network is a subnetted network.

- Keep all subnets within one area.

- Make sure the AS Border Router parameter is enabled if the router has any non-OSPF interfaces, and if you want that information propagated.

- Configure virtual links for each area border router that does not reside within or directly interface the backbone. Every border router must have a configured path to the backbone.

- If you have a preferred path to a destination, edit the Metric Cost parameter of your interface. OSPF will then choose the path with the lowest cost.

- Configure your routers that are running OSPF with the same timer values that coincide with the timers in your other devices.

- If there is a topology change, such as a change to an area or moving routers, you must reconfigure the appropriate OSPF elements, such as the interfaces, virtual links, and so on.

For Managers

Managing and Decision Making in an Information Systems Department

As the manager of an Information Systems department you will be required to be the sounding board for an entire department of intelligent, dynamic, and often strong-minded individuals. With this comes the need to sort out every IT member's thoughts, aspirations, and goals for the network. The feelings expressed may not be parallel with your thoughts and goals, and may contradict you and many others in your department. If this happens, you have to listen closely to what

Continued

each member of your team is saying. You must value their opinion, but in the end, it is just their *opinion*. You may have to meet with team members individually, and also in a group forum. If you do not reach common ground, and fear that a decision can never be made, you may find yourself in the predicament of making a decision. Just make sure you have completed the following when making a decision that is crucial to the entire department:

- Gather plenty of information in order to make your decision
- Identify needs and goals that you are trying to meet
- Identify alternatives to achieving the goal at hand
- Solicit input from everyone involved
- Test all of the products in an environment that simulates the actual environment
- Read as much information as you can about the solution
- Document the entire process
- Eliminate ideas that will not achieve the goal as you continue
- Make a decision, and stick by that decision.

There is the possibility that even after all the intense discussions, tests, and decision-making, you will end up not reaching your goal. This happens from time to time. Falling short of a goal is not the worst thing in the world; making a decision without the proper information, however, is worse.

BGP Requirements

Border Gateway Protocol (BGP) is the de-facto standard for routing between Autonomous Systems on the Internet. BGP was developed to address the limitations with Exterior Gateway Protocol (EGP), which was not the strongest routing protocol, although it was widely used. BGP can be thought of as the next generation of EGP. All communications between Internet Service Providers (ISP) is handled via BGP-4, which is *required* for CIDR. BGP-4 differs from BGP-3 just as RIP-2 differs from RIP-1. BGP-4 is also known as BGP4 without the hyphen.

BGP allows the use of announcements of classless routes, routes that are not strictly on class A, class B, or class C networks. These classless routes can be subnets or supernets. For more information on supernets, refer to the section on CIDR.

The primary purpose of BGP is to advertise routes to other networks, which are called Autonomous Systems (AS). BGP is also useful for advertising routes to upstream providers about what routes are available inside your network. When you are communicating with another ISP over the Internet, you are communicating with their network, or autonomous system, which is the more appropriate wording when speaking of routing with BGP. The border routers separate your AS from their AS. Every router in your AS should know the route to that destination AS. All AS routers in your area should contain the same routing information, and you should be advertising only routes that you know how to get to. The sin of BGP routing is advertising routes that you do not know how to reach.

There are three types of configurations in a network:

Stub areas. Always end points. This is usually a single, statically-routed connection from a central site, such as an ISP, to a remote location, such as a home or office. BGP is not needed in stub area configurations.

Multihomed areas. Central sites with at least two statically-defined or dynamically-routed connections to remote locations. Data will only flow to and from the remote locations. BGP is also not needed in this multihomed configuration.

Transit areas. Central sites with at least two connections to remote locations. One connection is to a remote location with an Internet connection, and another connection is to an additional Internet connection. Each of these locations is an autonomous system (AS). BGP is required in this configuration.

BGP is needed in the configuration if the customer has multiple locations with multiple routers, but he or she does not want each location's routing tables to affect the others. Defining these autonomous systems makes its possible to use these trusted paths between locations. This is the strategy that is used on the Internet to ensure better reliability and higher performance.

Figure 6.10 should clearly illustrate the purpose of BGP single-homed connections to an upstream provider.

Figure 6.10 Routing BGP in single-homed connections.

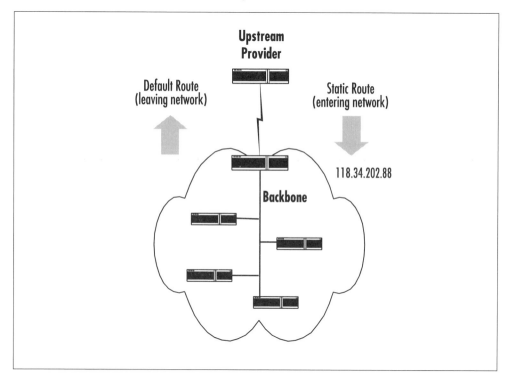

You can see how the default route for the AS is routed through the default route. This default route makes perfect sense on a sin-gularly-homed network, with only one connection to an upstream provider. From the upstream provider, it is also much easier, because your AS does not have a multihomed link to more than one upstream provider. This upstream provider can configure a static route to your AS. It would make no sense to configure this connection between the two ASs with a dynamic routing protocol, because this link between the ASs will rarely change. If this IP address to your AS were to change, you would simply have the upstream provider change the static routing address to your AS.

You have been hearing about the autonomous system—now, we need to describe the autonomous system number, which is used to represent the autonomous system to the Internet. Most networks will have only one autonomous system number. When you are exchanging routes with another router speaking BGP (called a *peering session*), it will start out like the following:

```
router BGP 14290
 neighbor 204.118.35.166 remote-as 802
 <the rest is omitted>
```

This communication starts out by saying, "I would like to connect to ASN (autonomous system number) 14290 using BGP." The list of commands that would initiate the routing table transfer is omitted.

If a node wishes to connect with BGP peer node, the node will open a connection on TCP port 179, which is the default port. A significant amount of information is transferred, such as the identification numbers, authentication information, and protocol version numbers before the BGP update of the routing tables can take place. The update will not take place if the authentication has not been successful. If the update is successful, the changes will then be propagated to neighboring BGP routers.

When you communicate to other hosts and routers using BGP, you can make semi-intelligent routing decisions, which include the best path to reach a destination. This route contains more than just the first router to route the packet to; it can include the complete route to the destination. You can also advertise your routes to neighboring routers, and have those routers in turn advertise your routes to their neighboring routers.

BGP selects only one path as the best path to a destination. This path is now propagated to the neighboring BGP routers. Unlike some routing protocols, BGP does not need a periodic routing table refresh. The initial exchange between two BGP routers is the full routing table, but from then on, only the optimal paths are advertised in update messages to the neighboring BGP routers. This makes long running sessions between BGP routers more efficient than short sessions, because the amount of times the full routing table is exchanged on initial contact is less.

There are actually two types of BGP that differ in terms of advertising routing information. The first is EBGP, basically referred to as BGP, which is what we have been discussing thus far. This is used to advertise routes to different autonomous systems, whereas IBGP is used to advertise routes within the same autonomous system.

Figure 6.11 Differentiating between interior and exterior routing with IBGP and EBGP.

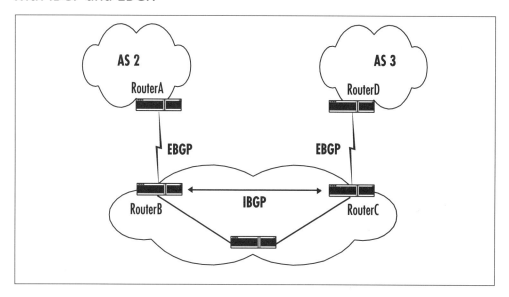

Figure 6.11 demonstrates the use of both types of BGP protocols and the autonomous system.

In the network example shown in Figure 6.11, BGP first makes sure that networks within the interior AS are reachable. Then, border routers can exchange routing information with each other regarding the status of networks within their autonomous systems. EBGP is used to communicate with border routers, and IBGP is used within the AS.

Just like RIP, IBGP is an interior routing protocol that can be used for active routing within your network. IBGP does not distribute routes as much as EBGP. Each router in an IBGP configuration must be configured to peer into every other router to exchange this information, whereas this is not needed with straight BGP. However, IBGP is more flexible and provides a more efficient means of controlling and exchanging the routing information from *within* an AS.

IBGP and EBGP Requirements

BGP requires a combination of hardware and software to support. The most commonly used implementations of BGP are with Cisco routers, Nortel routers, UNIX variants, BSD, and Linux. Nortel and Cisco routers are by far the most common types of routers currently supporting BGP.

We will now discuss the steps required to enable and configure BGP. First, we will assume that we want two routers to communicate using BGP. These routers will be called Router1 and Router2. These routers belong in two unique autonomous systems, called AS 1 and AS 2, as illustrated in Figure 6.12.

Figure 6.12 An example of routing between two separate autonomous systems.

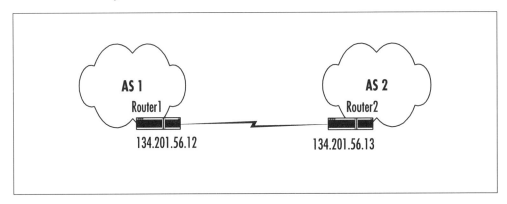

We now need to enable BGP on the routers one at a time, starting with Router1:

```
router bgp 1
```

and now the same step on Router2:

```
router bgp 2
```

These statements enable BGP on the router for the AS in which they belong. We will now define the neighbors that we wish to communicate with via BGP. Establishing a connection between two neighbors, or peers, via BGP is made possible by the TCP protocol. The TCP connection is essential for the BGP routers to establish a connection and exchange routing updates.

The *neighbor* command is used to establish a TCP connection:

```
router bgp 1
neighbor 134.201.56.13 remote-as 2
```

```
router bgp 2
neighbor 134.201.56.12 remote-as 1
```

These statements use the TCP/IP address of the directly connected routers for the EBGP connection. Note that EBGP will be used because we are communicating with an external autonomous system.

If we were to make the configuration more difficult, we could add another router called Router3 *within* our AS 1, and create another AS called AS 3, as illustrated in Figure 6.13.

We need to modify the statements on the routers as follows:

```
Router1#
router bgp 1
neighbor 134.201.56.13 remote-as 2
```

```
neighbor 134.201.56.14 remote-as 3
```

```
Router2#
router bgp 2
neighbor 134.201.56.12 remote-as 1

Router4#
router bgp 3
neighbor 134.201.56.12 remote-as 1
```

In the preceding example, Router1, Router2, and Router4 are running EBGP. Router1 and Router3 are running IBGP. The difference between running IBGP and EBGP is that the **remote-as** number is pointing to an external or internal AS.

Notice also that Router1 and Router3 are not directly connected, which is the case for router1 being directly connected to Router2 and Router4. This is acceptable because the router is within your AS. As long as there is some IGP running to connecting the neighboring routers within the same AS, this is acceptable.

Figure 6.13 Example of routing among three autonomous systems.

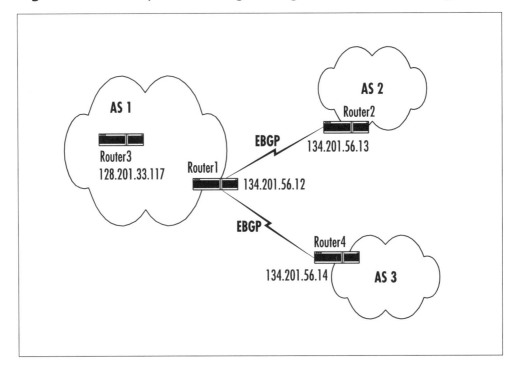

Loopback Interfaces

Another feature of IBGP is the use of loopback interfaces, which eliminate a dependency that occurs when you use the IP address of a router (the physical interface to the route). Figure 6.14 illustrates the use of a loopback interface specified on Router2.

Figure 6.14 Specifying the loopback interface for reliable routing.

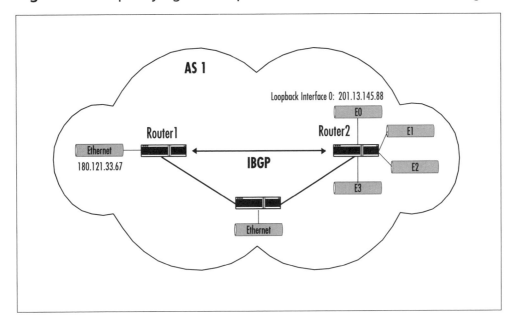

In Figure 6.14, Router1 and Router2 are both running IBGP in AS 1. If Router1 were to communicate with Router2 by specifying the IP address of the Ethernet interface 0, 1, 2, or 3 (as shown in the figure as "E" for Ethernet—E0, E1, E2, and E3), and if the specified interface is not available, a TCP connection was not possible. These two routers could not communicate. To prevent this from happening, Router1 would specify the loopback interface that is defined by Router2. When this loopback interface is used, BGP does not have to rely on the physical interface availability when making TCP connections. The following commands on both of the routers illustrate the use of specifying a loopback interface:

```
Router1#
router bgp 1
neighbor 201.13.145.88 remote-as 1

Router2#
loopback interface 0
IP address 201.13.145.88 255.255.255.0
router bgp 1
neighbor 180.121.33.67 remote-as 1
neighbor 180.121.33.67 update-source loopback 0
```

Router1 will specify the address of the loopback interface (201.13.145.88) of Router2 in the **neighbor remote-as** configuration command. The use of this loopback interface requires that Router2 also includes the **neighbor update-source** router configuration command in its own configuration. When this **neighbor** *<IP address>* **update-source loopback** command is used, the source of the BGP TCP connections for this specified neighbor is the IP address of the loopback interface, and not the IP address of the physical interface.

Summary

In this chapter we discussed the need for routing protocols and the many types of routing protocols available. As networks vary in size and complexity, it is important to implement the correct routing protocol to handle the network requirements. We learned that smaller networks have different needs than larger, more complex networks. With this in mind, a protocol designed for smaller networks cannot address the needs of the larger network, and any attempts to do so will impose restrictions and inhibit growth. This is evident with the Routing Information Protocol (RIP), which is a very popular routing protocol that works beautifully in smaller, less complex networks, but is incapable of performing on a complex network such as the Internet.

We also discussed the threat of IP address exhaustion on the Internet and the concern for large global routing tables with the influx of new networks on the Internet. One of the protocols responsible for addressing these issues is Classless Interdomain Routing (CIDR). CIDR can also implement supernetting to aggregate IP addresses into a large block that global routers can use instead of advertising each individual address.

We also learned that internal networks have different routing needs when maintaining routers inside a specific area. These routers use a routing protocol, such as the distance-vector-based Interior Gateway Routing Protocol (IGRP), to keep an accurate assessment of the network topology. Routers update their routing tables with neighboring routers and assign costs to network links that make one route more efficient than another.

Enhanced Interior Gateway Routing Protocol (EIGRP) has improved on IGRP in many areas, such as convergence, which implements a new algorithm that enables all routers involved in a topology change to synchronize their internal routing tables at the same time.

Routing Information Protocol (RIP) version 2 has also improved on its predecessor, RIP. Although the first version of RIP was limited for large network use, RIP-2 has addressed some of these issues, such as the addition of authentication, support for the subnet mask, and maintaining its small size and ease of implementation.

Open Shortest Path First (OSPF), like RIP, is another Interior Gateway Protocol (IGP). We learned that OSPF is much more robust than RIP, although RIP still is very effective in some implementations. OSPF uses a link-state technology and Shortest Path First algorithm that can determine the most efficient route much better than RIP, because OSPF can also determine the speed of the link. OSPF also makes use of areas, which are used to group hosts into logical groupings, much like a domain. OSPF can route to some of these areas, but will require an Exterior Gateway Protocol (EGP) to communicate with other areas.

Finally, in this chapter we learned how information is routed outside of an area by use of a protocol such as Border Gateway Protocol (BGP). This protocol passes information through the network backbone to the autonomous systems. Communication between Internet Service Providers is done through BGP. Border Gateway Protocol addresses the limitations of EGP, and is the routing protocol of choice when it comes to exterior routing.

FAQs

Q: Do I need to carry a full routing table for the Internet when I am implementing CIDR?

A: You do not have to carry the full routing table if you have a connection to the Internet through only one ISP; you just need to point your default route to your ISP, and inform your ISP that they do not need to send you the full routing table.

Q: When do I not need to implement BGP?

A: When you are singularly-homed, which means you only have one connection to the Internet. You also do not need BGP if you are not providing downstream routing. Use a default route instead.

Q: When do I have to renumber if I am using CIDR?

A: If you move your site from one ISP to another and you have been using an allocated set of addresses from your original ISP's CIDR block, you will have to return those addresses to your ISP.

Q: I am determining whether to configure my new network with RIP or OSPF. Why should I choose one over the other?

A: If you are implementing a new network, you need to examine both protocols to determine the correct protocol for your environment. You should use OSPF if you have a larger, complicated network. RIP works wonderfully for smaller, less complex networks and is still very common in internal networks.

Q: Why would I want to implement CIDR within my network?

A: Because you can create smaller subnets than are available with a standard class C address. You can create subnets with 128, 64, or 32 hosts.

Chapter 7

Automatic Assignment of IP Addresses with BOOTP and DHCP Objectives

Solutions in this chapter:

- Introduction to Automatic Assignment of IP Addresses
- Address Management with These Tools
- Comparing BOOTP and DHCP
- BOOTP and DHCP and Routed Networks
- BOOTP Implementation Checklist
- DHCP Implementation Checklist

Introduction

This section starts with a general overview of dynamic addressing, along with a short history of the development of dynamic addressing protocols.

For IT Professionals

Understanding RFCs

To understand the history, evolution, and current status of networking standards, an IP professional should have an understanding of the Request for Comments (RFC) process, and the particular RFCs involved in defining a particular service or protocol. Copies of the RFCs are available on the Internet in a variety of locations, but one of the most accessible is www.rfc-editor.org/rfc.html. This site provides FTP downloads of individual RFCs, listed in numerical order, as well as the ability to download a compressed file containing all current RFCs.

The RFC process does not provide for revisions of a particular RFC, but rather they are revised by creating a new RFC with a new number. RFCs that are revisions of an earlier RFC will list the RFCs they are replacing. It can be interesting to follow the trail of RFCs back using this information, to see the evolution of the topic over time. For our purposes, the following RFCs provide a wealth of information about the process of dynamic address assignment, specifically BOOTP and DHCP protocols.

RFC951: Bootstrap Protocol (BOOTP)

This RFC was published in September 1985 and outlined the BOOTP protocol.

RFC1542: Clarifications and Extensions for the Bootstrap Protocol

This RFC, published in October 1993, was intended to clarify some issues relating to BOOTP, as well as deal with some new technology issues, such as Token Ring bit-ordering problems. This RFC also replaced an earlier RFC1532, which covered some of the same topics.

Continued

RFC2131: DHCP Protocol

This is a relatively recent RFC, published in March 1997. It supercedes an earlier RFC1541, which was published in 1993. It is a definitive reference for DHCP.

RFC2132: DHCP Options and BOOTP Vendor Extensions

This is also a recent RFC, published in March 1997. It is a compilation of all previous work done in the area of DHCP and BOOTP options. It also refers to several earlier RFCs on the same topic, including RFC1497 and RFC1533.

Most of the RFCs are not as complicated and technical as you might expect, and can make for interesting reading. They often reflect the current state of the technology at the time they were written, and don't always accurately predict the future, looking at them in retrospect. One example is the use of broadcasts for returning a BOOTREPLY message. The RFC writers envisioned this as a stopgap measure, until the protocol stacks could be redesigned to respond to unicasts prior to receiving an IP address assignment. However, a look at modern DHCP servers, such as Windows NT, reveals that they may still rely on the broadcast process to return replies to a client.

So, the next time you hear an RFC number mentioned in connection with a protocol or service, don't hesitate to dial up an FTP site and retrieve a copy of it. It will definitely be informative, may be interesting, and if nothing else, will cure occasional insomnia.

The Role of Dynamic Address Assignment

Over the last two decades we have witnessed a tremendous growth in the size of networks. This growth has occurred in the geographic spread of the network, as well as in the number of nodes per network. Just within the last two decades, the change from a host-based computing model using terminals, to a client/server model with user workstations, has caused an exponential growth in the average number of nodes per network.

These phenomena have driven the need for distributed management tools, where those charged with administering the network can remotely configure and manage network nodes from a central location.

One of these tools is *dynamic address assignment*, a process of using a database as a source of IP addresses and related parameters. The information in this database is provided by a server to clients needing address configuration. These servers match a client with their address records in the database and return the information stored there to the client. The client then sets its IP configuration using the parameter values returned.

Dynamic address assignment provides several benefits to the administrator. It greatly reduces the time spent in configuring clients, since the process occurs automatically across the network rather than having to visit each workstation. Instead, administrators spend their time configuring the database. It can also help prevent configuration problems such as duplicate address assignments or input errors. It may even provide a mechanism for recovering and reusing assigned addresses that are no longer being used.

A key feature of dynamic address assignment concerns the protocols that are used between the requesting client and the server who provides address information. These protocols define the process of obtaining configuration information. They specify the format of the packets used to convey information between client and server, and may define the range of information that can be distributed to the client. The rest of this chapter will focus on these protocols.

A Brief History

It's ironic to note that the original impetus for much of the development of dynamic addressing protocols was not fueled directly by the desire for remote IP address configuration. Rather, it was based on the need to define a protocol that could be used to boot a diskless host across the network. The focus on diskless booting was a product of the times, since during the 1980s, when the original BOOTP

RFC was released, there was a flirtation with the diskless workstation architecture not unlike the current interest in terminal servers and "network computers." Diskless workstations used centralized disk storage, which could reduce the total costs of mass storage during an era when these costs were very high. They also held the promise of greater control over the data, centralized backup and administration, and file sharing.

The central challenge posed by the diskless workstation was how to get it booted, when it had no drives to boot from. The solution involved the use of the network interface card, with a programmable ROM chip that contained enough code to figure out its IP address, locate a server to transfer down a boot file, and then execute the boot file to get the rest of its instructions. To enable this PROM to communicate with the servers providing addresses and boot files, several methods were devised. Early attempts at doing this involved the use of RARP (Reverse Address Resolution Protocol). RARP is a protocol that a client can use to request an address from a RARP server, using its MAC address as its identifier. Unfortunately, RARP was designed to operate directly on top of the data-link layer, and thus does not use network-layer (IP) addresses. It's therefore not routable, and can't be used in subnetted environments.

The BOOTP protocol was defined in RFC951, released in September 1985. It described a protocol that would use a UDP datagram, on top of IP, to exchange address and booting information. The BOOTP packet contained fields for the assigned address, address of the boot file server, and name of the boot file, and also provided a "vendor extensions or options" field, which could convey numerous other parameters. BOOTP also was designed specifically to be capable of operating across a subnetted network, using a *BOOTP Relay agent.*

The DHCP protocol, first defined in RFC1541 in October 1993, was designed to be a refinement and extension of the BOOTP protocol. It used the same packet structure as BOOTP, but made extensive use of the vendor field (now called the options field) to convey DHCP-specific information. Enhancements provided by DHCP included the ability to define ranges of addresses to be given out, rather than having to provide individual entries in a database for each client. It also provided the ability to lease an address for a finite time period, and recover addresses that were no longer being used.

Some of the more recent developments in this area include the tying together of DHCP servers and DNS servers, so that dynamic address assignments can be communicated to the DNS server. The DNS server then updates its host-name-to-address-resolution database with the proper addresses.

Address Management with These Tools

The following section will explain in detail both the BOOTP and DHCP processes, and will offer some comparisons between BOOTP and DHCP.

For Managers

When NOT to Use BOOTP and DHCP?

Having heard about all the wonderful things that BOOTP or DHCP can do, it can be tempting to think of this as an all-purpose solution to the task of IP addressing. However, it is important to remember that BOOTP or DHCP are not appropriate to all addressing situations. In fact, it is very important to know when NOT to use these dynamic addressing tools.

First, these protocols were not designed for configuring router interfaces. DHCP address assignments that use address pools may also be inappropriate for any network node that needs a consistent, predictable address. A particular problem in this area has to do with name-to-address resolution performed by DNS servers. Since most DNS servers do not have a dynamic update capability, allowing DHCP to give out a non-specific address to a node can result in a DNS record that does

Continued

not match the assigned address. This means no one can reach that host by name until the DNS record is updated. There are tools by many vendors that can provide for dynamic updates between DHCP and DNS, thus alleviating this problem.

In a client / server environment, it is often a common practice to use DHCP to address the client workstations, while using manual addressing, or at least a specific address reservation, for the servers.

DHCP servers, in particular, must be statically configured, since they can't issue their own address. Static address assignments must be considered when designing address pools for DHCP, since it is necessary to avoid duplicate address assignments. It frequently makes sense to set aside a contiguous range of addresses for static assignments that can be expressed easily as exclusions within an address pool range. It may also make sense simply to choose a range of the lowest or highest node numbers in a subnet range for static assignments and to define a dynamic address pool range that starts before or after these addresses, as appropriate.

This problem of duplicate IP addresses raises another issue. Because IP addresses have to be unique on the network, it is not possible to have two servers giving out the same range of IP addresses at the same time, unless the servers use some kind of synchronization mechanism. This makes it difficult to provide redundancy for your DHCP server. BOOTP servers are not subject to this issue, since they use a static database that explicitly matches each client with their assigned address.

The problem of redundant DHCP servers can be solved in the following way: Since a DHCP server can handle multiple address pools or *scopes*, two DHCP servers can be configured so that each has a primary scope that includes 75–80 percent of the addresses in their total address range. In addition, each server has a second scope that includes the 20–25 percent of the address range not handled by the primary server. Should one server fail, the other server has an emergency pool of addresses for the other server's address range that it can issue until the primary server comes back on line.

The BOOTP Packet

The BOOTP packet (see Figure 7.1) is a special-purpose UDP datagram, which is carried inside a standard IP datagram, on a variety of data-link frames. The source IP address for this packet will be the client's IP address if the client knows it, or 0.0.0.0 if it doesn't. The destination IP address will be set to the server address if known, or will be the local broadcast address, 255.255.255.255, if the server address is unknown.

The UDP header will contain BOOTP-specific source and destination port numbers. These numbers are 68 for the client, and 67 for the BOOTP server. The client sends requests using 67 (BOOTP server) as the destination port and the server replies using 68 (BOOTP client) as destination port.

Figure 7.1 BOOTP packet structure.

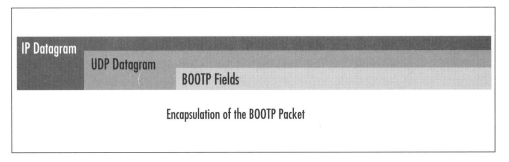

Table 7.1 represents the field definitions within the data field of the UDP datagram that make up the BOOTP packet structure. The fields are ordered according to their position in the table, reading from left to right, one row at a time.

Field Descriptions and Comments

This section explains each one of the field names listed in Table 7.1. It will explain the purpose of the field, as well as the possible values that the field can contain.

Table 7.1 Fields and Field Lengths for the BOOTP Packet

1st Octet	2nd Octet	3rd Octet	4th Octet
OP (1 byte)	HTYPE (1 byte)	HLEN (1 byte)	HOPS (1 byte)
XID (4 bytes)			
SECS (2 bytes)		FLAG (2 bytes)	
CIADDR (4 bytes)			
YIADDR (4 bytes)			
SIADDR (4 bytes)			
GIADDR (4 bytes)			
CHADDR (16 bytes)			Continues for 12 more bytes
SNAME (64 bytes)			Continues for 60 more bytes
FILE (128 bytes)			Continues for 124 more bytes
VEND (64 bytes) or OPTIONS (variable)			Continues for 60 more bytes

OP

This field is set to one of two values as follows:

```
1 = BOOTREQUEST, 2 = BOOTREPLY
```

The BOOTREQUEST op code is set by the client when they wish to request services from the BOOTP Server. The BOOTREPLY op code is set by the server when it replies to a client request. These codes are also used the same way with DHCP.

HTYPE

This is the hardware address type. This field will contain one of the values listed in Table 7.2. The most common values today would be 1 for 10MB Ethernet and 6 for Token Ring.

Table 7.2 Hardware Address Type Codes

Name	Number
Ethernet	1
Ethernet3	2
Ether	1
Ether3	2
Ieee803	6
Tr	6
Token Ring	6
Pronet	4
Chaos	5
Arcnet	7
Ax.25	3

HLEN

This is the length of the hardware address, expressed in bytes. For an Ethernet interface with the standard MAC address of 48 bytes, this field would contain 6.

HOPS

This field is used to indicate the number of routers or gateways through which the BOOTP packet has passed. It is set to zero by the client and then incremented as it passes through a router.

XID

This field is a transaction identifier. It is a random number generated by the client when it sends a BOOTREQUEST message. It will be returned in the server's BOOTREPLY message, so that the client can match its request with the appropriate reply.

SECS

This field is filled in by the client to indicate the elapsed time since it first sent a BOOTREQUEST message. Thus, the first message will have a value of zero in this field, and it will be incremented if the client has to send several requests before it gets a reply. Historically, there has been some inconsistency in the use of this field by different implementations, but it was intended to be used as a means of identifying packets that should be handled on a priority basis by a forwarding agent.

FLAG

In the original definition of the packet structure in RFC951 (September 1985), this field was labeled as unused, and was reserved for future enhancements. By the time that RFC1542 (October 1993) was written, the working group was struggling with the problem of returning boot replies to a requesting client. Since the client would not know his IP address until AFTER receiving the packet, it was often necessary to broadcast the reply back to the client. With this in mind, RFC1542 renamed this field and specified that the highest-order bit would be set by the client to indicate that a BROADCAST reply was required. The rest of the bits were reserved for future use, with a default setting of zero if unused.

CIADDR

This client uses this field to indicate its currently assigned IP address, if the client knows it. If not, it sets this field to 0.0.0.0. Since this protocol was designed for remote booting, BOOTP can be used for bootfile retrieval by a client that already knows its address.

YIADDR

The BOOTP server uses this field to indicate to the client the IP address it is being assigned. In those cases where the server unicasts a reply to the client, this address will be used as the destination.

SIADDR

This IP address is returned by the BOOTP server, which indicates the server that will be accessed to load the boot file used in the second step of the boot process.

GIADDR

Though this field is called the gateway IP address, this is a little misleading, in that it really refers to the address of a BOOTP relay agent. It is used to facilitate the transfer of BOOTP messages between a client and server located on different IP subnets. This agent will be a node on the client's network, and when the agent forwards a BOOTREQUEST, it changes this field from 0.0.0.0 to its own address. Then the BOOTP server can unicast its reply to this address on the client's subnet.

This field has been subject to some misinterpretation, in that it is sometimes confused with a router gateway address for the client. This interpretation has been fueled by the fact that a router can act as a relay agent, in which case the GIADDR may be a router interface. To alleviate this confusion, an option was defined in the VEND (options) field that explicitly defines a router (gateway) address. The client can use this when requesting its boot file, in the second stage of the BOOTP process.

CHADDR

This is the client's hardware address. It is interpreted in conjunction with the HTYPE (hardware address type) field and the HLEN (hardware address length). It is provided by the client in a BOOTRE-QUEST message, and is used by the server to identify the entries in the BOOTP database associated with this client. It was also designed to provide a server with a MAC address for the client, which it could store in its ARP cache to avoid having to use an all-ones broadcast in a BOOTREPLY.

SNAME

The client can use this field to specify a particular server from which it wishes to obtain a boot file. In this case the name would be a domain name that could be resolved using a DNS server or a HOSTS file. If this is left blank, the server will return an address in the SIADDR field that specifies the boot file server address for the client.

FILE

This field is used to indicate the name of the boot file to be downloaded by the client in the second phase of the BOOTP process. The client can use this field to request a particular boot filename, or the server can use this field to identify the boot filename in a BOOTRE-PLY message, based on a client's entry in the BOOTP database.

VEND/OPTION

This field originally was defined as a vendor-extensions field, with a fixed length of 64 bytes. Later, it was defined more generically as an OPTION field, with a variable length. It was intended to convey additional information to the client. Using this field, the client could specify its interest in additional parameters, and the server could supply parameters matching this request, provided that the requested information existed in the BOOTP database. To facilitate the interpretation of this field, the first four octets of the field describe a *magic cookie*, which is a value that identifies the format for the rest of the field. A vendor could use a specific set of octet values to define the field format, or a generic cookie could be used to indicate the standard option format, which will be described later in this chapter. The values used for a standard format are 99.130.83.99 in the first four octets.

BOOTP Process Details

The following section will outline in detail the process between the client and server. It includes a description of the packet contents in each direction.

Client BOOTREQUEST

The client will create a packet with the following settings:

- The IP destination address = 255.255.255.255.
- The IP source address and CIADDR = 0.0.0.0, if unknown, or client's address, if known.
- The UDP header length field is set to the length of the packet in bytes.
- The UDP source port = 68 (BOOTP Client).
- The UDP destination port = 67 (BOOTP Server).
- The OP field is set to 1 (BOOTREQUEST).
- The HTYPE field is set to the hardware address type.
- The HLEN field is set to the length of the hardware address.
- The XID field is set to a random value representing the transaction identifier.
- The SECS field is set to zero if this is the first boot request, otherwise it is set to the time since the first boot request.
- The FLAGS field has the high-order bit set to one if the client can only receive a broadcast BOOTREPLY; all other bits are set to zero.
- The GIADDR will be set to 0.0.0.0.
- The CHADDR is set to the MAC address of the client.
- The SNAME field may be filled in with the name of a server from which the client wishes to boot.
- The FILE field may be filled with the name of the boot file from which the client wishes to boot.
- The VEND field may be filled with a list of optional parameters the client is requesting.

If the client does not receive a reply to a BOOTREQUEST after a certain time period, the client will retransmit the packet with an updated SECS field, showing the elapsed time since the first BOOTP request.

Server BOOTREPLY

When a server receives a BOOTREQUEST message, it will perform the following checks:

- The SNAME field is checked, to see if the client requested a specific server. If it did, and the server does not match the current server, the packet may be forwarded using a BOOTP Relay agent function, and the GIADDR will be updated with the server's address, if it is not already filled in. Alternatively, it may be just discarded, depending on the server.

- The CIADDR field will be checked. If it is zero, the server will check the HTYPE, HLEN, and CHADDR fields and will use them to identify a record for this client in the database. If it finds a record, it puts the client's assigned address in the YIADDR field. If no record is found in the BOOTP server's database, the packet is discarded.

- The server will now check the FILE field. If a filename is specified, the server will check it against its database. If a match is found, the server will put the complete path to the filename in this field. If the filename doesn't match the database, the serve assumes the client is asking for a file this server does not know about, and it drops the packet.

- The VEND field is now checked for any special information or instructions that the client wishes to convey to the server. The list of vendor options will be covered later in this chapter.

The server then creates its reply packet with the following settings:

- The IP destination address = See Table 7.3 to determine the IP destination address.

Table 7.3 outlines the behavior of the server in passing back the BOOTREPLY packet, based on the field contents of the BOOTREQUEST packet from the client.

Table 7.3 Values in Client Fields and Corresponding Addressing Strategy for Server

BOOTREQUEST PACKET			BOOTREPLY PACKET		
CIADDR	GIADDR	Broadcast Flag	UDP Destination	IP Destination	Data-Link Destination
nonzero	0.0.0.0	X	BOOTPC (68)	CIADDR	Client MAC address
0.0.0.0	nonzero	X	BOOTPS (67)	GIADDR	Client MAC address
0.0.0.0	0.0.0.0	0	BOOTPC (68)	YIADDR	CHADDR
0.0.0.0	0.0.0.0	1	BOOTPC (68)	255.255.255 .255	Broadcast

Field Values in the BOOTREPLY packet

The server will create the BOOTREPLY packet with the following field values:

- The IP source address = the address of the server.
- The UDP header length field is set to the length of the packet in bytes.
- The UDP destination port = 68 (BOOTP Client) normally, unless returning to a BOOTP Relay Agent (see Table 7.3).
- The UDP source port = 67 (BOOTP Server).
- The OP field is set to 2 (BOOTREPLY).
- The HTYPE field is unchanged.
- The HLEN field is unchanged.
- The XID field is left unchanged, to match this reply with the client's original request.
- The SECS field is left unchanged.

- The FLAGS field is left unchanged if the broadcast bit is set. If zero, the server may set the BROADCAST flag if it knows the client can only receive broadcasted replies.

- The CIADDR is left unchanged.

- The YIADDR is set to the client's assigned IP address from the server's database.

- THE SIADDR is filled in with the server's own IP address, providing it will handle the next phase of the boot process, which involves serving the boot file.

- The GIADDR is left unchanged.

- The CHADDR is left unchanged.

- The SNAME field is left unchanged.

- The FILE field may be filled with the full path and filename of the boot file for this client, based on the database record.

- The VEND field may be filled with the list of optional parameters from the database record.

When the client receives the BOOTREPLY record from the server, it checks the fields in the packet to ensure that the reply is for it and not some other client. It looks for a match in the CIADDR, CHADDR, and XID fields.

The BOOTP Server Database

RFC 951 includes a section that outlines a suggested format for the BOOTP database. This database was envisioned as a flat text file database composed of two sections, separated by a line beginning with a percent (%) sign.

The first section contains a series of mappings from a generic (short alias) name to a complete path name for a boot file. If the client does not specify a filename, and the database does not contain a different filename for this client, the server will use the first name listed in this section as the boot filename returned.

The second section contains listings for each client, along with their assigned parameters. The client's hardware address type

298 Chapter 7 • Automatic Assignment of IP Addresses with BOOTP and DHCP Objectives

(HTYPE) and hardware address (CHADDR) fields are used as the index to match a record with the requesting client. Besides the hardware address type and the actual hardware address, each record contains the host name, the assigned IP address, and a reference to the generic filename from section one, which maps to a full path to the boot file. It may also include an optional suffix, which will be appended to the bootfile path to indicate a unique file, as in "filename.client1, filename.client2", etc. Comment lines can be indicated by beginning the line with a # symbol.

Following is a generic example of a BOOTP database file, as described in the RFC. There are variations to this file format between different BOOTP servers, but this offers a general idea.

 # Sample Database Format
Section one: generic name to path mappings
    bootfile1   usr\bootfiles\boot
    bootfile2   alt\bin\startup
% Section one ends, Section two begins
    host-one   HTYPE1 CHADDR1 IPaddress1 bootfile1 suffix1
    host-two   HTYPE2 CHADDR2 IPaddress2 bootfile2 suffix2

This server will match the HTYPE and CHADDR of a BOOTP request to a record in the database. For example, if these match the record for host-one, the server will return IPaddress1 to the client. It will also look at the generic name bootfile1 and translate it to the full path name using section one of the database file. It will then append the suffix1 to the filename and return it as the full path name in the FILE field of the BOOTREPLY packet. This full path would be usr\bootfiles\boot.suffix1.

How Does DHCP Work?

This section begins with an overview of the DHCP process. It is followed by a detailed description of the process, which includes explanations of the DHCP message types, as well as DHCP-specific option codes. It will also address the issue of BOOTP and DHCP interoperability, and will conclude with a discussion of DHCP address pools.

DHCP Process Overview

DHCP was designed to be an extension of, and replacement for, the BOOTP protocol. It uses the same packet structure, many of the same processes, and was designed for backward compatibility with BOOTP. It also has the ability to use BOOTP Relay Agents to enable client/server communication across subnet boundaries. It differs from BOOTP in that it provides a number of dynamic addressing methods not supported by the earlier protocol.

DHCP supports three address assignment methods. The first of these is called *manual address assignment*. This is roughly equivalent to the BOOTP process, where an administrator must manually configure entries in a database for each client, and the client then gets these parameters assigned through the BOOTP/DHCP process.

The second and third assignment methods involve the use of a DHCP-specific feature called an *address pool* or *scope*. In these cases, the administrator doesn't build a table correlating each client with a database record. Instead, a pool of addresses is defined. The addresses are handed out on an as-requested basis. There may also be a set of optional parameters defined for this address pool that are returned to each client along with an address. This alleviates the need to configure each client individually, but also makes it somewhat unpredictable which address a given client will receive.

One way addresses can be assigned from the address pool is to provide them to the client for a finite period of time, called a *lease*. This is referred to as *dynamic address assignment*. With a lease, a client is passed a parameter with the address that indicates the maximum time it can hold the address without renewing the lease. Each time the client reboots, it will renew the lease. If it stays booted for a long period of time, it will reach a point called the T1 time, when it will attempt to renew its address from the server it was originally acquired from. If it fails in this attempt, it will reach a second threshold called the T2 time, when it will attempt to renew its address by broadcasting to any available server, just as it did the first time it was assigned an address. The DHCP server keeps track of the addresses it hands out and the lease periods associated with them. If a client fails to renew its lease, the DHCP server will reclaim the address and reuse it with a different client. This feature is particularly useful for environments where addresses are scarce, or where the clients connect to the network on a temporary basis. It may be possible to use a *lease reservation* to reserve a specific address from the pool for a particular client.

The third assignment method, called *automatic address assignment*, uses the address pool, but instead of using a finite lease period, the addresses are simply handed out to the client indefinitely. Since BOOTP clients have no concept of a lease, and no lease renewal capability, this method would allow them to use the address pool feature of DHCP, but not the leasing feature.

One of the challenges for the DHCP server is to ensure that it does not hand out addresses that are already in use. There are a number of mechanisms that help achieve this. First, the server and/or client may perform a check by pinging the network for the address before it hands it out. If it gets a response, it knows the address is in use. For addresses that the DHCP server provides, it keeps a database of what addresses have been assigned to which clients, and their lease periods. Lastly, a DHCP server can specifically exclude from its address pool those addresses, or address ranges, that have been previously assigned to hosts through other means.

Both the DHCP server and the client maintain a persistent record of their address assignments. This means that if the server goes down, it will still remember all of its address assignments when it reboots. The client also maintains a record of its assigned address and other parameters, so that if it restarts it will be able to renew its existing assignments with the DHCP server, rather than looking like a new client. The process of assigning a set of parameters to a client is referred to as *binding*. A client remains bound to its parameters until either its lease period expires, or it relinquishes its assignments with a DHCPRELEASE message.

DHCP Process Details

DHCP uses the BOOTP packet format, with a few modifications, and also makes use of the packet exchange process between client and server. For example, the UDP ports for DHCP and BOOTP are the same. The OP codes used by BOOTP to indicate a client BOOTRE-QUEST and a server BOOTREPLY are also used by DHCP. DHCP differs in the extensive use of the VEND field.

In DHCP, the VEND (vendor extensions) field is renamed the OPTIONS field, and changed from a fixed length of 64 bytes to a variable length field. Each DHCP message will contain a DHCP Message Type option in this field, which identifies the packet's role in the DHCP process. In addition to the message types, DHCP also uses options to pass DHCP-specific parameters such as the lease period, as well as parameters common to DHCP and BOOTP, such as the subnet mask.

Each message sent from a DHCP client will have an OP code of 1 (BOOTREQUEST) and a destination UDP port of 67 (BOOTP Server). It may have different DHCP message types however, depending on whether it is requesting a new address, renewing a lease, or releasing an assignment. Similarly, each server message will have an OP code of 2 (BOOTREPLY) and a UDP port destination of 68 (BOOTP client) unless going through a BOOTP Relay agent.

Each DHCP packet, whether from server or client, will contain information in the OPTIONS field. The first four octets will contain the generic magic cookie, 99.130.83.99, discussed earlier. It will then contain a series of option parameters, of the following form:

TAG (option code)	SIZE	PARAMETER VALUE

Each option takes up one byte for the TAG code, one byte for the size, and then some number of bytes, as stated in the SIZE byte, for PARAMETER VALUE. Each DHCP packet must contain one of the DHCP Message type options, in addition to any other options defined.

Unlike the two-step process used by BOOTP, in which a client makes a BOOTREQUEST and the server responds with a BOOTREPLY, the

DHCP process normally requires four steps for a new client. In this process, the client broadcasts a BOOTREQUEST packet with a DHCP message type, DHCPDISCOVER. This means it is looking for a DHCP server. The server responds with a BOOTREPLY message using the DHCP message type, DHCPOFFER. This means the server is offering a set of parameters to the client. The client will then issue another BOOTREQUEST packet with the DHCP message type, DCHPRE-QUEST. This informs the server that the client accepts the offered parameters. The server then issues a final BOOTREPLY packet containing the DHCPACK message type, indicating an acknowledgement of the client's acceptance. This process is outlined in Figure 7.2.

Figure 7.2 Normal DHCP transaction.

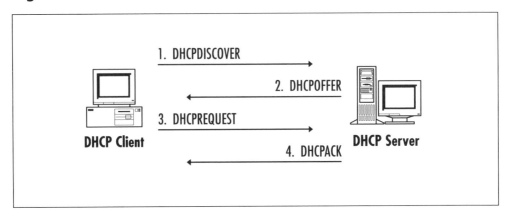

There is a great deal of flexibility, and therefore a great deal of variation, in the DHCP process. For example, a client may request certain parameters in its DHCPDISCOVER or DHCPREQUEST packets. The client may also be doing a lease renewal, rather than an initial discovery, in which case the process will only include a DHCPREQUEST from the client, followed by a DHCPACK from the server.

To preserve backwards compatibility with BOOTP, the server will return the assigned IP address in the YIADDR field of the BOOTP packet. It may also include various configured options in its reply, conveyed within the OPTION (VEND) field of the packet.

One way of discovering the flexibility of the DHCP process is to look at the various DHCP Message Types and their purpose, outlined in Table 7.4.

Table 7.4 DHCP Message Types

DHCP Message Type	Message Name	Explanation
1	DHCPDISCOVER	Client broadcast to locate available servers.
2	DHCPOFFER	Server to client in response to DHCPDISCOVER with offer of configuration parameters.
3	DHCPREQUEST	Client message to servers either (a) requesting offered parameters from one server and implicitly declining offers from all others (b) confirming correctness of previously allocated address after system reboot or (c) extending lease.
4	DHCPDECLINE	Client to server indicating network address is already in use; implies that the client is checking for duplicates.
5	DHCPACK	Server to client with configuration parameters, including committed network address.
6	DHCPNAK	Server-to-client network address is incorrect or client's lease has expired.
7	DHCPRELEASE	Client to server relinquishing network address and canceling remaining lease.
8	DHCPINFORM	Client to server asking only for local configuration parameters. Client already has externally configured network address.

DHCP-Specific Options

In addition to the DHCP Message Type options, there are a number of other DHCP-specific options that convey information useful to the DHCP process. This section lists the option types that can be listed in the VEND/OPTIONS field. In some cases, the option codes are used primarily by the server; in others, they can be used by either the client or the server. The remainder of the options, which are common to both DHCP and BOOTP, will be listed later in this chapter.

Requested Address

Option Code	Length (Bytes)	Parameter Value
50	4	Requested IP address

The client can use this option during a DHCPDISCOVER to request a particular IP address.

Lease Time

Option Code	Length (Bytes)	Parameter Value
51	4	Lease time (secs)

This option is used in a client's DHCPDISCOVER or DHCPRE-QUEST packet to request a specific lease time for an address. It is also used by the server in its DHCPOFFER packet to specify the lease time to the client.

Field Overload

Option Code	Length (Bytes)	Parameter Value
52	1	Field overload (1-3)

This is an interesting field. It is used in those situations where the client and server have defined a maximum packet size, and then have run out of room for options in the OPTIONS field. In this case, it is possible to use the FILE field and/or the SNAME field to hold additional options. This field indicates the intention to use those fields according to Table 7.5.

Table 7.5 Field Overload Codes

Parameter Value	Fields Being Used
1	FILE field
2	SNAME field
3	Both Fields

TFTP Server Name

Option Code	Length (Bytes)	Parameter Value
66	Variable	Alternative TFTP server field

If we have chosen to use the SNAME field to hold additional options, this option can be specified as an alternative way to indicate the server holding the desired boot file for a remote boot.

Bootfile Name

Option Code	Length (Bytes)	Parameter Value
67	Variable	Alternative file field

If we have chosen to use the FILE field to hold options, this option provides an alternative way of conveying the name of the desired boot file.

DHCP Message Type

Option Code	Length (Bytes)	Parameter Value
53	1	DHCP message number (1-8)

This option is used to convey the type of the DHCP message, as described in the preceding section. Table 7.6 outlines the message numbers and associated definitions.

Table 7.6 DHCP Message Option Codes

DHCP Message Number	Message Type
1	DHCPDISCOVER
2	DHCPOFFER
3	DHCPREQUEST
4	DHCPDECLINE
5	DHCPACK
6	DHCPNAK
7	DHCPRELEASE
8	DHCPINFORM

Server Identifier

Option Code	Length (Bytes)	Parameter Value
54	4	DHCP server address

Servers may include this in DHCPOFFER messages and may also include it in DHCPACK and DHCPNAK messages. This allows the client to know what DHCP server provided the offer, and the client will store this information for use when it renews its address with a DHCPREQUEST packet. DHCP clients can also include this in a DHCPREQUEST packet to indicate which offer it is accepting, when it has received offers from more than one DHCP server. This option was designed to allow the DHCP server to identify itself in a reply, while reserving the SIADDR field in the BOOTP packet for the address of the TFTP server serving the boot files for the remote boot process.

Parameter Request List

Option Code	Length (Bytes)	Parameter Value
55	Variable	List of parameters (options codes)

The client can use this option to specify a list of parameters it wishes to obtain from the DHCP server. This list consists of a series of valid option codes, each taking up one byte.

Error Message

Option Code	Length (Bytes)	Parameter Value
56	Variable	Error Message–Used with DHCPNACK or by a client in a DHCPDECLINE

If a server returns a DHCPNACK to a client, indicating that it cannot fulfill the client's request, or the client issues a DHCPDE-CLINE, refusing the offer from a server, this field can be used to convey additional information.

Maximum DHCP Message Size

Option Code	Length (Bytes)	Parameter Value
57	2	Max. DHCP message size

The client used this option, in a DHCPDISCOVERY or DHCPRE-QUEST message, to indicate the maximum message size it is willing to accept.

T1 Renewal Time

Option Code	Length (Bytes)	Parameter Value
58	4	T1 renewal time value (secs)

The server uses this option to define the time at which the client should begin to attempt renewal of its lease. A typical value for this parameter is 50 percent of the lease time.

T2 Rebinding Time

Option Code	Length (Bytes)	Parameter Value
59	4	T2 rebinding time value (secs)

The server uses this option to define the time at which the client should give up trying to renew a lease with the original server and instead, start trying to rebind to a new DHCP server. The default time is 87.5 percent of the lease time.

Vendor Class ID

Option Code	Length (Bytes)	Parameter Value
60	Variable	Vendor class ID

The original BOOTP packet definition provided the VEND field, now called the OPTION field, to convey vendor-specific information. The mechanism for doing this included using the first four octets of the VEND field to denote a vendor-specific magic cookie. If the field was being used generically, it would have the values 99.130.83.99 in these four octets. With the DHCP extension to BOOTP, every packet now uses this generic cookie value. Therefore, another method had to be provided with DHCP, to denote vendor-specific information. This option was designed to fulfill that purpose. A client will include this option in a DHCPDISCOVER message when it wishes to receive vendor-specific parameters. If the DHCP server can't respond to these vendor-specific requests, it ignores them. If it can respond, it returns the vendor-specific parameters in the OPTION field using an option code of 43 along with the requested parameters.

Client Identifier

Option Code	Length (Bytes)	Parameter Value
61	Variable	Client identifier

This option is used by DHCP clients to specify a unique identifier. This identifier will be used by the DHCP server to match a specific database record to a client, in the same fashion as a BOOTP server. This field can use the HTYPE and CHADDR values (hardware address type and the hardware address itself) just like a BOOTP server, or it can use an alternative identifier, such as a system's domain name. The identifier is required to be unique, in order to match the database record and the client properly.

Interoperation between DHCP and BOOTP

Because DHCP was designed to be a replacement for BOOTP, there are often mechanisms built into a DHCP server that preserve the backward compatibility between a BOOTP client and a DHCP server.

A DHCP server provides this compatibility by accommodating both DHCPDISCOVER requests, as well as a BOOTREQUEST from a BOOTP client. The server can distinguish between the two because a DHCP client is required to include a DHCP Message Type option, but a BOOTP client is not.

A DHCP server may maintain both a BOOTP-type database mapping individual clients to a set of specific parameters, and an address pool, with a common set of parameters that are routinely handed out with the addresses. The server may also reserve portions of its address pool for specific clients, and exclude ranges of addresses within the pool that are known to be preassigned. When receiving a client request, the server may check its database to see if a specific record for that client exists. If so, it returns the parameters in the database record. If not, it can assign parameters based on the configuration of its address pool. In this way, a BOOTP client can be assigned an address from a DHCP address pool.

There are some considerations to bear in mind when a BOOTP client gets an address from a DHCP server address pool. First, the client has no concept of leases, so the address must be given out with an infinite lease period. Also, there is no ability for the client to renew an existing lease, so if the client reboots, it will make a new BOOTREQUEST, which will result in it being assigned a new address from the pool. Meanwhile, the DHCP server has stored the client's original address as an infinite lease, and cannot recover it for reuse. The client will also not engage in the DISCOVER-OFFER-REQUEST-ACKNOWEDGEMENT process, so the server must store the address assignment as soon as it sends the BOOTREPLY, rather than waiting for a client request, in response to its offer.

It is also possible that a DHCP client may be able to obtain address information from a BOOTP server. Since the address information in each case is returned in the YIADDR field of the packet, and any options are returned in the OPTIONS/VEND field, there is a high degree of cross-compatibility. A DHCP client in this case would check the OPTIONS field to determine if the BOOTREPLY from the server included a DHCP message type, and if not, it would assume it was talking to a BOOTP server. In cases where both a DHCP and BOOTP server respond, the DHCP client should always choose the DHCP server.

DHCP Address Scopes

In the previous section on BOOTP, we discussed the format of the BOOTP database file. DHCP servers can also provide this functionality, which maps a specific client identifier to a set of parameters recorded in the database for that particular client. In addition, DHCP provides the ability to define a range of addresses, called an *address pool* or *scope*.

An address scope is simply a range of addresses that can be used in response to client requests. There is no one-to-one mapping of clients to parameters, but rather it is a first-come-first-served approach to address assignments. As the server gives out the addresses, it records the client who received the address, and flags the address as having been assigned, so it doesn't use the address again.

In addition to addresses, an address scope may be configured with a set of options that will be returned to each client with their address assignments. These can be defined at a scope level, so that rather than configuring each client record in a database, these parameters are shared with all clients. Typical parameters might be the subnet mask, default gateway, DNS servers, etc.

A DHCP scope has the ability to exclude some addresses within its range, to avoid duplicate assignment of addresses already in use by statically configured hosts, or those getting addresses via some other means.

A DHCP server can also maintain multiple scopes, with each scope and its associated options being defined for a given subnet. Through the use of BOOTP Relay agents, a DHCP server may service clients on multiple subnets. It can use the GIADDR field in the BOOTREQUEST packet to determine which subnet the request is coming from, and will respond with information from the appropriate scope for that subnet.

To reduce the randomness of the address assignments from the address pool, an address within the pool may be set aside for a specific host through a *reservation* process. This allows us to predict which address will be assigned to that client, while preserving its ability to obtain common parameters from the scope-defined options.

Comparing BOOTP and DHCP

Both BOOTP and DHCP use a server to provide automatic IP address configuration to clients. They also use the same packet format, which was designed originally for BOOTP and adopted later, with modifications, for DHCP. Both protocols provide the means to issue an IP address to a client. They also provide a way to indicate a server and filename on that server, which can be downloaded and used to boot the client. They both also include the ability to convey other configuration parameters as well, such as the gateway address, or the address of DNS servers.

DHCP and BOOTP can both use databases that are indexed using a client identifier such as the hardware address. By matching this client identifier to a record in the database, the server can locate the information requested by the client, and transmit it back in a reply message. Both DHCP and BOOTP can make use of BOOTP Relay Agents, which allow a client and server on different subnets to exchange BOOTREQUEST and BOOTREPLY messages.

DHCP protocol is an extension of the BOOTP protocol and is intended to be a replacement for that earlier protocol. DHCP makes extensive use of the VEND field (later called the OPTIONS field) in the original BOOTP packet to convey additional information between the client and server. In addition to BOOTP's ability to transmit addresses and information based on one-to-one entries in a database, DHCP can also assign addresses based on a stated range of addresses, sometimes called the *address pool* or *scope*. It also differs from BOOTP in that BOOTP assigns addresses permanently, whereas DHCP can be configured to lease addresses for a finite period of time. It will recover these addresses and reuse them if the client does not renew its lease on the address.

How BOOTP Works

The following section will provide an overview of the BOOTP process. This will be followed by a detailed description of the BOOTP packet structure. We will then take a more detailed look at the client and server processes that occur during a BOOTP exchange. Lastly, we will look at an example of a BOOTP database file.

BOOTP Process Overview

The BOOTP process consists of two phases. The first phase is the address and parameter acquisition phase, which is the focus of our interest. The second phase involves accessing a file server, typically a TFTP server, and downloading a file that can be used to boot the client. The BOOTP client functionality was designed to reside on a PROM that is generally located on the client's network interface card.

Both the client and the server communicate using a standard packet format, which is referred to as a BOOTP packet. A client makes a BOOTREQUEST and the server responds with a BOOTREPLY.

A client may use packet fields to indicate pieces of information it already knows, such as its IP address, or the boot filename it wishes to retrieve, or it may leave those fields blank when it wants to learn the values from the server.

The BOOTP process also provides for a forwarding function, to be performed by a BOOTP Relay Agent. This agent is a node on the same subnet as a client, which is configured to pass request and reply messages between clients and servers when they reside on different subnets.

DHCP / BOOTP Options

The last field in the original BOOTP packet specification was a field called the VEND field, used to convey information called vendor extensions. Later RFCs modified not only the name of this field, changing it to OPTIONS, but also changed it from a 64-byte fixed length to a variable length. Similarly, the information conveyed in these fields were renamed simply, options.

Each option has been through a review process by the IANA (Internet Assigned Number Authority) and has a code, sometimes called a *tag*, assigned by them. New options can be proposed by requesting a new tag code and then submitting a description of the option for approval.

Each option is expressed as a series of bytes that use up space in the BOOTP packet's VEND/OPTION field. The format of each option is as follows:

First Byte	Second Byte	Succeeding Bytes
Tag or Option Code	Length of data portion	Data portion

All the options originally defined as BOOTP vendor-extensions have been incorporated as options by DHCP. In addition, there are a series of DHCP-specific options that are not recognized by BOOTP. These options were discussed in the previous section dealing with the DHCP process, and will not be repeated here. For the sake of organization, these will be grouped into sections that share a similar function.

Due to the number of options available, it is not possible to explain the function of each one. Some will be familiar, whereas some others may be extremely obscure, having become obsolete, or else intended for specific environments that existed at the time the option was formulated. They are listed here for the sake of completeness.

BOOTP Options from RFC1497

The source used for the following options list is RFC2132, published in March of 1997, which incorporated option information from a number of earlier RFCs, including RFCs1497 and 1533. This first section includes those options defined in RFC1497. The organization of the rest of this section will also follow the format of RFC2132, since it presents the option codes roughly in ascending numerical order.

Pad

Option Code	Length (Bytes)	Parameter Value
0	1	Align on word boundaries (no data)

This option is used as a filler to extend the option fields to 32-bit word boundaries or to pad out the VEND field after an END option.

End

Option Code	Length (Bytes)	Parameter Value
255	1	End of data in field (no data)

This code indicates the end of information in the vendor/option field.

Subnet Mask

Option Code	Length (Bytes)	Parameter Value
1	4	Client subnet mask

This code specifies the client's subnet mask.

Time Offset

Option Code	Length (Bytes)	Parameter Value
2	4	Time offset from GMT

This code can be used to define the client's time zone relative to Greenwich Mean Time.

Router List

Option Code	Length (Bytes)	Parameter Value
3	Multiples of 4	List of router addresses

This specifies a list of routers available to the client, listed in order of preference.

Time Server List

Option Code	Length (Bytes)	Parameter Value
4	Multiples of 4	List of time server addresses

This specifies a list of time servers available to the client, in order of preference.

Name Server List

Option Code	Length (Bytes)	Parameter Value
5	Multiples of 4	List of name server addresses

This specifies a list of IEN 116 Name Servers available to the client, in order of preference.

DNS Server List

Option Code	Length (Bytes)	Parameter Value
6	Multiples of 4	List of DNS server addresses

This specifies a list of DNS Servers available to the client, in order of preference.

Log Server List

Option Code	Length (Bytes)	Parameter Value
7	Multiples of 4	List of log server addresses

This specifies a list of MIT-LCS UDP log servers available to the client, in order of preference.

Cookie Server List

Option Code	Length (Bytes)	Parameter Value
8	Multiples of 4	List of cookie server addresses

This specifies a list of RFC865-compliant cookie servers available to the client, in order of preference.

LPR Server List

Option Code	Length (Bytes)	Parameter Value
9	Multiples of 4	List of LPR server addresses

This specifies a list of Line Printer Remote (LPR) Servers available to the client, in order of preference.

Impress Server List

Option Code	Length (Bytes)	Parameter Value
10	Multiples of 4	List of impress server addresses

This specifies a list of Imagen Impress servers available to the client, in order of preference.

Resource Location Server List

Option Code	Length (Bytes)	Parameter Value
11	Multiples of 4	List of resource location servers

This specifies a list of RFC887 Resource Location servers available to the client, in order of preference.

Host Name

Option Code	Length (Bytes)	Parameter Value
12	Variable	Host name of client

This option specifies client's name, which may or may not include the domain name.

Boot File Size

Option Code	Length (Bytes)	Parameter Value
13	2	Boot file length (512KB blocks)

This option specifies the size of the client's default boot file.

Merit Dump File

Option Code	Length (Bytes)	Parameter Value
14	Variable	Merit dump file name

This option is used to define the path and filename for the file to be used as a core dump repository, if the client should crash.

Domain Name

Option Code	Length (Bytes)	Parameter Value
15	Variable	Client's Internet domain name

This option lists the DNS domain name that the client should use.

Swap Server

Option Code	Length (Bytes)	Parameter Value
16	4	Swap server's IP address

This option lists the address of the client's swap server.

Root Path

Option Code	Length (Bytes)	Parameter Value
17	Variable	Pathname to client's root disk

This option is used to define a path designated as the root drive for this client.

Extensions Path

Option Code	Length (Bytes)	Parameter Value
18	Variable	File name of extensions file

This option can be used to define the filename of a file that can be used as an extension to the VEND/OPTIONS field. It uses exactly the same format for listing options, and is designed to be retrieved using TFTP.

IP Layer Parameters per Host

Options in the following section are concerned with IP network-layer parameters, as they relate to the host globally, rather than to a particular interface configuration.

IP Forwarding Enable/Disable

Option Code	Length (Bytes)	Parameter Value
19	1	IP forwarding (enable=1)

This option specifies whether the client should configure its IP layer for packet forwarding. A value of 0 means disable IP forwarding, and a value of 1 means enable IP forwarding.

Nonlocal Source Routing Enable/Disable

Option Code	Length (Bytes)	Parameter Value
20	4	Source route forwarding (enable=1)

This option configures the client behavior in regard to whether or not it will forward packets with source-routing information.

Policy Filter Option

Option Code	Length (Bytes)	Parameter Value
21	Multiples of 8	Allowed source routing destination IP address/mask pairs

This option contains a list of IP address and mask pairs used to specify a list of source-routing next-hop addresses used for filtering. Any source-routed datagram whose next-hop address does not match one of the filters should be discarded by the client.

Maximum Datagram Reassembly Size

Option Code	Length (Bytes)	Parameter Value
22	2	Maximum datagram reassembly size in bytes

This option is used to define a maximum allowable size for the reassembly of an IP datagram that has been fragmented during transmission across the network.

Default IP Time-to-Live

Option Code	Length (Bytes)	Parameter Value
23	1	Default IP TTL (1-255)

The value of this option will be used as the default value for TTL in the IP header of outbound datagrams.

Path MTU Aging Timeout Option

Option Code	Length (Bytes)	Parameter Value
24	4	MTU aging timeout (secs)

The MTU (Maximum Transmission Unit) is the maximum packet size allowed on a given network segment. It is periodically tested using a polling mechanism called Path MTU Discovery. This option can set the polling interval.

Path MTU Plateau Table

Option Code	Length (Bytes)	Parameter Value
25	Multiples of 2	List of MTU sizes to check

The Path MTU Discovery process works by cycling through a set of potential MTU values, to find the maximum suitable value. This option contains a list of MTU sizes, arranged from smallest to largest, that this polling process can try.

IP Layer Parameters per Interface

Options in this section are intended to apply to a particular interface on a client. If multiple interfaces need to be configured, the client should issue individual requests for each interface.

Interface MTU Option

Option Code	Length (Bytes)	Parameter Value
26	2	MTU value for interface (bytes)

This option assigns an MTU value for a specific interface.

All Subnets Are Local Option

Option Code	Length (Bytes)	Parameter Value
27	1	All subnet MTUs are the same (1=yes)

This option tells the client whether or not all subnets the client is connected to share the same MTU value. A value of zero indicates that some subnets may have smaller MTUs.

Broadcast Address

Option Code	Length (Bytes)	Parameter Value
28	4	Subnet broadcast address

This option specifies the address used for subnet broadcasts on the interface subnet.

Perform Mask Discovery

Option Code	Length (Bytes)	Parameter Value
29	1	Enable subnet mask discovery (1=yes)

This option determines whether or not the client will perform ICMP mask discovery.

Mask Supplier

Option Code	Length (Bytes)	Parameter Value
30	1	Respond to subnet mask ICMP request (1=yes)

The ICMP mask discovery process relies on a host to respond to the mask requests. This option enables the host to reply to mask discovery requests.

Perform Router Discovery

Option Code	Length (Bytes)	Parameter Value
31	1	Perform router discovery (yes=1)

This option determines whether or not the client should perform router discovery (RFC1236).

Router Solicitation Address

Option Code	Length (Bytes)	Parameter Value
32	4	Address of server for router discovery requests

This option provides the address of the node servicing router discovery requests.

Static Route List

Option Code	Length (Bytes)	Parameter Value
33	Multiples of 8	Static routes listing destination address, next-hop router address

This option provides a list of static routes. Each entry includes the destination network and the next-hop router address for that destination.

Link Layer Parameters per Interface

Options in this section apply to a particular interface, and contain parameters related to the data-link layer.

Trailer Encapsulation

Option Code	Length (Bytes)	Parameter Value
34	1	Use trailers with ARP (yes=1)

This option determines whether or not the client will negotiate the use of trailers with the ARP protocol as specified in RFC 893.

ARP Cache Timeout

Option Code	Length (Bytes)	Parameter Value
35	4	Timeout value for ARP cache entries (secs)

This option specifies a maximum age for ARP cache entries.

Ethernet Encapsulation

Option Code	Length (Bytes)	Parameter Value
36	1	Encapsulation type (Ethernet II=0, 802.3=1)

This option is used to specify the Ethernet encapsulation type. Valid values are Ethernet II or 802.3 Ethernet.

TCP Parameters

This section contains per-interface parameters dealing with TCP.

TCP Default TTL

Option Code	Length (Bytes)	Parameter Value
37	1	TCP default TTL (1-255)

Outbound TCP packets will have the value defined in this option entered into the IP-level TTL field.

TCP Keepalive Interval

Option Code	Length (Bytes)	Parameter Value
38	4	Keepalive interval (secs)

This option defines an interval between keepalive messages on the TCP connection. A value of 0 disables periodic keepalive messages.

TCP Keepalive Garbage

Option Code	Length (Bytes)	Parameter Value
39	1	Send garbage octet (yes=1)

This option is used to preserve compatibility, without older TCP implementations that require an octet of random characters as part of the keepalive message.

Application and Service Parameters

Options in this section deal with miscellaneous parameters related to services or applications.

Network Information Service Domain

Option Code	Length (Bytes)	Parameter Value
40	Variable	Name of client's NIS domain

This option specifies the client's Network Information Service (NIS) Domain.

Network Information Server List

Option Code	Length (Bytes)	Parameter Value
41	Multiples of 4	List of NIS server addresses

This option specifies a list of NIS server addresses available to the client, in order of preference.

Network Time Protocol Server List

Option Code	Length (Bytes)	Parameter Value
42	Multiples of 4	List of NTP server addresses

This option specifies a list of Network Time Protocol (NTP) server addresses available to the client, in order of preference.

Vendor-Specific Information

Option Code	Length (Bytes)	Parameter Value
43	Variable	Vendor-specific information

This option is used in conjunction with option code 60, The Vendor Class Identifier, to pass vendor-specific parameters. These parameters will use the same Tag-Length-Parameter arrangement as a standard option code.

NetBIOS over TCP/IP Name Server List

Option Code	Length (Bytes)	Parameter Value
44	Multiples of 4	List of NBNS server addresses

This option contains a list of NetBIOS name servers that can perform NetBIOS name-to-address translation for the client.

NetBIOS over TCP/IP Datagram Distribution Server List

Option Code	Length (Bytes)	Parameter Value
45	Multiples of 4	List of NBDD server addresses

This option specifies a list of NBDD server addresses available to the client, in order of preference.

NetBIOS over TCP/IP Node Type

Option Code	Length (Bytes)	Parameter Value
46	1	NetBIOS Node type code

This option defines the NBT Node type of the client. This node type defines what methods the client will use to do NetBIOS name resolution. The values and meanings are listed in Table 7.7.

Table 7.7 NetBIOS over TCP/IP Node Type Codes

Hex Value	Node Type	Behavior
0x1	B-node	Broadcast
0x2	P-node	Use name server
0x4	M-node	Broadcast, then use name server
0x8	H-node	Use name server, then broadcast

NetBIOS over TCP/IP Scope

Option Code	Length (Bytes)	Parameter Value
47	Variable	NetBIOS scope name

This option defines the client as a member of a NetBIOS scope.

X Window System Font Server List

Option Code	Length (Bytes)	Parameter Value
48	Multiples of 4	List of X Windows Font server addresses

This option specifies a list of X-Windows Font server addresses available to the client, in order of preference.

X Window System Display Manager List

Option Code	Length (Bytes)	Parameter Value
49	Multiples of 4	Address list of systems running X Windows Display Manager

This option specifies a list of systems available to the client that are running the X Window System Display Manager.

Network Information Service+ Domain

Option Code	Length (Bytes)	Parameter Value
64	Variable	Name of client's NIS+ domain

This option lists the client's NIS +(Network Information Service Plus) domain.

Network Information Service+ Servers List

Option Code	Length (Bytes)	Parameter Value
65	Multiples of 4	List of NIS+ server addresses

This option provides a list of the NIS+ Servers available to the client, in order of preference.

Mobile IP Home Agent

Option Code	Length (Bytes)	Parameter Value
68	Multiples of 4, usually 4 or 0	List of Mobile IP Home Agent addresses

This option provides a list of the Mobile IP Home Agents available to the client, in order of preference. Usually there is either one of these, or none.

Simple Mail Transport Protocol (SMTP) Server List

Option Code	Length (Bytes)	Parameter Value
69	Multiples of 4	List of SMTP server addresses

This option provides a list of the SMTP Mail Servers available to the client, listed in order of preference.

Post Office Protocol (POP3) Server List

Option Code	Length (Bytes)	Parameter Value
70	Multiples of 4	List of POP3 server addresses

This option provides a list of the POP3 Mail Servers available to the client, in order of preference.

Network News Transport Protocol (NNTP) Server List

Option Code	Length (Bytes)	Parameter Value
71	Multiples of 4	List of NNTP server addresses

This option provides a list of the NNTP News Servers available to the client, in order of preference.

Default World Wide Web (WWW) Server List

Option Code	Length (Bytes)	Parameter Value
72	Multiples of 4	List of WWW server addresses

This option provides a list of the Web Servers available to the client, in order of preference.

Default Finger Server List

Option Code	Length (Bytes)	Parameter Value
73	Multiples of 4	List of Finger server addresses

This option provides a list of the Finger Servers available to the client, in order of preference.

Default Internet Relay Chat (IRC) Server List

Option Code	Length (Bytes)	Parameter Value
74	Multiples of 4	List of Finger server addresses

This option provides a list of the IRC Chat Servers available to the client, in order of preference.

StreetTalk Server List

Option Code	Length (Bytes)	Parameter Value
75	Multiples of 4	List of StreetTalk server addresses

This option provides a list of the StreetTalk Servers available to the client, in order of preference.

StreetTalk Directory Assistance (STDA) Server List

Option Code	Length (Bytes)	Parameter Value
76	Multiples of 4	List of STDA server addresses

This option provides a list of the STDA Servers available to the client, listed in order of preference.

RFC2132 completes this list with the DHCP-specific option codes that were covered in the DHCP section of the chapter, and then a section on how to propose new option codes.

BOOTP, DHCP, and Routed Networks

From the first definitions of the BOOTP protocol, a mechanism was specified that could allow a BOOTP client and server on different subnets to exchange BOOTP information. This mechanism was first called a BOOTP Forwarding Agent, but the name was later changed to avoid confusion with a router that provides routine packet forwarding. It's now referred to as a BOOTP Relay Agent.

Since DHCP was designed to be an extension of BOOTP, it was also designed to use BOOTP Relay Agents. From the standpoint of the agent, it does not care if the packet is a standard BOOTP pack-et, or a BOOTP packet with DHCP Message type options in the VEND/OPTIONS field. Either way, the process is the same.

The BOOTP Relay Agent

When a BOOTP client issues a BOOTREQUEST packet, typically it does not know the address of the BOOTP server that is going to reply. It therefore sends this packet out as a local broadcast with a destination address of 255.255.255.255. Since local broadcasts are not forwarded between subnets by a router, this message will never reach the server if it is not on the same subnet as the client. To allow this packet to be forwarded, a BOOTP Relay Agent must exist on the same subnet with the client. The Relay Agent recognizes that this broadcast is a BOOTREQUEST based on the destination UDP port number of 67, which is the BOOTP Server port. The agent will then forward this packet as a unicast, with the destination set to the IP address of the BOOTP Server. It knows what address(es) to use in forwarding these packets because the addresses are part of the agent configuration. It will also receive a BOOTREPLY unicast message back from the server, and then send it back to the client on the local subnet, typically as a local broadcast.

The definition of the BOOTP Relay agent did not specify whether this function should be incorporated into a router (gateway) or whether it could be another host on the same subnet as the client. Either implementation is acceptable since the main requirements are that:

- The Agent has to be a node on the same subnet as the client.
- It has to recognize and forward the client request as a unicast message to the server.
- It has to accept unicast messages back from the server that it then resends out on its local subnet to the requesting client.

In spite of the fact that either a host or a router could perform the relay agent function, it was suggested in several RFC discussions that a router provided a logical place to implement this functionality. Therefore, it is common to hear references to an RFC1542-compliant router, which implies BOOTP Relay Agent's capability in the router (see Figure 7.3). Although it was a valid point, it contributed to the confusion between forwarding agents and relay agents, and also contributed to a related confusion in the meaning of the GIADDR field in the BOOTP packet.

Figure 7.3 The BOOTP Relay Agent Process

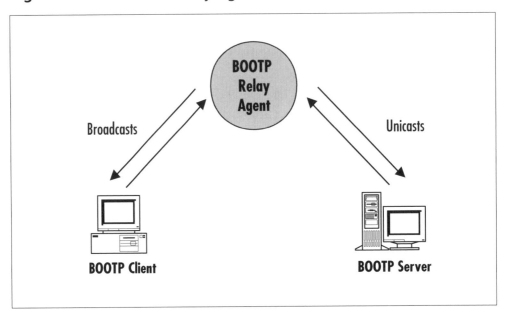

The Role of the GIADDR

The GIADDR field in the BOOTP packet plays a significant role in the functioning of BOOTP and DHCP across a routed network. We have learned that the GIADDR is set to 0.0.0.0 by the client when it transmits a BOOTREQUEST. If the BOOTP/DHCP server gets a BOOTREQUEST with the GIADDR set to all zeros, it knows the client is on the local subnet, and will respond directly to it, using UDP destination port 68 (BOOTP Client).

If the server is not local to the client, a BOOTP Relay Agent must exist on the client's subnet to forward the packet. If this is the case, the agent will examine the GIADDR field of the request, and if the field is all zeroes, it will place its own address in this field. This provides a unicast return address for the server to use in returning its BOOTREPLY message to the client's subnet. If the GIADDR is not zero, the agent assumes the existing value represents a node on the client's home subnet, and does not modify it.

When a BOOTP/DHCP server receives a BOOTREQUEST packet with a nonzero GIADDR, it recognizes that the packet was forwarded from a BOOTP Relay Agent. In this case it modifies its response in the BOOTREPLY packet, sending it to the GIADDR as the destination address, and sending it to port 67 (BOOTP Server) instead of port 68 (BOOTP Client). This is necessary because the agent only responds to the server port number, whether the message is a client request or a server response.

Another use of the GIADDR is DHCP-specific: The DHCP server uses the address listed in the GIADDR field to ascertain the client's subnet. Using this information, the server can determine which scope of addresses, if it has multiple address scopes, to use in responding back to the client.

Other Fields Involved

In addition to the GIADDR field, there are a number of other fields in the BOOTP packet that may be modified by the BOOTP Relay agent, outlined here.

HOPS

The HOPS field in a BOOTREQUEST from a client is initially set to zero. Each time the request packet crosses another router boundary, this field should be incremented by one. There is some ambiguity in the RFCs as to whether this should happen only if the agent is a router, or if the agent should do this regardless of role. It seems more appropriate to a router, since a properly configured relay agent and server will directly unicast between themselves, without the need for any intermediary agents.

The HOPS field was also intended to tell how far away a client was from a server, allowing a threshold to be set beyond which the packet will no longer be forwarded.

CHADDR, YIADDR, HTYPE, HLEN, FLAG

These fields all have a role to play in helping the server and agent determine how they should send back a BOOTREPLY to the client. A previous section of this chapter outlined the various options the BOOTP Server might use to reply to the client based on whether the client can accept unicasts or broadcasts. Since the BOOTP Relay Agent is acting on behalf of the BOOTP server, it will do the same evaluation of these fields to determine the appropriate method, unicast or broadcast, to return a reply to the client.

SECS

This field allows the client to communicate how long it has been trying to boot. If the client is forced to retransmit its BOOTREQUEST, this value will be nonzero, and can be used to initiate priority handling on the part of the agent and/or the server.

UDP Port Number

Normally, the client always uses UDP port 67 (BOOTP Server) as a destination port, and the server uses UDP port 68 (BOOTP Client) as its destination port in a BOOTREPLY. However, a BOOTP Relay agent responds only to packets with the UDP port set to 67. This means if the server is sending a BOOTREPLY message back through a relay agent, it must address this BOOTREPLY message to the agent's address (GIADDR) with a UDP destination port of 67 rather than 68. The relay agent will change the destination UDP port number to 68 before it forwards the packet back to the client.

IP TTL Field

A relay agent either will set the TTL field in the IP Datagram header to a configured default value, or it will take the existing value it received, and decrement it by one. This seems to be another specification in the RFC that is more suitable to a router-based relay agent, rather than some other host performing a relay function.

ALL Other Fields

All other fields in the BOOTP packet should be passed between server and client without any modification.

BOOTP Implementation Checklist

Use the following list as a rough guideline to the steps you should take in implementing BOOTP Servers:

1. First determine if you really need to use BOOTP. If you are implementing dynamic addressing it is very possible that DHCP would be a better choice, since DHCP server implementations can often accommodate older BOOTP clients, as well as DHCP clients.

2. Determine the range of addresses you will be issuing, as well as any BOOTP options that you wish to convey along with the address assignment.

3. Gather a list of the hardware addresses and address types for each of the BOOTP clients.

4. Determine if you will be using the remote boot features of BOOTP, or just the address assignment phase. If you are doing remote booting, prepare the appropriate boot files and determine the directory paths for these files.

5. Create the BOOTP database file, using all the information you have gathered.

6. Install and configure the BOOTP server.

7. Configure the clients to act as BOOTP clients.

8. Test the functionality of the BOOTP server.

9. Consider the needs for cross-subnet communication between clients and servers, and configure and test BOOTP Relay agents where appropriate.

DHCP Implementation Checklist

Use the following list as a rough guideline to the steps you should take in implementing DHCP Servers:

1. Determine the range of clients that will use DHCP. Also determine which hosts on the network will have static or reserved address assignments. Consider whether any BOOTP clients exist, and the strategy that will be used by DHCP to assign their addresses.

2. If necessary, configure a BOOTP database file for use by the DHCP server in servicing BOOTP clients. Ensure that any addresses included in this file are not part of any DHCP address pool.

3. Determine the range of addresses that will constitute the address pool. If the DHCP server will service multiple subnets, determine the appropriate address scopes for each subnet and the associated parameter options that you may wish to convey along with the address.

4. Install and configure the DHCP server or servers based on the address ranges, exclusions, reserved addresses, and options that will be associated with each address scope. Also decide on and configure an appropriate lease duration for the addresses.

5. If multiple servers are used, consider partitioning each address pool between two servers, to enhance reliability by providing some redundancy.

6. If clients and servers need to communicate across subnet boundaries, configure BOOTP Relay Agents in appropriate locations.

7. Configure clients to use DHCP.

8. Test the functionality of the DHCP server and Relay Agents.

Summary

In this chapter we discussed the dynamic assignment of IP addresses using the BOOTP and DHCP protocols. We covered the reasons for, and the history behind, the development of these protocols and learned in detail how they work.

BOOTP and DHCP are closely related protocols. Both make use of a specially defined packet that uses a UDP datagram addressed to specific UDP ports, namely port 68 (BOOTP client) and port 67 (BOOTP server). This packet has a payload consisting of fields that allow it to convey address assignments and other parameters, as well as the information a client may need to affect a remote boot across the network. Clients initiate this process with a BOOTREQUEST packet to a server, and the server responds with a BOOTREPLY packet. The BOOTP packet contains a Vendor extensions or Options field that is used to pass additional parameters to the client. BOOTP issues address assignments and other parameters based on a flat-file database that matches a client identifier, usually its hardware address, with the set of parameters listed for that client. Configuration of this file is a manual administrative task.

DHCP was designed to be an extension of BOOTP. It uses the same packet definition, same UDP ports, and the same BOOTREQUEST and BOOTREPLY messages, but it relies very heavily on the Vendor extensions field, which is now called simply the Options field. Each DHCP message uses a DHCP message type option code, to define a part of the DHCP process, as well as other option codes to pass DHCP-specific, as well as generic client configuration parameters.

DHCP provides more options in terms of address assignments. It can hand out addresses from a BOOTP-like database file, or it can hand addresses out on a first-come, first-served basis from an established address pool, sometimes called a scope. DHCP configuration can be much simpler than BOOTP, since it is not necessary to match each client manually to an individual address assignment. An address scope can be defined with a set of parameters, such as mask, default gateway, default DNS servers, etc., that can be distributed to all DHCP clients in that scope. DHCP can also accommodate multiple scopes for different subnets, each with its own set of parameter options.

Unlike BOOTP, DHCP can also be configured to assign addresses for a finite time period, called a lease. DHCP clients are required to renew their lease on an address periodically, or it will be reclaimed by the server once the lease period expires, and will be reassigned to a new client. This is a very useful feature when clients connect temporarily to a network, or where there is a shortage of IP addresses available. DHCP servers maintain a database of all the addresses they have assigned, to whom they were assigned, and how long the lease period is. This prevents the server from handing out duplicate addresses.

To accommodate client requests that cross subnet boundaries, the BOOTP specification includes the definition of a BOOTP Relay agent, which listens for client requests on its local subnet, and forwards them as unicast messages across router boundaries to the server. It performs the reverse function for the server as well. Both BOOTP and DHCP can make use of BOOTP Relay agents.

FAQs

Q: How do I know if my host can be a DHCP or BOOTP client?

A: The ability to act as a DHCP or BOOTP client is built into the IP protocol stack being used by the client. The protocol stack should include the ability to configure itself for dynamic address assignment, in addition to the usual manual configuration. Whether the client uses BOOTP or DHCP is often a function of how old the protocol stack is. Most newer protocol stacks will be configured to use DHCP, since it was designed to replace BOOTP. The documentation provided with the protocol stack should indicate what dynamic addressing capabilities are supported.

Q: When would I use BOOTP instead of DHCP?

A: In most cases it is better to use DHCP instead of BOOTP, if the clients support it. This is because DHCP will do everything that BOOTP will do and more. The configuration process with BOOTP is entirely manual, and can be a formidable task for a large network. By contrast, DHCP can be relatively easy to configure, even for large networks, since you only need to define an address range and a common set of parameters for each address pool to service a large number of clients.

Q: What is an RFC 1542-compliant router?

A: This term is often found in documentation dealing with the implementation of DHCP and BOOTP. It refers to the definition of a BOOTP Relay Agent and the functions of that agent. Simply put, an RFC 1542-compliant router is one that can be configured to act as a BOOTP Relay Agent. Remember that the relay agent does not have to be a router, but can be implemented on a host system that resides on the same subnet as the clients.

Q: If I configure multiple scopes on a DHCP server, how does the server know which scope to use for a given client?

A: The way that a DHCP server decides on which scope is to be used for a given client depends on the subnet to which the client is connected. This subnet information comes to the server by means of the GIADDR field in the BOOTP packet. This field is empty when a client is on the same subnet as the server, and contains the address of the BOOTP Relay Agent otherwise. This agent address is on the same subnet as the client, so the server can read this address to determine the client's connected subnet.

Q: How does DNS work with DHCP?

A: The short answer is, "Not very well." The problem is that unless each client is assigned a specific address reservation, it is not possible, until after the fact, to determine which IP address was assigned to a client. Since traditional DNS server implementations use a statically-configured database, this can pose some problems. There are several workarounds to this. There are products commercially available that will link DHCP servers and DNS servers, so that when an address assignment is made, the DNS server database is updated. In Microsoft environments, this problem has been handled using a WINS (Windows Internet Name Service) server. WINS clients register themselves dynamically with the WINS server after they have received a DHCP address assignment. The name resolution process checks both DNS and WINS servers to obtain a name resolution. As long as the same name is being used for the NetBIOS name and the Internet host name, this process will result in a name-to-address translation for either name type.

Chapter 8

Multicast Addressing

IP Multicast is an excellent example of using IP addresses for special purposes. In fact, apart from the rich IPv6 addressing structure, multicast is probably the most special use of addresses in the IP technology.

Solutions in this chapter:

- **What is multicast?**

- **Multicast addresses**

- **IP stacks**

- **Why use multicast?**

What Is Multicast?

Multicast is a technology used to address multiple hosts as a group. A host multicasts to a group of hosts by sending an IP packet to a special IP address that identifies the group. An IP address is used to designate a group of hosts. The IP address that defines a multicast group is in the range of 224.0.0.0 to 239.255.255.255, defined as Class D addresses. Each group has its specific IP address in that range, so many groups can be defined at the same time by using a different IP address.

The membership in a group is dynamic because hosts can join and leave the group as they want. The multicast standard is described in RFC1112.

Multicast is similar to broadcast since only one packet is sent to all hosts, whereas unicast means that one packet is sent to one host. However, multicast differs from broadcast because broadcasting involves sending a packet to all hosts, without exception, on the specified network, whereas multicast sends a packet to the group of hosts. Those hosts that are not part of the group will not process the multicast packet since it is not addressed to them.

One typical example of multicasting is to listen to a videoconference using a 2 Mbits/sec channel on a network. Not all users of a network may want to listen to the videoconference, so the idea is to join the group, or the videoconference in this case. Furthermore, if 10 users of the same physical network want to listen to this videoconference, then using unicast technology means using 2Mbits/sec * 10 users = 20 Mbits/sec sustained for those users. More users means more bandwidth used. By using multicast, only one channel of 2Mbits/sec is used, independently of the number of users: even 1000 users will still use only 2Mbits/sec.

Multicast Saves Bandwidth

One advantage of IP multicast is a very important saving in bandwidth for protocols that are "broadcast-type" by nature, like videoconferences.

Multicast traffic is bidirectional: a host can receive or send multicast packets.

Mapping IP Multicast to the Link Layer

Like any other IP packets, IP multicast packets have to be mapped to the link layer addresses. Multicast has been defined for the link layers of Ethernet, Token Ring, and others, like ATM. On Ethernet, the low-order 23 bits of the IP multicast address is placed in the lower part of the Ethernet multicast address 01-00-5E-00-00-00. RFC1469 describes multicast over Token Ring and RFC2022 describes ATM networks.

Joining the Group

To join a multicast group either by a user who wants to listen to a multimedia channel or by a specific application, it is actually very simple: the kernel has to be configured to process the IP multicast address of the group or channel. Then, all packets with an IP destination address as the group IP multicast address will be processed by the host and sent to the upper layer applications.

But, if the multicast channel comes from far away (meaning that it comes from another network), it is possible that this channel is not currently multicasted on the local network of the host. In this case, the host will have to tell its neighbor router that it wants to listen to this multicast channel. This is done using the Internet Group Management Protocol (IGMP), documented in RFC2236. Then this router will try to get that channel from its source and send the multicast packets of that channel to the local network. This entire process involves routing multicast over the larger network.

IGMP

When a host joins a multicast group, it sends a report to the all-hosts group (224.0.0.1) on its local network. Routers can then learn who is joining which group. When a host is leaving a multicast group, it sends a report to the all-routers group (224.0.0.2) on its local network.

Routers also send queries periodically to an all-hosts group address to request reports of group membership to all hosts on each multicast network to which it connects. In this way, a multicast router knows the membership of all groups for all multicast hosts.

RFC2236 describes in detail all the state diagrams and transitions of IGMP for hosts and routers.

Multicast Routing Protocols

Since multicast needs special processing for routers, the IETF defines multicast routing protocols to help routers control the routing of those multicast channels over the networks. The first one was Distance Vector Multicast Routing Protocol (DVMRP), which has been used a lot; however, the RFC (RFC1075) now has experimental status, which means that its implementation is not recommended. This multicast routing protocol was based on the Routing Information Protocol (RIP), and inherits its simplicity. Other protocols have been developed for multicast routing, like the Protocol Independent Multicast (PIM) protocol and Multicast extensions to OSPF (MOSPF).

Within the IETF, there has been work on enhancing the multicast routing and other related issues, mostly under the mboned, idmr, pim, and malloc working groups.

Stay Up to Date on Multicast Routing

Although multicast routing is not too difficult, it has undergone many revisions in the multicast routing protocols at the IETF. If you want to deploy multicast in your organization network, you should get the latest information on the best current practices.

Mbone

It is often really important to test standards on a real network with real users. The Mbone (Multicast backbone) is an initiative of volunteers who test multicast technology over the Internet. It is still used frequently during multicast events and to test new protocols or applications.

Because not all the ISPs support multicast natively in their infrastructure and routers, the Mbone was created by using a mix of tunnels and native multicast links.

Practical Experience of Multicast

If you want to understand and learn about multicast networks, you should connect to the Mbone. It is an easy way to try this great technology. Although you will probably find that Mbone is not as stable as a production network, it serves its original purpose: to experiment this technology in real world, in order to send feedback to the IETF engineers and developers.

Multicast Addresses

Multicast addresses are in the 224.0.0.0 to 239.255.255.255 range, or in binary have the four high-order bits as 1110. This is defined as Class D addresses. Class E addresses, which cover the 240.0.0.0 to 255.255.255.255 range, have been reserved for future addressing modes.

Transient and Permanent Addresses

Two types of multicast addresses can be defined: the permanent and the transient. The permanent addresses are defined in the protocol itself, as the all-hosts and all-routers described in the next section. Permanent addresses can also be assigned by the IANA for other protocols or other uses.

Transient addresses are used for some period of time. For example, a transient address will be used to multicast a videoconference of an event. After the event is finished, the transient address can be reused. In this way, there should be coordination of transient addresses used to be sure that two people or organizations will not use the same transient address for different needs. Back in the old days of the Mbone, you either preannounce it on a specific Mbone channel or on a Web page. Currently, IETF working groups are defining a more protocol-based approach.

Generic Assignments

In the protocol definition, some addresses have already been reserved. The address 224.0.0.0 is reserved and guaranteed not to be assigned to any group. The address 224.0.0.1 is assigned to all IP hosts on the directly connected network. In other words, it is a link-local address. Any hosts, including routers, printers and the like, are members of this group. So as soon as an IP device is configured for multicast, it is automatically and statically a member of this group. The address 224.0.0.2 is assigned to all IP routers on the directly connected network. Only routers are members of this group.

IANA Assignments

RFC1112 didn't define permanent addresses other than the all-hosts address. But the task of assigning permanent multicast addresses has been done by the Internet Assigned Numbers Authority (IANA).

IANA assigns addresses in the 224.0.0.0 to 224.0.0.255 range "for the use of routing protocols and other low-level topology discovery or maintenance protocols, such as gateway discovery and group membership reporting. Multicast routers should not forward any multicast datagram with destination addresses in this range, regardless of its TTL." For example, in that range, multicast addresses have been assigned for the use of some protocols:

```
224.0.0.4  DVMRP    Routers
224.0.0.5  OSPFIGP  OSPFIGP All Routers
224.0.0.6  OSPFIGP  OSPFIGP Designated Routers
224.0.0.9  RIP2 Routers
224.0.0.12 DHCP Server / Relay Agent
224.0.0.13 All PIM Routers
224.0.0.18 VRRP
224.0.0.22 IGMP
```

In the 224.0.1.0+ range, multicast addresses are defined for protocols but can be forwarded by routers like:

```
224.0.1.1  NTP      Network Time Protocol
224.0.1.3  Rwhod
SUN NIS+   Information Service
224.0.1.22 SVRLOC Service Location Protocol
224.0.1.75 SIP Session Initiation Protocol
```

Or, addresses are assigned to "permanent" conferencing, like the IETF events:

```
224.0.1.10 IETF-1-LOW-AUDIO
224.0.1.11 IETF-1-AUDIO
224.0.1.12 IETF-1-VIDEO
```

```
224.0.1.13 IETF-2-LOW-AUDIO
224.0.1.14 IETF-2-AUDIO
224.0.1.15 IETF-2-VIDEO
```

For IPv6, the first assignments are defined in RFC2375. Others are handled by IANA. The current list of assignments is available at: ftp://ftp.iana.org/in-notes/iana/assignments/multicast-addresses.

Scope of Multicast Addresses Using TTL

When holding an internal videoconference inside the company, we would like to ensure that this conference will not be received or seen on the Internet or outside the company. Even within the company network, we also might want to restrict the conference to one subnet.

Scoping has been realized by using the TTL field in the IP header. By using TTL = 1, this tells any IP router not to forward this packet to another network, since each router must decrease by 1 the TTL field, and if the TTL = 0, then the packet should not be forwarded. TTL was there to detect routing loops, as described in previous chapters.

In multicast, scoping of multicast addresses was based on the TTL value of the IP packet, and so is controlled by the source host. By defining specific thresholds and by configuring appropriately the multicast routers, Mbone people were able to scope many but not all of the situations.

Scoping using the TTL works has some limitations, because it is based on the number of routers in the network topology, not on the administrative boundaries. Also it conflicts with some routing functions, like pruning.

Administrative Scopes

A new scoping approach based on special multicast addresses in the range 239.0.0.0 to 239.255.255.255 has been defined in RFC2365. It is based on an administrative scope instead of a network topology scope. So the network manager can configure the administrative scope as needed, without taking care of the network topology.

The following scopes are defined:

- The IPv4 Local Scope, defined as 239.255.0.0/16, is for any local multicast channels. The locality is site-dependent, but we can define local scope to have one site in a city by configuring its site boundary routers not to forward local scope multicast packets.

- The IPv4 Organization Local Scope, defined as 239.192.0.0/14, is for an organization scope that can include many sites.

- Link-local scope, defined as 224.0.0.0/24.

- The global scope (meaning the full Internet) is defined as 224.0.1.0-238.255.255.255.

For Managers

Managing Multicast with Administrative Scopes

By using administrative scopes, it is much easier to manage multicast routing, so it enables organizations to deploy multi-cast with the control they need.

IP Stacks and Multicast

Most current IP stacks support multicast, either installed by default or configured to do so. It is not easy to find whether the kernel of a computer supports multicast. The basic way is to find if the host has the all-hosts address (224.0.0.1) configured, since, by definition, if a host is multicast-enabled, this address is configured. Another (harder) way is to send an all-hosts (224.0.0.1) packet on the local network and have a network sniffer see who responds to it. Another way is to use commands that show the 224.0.0.1 address. On Unix and NT, using netstat –rn can show a route to the multicast group

224.0.0.1. Figure 8.1 shows an example of a netstat command on a Sun Solaris 2.6 computer.

Figure 8.1 Netstat command on Solaris.

```
Sun Microsystems Inc.   SunOS 5.6       Generic August 1997
host1% netstat -rn


Routing Table:
   Destination       Gateway          Flags   Ref   Use    Interface
------------------ ---------------- ------ ----- ----- ----------
198.202.48.128     198.202.48.134    U       3     9310   hme0
224.0.0.0          198.202.48.134    U       3     0      hme0
default            198.202.48.131    UG      0     153900
127.0.0.1          127.0.0.1         UH      0     0      lo0
```

The second line in the routing table shows that 224.0.0.0 network is available, which means that multicast is enabled on that computer.

Why Multicast?

The first and most well-known use of multicast is to save bandwidth when casting a videoconference to a number of users. But multicast can do more.

Efficiency of Bandwidth Usage and Scaling

As discussed in this chapter, multicast has been used since the beginning to save bandwidth, especially for any content that is for many users, for example, audio and video. Other examples are net-news sent to many servers and software upgrades for a whole network sent to all hosts. All these examples save bandwidth by sending only one copy of the content whatever the number of clients, instead of one copy per client in the standard unicast way.

Discovering

Many discussions on IP are related to making it easier and autoconfigurable, and enabling devices to discover "automatically" servers, services, and the like. Examples of this are wireless and small devices that do not have permanent memory, and have to discover where they are, who they are, and which services are available. Another example is the famous "dentist office," meaning that IP should be able to be more plug-and-play, so a dentist can deploy an IP network of many devices without a network administrator. Although IPv6 helps a lot in this and is the key technology for that purpose, multicast is very interesting, because hosts that need to discover things can multicast their request on specific channels in order to get more information from listening servers. This is actually being implemented in the Service Location Protocol (SLP), described in RFC2608. IPv6 uses multicast to get this autoconfiguration working. Even more, IPv6 uses multicast for renumbering a whole network, when the organization changes its ISP and needs to renumber. In comparison, in IPv4, renumbering is a complex and very difficult task. Chapters 9 and 10 cover IPv6.

Efficient Channel

Without multicast, the only way to send a packet to computers that have the same characteristics (like running a specific protocol) or are routers, was either to know the addresses of them, which is a very difficult task when the number is important, or to use broadcast. If broadcasts were used for all those purposes, then all computers would have to process those packets, even if the packet is not for them. Not only that, but broadcast is limited to the link-local, where multicast can be used over multiple networks. So multicast is an easy way to send information to unknown parties that share the same characteristics without disturbing others.

Industry

The history of multicast shows that industry was not very support-ive. But now, an industry consortium has been formed on IP multi-cast by Stardust Inc. This will help multicast to be used and deployed, and to deliver products to the market. Information is available at http://www.ipmulticast.com. They provide very good information on everything related to IP multicast and also organize events and meetings. Excellent technical white papers and refer-ences are available at this site.

Summary

Multicast is a great technology that enables a group of computers sharing a multicast address to communicate together. The IP addresses used in multicast are from 224.0.0.0 to 239.255.255.255, defined as Class D addresses. Class E addresses are reserved for future addressing needs. With IGMP and multicast routing proto-cols, a network with subnets as well as the Internet by the Mbone, can be configured to use and forward multicast packets. Hosts can report they are joining or leaving a group using IGMP.

Although a few addresses, like 224.0.0.1 as all-hosts and 224.0.0.2 as all-routers, on the local network are defined in the pro-tocol, IANA is the authority that assigns other multicast addresses.

Scoping is an important issue of multicast. The traditional way uses the TTL IP header field to manage the scope, but it has some limitations depending on the need. A new range of multicast addresses have been assigned and defined as Local Scope and Organizational Local Scope to help organizations manage the scope of the multicast traffic.

Multicast can be used for effective bandwidth usage, discovery, and efficient channels. IPv6 uses multicast in its core functions and industry is supporting it. You are invited to join the Mbone if you wants to learn by practice.

FAQ

Q: Where can I find information about IP multicast support in industry?

A: IP Multicast Initiative: http://www.ipmulticast.com/.

Q: Which IP multicast addresses have been allocated?

A: Allocation of IP multicast addresses is done by IANA (http://www.iana.org). The current list of assignments can be found at ftp://ftp.iana.org/in-notes/iana/assignments/multicast-addresses.

Q: Who is working on multicast protocols and standards?

A: Many IETF working groups are working on multicast. Please refer to the IETF working group pages to get the most current work (http://www.ietf.org).

References

[RFC1075] "Distance Vector Multicast Routing Protocol." D. Waitzman, C. Partridge, S.E. Deering. Nov-01-1988. (Status: Experimental)

[RFC1112] "Host Extensions for IP Multicasting." S.E. Deering. Aug-01-1989. Obsoletes RFC0988, RFC1054; updated by RFC2236 and STD0005. (Status: Standard)

[RFC1469] "IP Multicast over Token-Ring Local Area Networks." T. Pusater. June, 1993. (Status: Proposed Standard)

[RFC2022] "Support for Multicast over UNI 3.0/3.1 based ATM Networks." G. Armitage. November, 1996. (Status: Proposed Standard)

[RFC2236] "Internet Group Management Protocol, version 2." W. Fenner. November, 1997. Updates RFC1112. (Status: Proposed Standard)

[RFC2608] "Service Location Protocol, version 2." E. Guttman, C. Perkins, J. Veizades, M. Day. June, 1999. Updates RFC2165. (Status: Proposed Standard)

Chapter 9

IPv6 Addressing

Solutions in this chapter:

- IPv6 Addressing Basics
- IPv6 Addressing Scheme Characteristics
- IPv6 Benefits
- The Need for Further Development

Introduction

First, in order to understand how IP version 6 (IPv6) can solve some of the current and future problems encountered with IP version 4 (IPv4), we must understand the motivation for its inception. This chapter will give a short introduction to the history and development of the IPv6 protocol, through its current accepted form.

Second, we will look at some of the key aspects of IPv6 that separate the protocol from IPv4, and look into the benefits that we can gain by utilizing IPv6 and its addressing schemas to build a more scalable network. From there, we can begin to build real-world examples of how this addressing can be deployed in Internet-connected networks to come.

Finally, we will look into some of IPv6's outstanding issues and its addressing schemes, and some of the proposed solutions to cope with these yet unsolved issues. Also in this section, we will give a brief introduction to the IPv6 test network, the 6Bone.

IPv6 Addressing Basics

By the early 1990s, it was clear that the Internet was going to take off. The average person was becoming aware of its existence, and the killer-apps of today (Web browsers) were coming into their own. This dramatic increase in usage of the Internet, which stemmed from outside the research community, was clearly not going to go away. Address space delegations increased at an alarming rate, and it was clear that the Internet Protocol version 4 had a foreseeable upper limit in terms of the number of entities it could connect to the ever-increasing worldwide Internet. The Internet Engineering Task Force (IETF), the standards group from which a large portion of Internet technologies emerge, was beginning to see this as an issue that needed to be tackled earlier rather than later. At present, for example, regional numbering authorities (such as ARIN, RIPE, APNIC, etc.) are delegating numbers from within the 216/8 network block. In 1996, by contrast, ARIN was only delegating in the 208/8 range. This would mean that just over 150 million hosts were added to the Internet in this three-year span (if delegations and address assignments were made efficiently). We calculate this by raising 2 to the power of 24 (for each /8) and multiplying by 9.

Although the Internet *is* growing at an alarming rate, and slowly working its way into our day-to-day lives, it is clear that 150 million hosts were not added. There was a major problem with address allocation, even after the efforts of CIDR (Classless Inter-Domain Routing) were implemented. Address space was being wasted. Furthermore, we know that 224/8–239/8 is set aside for multicast, and that 240/8–255/8 is reserved. From this, we can see that we are nearing our end (although some of the addresses in the middle, from 64/8–128/8, are just now being delegated, so it will buy a little more time than expected).

Now we see that not only was there not enough space to take us far beyond the millennium, but also much of the currently delegated address space was being wasted. Additionally, a greater need for enhanced Network-Layer (Layer 3 on the OSI stack) features was beginning to emerge, for example, end-to-end encryption, authentication of packets, source-routing, and Quality of Service. For all of these reasons, it was becoming apparent that a new Internet Protocol, or IP, was going to have to be conceived and adopted for the future of the Internet. This is where the fun began.

As people began to see these factors as a reality, many proposals for a new Internet Protocol emerged. The first draft that gained widespread notice was loosely based on the CLNP (Connection-Less Network Protocol), which was based upon another protocol suite, the OSI stack. This stack originally ran on the early Internet, but was quickly replaced by IPv4 when the Internet began to take on size and popularity. The proposal was coined TUBA (TCP/UDP over Bigger Addresses). CLNP does provide for a much larger address range than the current IPv4. Its Network Service Access Point (NSAP) address consisted of 20 octets, and would provide adequate addressing ranges for the Internet's foreseeable future. However, this proposal was rejected because CLNP lacked some of the value-added features that were already installed into the current IP (Quality of Service, multicast, etc.), and these were determined to be important to the Internet's future growth.

There was a proposal that attempted to create a packet format compatible with current IP, CLNP, and IPX. Yet another proposal, known as SIPP (Simple IP Plus), simply advocated increasing the current IP addressing format to 64 bits, and fine-tuning some of the feature sets of IPv4, as well as establishing better routing strategies. SIPP turned out to be the closest match for what the Internet needed, after some modifications. The addressing range was changed from 64 to 128 bits, and the name was changed to IP version 6, or IPv6 (IPv5 was already delegated to another protocol). This would be the protocol to solve the Internet scalability problems, and put us into the next millennium (and the foreseeable future).

In this chapter, we will learn more about the specifics of IPv6. We will begin by looking at IPv6 addressing schemes, and discuss how they can improve routing stability and efficiency. Then we will look at how the protocol design will aid in numbering and renumbering networks. Finally, we will discuss some of the value-added services that come with IPv6, and how they can benefit both residential users and big businesses on the Internet. We will also go into some details about the 6Bone, the IPv6 proving ground, where deployment and transition strategies are developed and tested.

IPv6 Addressing Scheme Characteristics

Now that we have looked at some of the history of IPv6, as well as some of proposals that competed with IPv6 as the new Internet standard, let us take a look at some of the generic characteristics of IP version 6. A full discussion of IPv6 can be found at www.ietf.org/rfc/rfc2460.txt. Figure 9.1 is the IPv6 packet header, taken from this RFC.

Figure 9.1 IPv6 header format.

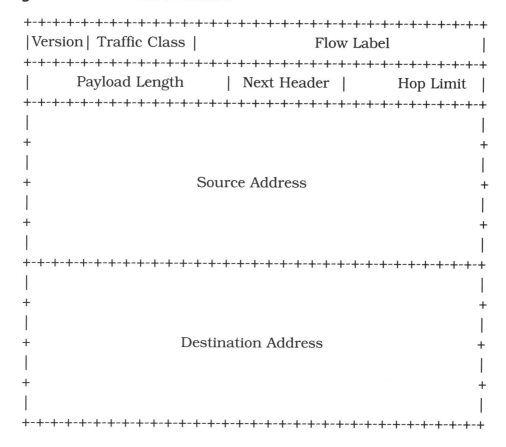

Let's look at these fields in a little detail (the next chapter will provide a more intense study of the specifics of the IPv6 protocol).

Version

The version field in the IPv6 header is present so that Internet mechanisms that know how to route, or even speak routing protocols, will know what type of routing protocol they are about to deal with. Notice the similarities to IPv4. In the case of IPv6, the version field is a 4-bit integer, with the value of 6 (0110 in binary), to designate this packet as an IP version 6 packet.

Traffic Class

The Traffic Class field is an 8-bit field in which some sort of traffic differentiation identifier can be placed. Currently, in the IETF, many working groups are dedicated to coming up with the best way to utilize this type of differentiation mechanism (though they mostly concentrate on IPv4 today). One example of such a group is the DiffServ (Differentiated Services). The members of DiffServ are trying to come up with a way to give more important traffic a higher priority for routing on the Internet today. This field was designed for things such as IP Precedence bits (giving certain values of this field higher priority, and then using differentiated queuing strategies in the router to tell "who goes first"). You can learn more about DiffServ on the Web at www.ietf.org/html.charters/diffserv-charter.html. A number of drafts and RFCs have been written with ideas as to how to implement such a policy. The list of current open drafts (they are only good for six months after writing, at which time they need to be resubmitted, just to keep things current) and RFCs is at the bottom of the aforementioned URL.

Flow Label

This is a 20-bit field used when special handling of a packet is needed. Common interpretation of this field at the time of this writing is that the field will assign flow labels in order to engineer different traffic patterns in an IPv6 network. The major player in this (though for mostly IPv4 at this time) is the MPLS (Multi-Protocol

Label Switching) working group. To see the group's charter, please see www.ietf.org/html.charters/mpls-charter.html. This group's main intention is to come up with an efficient way to assign labels to flows, and to come up with an efficient and scalable way to route based on these flows. A flow can be defined as any class of traffic going from one point to anther, whether point-to-point traffic, or a TCP flow from one end-station at a given port to a destination end-station at a given port. The possibility of assigning flows opens up many interesting options for deployment. Perhaps Quality of Service (quite a buzzword in the field today!) can be deployed with scalability this way. Many Internet providers are keeping their eyes wide open as this working group develops, since advanced services that the MPLS working group sees as feasible could lead to ground-breaking new developments in the Internet industry as a whole.

Payload Length

This 16-bit integer is used to designate the length of the payload (the data) in the IPv6 packet, in octets. Notice this field is 16 bits long (2 raised to the power 16), which gives us over 64,000 different possibilities, allowing IPv6 to have fairly big packets (over 64,000 octets). To have the ability to make big packets can increase the efficiency of the Internet as a whole. When your packets are bigger, the number of packets needed to send a given amount of data becomes smaller for a given flow. When there are fewer packets to route, then a router has more time to route other packets, or perform other tasks (routing table maintenance, cache aging, etc.). You can see how this can help to increase Internet efficiency altogether. Note that any extension headers (see later) outside of this header are included in the total packet length in this case. Compare this with the IPv4 case (RFC791) where the total length field *includes* the IPv4 main header.

Next Header

This field is designated to tell routers if there are any other headers that need be looked at for the packet to route according to instruction. This differs drastically with the IPv4 case, where there is only one header with a fixed length. The IPv6 main header is fixed length as well (allowing routers to know beforehand how much of the packet they need to read), but has built-in functionality to stack other headers that provide other value-added services, on top of the main header. This field is 8 bits in length, allowing for up to 255 types of next-headers. Currently, only a finite amount of next-headers are developed. Here is a list of the ones currently on the plate:

1. Hop-by-Hop Options Header
2. Destination Options Header I
3. Routing Header
4. Fragment Header
5. Authentication Header
6. Encapsulating Security Payload Header
7. Destination Options Header II

The preceding list shows the selection of Next Header fields that can occur in an IPv6 packet. These headers are listed in order of the appearance they would make in an IPv6 packet utilizing this extra functionality. All of these headers will be discussed in detail in the next chapter, but for now, we can give a brief explanation of each one, and why they are in a particular order.

Hop-by-Hop Options Header

This header designates properties that are to be examined by each IPv6 speaking node in the path.

Destination Options Header I

This header is reserved for options to be performed by the destination concerning handling of the packet. Notice this header is the first of two with the same name. In the case of IPv6 packets, with the Hop-by-Hop header in use, the destination can be the next hop on the router. This is the motivation for putting the Destination Options header right behind the Hop-by-Hop header. For a full description of this header and its options, read on, and see RFC2460, the protocol specification.

Routing Header

The routing header designates a list of intermediate nodes that a packet must traverse prior to arrival at the final packet destination. This is analogous to the functionality in IPv4 known as Loose Source Route and Record. This allows you to designate, at the very least, a set of routing devices that a packet must travel through on the way to its destination.

For IT Professionals

How Much of IPv6 to Enable

As an Internet Backbone engineer, you can see that this may not be something that Service Providers would want to enable on their networks. Think of the ramifications: Suddenly, the way that you design your network can become irrelevant! Customers can now pick and choose their path through the network. This can lead to very difficult build-out strategies. Although this may have benefits for organizations savvy enough to route around congested areas, I believe there are other considerations to look at prior to deploying this on a live Backbone.

Fragment Header

This header is used by the source to send packets that are bigger than the defined Maximum Transmission Unit, or MTU of the path. Normally, in IPv4, intermediate nodes may fragment packets in order to fit the standards of given media that the packet may traverse. Each media, be it Ethernet, FDDI, or other, is designed with a specific MTU in mind for optimal performance of the given media. In contrast, IPv6 does not allow for fragmentation of a packet at an intermediate point through the path. Instead, the IPv6 speaking device will undergo MTU Discovery. In this, IPv6 will use ICMPv6 (Internet Control and Message Protocol version 6) to send packets hop-by-hop through the path from source to destination, each time reporting the MTU for that particular link between hops. The lowest value for MTU is used as the maximum size packet that the source will send (again, this can increase routing stability and efficiency, since routing entities now don't have to spend time and CPU fragmenting packets, but can concentrate on simply routing them). This header is used when the source wants or needs to send a bigger packet than the largest MTU that was discovered.

Authentication Header

This header is used if the need for end-to-end authentication exists. It contains a method of authentication so that a destination can be sure that a given packet is, in fact, from the source that it says it is. Please note the order of this header in the line. We allow for the preceding headers to come first for good reasons. For instance, if a source and destination are using complex authentication, but we still want to utilize the Hop-by-Hop header, no authentication information needs to be read or tampered with along the path. Think of the extra CPU time if all routers had to authenticate packets prior to routing them! We can still use the Hop-by-Hop or Destination Options I (the hop-by-hop destination) without having to check or tamper with the authentication.

Encrypted Security Payload Header

Now that we have methods to ensure that packets come from the source that they say they do, we need some way to ensure that no one can read the payload of the packet along the way. The Encrypted Security Payload (ESP) header allows for encryption of both the data in the packet, and all headers behind it, in order to ensure security of the data in the packet. Details of this header can be found later in the next chapter, or in the RFC archives. The combination of this header and the Authentication header makes up IPSec (IP Security). This is currently being implemented with IPv4, but since it is not inherent in the protocol, the IETF is challenged to make this work in a way that is not severely performance-enhancing. This is one of the benefits of IPv6: It is already built into the protocol, so minimal per-formance hits are required to enable this functionality.

Destination Options Header II

This is similar to the Destination Options header I, except this header is designated for options destined for the final destination only. Note that the ESP and Authentication headers come prior to this header in order. This will allow secure Options to be passed without worrying about someone learning something valuable about the destination while the packet is in transit across the Internet.

So as we can see, the next header field is of vast importance to security and value-added services associated with IPv6. Also of note, Service Providers may not always have their Backbones listen to certain next headers, as they can cause routing inefficiency. Notice the VPN solutions that can result from the Authentication and ESP headers alone. Does this mean that Internet data will now be secure? At the time of this writing, it definitely looks like a good attempt at data security over the Internet. Ramifications of IPv6 deployment with full functionality could include the collapse of the "Intranet" ("secure" Internet), which uses physically separate back-haul facilities in order to prevent data or machines from getting attacked or stolen by mean Internet users.

Hop Limit

This is similar in function to the TTL field in IPv4. It specifies the number of Layer 3 (Network Layer) hops that a given packet can traverse before a routing system will discard the packet. Having a limit such as this is of vital importance. If a routing loop occurs on the Internet, as they sometimes do even today, packets have the potential to circle around and around to infinity. If a user gets tired of waiting, and sends more packets, you can see how quickly this can bring certain areas where a loop exists to its knees. To fix this, the TTL field is used in IPv4. This originally was meant as a Time To Live (in seconds) parameter, by which a packet will be discarded if it exists on a network for a specified amount of time. It was quickly determined that this was not the best approach, so the concept of Hop Limit came into being. Every time a router receives a packet, the TTL field is decreased by 1. When a packet is received with a TTL of zero, the packet is discarded. This helps to ensure that packets do not exist forever on the Internet, taking up valuable CPU cycles and bandwidth. In IPv6, the Hop Limit field is 8 bits long, giving a maximum of 255 routed hops between source and destination. Although we would be extremely dissatisfied if we had to traverse even 100 hops from a source to a destination today, this field is given a high available maximum value to ensure that future routing requirements are met. Who knows how many hops your home refrigerator will be from your office?

Source Address

This is the IPv6 address of the machine that originates the packet. This is discussed in detail later in the section.

Destination Address

This is the 128-bit IPv6 address of the destination for the packet (note that based on the Next Header field discussed earlier, this can be the final destination, or an intermediary destination, depending on which next headers are used).

More Bits!

Internet Protocol version 6 was developed to rescue the Internet from current problems discussed in the Introduction section of this chapter. First and foremost of these problems is the address scalability problem that the Internet faces today. The current Internet Protocol address field, being only 32 bits in length (see IPv4 Figure 9.2), can be shown to have scaling problems given current Internet growth. It is becoming clear that the number of Internet-connected entities will only increase as time passes. Eventually, everyone will be connected, and given population expansion alone, we can see scaling problems already (a 32-bit address field provided for roughly 4.2 billion addresses). When you take into account other devices that either already are, or may be, connected to the Internet in years to come (phones, television, routers, radios, diagnostic equipment, Web servers, refrigerators!), we can see this problem only getting worse. If you then factor in the legacy problems with IP wasting (owning more IP addresses than you have assigned to Internet entities), it is clear that another solution is needed.

Figure 9.2 IPv4 packet header format.

```
 0 1 2 3 4 5 6 7 8 9 0 1 2 3 4 5 6 7 8 9 0 1 2 3 4 5 6 7 8 9 0 1
+-+-+-+-+-+-+-+-+-+-+-+-+-+-+-+-+-+-+-+-+-+-+-+-+-+-+-+-+-+-+-+-+
|Version|  IHL  |Type of Service|          Total Length         |
+-+-+-+-+-+-+-+-+-+-+-+-+-+-+-+-+-+-+-+-+-+-+-+-+-+-+-+-+-+-+-+-+
|         Identification        |Flags|      Fragment Offset    |
+-+-+-+-+-+-+-+-+-+-+-+-+-+-+-+-+-+-+-+-+-+-+-+-+-+-+-+-+-+-+-+-+
| Time to Live  |    Protocol   |         Header Checksum        |
+-+-+-+-+-+-+-+-+-+-+-+-+-+-+-+-+-+-+-+-+-+-+-+-+-+-+-+-+-+-+-+-+
|                        Source Address                          |
+-+-+-+-+-+-+-+-+-+-+-+-+-+-+-+-+-+-+-+-+-+-+-+-+-+-+-+-+-+-+-+-+
|                      Destination Address                       |
+-+-+-+-+-+-+-+-+-+-+-+-+-+-+-+-+-+-+-+-+-+-+-+-+-+-+-+-+-+-+-+-+
|            Options             |         Padding               |
+-+-+-+-+-+-+-+-+-+-+-+-+-+-+-+-+-+-+-+-+-+-+-+-+-+-+-+-+-+-+-+-+
```

IPv6 does a good job at handling this problem. Rather than the 32-bit address field of IPv4, IPv6 was designed with four times as many bits for addressing. With 128 bits for addressing (see IPv6 Figure 9.3), we are left with enough address space to accommodate future growth as predicted within the IETF (128 bits is roughly enough for 4.2 E37 (4.2 *10 to the power of 37) Internet-connected entities. This is roughly equivalent to having 8.27E+016 unicast Internet addresses for each square millimeter of the Earth's surface! As we can see, this appears to scale to future growth for what hopefully will be a long time.

Figure 9.3 IPv6 packet header format.

```
+-+-+-+-+-+-+-+-+-+-+-+-+-+-+-+-+-+-+-+-+-+-+-+-+-+-+-+-+-+-+-+-+
|Version| Traffic Class |            Flow Label                 |
+-+-+-+-+-+-+-+-+-+-+-+-+-+-+-+-+-+-+-+-+-+-+-+-+-+-+-+-+-+-+-+-+
|         Payload Length        |  Next Header  |   Hop Limit   |
+-+-+-+-+-+-+-+-+-+-+-+-+-+-+-+-+-+-+-+-+-+-+-+-+-+-+-+-+-+-+-+-+
|                                                               |
+                                                               +
|                                                               |
+                      Source Address                           +
|                                                               |
+                                                               +
|                                                               |
+-+-+-+-+-+-+-+-+-+-+-+-+-+-+-+-+-+-+-+-+-+-+-+-+-+-+-+-+-+-+-+-+
|                                                               |
+                                                               +
|                                                               |
+                   Destination Address                         +
|                                                               |
+                                                               +
|                                                               |
+-+-+-+-+-+-+-+-+-+-+-+-+-+-+-+-+-+-+-+-+-+-+-+-+-+-+-+-+-+-+-+-+
```

Before we dive into the addressing schemes inherent to IPv6, let us first look at the new convention for expressing IPv6 addresses. Contrary to IPv4, which uses dotted decimal notation, with one number per octet of its 32-bit address, IPv6 utilizes hex notation for describing its addresses. Although dotted decimal notation is well suited for the relatively short IPv4 host address, it does not scale well to the 128-bit IPv6 host address (with dotted decimal notation, we would need 16 numbers to designate each host). With hex notation, each digit signifies 4 bits of address space, cutting address length, when written, substantially. Table 9.1 summarizes how hex notation differs from dotted decimal notation. Notice that hex notation has 16 values, instead of the classical 10 values of decimal notation. This allows a byte of data to be summarized by two digits. Therefore, an address in IPv6 will look a little different from what you are used to. However, with a little practice, hex notation becomes easy to use. For instance, the IPv4 address 24.172.96.240 can be written in hex (with dots in the same place) as 18.AC.60.F0.

For IT Professionals

This Is the Trick

This is something to become proficient at as soon as possible when deploying IPv6. Subnetting, as you have known it, is usually the hardest part to master with hex notation. Practice, however, will make this easy. The trick is to stop trying to translate between dotted decimal and hex. Instead, allow yourself to actually think in hex, and things will become a lot easier much more quickly.

Hex notation is useful for condensing large numerical expressions. Each digit expresses 4 bits of the address. The next convention to know about that differs from IPv4 is that addresses are grouped together in groups of 16 bits. For instance, a sample IPv6 address may be 3FFE:2900:B002:CA96:85D1:109D:0002:00AD. The colon (:) is used as a delimiter in IPv6 addresses. Most implementations will support dotted decimal notation as well, to aid in a smooth transition in the networking community (old habits are hard to break, you know), but the agreed upon convention will be hex with colon delimiters.

Now that we see how IPv6 addresses are formed, we can use a couple of additional conventions to aid in IPv6-address hex expressions. The convention carries over from IPv4: All zeroes that are to the left of a given 16-bit expression may be left out. For instance, the IPv6 address 3FFE:2900:C005:001A:0000:0000:0AD0:0001 can be reduced to 3FFE:2900:C005:1A:0:0:AD01:1, which saves substantial time. This is analogous to the writing of the addresss (for example) in IPv4 of 199.000.055.085 as 199.0.55.85. The second convention helps even more. It states that if there is more than one string of 16 binary zeroes in a row, they can be omitted. In place of the zero strings, we simply use the double-colon (::). From the preceding address, we can express this address as 3FFE:2900:C005:1A::AD0:1, which shortens the expression even further. Please note that the double colon can only be used once in an address. Since the length of the zero string is unknown, any IPv6 node interpreting the expression would not know how many 16-bit zero strings to pad the address with, if this shortcut were to be used more than once. For instance, 3FFE:2900:1::1::2 could be 3FFE:2900:1:0:1:0:0:2 or 3FFE:2900:1:0:0:1:0:2.

When we look at both of these shortcuts in full use, we can see that addresses can become especially easy to express. For instance, the IPv6 6Bone address 3FFE:2900:0000:0000:0000:0000:0000:0001 can be written as 3FFE:2900::1. This dramatically reduces both the time to write IPv6 addresses, and the thinking associated with making sure that you get all 128 bits into your expression. Now that we have all of these rules down, we can begin to look at the protocol addressing scheme in more detail. Familiarize yourself with Table 9.1 prior to moving into the next sections of this book, as hex will be the normal method for expressing IPv6 addresses from here on out.

Table 9.1 Hex-to-Decimal Translation Cheat Chart

Value	Hex Notation	Decimal Notation	Binary
0	0	0	00000000
1	1	1	00000001
2	2	2	00000010
3	3	3	00000011
4	4	4	00000100
5	5	5	00000101
6	6	6	00000110
7	7	7	00000111
8	8	8	00001000
9	9	9	00001001
10	a	10	00001010
11	b	11	00001011
12	c	12	00001100
13	d	13	00001101
14	e	14	00001110
15	f	15	0000111

Now that we have more bits from which to address Internet entities, we need to make sure that we have sufficient means for all of these machines to talk with one another. In other words, we must also incorporate into the new Internet Protocol ways for routing to maintain an efficient state. Just imagine the processing power Internet Backbone routers would need to have in order to retain and process against a list of every host in IPv6! At the time of this writing, there are between 62,000 and 65,000 classless routing entries in the Internet default-free Backbone routing tables. This number is increasing, but at a much slower rate than address allocations (providers are delegating address space that can be aggregated into supernets; this keeps global routing table growth less than that of Internet-connected entity growth). We need to ensure that the upper limit of routing entries with IPv6 is still within foreseeable limits of what Backbone routers can hold, and process upon, quickly. In the following sections, we will first look at how IPv6 addressing works, and then look at how this addressing scheme ensures that these concerns are sufficiently addressed.

A More Flexible Hierarchical Organization of Addresses

As stated earlier, any protocol that replaces the current IP will need to not only provide for more Internet-routable addresses, but it will also have to contain inherent mechanisms to ensure a stable and efficient Backbone routing system. If we were to adopt an Internet Protocol without addressing this issue, we may solve an address space problem, but getting from one point in the Internet to another will become cumbersome for Backbone routing equipment and could lead to a less stable Internet as a whole. Many Internet gurus today envision the Internet replacing all prior means of communication, be it phone, television, radio, etc., so the routing stability issue has to be held in high priority for this dream to become reality. In this section, we will look at one of the main improvements IPv6 attempts to make over IPv4, and study the effects this can have on Backbone routing tables.

Although IPv4 first routed based on classful entries (Class A, B, C blocks), it was apparent that this was not sufficient for wide-scale deployment. Then, the concept for Classless Inter-Domain Routing was developed. With CIDR, the concept of classes went away, allowing the ability to aggregate smaller networks into supernets, or to break up big blocks into subnets. This increased the efficiency of network addressing, because we could now address a network with the appropriately-sized network block, regardless of what class the address fell into. With this new development, IPv4 addresses were now used more efficiently, but there was a side effect on the Backbone routing tables of the Internet. Instead of carrying the first 128 blocks of network space with 128 entries, these networks could now be spread out over large noncontiguous geographic areas. This caused routing table size to grow at an increased rate.

Let us perform a mental exercise to help demonstrate this point. Suppose that Internet-connected Network I has two Internet Providers, A and B. Network I has been delegated a subnet from Provider A from which to address their Internet-connected machines, to provide for Internet routability. When this provider runs BGP, it announces this subnet up to both providers. This is where the problems occur. If Provider A decides to announce to its peers only the aggregate of the Address block from which Network I was given a subnet, only traffic originating on Provider A's network (and sometimes not even that) would use the connection from Provider A to Network I to get to Network I. Since Provider B receives, and passes on, the subnet that Network I announces, all Internet traffic will use Provider B's connectivity to Network I for its best path (via the longest match routing rule). We can see that this limits a downstream network's ability to load-balance between multiple provider links. The only solution that would allow Network I to control its traffic load on either connection would have to include the external announcement of both the aggregate and the subnet from Provider A to its peers.

For IT Professionals

BGP Functionality

BGP4 (Border Gateway Protocol version 4) will do this automatically, since the originator of the subnet will be the Autonomous System of Network I in this example. The route will be announced to both providers, unless either one has a policy in place to filter this announcement. This is how most Internet Backbones today take care of this problem. This is also why most Tier 1 providers will not allow a customer to use static routing between the Provider and the customer, if that customer is multihomed to multiple providers, since this would break this model of deaggregation via BGP4.

So as we can see, the inception of CIDR provided for more efficient use of Internet-routable addresses, but in turn, it also reduced the efficiency of Internet routing tables. When this example is expanded to the global Internet, we can see that this is a problem. IPv6 makes some good modifications in policy to rid the Internet of both problems.

The IPv6 address consists of 128 bits. One advantage that IPv6 has over CIDR is a built-in, well-defined set of boundaries from which to define sets of address space to delegate downstream to other people who get Internet connectivity from you.

Figure 9.4 Globally-routable IPv6 addressing architecture.

```
| 3 |  13  | 8 |  24  |  16  |          64 bits              |
+---+------+-----+--------+---------+------------------------------+
|FP| TLA |RES|  NLA |  SLA |      Interface ID            |
|   | ID  |   |  ID  |  ID  |                              |
+--+------+-----+--------+---------+------------------------------+
```

Notice in Figure 9.4 that the IPv6 globally-routable unicast prefix is divided into six different sections. Let us look at each section in detail.

FP: Format Prefix

The Format Prefix for globally-routable unicast prefixes will always have the same three bits (in the initial deployment of IPv6). These first three bits will always be set to 001, and are there to designate (to any routing entity on the Internet) that this address is a globally-routable unicast address. For each type of IPv6 address that we discuss, the FP will be unique to that type of address, thus making it easier for routing entities to discern packet types, and process them according to the rules that apply to the respective packet type. For instance, multicast packets and unicast packets are routed in very different ways. Unicast packet routing is 1-to-1 (a packet with an IPv6 Globally-Routable Unicast destination originates from one host, and is delivered to one host), and multicast packets are 1-to-N (one multicast packet may be delivered to N interested destination hosts), or N-to-N (N sources delivering packets to N destinations), so these packets are handled in vastly different ways on an Internet backbone. The FP serves as a delimiter, so a routing device can make a quick decision as to how to handle the incoming packet, and ensure that it is handled correctly. Note that using the first few bits of an address to designate type of address is more efficient than putting it into the packet, because now we can utilize more of the packet for other valuable features, discussed earlier.

TLA ID

This is the Top Level Aggregator Identifier, 13 bits used to signify to which Top Level Aggregator the address belongs. A Top Level Aggregator is a Network Provider that sits at the top level of aggregation of Internet traffic. In unicast terms, Top Level Aggregators are sometimes referred to as "Tier-1 Providers." These are Internet Providers who make up the core of the Internet Backbone. They usually have equal part peering (they don't pay the other provider to receive the other provider's routes) relationships with other TLAs (nonpaid connectivity to other TLAs), encompass a large area of the globe with coverage of Internet core routing, and provide the high-speed transport that moves packets from one part of the globe to another. Their Backbones are composed of highly sophisticated, fast-routing devices, and their cores carry full Internet routes. Current examples of Top Level Aggregators include Sprint and WorldCom. In IPv6, providers of this caliber are given blocks of IPv6 Globally Routable Unicast addresses (a TLA assignment), and they, in turn, delegate pieces of this block down to their customers.

RES

These bits are reserved for now. It has not been determined by the IETF what course of action should be used for these bits. At this stage, it is appropriate for TLAs to subnet their assignment using these 8 bits to increase the amount of Globally Routable Unicast address space that a TLA can use to delegate to their customers, or use on their Backbone.

NLA ID

These 24 bits depict the Next Level Aggregator Identifier. A Next Level Aggregator can be thought of today as a Tier-2 Network Service Provider or ISP. An NLA can range from a small organization with one TLA connection, to a large, regional Provider with many upstream TLA connections, and complex Backbones. An NLA will receive an NLA ID from their upstream TLA, and in turn, will break their NLA ID into chunks, which will be delegated to their customers.

SLA ID

A Site Level Aggregator Identifier describes an entity that has no downstream customers who are network service providers. A SLA could be a small to large business, or a small Service Provider who does not delegate address space to its providers (for instance, today's cable-modem providers could fit into a SLA arrangement).

Interface ID

The final 64 bits of the globally routable IPv6 unicast address is reserved for the Interface Identifier. In IPv4 terms, this is known as the host id. These 64 bits will be designated to distinguish one host from another on a given network segment. Each Interface ID on a given network segment must be unique. We will see that IPv6 builds in a clever way to ensure this is so.

Aggregation Realized

Now that we know how the IPv6 Globally Routable Unicast address format is split up, we can begin to see how aggregation based on this format is possible. Figure 9.5 depicts a TLA that has a variety of customers for which they provide transit Internet connectivity. By

delegating a subset of their address space (TLA ID) to each customer, depending on that customer's purpose, they are ensured that
all address space that is advertised to them from their downstream
customers is a subset of their address space. This brings up a good
point regarding the political changes surrounding IPv6. With IPv6,
small to regional Network Service Providers as well as end-users will
no longer have the ability to obtain address space directly from registries. Instead, Top Level Aggregators will be assigned address
blocks, which they will in turn be in charge of managing and delegating to their downstream connections (NLAs and SLAs). This shift
in address management is thought to be much more efficient than
the current address management policies of today. If a small-to-
midsize ISP/NSP can no longer get address space from registries,
and therefore puts a burden on Backbone TLA core providers to
carry these routes as transit, then the possibility of aggregation
beyond what IPv4 can do today becomes a reality. In the next section, we will look at how this aggregation works, and why it will
increase the stability of the Internet as a whole.

Figure 9.5 A generic IPv6 Internet.

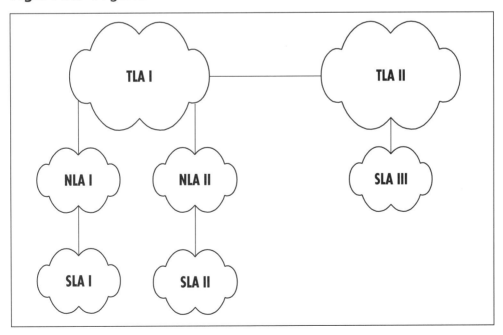

Minimizing the Size of Routing Tables

As we have discovered, IPv6 will allow ample address space for the future of the Internet. With 128 bits of address spacing, there should be adequate addresses for Internet-connected entities to grow in number and complexity. With a well-defined format for IPv6 addressing, we can see that addressing becomes more organized than classical IPv4. From this, we will now look at how the addressing scheme for IPv6 helps to minimize the number or Internet Core routing entries that need to be carried, thus limiting the scope of future Internet routing complexity. In Figure 9.6, we see two TLAs, with various connected customers of both the NLA and SLA variety. Let us look at the routing announcements necessary for this scenario to function with stability and efficiency.

Figure 9.6 Generic addressed IPv6 Internet.

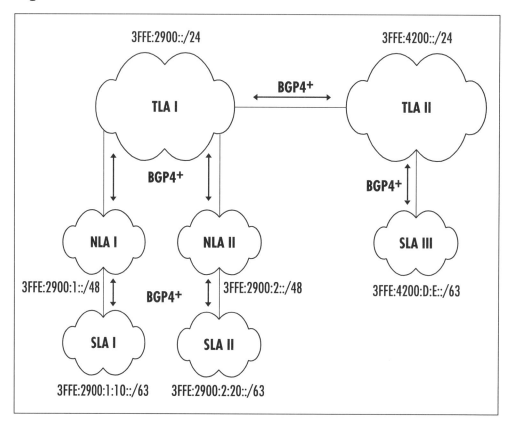

In Figure 9.6, we have two TLAs (Tier 1 Network Service Providers) and a variety of NLAs and SLAs in various configurations. TLA I is in a bilateral peering arrangement for TLA II, and both exchange routes via BGP (there are changes to BGP that are currently in IETF working groups to support different types of NLRI (Network-Layer Reachability Information), so BGP4 very well may not be the standard BGP by the time IPv6 is deployed; for the purposes of this example, BGP4 will serve adequately). TLA I owns a Top Level Aggregator Block. In this example, we designate TLA I with 3FFE:2900::/24 as its TLA delegation, and TLA II with 3FFE:4200::/24 as its TLA delegation. So we know that TLA I and TLA II must supply each other with these routes at a minimum for routing to operate properly between TLA I and TLA II Backbones.

TLA I will subdelegate blocks of address space to its NLA and SLA customers. In this case, let us assign NLA I with 3FFE:2900:1::/48, and NLA II with 3FFE:2900:2::/48. Furthermore, these NLAs must delegate blocks down to their customers out of this block. Let us assume SLA I will be given 3FFE:2900:1:10::/63, SLA II 3FFE:2900:2:20::/63, and SLA III 3FFE:4200:D:E::/63.

Starting at the bottom aggregators, SLA I must announce its block 3FFE:2900:1:10::/63 up to NLA I. Because this is a subset of NLA I's space, NLA I is not required to announce this SLA (from SLA I) up to TLA I. A similar situation exists with NLA II. TLA I only needs to hear the NLA aggregations that it delegated down to these two NLAs, regardless of how that NLA has subdelegated its space.

So from this, we can see that at this point, TLA I has to carry only three announcements for nonbackbone space:

3FFE:2900:1::/48 (from NLA I)
3FFE:2900:2::/48 (from NLA II)
3FFE:4200::/24   (from TLA II)

Even further, we notice that the first two of these announcements are simply subsets of the block assigned to TLA I. Therefore, in the bilateral peering between TLA I and TLA II, we can see that only one route needs to be exchanged between these peers.

Although this is a limited example, we can see the routing simplicity that has come to pass as a result of this aggregation. The beauty of this comes from two facts.

Figure 9.7 Routing advertisements along aggregation paths.

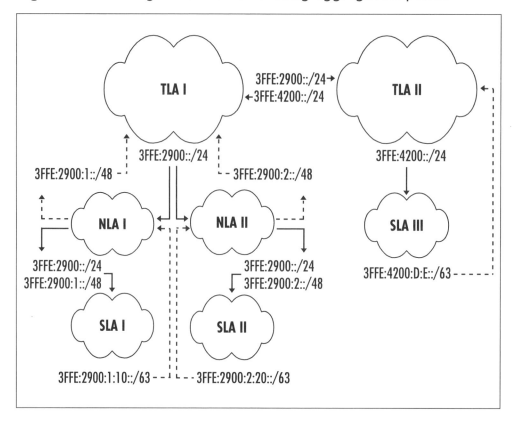

The first is that *no address blocks are portable.* Today, a large part of IP space is known as portable. A portable address block is a block that can be taken with you when you leave a certain service provider's jurisdiction, and go to another provider. This leads to many extraneous announcements in the core of the Internet Backbone, as Network Service Providers lose the ability to aggregate announcements properly. For example, if a service provider is given the classless block 71.16.0.0/16, and loses one part of this, say 71.16.241.0/24, from its possession (a customer takes it with them when they leave), we are left with a suboptimal routing scenario. Now,

1. The Service Provider has to announce this block one /16 to peers and customers as many different subnets—in this case, eight announcements (71.16.0.0/17, 71.16.128.0/18, 71.16.224.0/19, 71.16.240.0/24, 71.16.242.0/23, 71.16.244.0/22, 71.16.248.0/21).

2. The Service Provider has to update its filters to peers to allow this lost block to be heard via BPG from peers. Normally, this block would be denied, to prevent routing loops (see the note regarding BGP in a previous section of this chapter; the BGP4 provider helps a little due to the originating ASN). Not only is this a management nightmare for Network Service Providers, it is also extremely inefficient for the Internet core.

So by removing portability, we have greatly increased the long-term efficiency of the Internet Backbone routing tables. Some may ask, "Why don't we eliminate this in IPv4?" This has been done, for the most part; however, legacy portability has taken its toll on the Internet. Second, pressure still remains from downstream Internet entities. The argument is that not allowing IP blocks to be portable puts the customer under pressure not to change providers, because a big network is cumbersome to renumber with new IP space (DNS entries, as well as host reconfiguration is required). There is no way for IPv4 to provide a smooth transition from one Provider-delegated block of IPv4 addresses to another. IPv6 will need some mechanism to allow for smooth migration from one provider's address space to another. We will see that this is the case. The use of anycast addressing, as well as auto-configuration of interfaces, aids in the pain of renumbering upon switching providers, or renumbering for any other reason. But let's put this aside for the moment to complete our study of routing tables. We will discuss strategies for renumbering in the next section.

The second reason is that *only* TLAs will be assigned address space from the Numbering Authorities. Today, IANA (the Internet

Assigned Numbers Authority) is the responsible party for numbering, which in turn delegates numbers to Regional Registries, such as ARIN, RIPE, and APNIC. These regional numbers authorities in turn assign IPv4 address space to Internet providers, or businesses and organizations that can demonstrate sufficient need for their own IP blocks. Notice how this leads to more small blocks being carried in the core Internet table. This all goes back to renumbering problems. If renumbering were simple, then getting IP space directly from our upstream providers of connectivity would not be a big deal. If we are dissatisfied with service, we can simply get another provider, and then renumber. Many businesses today feel restricted in doing this, as renumbering in IPv4 is sufficiently complex to sway people away from going somewhere else when their provider is not satisfactorily providing service. By ensuring that only TLAs get address space, the Internet is assured that only big blocks of space are delegated, which will make sure that aggregation can always occur.

For IT Professionals

Not All Allocations Are as Depicted

It is important to note that not all allocations will go exactly as we cited earlier (in the IPv6 Internet example corresponding to Figures 9.6 and 9.7). NLAs generally will be given whatever address space is necessary for them to operate. They should be given as much address space as they can deploy efficiently, or delegate down to SLAs. So in reality, a TLA will delegate down a /X prefix, where 24<X<48, depending on what the NLA needs. The same scenario applies to the SLA. We don't want to waste IPv6 address space, but we don't want to limit business or world interconnectivity either.

Global Addresses for the Internet and Local Addresses for Intranet

Now that we can see how the Internet core can benefit from IPv6, and we have touched on some of the nice things it provides to end-user networks, let us look at how a typical LAN will be addressed, and how its routing allows for robust and easily managed connectivity.

So far, we have learned that Globally-Routable Unicast IPv6 addresses follow a strict aggregation scheme. But does every machine need to have a Globally Routable Unicast address? Most companies today that are connected to the Internet have some sub-set of systems that route and speak IPv4, but do not necessarily need to be routed across the Internet, nor do they need to have their very own Globally Routable Unicast address. Certain systems, such as internal-only servers, printers, and other systems need be able to route on a company network, but do not need to be globally routed across the Internet. Furthermore, many companies wish there were a way to ensure that these systems could not be seen from the outside world. Today, this is remedied through security precautions: the firewall and the packet filter are the best ways to ensure (or hope to ensure) that some secret or important machines are not accessible from the outside. Although security is important, and will not go away with the invention of IPv6, there are other possibilities. IPv6 incorporates the idea of scoped addressing into its protocol stack. Scoped addressing, in addition to providing other functionality, provides for this problem.

Addresses are said to be *scoped* when the address in question has a well-defined boundary in which it will route. Furthermore, the scoped address does not route outside of this boundary, nor does it have a routing entry associated with it that leaves this boundary. To better understand, let us look at a diagram of a simple IPv6 network, and a generic example of how scoping can be used to ensure that machines operate only within their jurisdiction. Refer to Figure 9.8 to picture this type of scenario.

Figure 9.8 A scoped IPv6 network.

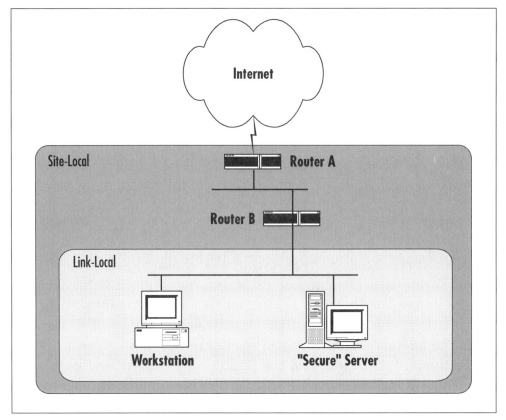

The machine labeled "secure" server cannot route outside of the boundary of its network, because it does not know about the rest of the world (it has no default route). The rest of the world does not know about it either (no routing entry is advertised to other routers about the existence of the link-local network.)

In this network, we have some people who may be in another side of the building, who need to access Machine A. Also, Machine A can talk to other parts of the building. We still have the ability to use filters and firewalls (or some sort of security measures) to ensure this machine is invisible from the outside. However, classically, this can be dangerous, as most operators, no matter how good and careful, can make mistakes. Addresses that are not supposed to get announced to the rest of the world eventually will get announced, even if by accident and for a short period of time, when a mistake gets made. RFC1918 designates reserved address space for IPv4 (RFC1918: Address Allocation for Private Internets, www.ietf.org/rfc/rfc1918.txt). Note that in IPv4, it is left to the competence of the Network Operator to ensure that reserved address space is not announced globally. In IPv6, it is conceivable that a routing system will automatically know not to route link-local or site-local space between ASs.

As you have probably guessed by now, IPv6 addresses this problem, and does what many feel IPv4 has tried to do too late. IPv6 has a set of address space that is scoped for different types of applications. Table 9.2 summarizes delegation of IP spaces.

Table 9.2 summarizes how the first few bits of the IPv6 address will tell us what type of address it is. Notice that in three bits, we can see whether or not a given address is a Globally Routable Unicast address or not (001; which leaves as hex, either 0010 (2) or 0011 (3)). As a side note, this is pretty nice for routing systems!

So we can see that there are two levels of unicast scoped addresses. The first type of scoped address for IPv6 is the Link Local Unicast address, which exists only on the media that connects two or more machines together. For instance, on a PPP link (or HDLC, Frame-Relay, Ethernet, Token Ring) there will be a specific set of address space especially designed for that link. The motivation for this was to allow IPv6 speaking machines to have a set of addresses from which to link groups of machines together in order to communicate functions that are specific to that link. For instance, Link Local addresses can be used for things like Neighbor Discovery, or Auto-Configuration (discussed later). This allows all machines to have an address that allows them to talk to other directly connected machines (directly connected at Layer 1 or 2 in this case; consider two machines that are on the same Ethernet subnet as being directly connected). Notice that in itself, this relieves some of the burden of renumbering. Although an administrator renumbers a network, for whatever reason, at least machines that need to talk to each other can still do so outside of the Globally Routable Unicast address. Link Local addresses are to be routed only on that link, and are not to be sent into any IGP (Interior Gateway Protocol) or EGP (Exterior Gateway Protocol; to other routing domains), for obvious reasons. They are Link Local after all! Most routing systems for IPv6 today have this functionality built into their operating systems (it is unclear whether routing systems will need to have this automatically built in at this time, but it seems to make the best sense that they do).

Table 9.2 IPv6 Address First-Bits Standards

Allocation	Prefix (binary)	Fraction of Address Space
Reserved	0000 0000	1/256
Unassigned	0000 0001	1/256
Reserved for NSAP Allocation	0000 001	1/128
Reserved for IPX Allocation	0000 010	1/128
Unassigned	0000 011	1/128
Unassigned	0000 1	1/32
Unassigned	0001	1/16
Aggregatable Global Unicast Addresses	001	1/8
Unassigned	010	1/8
Unassigned	011	1/8
Unassigned	100	1/8
Unassigned	101	1/8
Unassigned	110	1/8
Unassigned	1110	1/16
Unassigned	1111 0	1/32
Unassigned	1111 10	1/64
Unassigned	1111 110	1/128
Unassigned	1111 1110 0	1/512

Continued

Allocation	Prefix (binary)	Fraction of Address Space
Link-Local Unicast Addresses	1111 1110 10	1/1024
Site-Local Unicast Addresses	1111 1110 11	1/1024
Multicast Addresses	1111 1111	1/256

The second type of scoped address is the site-local address. This address designates a routing domain, or subset of a routing domain. Machines that are addressed site-locally will be able to communicate with other designated subnets through this addressing scheme, but will not route globally on the Internet. This can benefit us in some ways as well. Perhaps there is a need for a machine to speak with other internal machines at an office, but the administrator wants to make sure that that particular machine (perhaps an accounting machine for a company, for example) cannot route through the Internet. Through the use of Site Local addressing, we can accomplish this, without the intervention of complex security schemes to ensure that a machine is invisible to the bad guys out there who want to cause trouble (this does not substitute for a network security, but does ensure that packets coming from this host do not reach the global internet). The basic routing principles associated with Site Local addresses are common sense. A Site Local address may be routed through an IGP, but should never pass into an EGP. Again, most of the time, an intelligent routing system will have the ability to discern these routes by their unique addressing, and make sure that they are not leaked to the Internet.

So as we can see, IPv6 makes an attempt (and a pretty good one at that) for separating out addresses that are internal to a routing domain, or internal to a given network or link, and makes sure that the Internet routing table integrity is maintained. Now that we have an idea of what types of local addressing IPv6 has for us, let us look at some of the benefits of scoping. Figure 9.9 shows addresses that have been assigned to hosts in the Site Local, Link Local, and Globally Routable Unicast space.

Figure 9.9 Scoped addresses on a LAN.

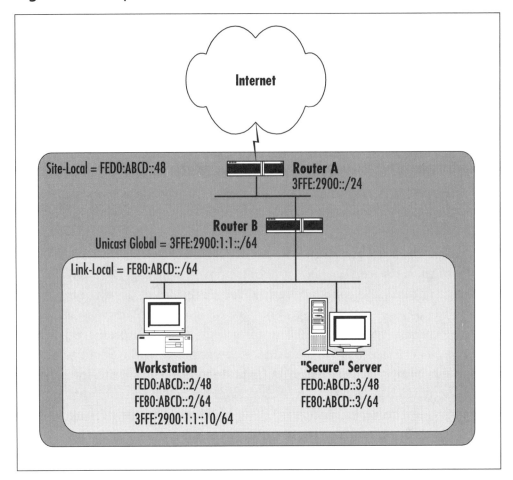

Now that we have machines that can speak to each other on a LAN or link with well-known addresses that are always in the same range, we can look at some of the benefits associated with this scenario. Earlier in the chapter, we mentioned the problems associated with renumbering today in IPv4. Renumbering a network is rather complex with IPv4, because not only would you have to sit at every machine (or DHCP server at the least) for every network and reconfigure the LAN to use new IPv4 addresses, but also there would be considerable downtime with this approach. Furthermore, services such as Domain Name Service potentially could be drastically impacted by this undertaking, in that zone files would need to be changed to reflect new forward and reverse DNS entries for machines. If you are in the Internet business, providing access to services or information that needs to be reachable to consumers at any time, you can see how this can cost businesses money. Today, downtime is becoming more and more pricey as people begin to rely more and more upon Internet availability for business-critical applications and information. We will see in the following sections how IP version 6 will help us to minimize downtime, while also helping administrators (those poor fellows) to keep up with network changes such as renumbering, more efficiently.

NOTE

I am not implying that using Site Local addressing only on secure machines is the only security precaution that needs to take place. For instance, someone who wants this information can always capture control of a machine that is at the same site, but has a Globally Routable Unicast address and can then attack the site-locally-addressed machine. Security concerns do not go away, but obscurity does increase with this method.

IPv6 Benefits

Now that we have looked into the promise that IPv6 gives to the Internet of the future, let us discuss some of the benefits of IPv6 in more detail, in order to see how this protocol attempts to deal with the Internet and business network problems of today. We will look at the two main problems that IPv6 solves—address depletion and routing scalability—in more detail, and then look at some of the added benefits that IPv6 gives to network designers and administrators.

Increased IP Address Size

We now understand that IPv6 has 128 bits for reserving. Let us look at this closer and appreciate the vastness of this degree of address space. 128 bits of address space means that there are 2^{128} different addresses available. Because we already know that the first three bits of 001 are reserved for Globally Routable Unicast addresses, we now have 125 bits left to play with (128–3=125). So now we have 2^{125} addresses available before Globally Routable Unicast address space is depleted, roughly, 4.25 E+037 addresses. To put this into perspective, let us compare this to IPv4. In IPv4, we use all address space between 0.0.0.0 and 223.255.255.255 for unicast routing (we will not take into account the addresses delegated as nonroutable reserved addresses as defined by RFC 1918), which is approximately 2.15E+09 addresses (3 times 2^{29}, as there are three legal possibilities for the first three bits, 000, 100, 110, and 101). This means that there 2^{31} more addresses than IPv4! Clearly, 128 bits provides enough address space to take current Internet trends *well* into the future. We could even argue that this is a seemingly inexhaustible amount of address space. Although this number is big, we will see, when we get into the details of LAN and WAN configuration, that this is not quite the case, but there is still many times the address space of IPv4.

One thing to get used to thinking of in order to appreciate IPv6 is the number of *networks* that IPv6 can support. From the address format discussed previously, we know that, in an IPv6 address, the last 64 bits describes the host ID for a system on a network. Did this seem fishy when you read it? It probably should have. IPv6 actually uses the last 64 bits of the address to distinguish hosts from one another. Whether using the Link Local, Site Local, or Globally Routable Unicast address format, the last 64 bits on a machine will remain the same. This is because IPv6 uses the Layer 2 MAC address (the address that is burned into all Layer 2 hardware; for example, Ethernet cards or other Network Interface Cards) as the host ID for a machine. This does, in fact, limit the number of addresses that are out there, because there will rarely be 2^{64}

addresses in use on a typical Ethernet LAN (we could argue that there will never be 2^{64} machines on a LAN; especially on 10 or 100 Meg Ethernet!). Some address space definitely gets wasted. However, if you remove the 64 bits used for host id, and the first three bits of address space to designate Globally Routable Unicast addresses, you get 2^{61} possible (2.31E+018) networks, compared to 1.07E+09 that IPv4 provides (assuming that *every* network in IPv4 is a /28, of which most are not; this number is derived by multIPlying 4 times the first 28 bits of address space). Notice that this is still 2.1 billion times as many networks as IPv4 allows, and IPv6 does not have the network restriction that we assume here for IPv4 (the number of IPv4 networks used here is for the number of LANs if all IPv4 networks were subnetted down to /28s; 13 hosts, one default router, one reserved, and one broadcast for the network). So we see that we have 2.1 billion times as many networks as this, and the IPv6 networks here can have up to 1.8E+19 hosts on each network (minus one for the default router). So even without using all of the addresses that IPv6 can use, we have the scaling ability to take us well beyond the future of IPv4, and in all likelihood, the scaling ability to take all of us through all of our careers in the IT field (or any other field). Clearly, IPv6 frees up the ability to use Addressing efficiently, without having to worry about running out. Please keep in mind that I do not mean to say that address space should be used in a carefree manner. This is how IPv4 came into the predicament that it is in so early in its life cycle!

Increased Addressing Hierarchy Support

As we learned earlier in the chapter, IPv6 addressing has restructured the means by which address blocks are delegated. Although IPv4 first used the classful IP assignment rules, and then began to assign based on the princIPles of CIDR, IPv6 corrects the deaggregation problems associated with each by splitting the IPv6 address into a set of definite scopes, or boundaries, by which IPv6 addresses are delegated.

The Format Prefix is used to show that an address is Globally Routable Unicast, or another type of address, and is always set to the same value. This allows a routing system to discern quickly whether or not a packet is Globally Routable Unicast, or another. By knowing this quickly, the routing device can more efficiently pass the packet off to routing subsystems for proper handling.

The Top Level Aggregator ID is used for two purposes. First, it is used to designate a big block of addresses from which smaller blocks of addresses are carved, in order to give downstream connectivity to those who need to get to the Internet. Second, it is used to distinguish where a route has come from. If big blocks of address space are given out to Providers only, and then in turn delegated down to customers, it becomes easier to see which transit network a route has traversed, or from which transit network the route first originated. With IPv4, in which, historically, many addresses were portable, and the numbers authorities were delegating blocks down to small businesses, it became impossible to know where a route came from without tracerouting back towards the source of the packet. Now, with IPv6, the possibilities for determining the source of a route are more feasible. Imagine an Internet consisting of 500 Tier 1 providers. If this were the case (which is most likely not too far off from today, though what makes a provider a Tier 1 provider is very ambiguous) then at the very least a quick search through a text file could tell you where a route originated, based on the TLA ID of the longest match route. It's even possible to contain software that has this functionality built into it (though I know of none currently in existence, and this software would most likely become outdated quickly, as new delegations were assigned).

Let us look at the size of the TLA in more detail. We discussed in prior sections how the address space would be given only to providers, or those who needed their own IPv6 space (the term needed is used cautiously here, as it is ambiguous as well—there are currently no set boundaries or requirements with respect to what need means). This way, we are able to sufficiently aggregate prefixes into big blocks at the Internet core, and pass fewer routes between routing domains, as well as internally, which will increase the efficiency of the Internet core.

For fun, let us assume that we have the delegation 3D00::B234::/24. Let us further assume that all of our customers have sufficient need for a /48 delegation for their networks. This leaves us with 24 bits of addressing to delegate out! This is quite a lot of address space. The number of *networks* we can support with this scheme is equivalent to the number of *hosts* that we could support with a classful Class A IPv4 address block! You can see that there will be much more pressure on Tier 1 Service Providers to efficiently track the delegation of address space that they make. Today, a Tier 1 Service provider gets addresses in blocks of perhaps /16 or less. If we assume that a Service Provider today only delegates addresses up to /24, that leaves only 256 delegations (8 bits) that the Service Provider can make prior to applying for more address space. Most Tier-1 Service Providers today are required to sub-net delegations down to at least /28 in order to qualify for more address space, so this example may not be entirely realistic, but we can still grasp the size of a TLA as being monumental compared to that of the assignments that happen today.

For IT Professionals

Think Ahead

We can see that this amount of address space presents tremendous support infrastructure problems. Service Providers that today provide DNS service for their downstream customers will have to think long and hard of the best way to implement these support structures, prior to getting into the IPv6 market.

As we can see from the previous example, Tier 1 Service Providers will have an extremely big set of address space to deal with. This will not only eliminate much of the politics surrounding address delegation and obtaining more address blocks, but will also provide motivation for major support and automation infrastructure upgrades within an organization. Many Service Providers today have difficulty in upgrading support structure due to the engrained functionality and interdependencies of many support platforms integrated together. IPv6 provides for great challenges and opportunities not only in network engineering and architecture, but also in IT development and integration. The trick will be making a move from the old to the new world look like a fresh start, rather than a workaround for support.

The Next Level Aggregator address block is a block of addresses that are assigned to a downstream out of a TLA block. We know that these addresses are to be aggregated as much as possible into bigger TLA blocks, when they are exchanged between providers, in the Internet core. Let us look at the benefits of this type of addressing structure from the NLA perspective.

There are two main values in getting address space from a provider. The first advantage or value has to do with individual Backbone routing stability. If we are a NLA and wish to provide downstream service to our customers, we will most likely wish to provide the fullest, most robust service we can to our client base in order to retain current clients, and to gain market share. Perhaps we wish to allow customer to connect to us at multiple locations, as we are fairly geographically diverse for a given region, and have rich connectivity upstream to Internet Tier-1 (the core) providers. Furthermore, we want to allow our customers to receive a full routing table should they desire one, if they want to use explicit routes to form their routing policy. Perhaps they wish to load-balance between two connections, using some destinations preferred through one connection, and the rest preferred through the other connection to us. To do this, we have to carry full routes in our Backbone, so we may pass them down to our customers. Though an Internet core is usually composed of very modern, robust routing equipment, a Tier-2 provider may not be able to afford to upgrade their Backbones constantly in order to keep up with new technology, as well as increased routing table size. Luckily, processing power is not as big of a worry as it could be with IPv6. Because the

Internet core is fundamentally aggregated efficiently, we now have a much smaller routing table to maintain. We can provide full routes to a customer, and that set of routes may not be too big for us to handle. So by everyone "playing nice" and following aggregations strategies, we are able to reap the benefits of the core's minimized routing table size in our own Backbone.

The second benefit to NLA aggregation has to do with actual route stability of our routes across the Internet core globally. A little background is needed in order to fully appreciate this point. In the beginning of the Internet explosion in size, there were times when the Internet was not very stable. BGP speakers would lose routes, due to Backbone links failing, immature software, and the like. Because of this, routes were constantly being advertised, and then withdrawn (when the route became unreachable), causing consider-ably more processing to take place on core routers, which are required to keep an up-to-date set of full Internet routes at all times. To combat this BGP instability, the concept of *route dampen-ing* came into being. Essentially, route dampening works in the fol-lowing way: Every time a route is withdrawn and readvertised, it is assigned a penalty, which is recorded at the place of instability (usually an EBGP session). The more the route flaps, the higher the penalty associated with that route gets. When the penalty associated with that route reaches a certain level, the route is withdrawn, and not accepted for advertisement for a given period of time. When this happens, the route is known as *dampened*. The dampened route must undergo some period of wait time, without flapping more (or the penalty gets even higher) before it can be re-introduced into a router's BGP table. When the route goes for a long enough period of time without flapping (the penalty decreases with time) then the route is again allowed, and it is inserted back into the router's BGP table, and treated like other routes. This route dampening allowed a way for the Internet core to deal with instabilities in a manner that minimized the cost of other crucial processing.

Now that we understand route dampening, we can appreciate the second benefit of aggregation. When our upstream provider aggregates this route for us, and only announces the aggregate to their peers, this aggregate will in all likelihood remain stable, without respect to the stability of our own network. Because of this, we are virtually certain that another provider will never dampen our routes somewhere else in the Internet. None of the more specific routes that we use need be spread across the Internet core, outside of our own upstream provider. This improved routing stability is a major benefit to aggregation as a whole, both in IPv4, and in IPv6. The good part is that it is required in IPv6, instead of only being recommended. So now, the only place that we may need to worry about being dampened is within our own upstream provider's network. Fortunately, because in most cases, we are paying for our upstream connectivity, it is substantially easier to get our own upstream provider to help us to remove the penalties on dampened routes than it is with another provider, to whom we have no financial obligation.

So as we can see, with the exception of more addresses and smaller routing table sizes, there are more ramifications of IPv6 aggregation schemes than first meet the eye.

The Site Level Aggregator enjoys most of the benefits that an NLA does, except for its size. The Site Level Aggregator is usually a network or network provider with a much smaller network. Because of this, a smaller delegation of address space is needed. It retains the values of aggregations, in that its routing tables are kept smaller, even when receiving a full Internet routing table from its upstream provider. It also enjoys the benefits of global route stability, in that its upstream providers, whether an NLA or a TLA, aggregate according to the principles of the IPv6 aggregations model.

Simplified Host Addressing

As we have studied earlier, the IPv6 model defines 128 bits of address space. The first 64 bits are used for network numbering, and the last 64 bits are used for host numbering. We also remember that the last 64 bits of the host ID are obtained from the MAC address of the host's Network Interface. You may wonder how the

64-bit address is derived from a MAC address, which is classically only 48 bits. In this section we will look into how address is derived, and what developments we may see in the future as a result of the IPv6's addressing scheme.

When assigning a host in IPv4, by convention, one will break up the subnet given, and assign host addresses based upon the addresses that are available. Normally, again by convention, the first address is given to the designated router, and the rest of the addresses get assigned to hosts on that subnet, reserving the last address in the subnet for the broadcast addresses for that subnet. In IPv6, the situation changes somewhat. With IPv6, we know that the host ID is a 64-bit address that is obtained from the MAC address. Although the MAC addresses of today are classically 48 bits, we need a way to get the host ID to come out to 64 bits.

The answer to this problem is to pad the MAC address with some well-defined set of bits that will be known by routing systems on that subnet. Today, we use the string 0XFF and 0xFE (:FF:FE: in IPv6 terms) to pad the MAC address between the company ID and the vendor-supplied ID of the MAC address (MAC addresses are delegated in much the same way as IP addresses today, except companies who make NIC cards are given a piece of MAC space, rather than providers being given IPv4 space). This way, every host will have a 64-bit host ID that is related to their MAC address in the same way. Furthermore, we know that the 64-bit MAC address will be unique on a given network, because every NIC card will have a unique MAC address. By using this well-defined padding, it now becomes possible to learn IPv6 addresses (or at least host IDs) of other machines on the subnet, simply by learning the Layer 2 MAC information.

One interesting debate is whether or not MAC addresses will need to become 64 bits in length prior to the widespread deployment of IPv6. If there is a need for MAC addresses to become longer (if all MAC addresses are used) then 64 bits will most likely be the next option for length, as this will supply over 1.8E019 more MAC addresses to use (2^{64}–2^{48}). Moreover, if this becomes the case, we may simply stop the padding of the MAC address, and use the full 64 bits of the MAC address for the Host ID.

Now that we see where the Host ID comes from, let us now look into one of an administrator's favorite aspects of IPv6. Not only is Host ID already determined prior to configuring an IPv6-speaking machine, but the network on which it resides can be deduced as well.

Simpler Autoconfiguration of Addresses

Now that we understand where the Host ID comes from, let us look at one of the newest inventions of IPv6, its ability to autoconfigure. Before we go into detail about autoconfiguration, a new type of address will have to be brought into our repertoire, the multicast address.

A multicast address can be assigned to more than one machine simultaneously. It differs from an anycast address: anycast packets are routed to the destination (one of the set of machines with the same address) that is closest, but multicast packets are routed to *all* machines that are assigned this address. This is fundamentally different than a Globally Routable Unicast address, because more than one host can be numbered with the same address, so the address that a given host is assigned need not necessarily be unique for the given scope on which the multicast address is acting. All machines assigned this multicast address are said to be in a multi-cast group, whose address is the multicast address they use. Multicast-speaking machines send and receive data from more than one host (every member in that group). This type of addressing and routing classically has been used for 1 to N, or M to N type Internet transactions (when one or more people need to get identical infor-mation to more than one destination). Multicast provides the effi-cient means to do so.

Now that we understand the idea of multicast, if we unite this idea with the idea of Host ID coming from the hardware on a given machine, we can see how autoconfiguration is possible. When a machine first powers up onto a network, and realizes that it is connected and is supposed to speak IPv6, it will send a multicast packet–that is well known and defined by standard–out onto the LAN segment to which it is attached. This packet will be destined towards a locally-scoped (see earlier) multicast address, known as the Solicited Node Multicast address. When the router sees this packet come in, it can then reply with the network address from which the machine should be numbered, in the payload of the reply packet. The machine receives the packet, and in turn reads the network number that the router has sent. It then assigns itself an IPv6 address that consists of that network number, appending its Host ID (obtained from its MAC address of the interface that it connected to that subnet) to the network number, and it now has an IPv6 address. Not only does this not involve manual intervention by the administrator to configure this machine (though it may or may not involve manual configuration of the router on that subnet), but it also does not require any worry about the address being nonunique. The machine is guaranteed to have a unique address because the network number is assigned uniquely by the router on that network. The Host ID is unique because the MAC address of the interface by which that machine is attached is provided by the vendor and is unique. Furthermore, it can learn the default route that it needs in order to get off of that subnet, now that it has a routable address.

Notice the ease of configuration that we now have when we move from one network to another. Not only do we no longer have to reconfigure an end-station manually (and then reboot in most cases), we also no longer have to take time out of our network administrator's busy day for him to delegate an address in order to ensure its uniqueness. Also, the administrator no longer has to keep track of the addresses that he has assigned, and which ones are free at any given time! Certainly, this can be seen to save a network administrator much time, both in paperwork associated with keeping track of addresses used, and in reconfiguration that must occur for a network to be renumbered. Think of the things an administrator could be doing if he or she isn't constantly being hounded for IP addresses or network numbers! We will get into the concept of the multicast address, and its possible uses, in more detail in a later section. See Figure 9.10 for a graphical representation of autoconfiguration.

Figure 9.10 LAN discovery mechanism.

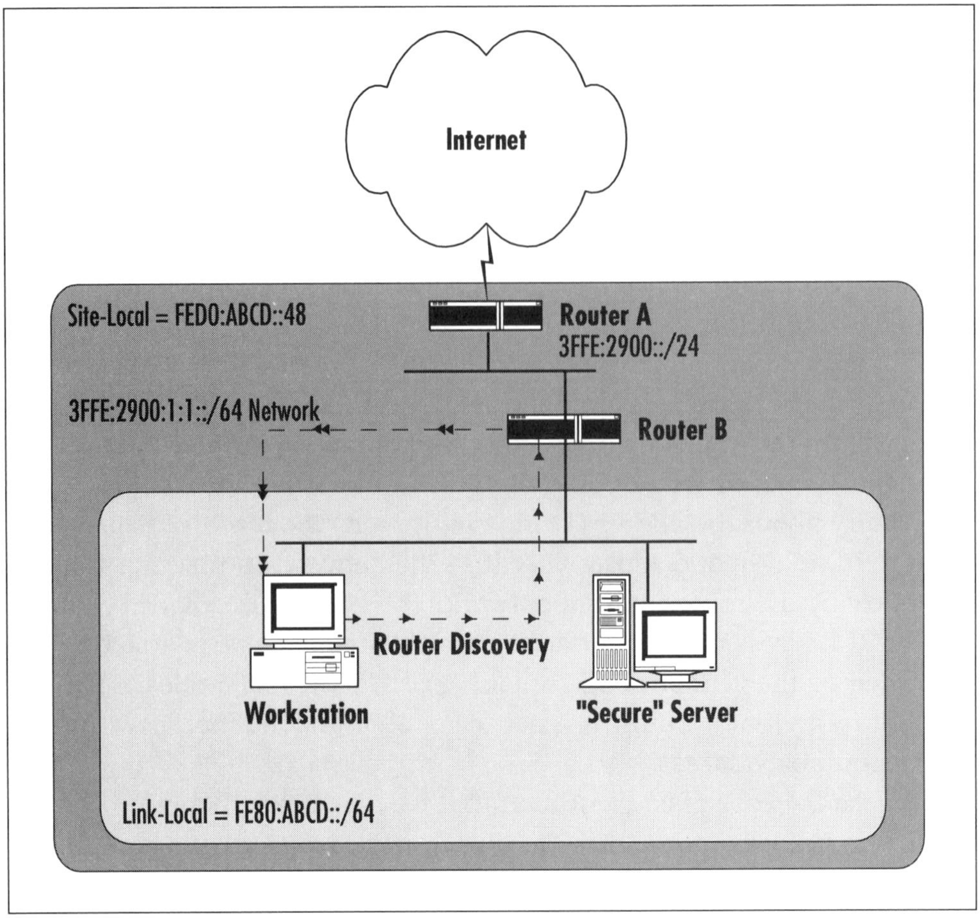

Improved Scalability of Multicast Routing

Now that we have studied unicast addressing, looked at the primary merits of multicast addressing, and discovered the potential of routing table size scalability on the Internet with IPv6, let us take a moment to discuss the multicast address in a little more detail. Multicast servers are perhaps the most misunderstood technology of today. Let's look into the concept of multicasting in general.

In the beginning, the Internet was primarily a research network upon which research data flowed from one university to another. This was not big business, so congestion problems were tolerated, and the data that people were sending was not dated (because data didn't need to be received in real-time). Today, by contrast, businesses and consumers are using the Internet for a vast array of applications. More and more, we are seeing different types of media going over the Internet, whether it is stock quotes, phone calls, or even our favorite TV channel. We see the need for media to not only arrive quickly, but also to be sent to an increased audience. Even things such as newsgroups are getting information out to millions of people each day.

This 1 to N transmission trend is bringing about a need for a new type of traffic sending, in which one person can send a piece of data to many people. In the past, if we wanted to send a piece of data to 10 friends, we would simply make 10 copies of that data, and send them to each person one at a time. However, as this type of transmission gains popularity, a scaling problem takes place. For instance, perhaps we have a video or a radio show that we wish to send out over the Internet. If we want to send this media to 10,000 people who all want to see this show in a fashion as close to real-time as possible, we run into a problem. Now in order to do so, we have to make sure that our upstream bandwidth is sufficient to handle up to 10,000 times the data rate of one transmission. We now must spend much more money in order to purchase this upstream bandwidth and satisfy our client base (our viewers or listeners). Fortunately, the concept of multicast was conceived some time ago, and has been in a testing phase for quite some time. The concept of taking one piece of data, and sending it to many interested parties at once, efficiently, becomes quite a complex routing problem, especially if we become caught in the unicast paradigm we are all used to. The concept of multicast addresses this problem.

In a multicast situation, we have a 1 to N (or M to N) relationship between the source and the destination. Instead of using a unicast address to designate that we are interested in receiving a given multicast feed, the concept of a multicast address is used. A multicast address, in IPv4, is usually referred to as a group address. This group address, when applied to a machine, or to an application on that machine, signifies that we are interested in listening to any data that is sent to that address. In IPv4, the address range from 224.0.0.0 through 239.255.255.255 is used to designate multicast group addresses. When someone wants to receive multicast feeds, they (temporarily or permanently, depending on the situation) address themselves with that address, and effectively listen for packets coming along that have that multicast address listed as a destination

The routing for multicast becomes rather complex, and is out of the scope of this book, but you are encouraged to read more about this. Good information can be found either in the Multicast Forum home page at http://www.ipmulticast.com, or in the IETF working groups regarding multicast. Some of the working groups you may wish to check out include the Mbone Deployment Working Group (www.ietf.org/html.charters/mboned-charter.html) or the Inter-Domain Multicast Routing Working Group (www.ietf.org/html.charters/idmr-charter.html). There are also a number of protocol-specific working groups currently active within the IETF, including the Multicast Source Discovery Protocol Working Group (MSDP) and the Protocol Independent Multicast Working Group (PIM). I leave it up to you to learn as much as you wish about the current updates to multicast routing in general. For the purposes of this book, let us assume that multicast works, and will help save us bandwidth, since now we only need to send one stream out of our Internet connection, and the Backbone will reproduce it as seen fit to make sure it gets to all the interested destinations.

IPv6 contains the concept of a multicast scoping. One of the nice uses of multicast can be in a corporate network. Perhaps a memo needs to be sent to all employees' workstations at once, or a live videoconference from the CEO needs to be sent over the corporate network to all employees. In a corporate network, we want to save as much money as possible on bandwidth, while maintaining an efficient routing structure. Multicast buys us just that. However, in most cases, we only want multicast information (streams) to get to the places that are supposed to see them. We do not want the whole Internet to hear our CEO talk about our newest secret initiative to take over our competition! For this, IPv6 has built in the concept of multicast scoping. With IPv6, we can designate certain multicast streams to be routed only within a certain area, and never to allow packets to get out of that area, for fear of who may see them. This scoping will be well known and understood by all routing entities, in order to ensure, through minimal configuration, that multicast data and multicast routes do not get outside the edges of the routing domain for which they are meant to exist. Figure 9.11 presents multicast addressing format in a little detail.

Figure 9.11 IPv6 multicast address format.

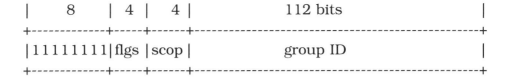

```
|    8    | 4 |  4 |                112 bits                      |
+-------------+-----+------+---------------------------------------------------+
|11111111|flgs |scop |              group ID                     |
+-------------+-----+------+---------------------------------------------------+
```

So as we can see, the multicast addressing architecture is a little different than that of the Globally Routable Unicast addressing format. Notice the first eight bits are all set to 1, which will allow a routing device to know immediately that the packet is multicast in nature, and subject to special handling associated with this packet type. The next four bits are used for flags. Currently, the first three bits in the flgs field are reserved, and undefined, so they should always be set to 0 (though you will find some implementers of protocols will use these bits fallaciously for some sort of proprietary signaling. This is fine, until the bits get standardized to something in the future, at which time incompatibilities arise). The fourth bit is known as the T bit (see RFC2460), and is used to decide whether the multicast address is a permanently assigned address (also known as *well-known*) or a temporary assignment (also known as *transient*). So this field will tell us if the multicast address being used is one that is standard (perhaps a group address used to contact all nodes within a given routing domain, for example) or a temporarily assigned address (perhaps the Monday night football game broadcast over the Internet). The next field is the one we are interested in here. The scope field will determine how far the multicast packet can go, in what areas of a routing domain the packet can travel, and the group address that can be advertised. The scope field values are in Table 9.3.

Table 9.3 Scope Definitions

0	reserved
1	node-local scope
2	link-local scope
3	(unassigned)
4	(unassigned)
5	site-local scope
6	(unassigned)
7	unassigned)
8	organization-local scope
9	(unassigned)
A	(unassigned)
B	(unassigned)
C	(unassigned)
D	(unassigned)
E	global scope
F	reserved

Depending on how we assign our multicast address, we can control how far the multicast packets will travel, and how far the routing announcements associated with that multicast group will get advertised. For instance, if you would like to advertise a multicast session of your fish tank in your office, and you would like the whole world to see it, you would assign a scope of E (1110 in binary). However, if you want to set up a multicast group so you and your coworkers can have a video conference over the corporate network, you would want to make sure to give the address used a scope of 5 (0101 in binary), or 2 if everyone involved is on the same LAN as you (0010 in binary). See how this makes life a little easier for controlling how far information gets propagated. Now, instead of relying on a Network Administrator to apply filters at the borders of each routing domain, we can rely on software (which generally is not susceptible to the same sort of random changes that networks are) to keep our traffic inside of the scope we want. This allows for privacy at a much easier level to implement. This is another benefit of IPv6. Not only are multicast boundaries well defined, they are also easy to maintain.

The Anycast Address

IPv6 defines a new type of address, known as the anycast address. Although this form of address is deployed in a limited fashion in IPv4, IPv6 integrates this address type into its operations, which improves routing efficiency. In this section we will explore some of the characteristics of the anycast address in detail, and discuss some of the interesting applications of the anycast address in the IPv6 Internet of the future.

An anycast address is an IPv6 address which is assigned to a group of one or more hosts that serve a common purpose or function. When packets are sent to the IPv6 anycast address, routing will dictate which member of the group receives the packet, via the closest machine to the source, as decided by the IGP (Interior Gateway Protocol: the routing protocol you use in your routing domain; e.g., RIP, EIGRP, IS-IS) of the network in question. In this way, it becomes possible to disperse functionality geographically across your network in a way that helps efficiency in two ways. This differs fundamentally with the multicast address. Although both the anycast and the multicast address are assigned to more than one host, the anycast address serves for data transmissions that are 1 to 1, whereas multicast addressing is used when a data transmission to multiple destinations is required. Let us look at the two main benefits of the anycast addressing scheme.

First, if you are going to the closest machine in a group, and it is irrelevant which group member you exchange information with in the anycast group, you are usually saving time by communicating with the closest (IGP-wise) group member. Second, when you are going to the closest anycast group member, you are saving bandwidth, because the amount of distance a packet has to travel is in most cases minimized by this approach. So not only do you save time with anycast, but you also save money (bandwidth IS money these days) with this approach.

The anycast address does not have its own set of bits to define it, however; instead, anycast addressing is derived from either scoped or Globally Routable Unicast addresses. From the point of an IPv6-speaking machine, the anycast address is no different than a unicast address. The only difference is that there may be other machines that are also numbered with the same scope of unicast address, within the same region for which that scope is defined (for instance, you may have more than one machine with a Site Local anycast address within a given site).

Now that we understand the differences between anycast and multicast addresses, let us look into some possible uses of the anycast address. One nice application that anycast can help with is DNS (Domain Name Service). If we were to offer DNS to many people or customers, as in the case of most Tier-1 Service Providers today, we would need to build our DNS in a way that can handle a large number of queries from all parties for which we provide this service. Because of this, it is more efficient to deploy multiple DNS servers, and spread them out geographically. This will allow for fail-over, if one DNS server becomes unreachable due to network failures, and will also allow us to spread the load of our DNS service between these servers. However, we do not want to make our customers assign too many different IP addresses of DNS servers, as most people only use one or two. Also, we want some way for one or two IP addresses to be used for all of our service geographically, for the fail-over reason just stated.

One way to do this would be to assign each DNS server that has identical configuration and authoritative information the SAME IP address. If we then inject routes to each of these DNS servers into our Backbone routing table, when someone wants to query our

DNS, the request will be sent to the geographically closest DNS server. This will allow us not only to split up the load between multiple DNS servers, but also will avoid backhauling DNS queries across our Backbone too much. So by this method of deployment, we are saving both time for our customers (DNS servers are close, so they the data transmission takes less time), and money for ourselves (bandwidth = money for Service Providers). Because DNS is UDP-based, rather than TCP-based, transactions between DNS servers and end-stations are quick, short, and not tracked with sequencing, error checking, etc. When we want to resolve a host name, a packet is sent to the DNS server requesting the address associated with a given Internet Domain Name, and a response is sent back with the answer. This makes the anycast-addressing model viable for this type of application. For more information on this specific type of deployment, you can read draft-catalone-rockell-hadns.00.txt.

For IT Professionals

Which Applications Are Good Candidates for Anycast?

Some applications may not be well suited for anycast deployment. For instance, TCP-based applications using anycast addressing for deployment will not provide the fail-over capabilities that the previous example provides. When we are using a UDP-based application, there is no sequencing information to keep track of. With TCP, we run into a problem: when a network problem occurs and users are in the middle of a TCP session with an anycast machine, the TCP sequencing will be all wrong when the traffic gets rerouted to the next-closest anycast server. In the case of Web traffic, which is largely TCP-based, the user would need to reload the Web page at least, to get to where he or she was when the failure occurred on the network. Other applications could have even more painful consequences associated with rerouting, so careful consideration should be given to which types of service are supplied using an anycast model.

The Need for Further Development

Although IPv6 does in fact present many new and useful ideas aimed at increased efficiency and ease of routing and configuration, the work that is needed prior to IPv6 deployment natively on the Internet is not done. In this section, we will look at one current issue that is gaining increased attention by the IETF working group IPNGWG (Internet Protocol, Next-Generation Working Group; please see http://www.ietf.org/html.charters/IPngwg-charter.html for more the working group's charter and the current status on their goals and how close they are to reaching them).

The Multihoming Problem

Now that we have basic familiarity with how IPv6 addressing and routing works, let us look at one of the potential problems associated with IPv6 routing. We know from earlier in this chapter that Tier 1 Service Providers will be given large chunks of address space, from which they will delegate smaller bits of that space to their customers, to number their own networks. We also know that fundamental to IPv6 is the concept of firm route aggregation, by which that Tier 1 Service Provider will need to announce the aggregate of their space only to other Tier 1 peers. This will keep the routing table size small, compared to what it could be without aggregation, and route stability maximized, as changes in small areas of one's network need not withdraw routes globally. This causes route dampening to affect reachability once a network failure occurs and is corrected.

However, what do we do when a smaller network, such as an ISP or a business, is buying Internet connectivity through multiple providers? Classically, in IPv4, the way to do this is to run BGP from that ISP or business to its upstreams, announcing the IP space that you obtained from one of your providers to both of your upstream providers. These announcements in turn will need to be announced everywhere, in order for the Network Administrators of this small ISP or business to retain the ability to load-share over both of these Internet connections inbound. So the subnet that is delegated now has to be accepted into the global route table. With IPv6, this violates fundamental principles regarding aggregation. If we look at the IPv4 scenario listed earlier in the chapter, and substitute IPv6 addresses, we are left with the identical problems. Not only will the Service Provider (the one that delegates the customer the address block) need to allow the smaller block announced from its customer, and heard through its peer (the one through which the customer also buys connectivity), but it will have to export the more specific route to all of its peers as well, so they automatically do not choose the other provider (from whom the address block was not delegated) as the more specific route advertisement, and therefore the best path to the customer. Both the IPNGWG and the NGTRAN-SWG (Next-Generation TRANSition Working Group) are looking into this problem. At the time of this writing, there are a couple of proposed solutions to this problem, but each of them presents other interesting dilemmas as well.

The first proposed solution to this problem is now written as an RFC (RFC2260). This approach, summed up, is to follow the aggregation principles as outlined previously in the chapter, until such time as a network failure occurs. When everything is working, the border router to upstream 1 sends only the prefix that was delegated by upstream 1 to upstream 1, and conversely, the border router that connects to upstream 2 announces only the prefix that upstream 2 has delegated, up to upstream 2. When a failure occurs, however, the border router that does not have a failure will announce both prefixes up to the upstream that is still working. When the connectivity failure is fixed, the illegal prefix is withdrawn, and the situation returns to normal. Although this proposal has merits, since it allows for fail-over for a downstream that is multi-homed and assigns addresses in its network from both providers, it does present some management problems for the upstream provider. If the upstream provider has an efficient routing policy towards its downstream customers, this usually includes a filter on the BGP session to that downstream that allows only routes that the upstream expects to hear from its downstream customer. Now the upstream would have to allow both the route it has delegated, and the route that the other upstream provider has delegated to its customer. Furthermore, the upstream provider who receives both prefixes has no way of knowing when or even if a network failure has occurred between its downstream customer, and the other provider. Also, the upstream provider has no way of determining when the downstream customer's other provider connection has been fixed, and the route should be withdrawn. The only way to know would be to rely on the downstream customer to have their configuration done correctly to avoid announcing both routes when everything works, and to have a software implementation that has the capability of automatically withdrawing the illegal route when the problem is fixed. A downstream customer in this case could easily misconfigure their outbound policy to announce both routes illegally, even when there is no failure. So in summation, although this proposal does have merits, the implementation specifics are not nearly as controllable as an upstream provider would like.

The second proposal, which is currently in use in the 6Bone IPv6 test network, is to assign each multihomed host an address for each upstream connection, and therefore IPv6 delegation, that the downstream customer has. For instance, if you are delegated two prefixes, one from Provider A, and one from Provider B, then each machine that wishes to use the benefits of multihoming would need to be assigned a prefix from each of the delegations received from Provider A and Provider B (let us call these delegations Prefix A and Prefix B). So each host now has two Globally Routable Unicast addresses, one from Prefix A and one from Prefix B. Then, each border router that speaks with the upstream providers can announce only the prefix delegated from that provider, and the routing is stable. In theory, if there is a network failure, and one provider becomes unreachable, then machines that were using the address associated with that provider can switch over to the address associated with the other provider, and connectivity is established.

This solution comes with its own host of problems. First, this approach is not that optimal when it comes to efficient delegation of IPv6 address space. Now each network with N upstream providers will have N addresses assigned to them. Furthermore, and perhaps more important, is that currently, TCP does not allow for address changing in the middle of a TCP session. The only solution is to adjust TCP to allow for this, which in itself seems easy, but the ramifications are far more than meet the eye. Most TCP applications are built in such a way that modifications of TCP would require modifications of the application. This could mean drastic reworking of current network software. Also, current operating systems themselves may need over-hauling in order to switch source addresses dynamically when a net-work becomes unreachable. How does a source know that a network failure has occurred in the right place? What if the destination had a problem? How would the source know if switching IPv6 source addresses would fix the problem? All of these factors lead us to believe that this is not a viable long-term solution either.

So as you can see, multihoming with IPv6 still has some work. It is currently of top priority in the IETF working group IPNGWG. Hopefully, their work will produce a solution that is both scalable, and able to accommodate the problems associated with either of the previous proposals. Stay tuned to this one!

The 6Bone

Now that we have the basis for understanding elementary IPv6 addressing and routing, let us look into current IPv6 deployment, and its successes and shortcomings. The primary example of IPv6 deployment is the IETF Next-Generation Transition Working Group (NGTRANSWG) 6Bone. The 6Bone is a network of IPv6-speaking entities interconnected over the classical IPv4 Internet. It consists of both native networks (where IPv6 is running without being tunneled through another Layer 3 protocol) and IPv4 tunnels between differ-ent IPv6 speaking entities. The purpose of this network is twofold. The first reason for the 6Bone is to provide implementers a means to test their IPv6 implementations in a large network where other vendors have deployed their own version of IPv6 implementations. By allowing this, we can ensure that IPv6 implementations are interoperable. This way, protocol developers can make sure that the protocol specifications are specific enough to allow for implementers to develop IPv6-speaking machines without ambiguity. The second reason for the 6Bone is to give network operators a chance to design networks and get their feet wet with the new protocol. Also, it allows operators to uncover any problems with the IPv6 protocol (such as the previous multihoming problems) that may have been missed or underappreciated during the protocol's conception.

Although the fathers of the IPv6 protocol were extremely meticulous in the protocol's design, it never hurts to get the new technology running on a live network somewhere prior to implementation on a grand scale. The 6Bone helps to work all of the details out, and test new features, prior to deployment, in a cooperative, multinational fashion. It follows all routing practices as defined by the IETF. For the most current IPv6 routing practices on the 6Bone, see www.ietf.org/internet-drafts/draft-ietf-ngtrans-harden-02.txt. (Note: This is an Internet draft. At the time of this writing it is in the last-call stage for RFC.) For more information on the 6Bone, please see http://www.6bone.net.

Summary

We can see that IPv6 provides for many of the presently needed improvements in the Internet. Not only does it solve the address depletion problems of today's IPv4, but it also makes for a more scalable Internet core, which can help improve routing efficiency of the Internet as a whole. By allowing for 128 bits of addresses, we can see that there is adequate address space for the future. By then aggregating this address space in an efficient manner, we may establish a firm upper limit on routing table size in the Internet core. This, in turn, can help us to build an Internet to take us into the future.

Although the two primary problems of the Internet can be solved with IPv6, the protocol improvements do not stop there. Also built into the IPv6 protocol are means for hop-by-hop routing, authentication of packets, encrypted packets, tag switching, Quality of

Service, and other things to make the protocol more versatile than its grandfather, IPv4. Furthermore, IPv6 has built into it the ability to use multicast and unicast routing in a manner such that boundaries easily can be scoped to ensure that data does not get to places where it is not allowed. IPv6 also introduces the use of an anycast address, for applications that may be serviced by multiple machines, but the need for distribution of these services in a scalable manner is required.

We can also see that IPv6 is already in testing, and is starting into production in some areas, connected via the 6Bone. This virtual backbone will provide for testing of both IPv6 implementations and the protocol itself. Clearly, we can see that IPv6 is getting more and more attention, and is looking like a promising aspect for the future of the Internet.

FAQ

Q: How can I get onto the 6Bone?

A: The 6Bone has a mailing list where operational issues associated with it, as well as new proposals for transition strategies, are discussed and collaborated. This list can be joined by sending e-mail to majordomo@isi.edu, with "subscribe 6bone" as the contents of the message. It is encouraged that all mailing list members of the 6Bone actually become IPv6 speakers on the 6Bone as well. Refer to the Web page www.6bone.net for information on how to get connected, and to find the nearest upstream provider to obtain a tunnel.

Q: Where do I get an IPv6 address?

A: IPv6 addresses are delegated out by the Providers who have them. When you join the 6Bone or any other IPv6 network, your upstream Provider is responsible for providing you with adequate IPv6 address space to take care of your needs.

Q: Where do I get the IPv6 protocol specifications for more details?

A: All protocol specifications are in the form of IETF RFCs (Requests for Comments). These can be found at www.ietf.org; there is a search engine where you can pull up all current IPv6 RFC and Internet drafts.

Chapter 10

The IPv6 Header

Solutions in this chapter:

- The changes from IPv4 to IPv6 and their implications on headers

- Additional functionality in IPv6: Flow Labeling and Security Features

- Formats of IPv6 header and extension headers and their usage

- Implications of IPv6 on upper-layer protocol

Introduction

The IPv4 has served us well in the past; however, some design decisions made a couple of decades ago have many shortcomings for supporting current and future networking. The IPv6 is the new IP protocol that is designed to meet the requirements for supporting future generation networking, while interoperating with the current IPv4.

With the growing popularity of internetworking, it has become apparent that the number of nodes in the Internet will outgrow the 32-bit address space used in IPv4. Further, as the number of addressable nodes increases, the size of the routing table is likely to grow. The larger routing table degrades the performance of the IP network; this, and the shortage of address space, are the primary concerns for continued use of IPv4.

These concerns raised the need for a new IP protocol, IPv6. In addition to solving these problems, several other features have been incorporated in the design of IPv6 to enhance the IP network.

The advances in hardware technology have resulted in the development of new applications, which may need special provisioning when deployed over the network. However, the connectionless, on-demand nature of IPv4 does not lend itself well for per–connection-based support. The design of IPv6 includes flow labeling for providing per–connection-based support.

For continued success of IP internetworking, the use of the IP network should be plug-and-play, similar to the use of a telephone system. To achieve the plug-and-play concept in the IP network, configuration of an IP node should be simple, if not automatic. Even with the continued autoconfiguration effort such as Dynamic Host Configuration Protocol, configuration of an IPv4 node has been non-trivial so far. The IPv6 has been designed to better support autoconfiguration of IPv6 nodes.

In recent years, the use of the Internet for many businesses has been increased drastically, and e-commerce has also gained popularity. It is necessary to implement security features in internetworking. The security features are mandatory in IPv6, making an IPv6 network more suitable for meeting security requirements.

Most importantly, the design of IPv6 has provided for the transition from IPv4 to IPv6. This transition cannot occur overnight; therefore, the IPv6 has been designed with the assumption that the IPv4 network will coexist with the IPv6 network for a long time, if not indefinitely. Many design decisions are in place for interoperability with IPv4 nodes. A lot of investment has been made in the current infrastructure of IPv4 networks. Without the ability to communicate with the existing network, no new protocol is likely to replace the current internetworking infrastructure successfully, regardless of its benefits.

The design of IPv6 has stemmed from limitations of what IPv4 offers, and from lessons learned in IPv4. First, this chapter covers the changes from IPv4 to IPv6. Expanded addressing, simplified header, improved extension and option support, flow labeling capability, and authentication and privacy capability summarize these changes. The first three changes are due to modifications to bases of IPv4 technology such as using 128-bit address size instead of 32-bit, not allowing intermediate routers to perform fragmentation, or embedding optional information in extension headers instead of including it in the IP header. The latter two changes include additional functionality incorporated into the design of IPv6 to satisfy the network support current and near-future applications demand.

This chapter also covers the format of the IPv6 header and extension header. The fields in the IPv6 header are discussed and compared to those in the IPv4 header. The formats of extension headers are provided, along with an example usage of each extension header.

Finally, upper-layer protocol issues imposed upon the use of IPv6 are covered.

Expanded Addressing

IPv4 uses 32-bit addresses, which potentially can address up to 2^{32} nodes. However, the combination of network and local address hierarchy and reserved address space for special handling, such as loopback and broadcast, reduces the number of addressable nodes. At the same time, the exponential growth of computer networks in recent years indicates the outgrowth of addressable node using 32-bit addresses.

Furthermore, the network and local address hierarchy in IPv4 address architecture leads to inefficient use of address spaces. For instance, an organization that needs far fewer than 2^{16} hosts, but more than 2^8 hosts, may waste much usable address space when using a 2-octet network address and a 2-octet local address.

Despite the inefficiency of the network address hierarchy, a flat network address (e.g., a sequential address assignment) is not realistic, since network operations such as routing would be impossible. When using a sequential address assignment, the size of routing tables would be unmanageable and routing would become a slow process because of the amount of data that needs to be scanned.

The IPv6 address size has been increased to 128 bits. The advantages of this increase are, one, more addressable nodes, and two, the ability to support more levels of addressing hierarchy. Better addressing hierarchy leads to more efficient network operations and network scaling. As more networks are added, the size of the routing table increases, and the routing process takes longer. A careful planning of addressing hierarchy can limit the growth of the size of the routing table, while routing packets efficiently. An organizational change often means configuration changes at each node that is affected. For instance, when an organization obtains a new Internet Service Provider (most often network address change), each node in this organization must be reconfigured to reflect this. However, despite continuous efforts of developing autoconfiguration mechanisms such as Dynamic Host Configuration Protocol, the reconfiguration process often needs to be done manually. The larger address space can support autoconfiguration better.

In addition to increased address size, IPv6 has eliminated broadcast address and added the notion of anycast address, which can be used to send a packet to any one of a group of nodes.

Simplified Header

IPv6 has evolved from the IPv4 technology; experiences learned from the IPv4 are reflected in the design of IPv6. The length of the IPv4 header varies between 20 and 60 bytes, and there are 11 fields within the first 20 bytes of the IPv4 header. The complexity of IPv4 can lead to inefficient router operations. By employing a simpler header, 8 fields in 40 bytes and fixed length of the header, IPv6 can enhance the performance of routers.

A couple of fields in the IPv4 header have been either removed or embedded in extension headers. Since options are embedded in extension headers, the length of the IPv6 header is no longer variable, thus eliminating the need for the Header Length field in the IPv6 header. In IPv6, only source node can perform fragmentation; therefore, the information necessary for fragmentation and reassembly is removed from the IP header. Since the upper-layer protocol, such as TCP and UDP, calculates the checksum for the entire packet, the Checksum field also can be removed from the IP header.

Improved Support for Extension and Option

Since the total length of the IPv4 header is variable, the Header Length field is used to indicate its length. The number of bits in this field, 4 bits, determines the maximum length of the IPv4 header. In particular, 60 bytes is the largest size of the IPv4 header, for this field specifies the header length in 4-octet units. Since the fixed portion of the IPv4 header is 20 bytes long, it places a stringent requirement on the length of options.

Length of Addressing Options in IPv4

This limit on the length of options has eliminated some options (such as the routing option), because they are ineffective in IPv4 network.

Aside from the limit on their length, options are examined at every router on the path, when included. However, often these options are information applicable only to the destination node. Including such options in the IPv4 header forces each router on the path to examine the packet, thus leading to inefficient router operations.

By embedding options in extension headers, the option length limit has been relaxed greatly, and options can be used more effectively in IPv6. Use of a proper extension header in IPv6 allows a packet to carry optional information that is applicable only to its destination node as well as to all intermediate routers more efficiently. The proper extension also allows hardware memory lookups, since the headers are fixed.

Flow and Flow Labeling

IPv4 was designed to be connectionless (or stateless); in other words, each packet belonging to the same session is routed independently, and two packets from the same session may arrive at the destination via different paths.

This approach works well under error-prone networks, such as the time when IPv4 was being developed. There is a cost associated with this, however—processing each packet at every hop adds to the delay, and it is not trivial to provide special services for a communication between selected source and destination.

With technological advances in networking, network failures, especially hardware failures, have been drastically reduced in recent years. Also, new applications are more tolerant to errors, but more sensitive to fluctuations in delay. It is inevitable that networks support such applications. In the design of IPv6, the notion of a flow has been incorporated in order to facilitate special handling of data belonging to an application with special requirements.

RFC 1883 defines a flow as a sequence of packets sent from a particular source to a particular destination for which the source desires special handling by the intervening routers. IPv6 provides a framework for an easier per-flow handling. A video application, which may have strict requirements on the maximum delay difference, may take advantage of flow and flow labeling in IPv6. The application marks each packet with a flow label, and routers on the path remember the state of packet transmissions on this flow. This state information will help a router to determine which packet to service next. A router may service a packet that has the largest elapsed time since its previous packet in the flow, for instance.

Authentication and Privacy

No real security features have been incorporated into the design of IPv4. However, the wide use of IP networks by the general public has led to the use of computer networks as a means of conducting various kinds of businesses. Thus, it is natural for the design of IPv6 to provide necessary security measures. RFC2401 defines the security architecture for the IP network, and IPv6 uses the Authentication Header and Encapsulating Security Payload extension headers to implement such features.

Both Authentication Header and Encapsulating Security Payload header can be used alone, or as a combination of source and destination or two security gateways. The former mode of operation is called Transport Mode and the latter is referred to as Tunneling Mode operation.

When used in transport mode, the source and destination of a packet is the sender and receiver of the Authentication Header, respectively. When used in tunneling mode, however, the security

gateway at the source of a packet would be the sender of the
Authentication Header, and the security gateway at the destination
of this packet would be the receiver of the Authentication Header.

The sender calculates secure and reliable checksum (message
digest) calculation over packets and places it in the Authentication
Header. The receiver recalculates it and compares it to the value
provided in Authentication Header. When these values differ, a
packet is assumed to be damaged during transmission.

Using Encapsulating Security Payload, a payload of a packet
may be encrypted, or the entire IP packet may be encrypted in tunnel mode via security gateways. When encrypted in tunnel mode,
real source and destination and some IP header information can be
hidden, thus making it more secure.

IPv6 Header

The IPv6 header is fixed in length and aligned at 8-octet boundary,
unlike the IPv4 header, which is variable-length and aligned at 4-
octet boundary. Most modern computer architectures are optimized
to read 8 octets at a time. Thus, the length of the IPv6 header or
extension headers is designed to be a multiple of 8-octets for 8-octet
alignment. With a fixed IPv6 header, a router can efficiently process
a packet. For instance, a router must decide if there are any options
in an IPv4 packet by reading the Header Length field. Processing a
variable-length header leads to inefficient router implementation.

The changes from the IPv4 header and IPv6 header will be covered in the subsequent section. In this section, each field in the IPv6
header and its intended role is described. Figure 10.1 shows the format of an IPv6 header.

The IPv6 header stores the information necessary to route and
deliver packets to their destination. The headers are processed by
each node along the path. The first 4-bit field, version, indicates the
version of the Internet Protocol being used, and its value is 6 for
IPv6. This field is necessary because it allows both protocols to
coexist on the same segment without conflicts. The next two fields,

traffic class and flow label, are used to provide differentiated services and support applications requiring special handling per-flow. The 8-bit traffic class field can be used to provide differentiated services based on the nature of data being transmitted. This field is similar to the intended use of the type of service field in the IPv4 header. For instance, an organization may set up its network to prioritize network traffic based on applications, source and destination information, etc., and hosts and/or routers use the traffic class field to differentiate the priority. The values and the exact use of this field are yet to be determined. The flow label, in combination with source and destination addresses, can uniquely identify a flow that requires special handling by intermediate routers. When a router identifies a flow the first time, it remembers the flow and any special handling this flow requires. Once per-flow handling has been set up, the processing of subsequent packets belonging to this flow can be shorter than processing individual packets. The 16-bit payload length field, similar to the total length field in the IPv4 header, indicates the length of the packet, not including the length of the IPv6 header. The 8-bit next header field is used to indicate the next header following the IPv6 header. The intended use of this field is identical to the use of the protocol field in the IPv4 header. The hop limit can be used to limit the number of intermediate hops a packet is allowed to visit, which can prevent packets from being circularly routed in a network. In IPv4, the time to live field has been used to prevent packets from being routed circularly. The name of this field has been chosen to reflect accurately the purpose of this field. As in IPv4 headers, IPv6 headers contain source and destination IP addresses. Unlike IPv4 nodes, IPv6 nodes use 128-bit addresses.

Figure 10.1 IPv6 header.

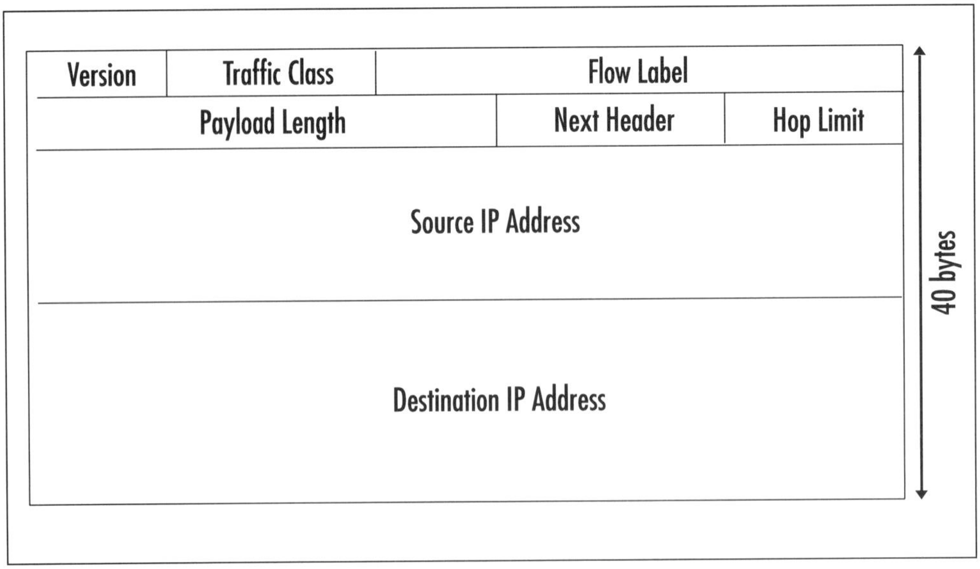

Version	Traffic Class	Flow Label		
Payload Length			Next Header	Hop Limit
Source IP Address				
Destination IP Address				

40 bytes

IPv4 Header

Figure 10.2 illustrates the format of an IPv4 header.

The first 4-bit version field in the IPv4 header is used to indicate the current version of the Internet Protocol (IP) being used. The same field is used in the IPv6 header and is necessary in order to make IPv6 backward-compatible.

The 4-bit header length field is necessary for the IPv4 header to indicate the length of the header since the total length of the IPv4 header is a variable length between 20 and 64 bytes, depending on the presence and the length of options in the option field. However, this field is not necessary in an IPv6 header, because an IPv6 header is a fixed length of 40 bytes.

The intent of this type of service field in IPv4 is similar to the traffic class field in the IPv6 header. Nevertheless, this field has not been widely accepted and used in IPv4 implementations.

Next, two fields in the IPv4 header, flags and fragmentation offset, are all related to the handling of fragmentation and the reassembly of packets in IPv4. In IPv4, an intermediate hop may further fragment a packet when the maximum transfer unit (MTU) on the outgoing link is smaller than the size of the packet that is to be transmitted on that link. Unlike IPv4, in IPv6, fragmentation processing takes place only at the source node, using a path MTU. Further, information related to fragmentation is encoded in the Fragmentation header as an extension header in a IPv6 packet. Therefore, identification, flags, and fragmentation offset fields are not necessary in the IPv6 header.

Figure 10.2 IPv4 header.

Version	Hdr Len	Type of Service	Total Length	
Identification			Flags	Fragment Offset
Time to Live		Protocol	Header Checksum	
Source IP Address				
Destination IP Address				
Options, if any				

20 bytes
up to 60 bytes

In the original design of IPv4, the time to live field is used to indicate the number of seconds to live in a network, thus preventing packets from being circularly routed, if a circular route exists in a network. However, in implementations, this field is used to limit the number of hops the packet is allowed to visit. At each hop, a router decrements this field, and when this field reaches 0, the packet is removed from the network. In IPv6, this field is renamed to hop limit, a more accurate description of the implementation.

The protocol field, which is used to indicate the next protocol (header) following this IPv4 header, is similar to the Next Header field in the IPv6 header.

The header checksum field is used to maintain the integrity of the IPv4 header. However, the higher layer calculates the checksum again for the entire packet, thus making this field redundant. Therefore, this field is not used in IPv6 header. If applications require a higher degree of integrity, they can achieve it through appropriate use of Authentication Header and Encapsulating Security Payload extension headers.

The source and destination fields in the IPv4 header remain the same in the IPv6, except that the IPv4 node addresses are 32 bits, and the IPv6 node addresses are 128 bits.

The use of options in IPv4 implies that each intermediate node in the path needs to examine the option field in the IPv4 header, although the options may be pertinent only to the destination node. This leads to inefficient router performance when options are used. In IPv6, optional information is encoded in extension headers.

Extension Headers

Extension headers, placed between the IPv6 header and the upper-layer protocol header, such as a TCP-header, are used to carry optional Internet-layer information in a packet. An IPv6 packet may carry zero, one, or more extension headers. The Next Header field in the IPv6 header and extension headers is used to indicate which extension header or upper-layer protocol header follows the current header.

For IT Professionals

Next Header Values and Corresponding Headers

Table 10.1 provides the Next Header value and the corresponding headers. Except for the Hop-by-Hop Options header, the Next Header value appears in the immediately preceding header. When the Hop-by-Hop Options header is used, it must follow immediately after the IPv6 header. Therefore, the Next Header value of 0 can appear only in IPv6 header.

Table 10.1 Next Value Headers

Next Header Value	Next Header
0	Hop-by-Hop Options header
4	Internet Protocol
6	Transmission Control Protocol
17	User Datagram Protocol
43	Routing header
44	Fragment header
45	Inter-Domain Routing Protocol
46	Resource Reservation Protocol
50	Encapsulating Security Payload
51	Authentication header
58	Internet Control Message Protocol
59	No next header
60	Destination Options header

When a TCP header immediately follows an IPv6 header without an extension header, the value of the Next Header field in the IPv6 header indicates that the following header is a TCP header. When a packet using TCP as its upper-layer protocol carries one extension header, Routing header, this extension header is placed between the IPv6 header and the TCP header. The Next Header field in the IPv6 header indicates that the Routing header follows the IPv6 header and the Next Header field in the Routing header indicates that the TCP header immediately follows the Routing header. The Next Header value of 59 indicates that there is no extension or upper-layer protocol header following the current header.

A full implementation of IPv6 includes the following extension headers: Hop-by-Hop Options, Routing (Type 0), Fragment, Destination Options, Authentication, and Encapsulating Security Payload. The recommended ordering of extension headers, when multiple extension headers are present in a packet, is as follows:

- IPv6 header
- Hop-by-Hop Options header
- Destination Options header (to be processed by all destination nodes appearing in the routing header)
- Routing header
- Fragment header
- Authentication header
- Encapsulating Security Payload header
- Destination Options header (to be processed only by the final destination of the packet) upper-layer header.

Except for the Destination Options header, each extension header should appear at most once in a packet. The Destination Options header contains information to be processed by the final destination node. When the Routing header is present, an additional Destination Options header may be used for options to be processed by all nodes listed in the Routing header; in this case, there will be at most two occurrences of Destination Options headers in an IPv6 packet.

When an IPv4 packet carries an option that is applicable only to its destination node, all intermediate nodes must examine and process the packet before forwarding, thus impacting the performance of the forwarding nodes.

For Managers

Should Options Be Used in IPv4 Networks?

Most often, routers are implemented in a way that packets containing options are often handled after handling packets without options. Therefore, the use of options is discouraged in IPv4 networks.

Except for the Hop-by-Hop Options header, extension headers are examined or processed only by the destination node (or nodes, in the case of multicast) of the packet. Thus, an IPv6 packet may carry optional information applicable only to its destination node, without impacting the performance of all intermediate nodes. The Hop-by-Hop Options header can be used to carry optional information that needs to be examined or processed at all intermediate nodes.

The value of the Next Header field in the current header determines the next action to be taken, and the semantics of current extension header determines whether to continue processing the next header. Thus, extension headers must be examined in the order they appear in a packet. A node discards a packet and sends an ICMP Parameter Problem message to the source of the packet, with an ICMP Code value of one, unrecognized Next Header type encountered, when it receives unrecognized Next Header value in a packet. Because the Hop-by-Hop Options header must immediately follow the IPv6 header, the Next Header value of zero in any header other than IPv6 header is treated as a packet with unrecognized Next Header value.

Currently, the Hop-by-Hop Options header and the Destination Options header carry a variable number of options, encoded in Type-Length-Value (TLV) format, as seen in Figure 10.3.

The Option Type identifiers are encoded in such a way that the highest-order two bits specify the action to be taken when the processing node does not recognize the Option Type, and the third-highest bit specifies whether or not the Option Data of that option can change en route to the packet's final destination. For instance, when a node encounters an unknown option type value of 130 (1000 0010), the highest-order two bits indicate that the node must discard the packet and send an ICMP Parameter Problem, Code 2, message to the source of the packet. Table 10.2 describes the encoding of Option Type and its meaning for handling unrecognized Option Type.

Figure 10.3 TLV-encoded option format.

Option Type	Opt Data Len	Option Data

Option Type   8-bit identifier of the type of option
Opt Data Len   8-bit unsigned integer. Length of the option Data
                field of this option, in octets.
Option Data   Variable-length field. Option-Type-specific data.

Table 10.2 Option Type Encoding

Highest-order two bits	Action to be taken
00	Skip over this option and continue processing the header.
01	Discard the packet.
10	Discard the packet and, regardless of whether or not the packet's Destination Address was not a multicast address, send an ICMP Parameter Problem, Code 2, message to the packet's Source Address, pointing to the unrecognized Option Type.
11	Discard the packet, and only if the packet's Destination Address was not a multicast address, send an ICMP Parameter Problem, Code 2, message to the packet's Source Address, pointing to the unrecognized Option Type.

Some Option Type values may change as the packet progresses through the route to its destination. The third highest-order bit of the Option Type is used to indicate if its data value can be changed en-route or not. The third highest-order bit is 0 when Option Data does not change en-route and 1 when it may change. When the

Authentication header is used, the source of the packet computes the authenticating value over the packet and places in the Authentication header. For Option Type whose Option Data may change en route, the Option Data is treated as zero-valued octets when computing the packet's authenticating value.

As stated before, extension headers are designed to be a multiple of 8-octets in length. To ensure that the end of the Option Data field is aligned with the 8-octet boundary, specific Option Types may be associated with alignment requirements in the form of xn+y, indicating that the Option Type must appear at an integer multiple of x octets from the start of the header, plus y octets. For instance, a 4n+2 alignment requirement indicates that the Option Type must start at any 4-octet offset from the start of the header, plus 2 octets, such as 2, 6, 10, 14, etc.

Two padding options, Pad1 option and PadN option, may be used to make headers containing options to be multiples of 8 octets in length. The Pad1 option, one zero-valued octet, is used to insert one octet of padding, and the PadN option is used to insert more than one octet of padding. The format of the PadN option is shown in Figure 10.4. To insert 2 octets of padding, Pad2, one octet with the value of 1 and one octet (Option Data Length field) with the value of 0 can be used. The Pad2 option is a special case in that there is no Option Data, or Option Data of 0 length is used.

Figure 10.4 PadN Option format.

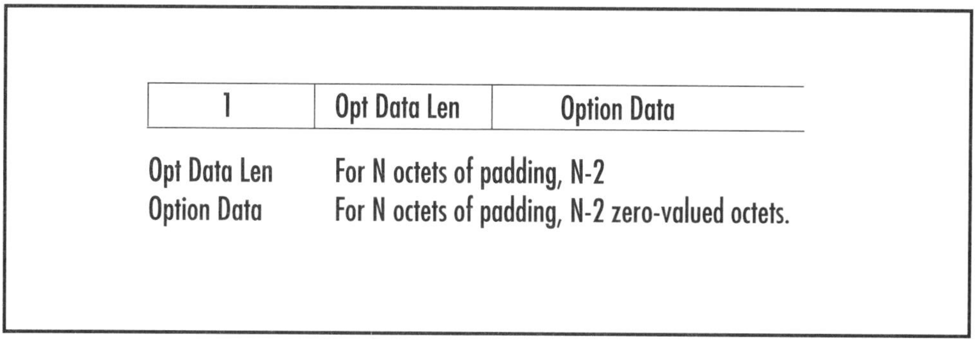

1	Opt Data Len	Option Data

Opt Data Len	For N octets of padding, N-2
Option Data	For N octets of padding, N-2 zero-valued octets.

Hop-by-Hop Option Header

The Hop-by-Hop Options header, identified by a Next Header value of zero in the Ipv6 header, carries optional information that must be processed by every node along a packet's delivery path. For instance, it may be necessary for a router to examine and process a packet containing control messages for new protocols, such as RSVP. The use of the Hop-by-Hop Options header allows routers to examine selectively packets for special handling, if necessary. The format of the Hop-by-Hop Option header is shown in Figure 10.5. Note that the Header Extension Length field is the length of the Hop-by-Hop Options header, in 8-octet units, not including the first 8 octets. In other words, when the length of TLV encoded option(s) is less than or equal to 6 octets, the Header Extension Length field is zero. Examples of Hop-by-Hop Options include Router Alert Option and Jumbo Payload Option.

Figure 10.5 Hop-by-Hop Options header.

Next Header	Hdr Ext Len	
	Options	

Next Header   8-bit selector. Identifies the type of header immediately following the Hop-by-Hop Options header. Uses the same values as the IPv4 Protocol field [RFC1700].

Hdr Ext Len   8-bit unsigned integer. Length of the Hop-by-Hop Options header in 8-octet units, not including the first 8 octets.

Options   Variable-length field, of length such that the complete Hop-by-Hop Options header is an integer multiple of 8 octets long. Contains one or more TLV-encoded options.

A call set-up control message using RSVP protocol needs special provisioning at each router along the path of the connection. Using the Router Alert Hop-by-Hop option, routers can provide special handling. Processing of a Hop-by-Hop option may result in processing of an upper-layer protocol such as RSVP.

The Option Type of the Router Alert option is 5 (00000101), indicating that nodes not recognizing this option should skip it and continue processing the header, and Option Data must not change its value en route. The Option Length of Router Alert option is 2; thus, the valid range of Option Data is between 0 and 65,535. Currently, only 0, 1, and 2 have been defined to indicate a packet containing ICMPv6 Group Membership message, RSVP message, and Active Network message, respectively. No alignment requirement has been associated with this option.

Figure 10.6(a) illustrates a packet containing a Router Alert Hop-by-Hop Option. The value of the Next Header field in IPv6 header is 0, indicating that Hop-by-Hop Options header follows. All nodes in the path of this packet are to examine and process this packet. The Next Header field of the Hop-by-Hop Options header indicates the next header following this Hop-by-Hop header—TCP header in this example packet. The Extension Header Length field is 0 since there is only one option, Router Alter option, and the total length of TLV encoding of this option is 4 octets. Since there is no alignment requirement associated with this option, its TLV encoded option is placed first and Pad2 Option is used to make the length of this Hop-by-Hop Options header to be exactly 8 octets.

The IPv6 header uses the 16-bit Payload Length field, which limits the maximum length of a packet to 65,536. However, the advances in hardware enabled the transmission of a jumbogram, a packet with payload larger than 65,536 octets. This option supports jumbograms up to 4,294,967,296 octets. When path MTU can support payloads larger than 65,535, this option may be used to transmit jumbograms.

The Option Type of Jumbo Payload Option is 192 (1100 0010), indicating that nodes not recognizing this option type must discard this packet and send an ICMP, Parameter Problem, Code 2, message to its sender only if the destination is not a multicast, and Option Data must not change en route. The Option Length field of this option is 4 octets, and the Option Data is the length of the IPv6 jumbogram, not including the IPv6 header. When this option is used, the Payload Length field in IPv6 is set to 0. This option has an alignment requirement of 4n+2.

Figure 10.6(b) illustrates a packet with Jumbo Payload Hop-by-Hop option. The Next Header field in the IPv6 header indicates that the Hop-by-Hop Options header follows. Note that the Payload Length field in IPv6 header is set to 0 in this sample packet. The Next Header field in this Hop-by-Hop options header indicates that the next header is TCP header. The Extension Header field is 0 because the total length of TLV encoded Jumbo Payload option is 6 octets. The value in Option Data of this packet indicates that the payload of this packet is 2,818,048 octets (0x002A FFFF). Since the end of Option Data is aligned with 8-octet boundary, no padding option is necessary in this sample packet.

Processing of a Jumbo Payload option must detect several format errors and send an appropriate ICMP Parameter Problem message. These format errors include the absence of the Jumbo Payload option when the IPv6 Payload is 0 and the IPv6 Next Header is 0, the use of the Jumbo Payload option when the IPv6 Payload is not 0, use of the Jumbo Payload option when actual payload is less than 65,535, and the use of the Jumbo Payload option when the Fragment Header is present.

For Managers

Do Not Use Jumbo Payload Option and Fragment Header Together

The Fragment header uses the 13-bit Fragment Offset field, in 8-octet units, to indicate the offset of the fragmented data, relative to the original packet. In other words, the maximum offset can be the 65,536th octet. Therefore, it makes little or no sense to use the Jumbo Payload option and Fragment header at the same time.

Figure 10.6 Packets with the Hop-by-Hop Options header.

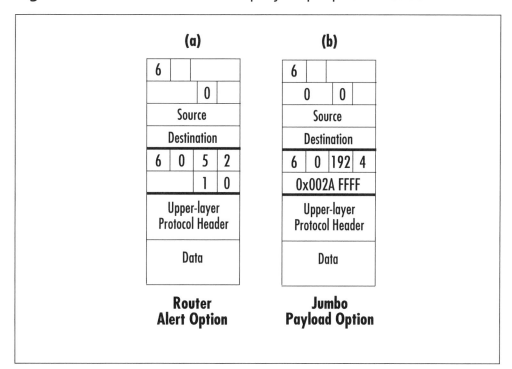

Routing Header

The Routing Header, identified by a Next Header value of 43 in the immediately proceeding header, allows an IPv6 source to determine routes to reach its destination by listing one or more intermediate nodes to be visited (very similar to IPv4's Loose Source and Record Route option). The format of the Routing Header is shown in Figure 10.7.

When a node encounters an unrecognized Routing Type, and Segment Left is zero, it ignores the Routing header and continues to process the next header. However, if Segment Left is nonzero, a node discards the packet and sends an ICMP Parameter Problem, Code 0, message to the packet's Source Address. Currently, only Type 0 has been defined, and Figure 10.8 shows the format of Type 0 Routing header.

Figure 10.7 Routing header.

Next Header	Hdr Ext Len	Routing Type	Segments Left
Type-Specific Data			

Next Header	8-bit selector. Identifies the type of header immediately following the Routing header. Uses the same values as the IPv4 Protocol field [RFC1700].
Hdr Ext Len	8-bit unsigned integer. Length of the Routing header in 8-octet units, not including the first 8 octets.
Routing Type	8-bit identifier of a particular Routing header variant.
Segments Left	8-bit unsigned integer. Number of route segments remaining, i.e., number of explicitly listed intermediate nodes still to be visited before reaching the final destination.
Type-Specific Data	Variable-length field, of format determined by the Routing Type, and of length such that the complete Routing header is an integer multiple of 8 octets long.

An example of Type 0 Routing header use is in supporting new protocols, such as RSVP. In RSVP, a connection path may be established, and all packets belonging to the connection follow the same path to reach the destination. Then the source of this connection may use a Type 0 Routing header to specify the path to its destination.

Another use of a Routing header is to communicate with a mobile node away from its home network without triangle routing. Without Route Optimization, which may or may not be supported, packets may have to be sent to the mobile node's home network and be forwarded by the home agent, creating triangle routing, when a mobile node is away from its home network. The source of such a connection can specify the path using a Type 0 Routing header to allow the source of a connection to specify its path and avoid triangle routing.

Figure 10.8 Type 0 Routing header.

Next Header	Hdr Ext Len	Routing Type=0	Segments Left
Reserved			
Address [1]			

·
·
·

Address [n]

Next Header	8-bit selector. Identifies the type of header immediately following the Routing header. Uses the same values as the IPv4 Protocol field [RFC1700].
Hdr Ext Len	8-bit unsigned integer. Length of the Routing header in 8-octet units, not including the first 8 octets. For the Type 0 Routing header, Hdr Ext Length is equal to two times the number of addresses in the header.
Routing Type	0
Segments Left	8-bit unsigned integer. Number of route segments remaining, i.e., number of explicitly listed intermediate nodes still to be visited before reaching the final destination.
Reserved	32-bit reserved field. Initialized to zero for transmission; ignored on reception.
Address[1...n]	Vector of 128-bit addresses, numbered 1 to n.

For the connection between source node s and destination node d via routers r1 and r2, source node s creates an IPv6 packet with the routing header, as shown in Figure 10.9(a). Notice that the destination field is r1, the first router in the path, instead of the final destination node d. Recall that except for the Hop-by-Hop Options header, all other extension headers are examined only by the packet's destination node. Since router r1 is the destination of this packet, after examining the IPv6 header, it continues to process the next header as indicated by the Next Header field in the IPv6 header. In this case, the Routing header will be processed by router r1.

The Extension Header Length field is 4, indicating that the length of the Routing header is four 8-octets, not counting the first eight octets. The value 4 is also twice the number of addresses (2 as indicated in the Segments Left field) in this Routing header. The first address in the Routing header is the next router in the path, r2, followed by the final destination node d.

Router r1 decrements the Segments Left field and swaps the values in the destination field in the IPv6 header and the first address in the Routing header. Figure 10.9(b) shows the packet sent from router r1 to router r2. Similarly, after examining the IPv6 header, router r2 continues to process the Routing header, since the destination field of the IPv6 is r2. Again, router r2 decrements the Segment Left field and swaps the values in the destination field in the IPv6 header and the second address in the Routing header. When processing the Routing header, the index of the address to visit can be computed using the Header Extension Length and the Segment Left fields (the Header Extension Length/2 – the Segment Left + 1). When the Segment Left is 0, the node handling this Routing header proceeds to process the next header in the packet, whose type is identified in the Next Header field in the Routing header.

When processing the Type 0 Routing header, format checking is performed. Recall that the Header Extension length is two times the number of addresses in the Routing header. Thus, the Header Extension length must not be an odd length. A node processing this packet discards the packet and sends an ICMP Parameter Problem, Code 0, message to the source node. Since the Header Extension length is two times the number of addresses in the Routing header, the largest value in the Segment Left field is at most half of the Header Extension length. If the Segment Left is larger than the half of the Header Extension length, the node handling the packet also discards this packet and sends an ICMP Parameter Problem, Code 0, message to the source.

Figure 10.9 Packets with a Routing header.

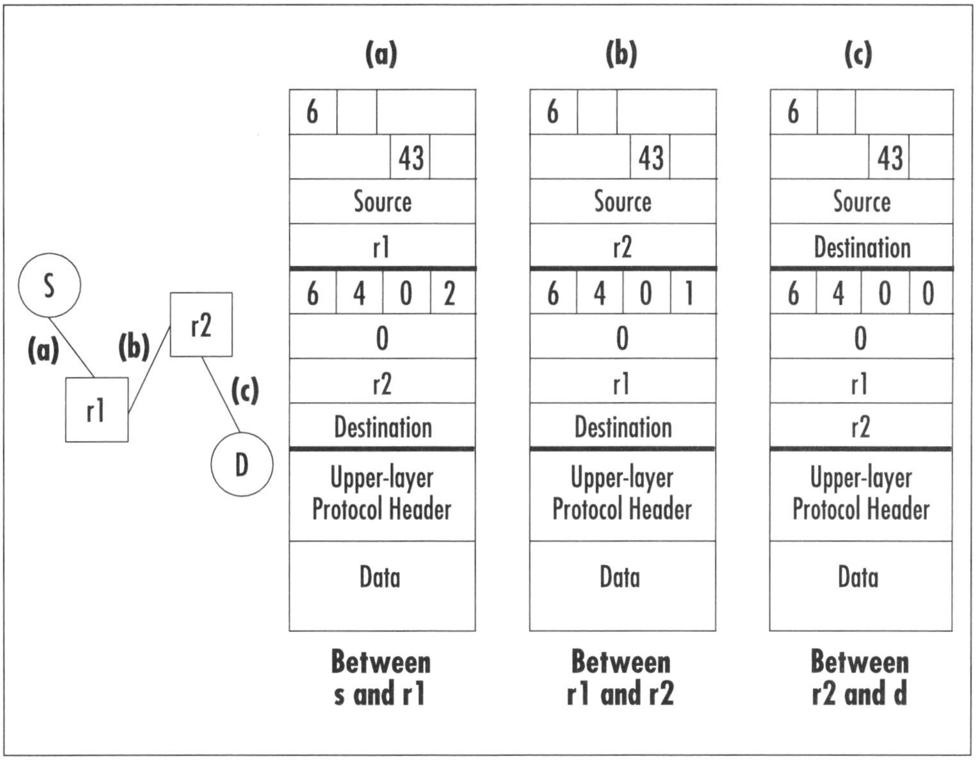

For IT Professionals

Type 0 Routing Header

The Type 0 Routing header is processed by all nodes appearing in the address field, and each node decrements Segment Left field and swaps the values in the destination field in the IPv6 node and the address. Thus, multicast addresses must not appear in the address in the Type 0 Routing header or in the IPv6 destination field of a packet containing the Routing header.

Fragment Header

The 16-bit Total Length field in the IPv4 header limits the maximum size of a packet to be 64k bytes. However, depending on the link technology used, the actual size of a packet may be further limited. In IPv4 packet transmission, each IP-layer is responsible for fragmenting packets if necessary to ensure that the packet size would not exceed the Maximum Transfer Unit (MTU). Thus, the user data sent in a single packet from a source node may arrive at the destination node in multiple packets if there is a link whose MTU is smaller than the link MTU at the source node. This approach, however, may not be the most optimal solution for the path.

For IT Professionals

Packet Fragmentation Overhead

Consider an application that transfers a segment of 3000 bytes at a regular interval, where the link MTU at the source is 3000 bytes. The next link MTU is 1500 bytes; thus, a packet is fragmented into two packets of 1500 bytes each. However, the following link MTU is 1000 bytes. Then each of 1500-byte packets will be further fragmented into two packets, 1000 bytes and 500 bytes. If the path MTU had been known at the source, the source node would have fragmented 3000 bytes in three packets. The overhead involved in transmission of 3000 bytes is 20 bytes, IP header alone without options. The overhead is higher when upper-layer protocol header overhead is considered.

In general, fragmentation involves high overhead, thus the use of fragmentation should be discouraged. Links with configurable MTU (e.g., PPP links) should configure their MTU to at least 1280 octets or greater, which is the required MTU in IPv6.

In IPv6, only source nodes perform fragmentation. A source node first finds the path MTU and then segments the fragmentable part of the original packet so that the length of each fragmented packet does not exceed the path MTU. The original packet before fragmentation consists of two parts: the unfragmentable part and fragmentable part. The IPv6 header and any extension headers that need to be processed at each hop on the way to the destination are unfragmentable, and extension headers processed only by the final destination node (or nodes in the case of multicast) are considered to be fragmentable.

When Hop-by-Hop Options header is present, but not the Routing header, the unfragmentable part of the original packet includes the IPv6 header and the Hop-by-Hop Options header. When the Routing header is present, the unfragmentable part includes the IPv6 header, the Hop-by-Hop Options header, the Destination Options header, and the Routing header, if the Hop-by-Hop Options header and Destination Options header are present.

The Fragmentation header is identified by the Next Header value of 44 in the immediately preceding header. Figure 10.10 shows the format of the Fragmentation header. The source node generates a unique 32-bit identifier for every fragmented packet sent to the same destination. Except for the last fragmented packet, the fragmentable part of the original packet is divided so that each fragmented part is of length integer multiples of 8 octets long. The Fragment Offset field is used to indicate the offset of the data following this Fragmentation header, relative to the start of the Fragmentable part of the original packet.

Consider the packet shown in Figure 10.11(a). This packet needs to be further fragmented by the source node since its path MTU is 1514 bytes. The unfragmentable part of the original packet in the example includes the IPv6 header and the Routing header (the Next Header of the IPv6 is 43). The original packet is broken into three parts. Since the Ethernet header is 14 bytes, the IPv6 packet including the IPv6 header cannot be longer than 1500 bytes. Since the Routing header is part of the unfragmented part, each fragment includes the Routing header. Further, the Fragmentation header (8 octets) is added, leaving 1412 bytes for user data. However, the Fragmentation Offset field in the Fragmentation header is in an 8-octet unit. Therefore, the maximum size of the fragmentable part of the original packet is limited to 1408. This explains 1456 in the Payload length field in the IPv6 of the first fragmentation as shown in Figure 10.11(b).

Figure 10.10 Fragmentation header.

Next Header	Reserved	Fragment Offset	Res	M
Identification				

Next Header	8-bit selector. Identifies the initial header type of the Fragmentable Part of the original packet. Uses the same values as the IPv4 Protocol field [RFC1700].
Reserved	8-bit reserved field. Initialized to zero for transmission; ignored on reception.
Fragment Offset	13-bit unsigned integer. The offset, in 8-octet units, of the data following this header, relative to the start of the Fragmentable Part of the original packet.
Res	2-bit reserved field. Initialized to zero for transmission; ignored on reception.
M flag	1=more fragments; 0=last fragment.
Identification	32-bit identifier.

The Next Header fields in the Routing header in all three fragments (Figure 10.11(b), (c), and (d)) are 44, indicating that the next header following this Routing header is the Fragmentation header. The Next Header field in the first fragment is 6, indicating that the upper-layer protocol header follows this Fragmentation header. However, the Next Header fields in the other two fragments are 59, indicating that there are no more headers following this

Fragmentation header. In this example, the hexadecimal of 0x12345678 is used to indicate that the same identifier is used for all fragments. The Fragmentation Offset field is used to indicate the offset, in 8-octet units, of the data following the Fragmentation header, relative to the start of the fragmentable part of the original packet. Thus, the Fragmentation offset in Figure 10.11(c) indicates that the data following this Fragmentation header should be positioned in the 176x8[th] byte in the fragmentable part when reassembled at the destination node.

Figure 10.11 Example of fragmentation.

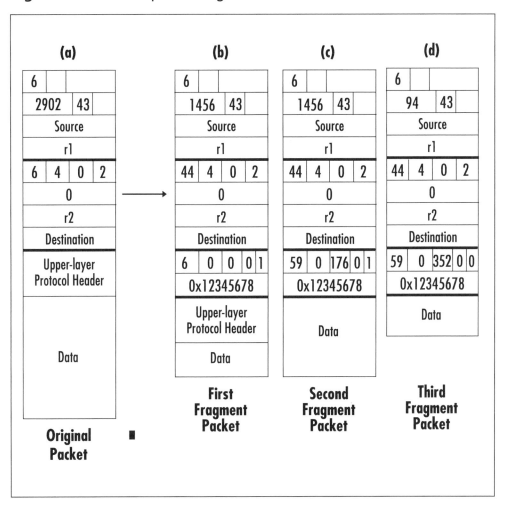

Authentication Header

In an IP network (both IPv4 and IPv6), the Authentication header is used to provide integrity and data origin authentication for IP packets and to protect against replays. However, in this section, all terms are provided based on the IPv6 network. The Authentication Header provides authentication for the IPv6 header and extension headers fields that may not change en route. For instance, the Destination Address field in the IPv6 header changes at every hop when the Type 0 Routing Header is used. In this case, the Authentication Header cannot provide the authentication of the Destination Address field. Figure 10.12 shows the format of the Authentication Header.

Figure 10.12 Authentication header.

Next Header	Payload Len	Reserved
Security Parameters Index (SPI)		
Sequence Number Field		
Authentication Data (Variable)		

Next Header	8-bit selector. Identifies the type of header immediately following the Authentication header.
Payload Len	8-bit unsigned integer. Length of the Authentication header in 4-octet units, not including the first 8 octets.
Reserved	16-bit reserved field. Initialized to zero for transmission; ignored on reception.
Security Parameter Index	32-bit unsigned integer. Combination of this field, destination address, and security protocol. Identifies the Security Association for this packet.
Sequence Number	32-bit unsigned integer. Monotonically increasing counter-value.
Authentication Data	Variable-length field containing the Integrity Check Value (ICV) for this packet. This field must be an integral multiple of 8-octet units in length.

Note that the Payload Length field is in a 4-octet unit (32-bit word), not including the first eight octets (or 2 units of 4-octet).

Thus, with 96-bit Authentication Data value, the Payload Length will be 4. For debugging purposes, the Null authentication algorithm may be used. In this case, the Payload Length field will be 2.

The Sequence Number field is used to provide protection against anti-replay. When a Security Association is established between source and destination nodes, counters at sender and receiver are both initialized to 0. It is mandatory for the sender to increment this field for every transmission; however, the receiver may elect not to process. This service is effective only if the receiver processes this field.

The Authentication Data field contains the Integrity Check Value (ICV) for this packet. The authentication algorithm, selected when the Security Association is established between the sender and the receiver, specifies the length of the ICV, the comparison rules, and the processing steps necessary. This is the value computed over the packet by the source node and verified by the destination node by comparing this value to the value recomputed at the destination node.

The Authentication header may be applied in transport or tunnel mode. The transport mode Authentication header, implemented in hosts, provides protection for the upper-layer protocol header and any fields in the IPv6 header, and extension headers that do not change in transit. The tunnel mode Authentication header is applied to the original IPv6 packet, encapsulating the original packet by constructing a new IPv6 packet using a distinct IPv6 addresses, such as security gateway.

In transport mode, the Authentication header, viewed as an end-to-end payload, is placed after the IPv6 header and Hop-by-Hop, Routing, and Fragmentation extension headers. Recall that the Destination Options header may appear once before the Routing header, the options in the Destination Options header are applicable to intermediate nodes specified in the Routing header. In this case, the Authentication header comes after the Destination Options header as shown in Figure 10.13.

Figure 10.13 Header order with Authentication header in transport mode.

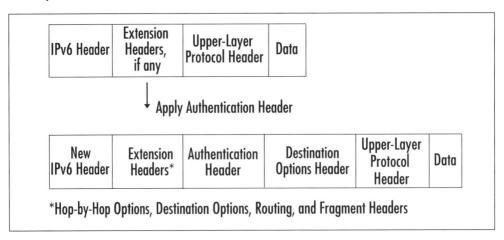

In tunnel mode, the Authentication Header is applied to the original IPv6 packet using distinct IPv6 addresses as communication end points (e.g., addresses of security gateways). A new IPv6 header is constructed with addresses of security gateways as source and destination addresses. Fragmentation processing may be necessary after applying the Authentication header. Thus, a newly constructed IPv6 packet may undergo further processing if necessary. Figure 10.14 shows the order of headers after applying Authentication header in tunnel mode.

Figure 10.14 Header order with Authentication header in tunnel mode.

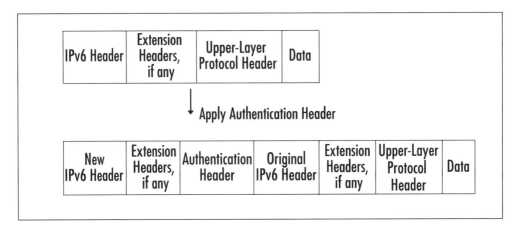

Encapsulating Security Payload

The Encapsulating Security Payload header, used in transport mode or in tunnel mode, also provides security services in both IPv4 and IPv6 networks. The security services provided through the Encapsulating Security Payload include confidentiality, authentication (data origin authentication and connectionless integrity), an antireplay service, and limited traffic flow confidentiality. Implementation and options chosen at the time of Security Association establishment determine the security services provided.

As in the case of the anti-replay service provided by the Authentication header, the source increments the Sequence Number; however, the destination node must check this field to enable the anti-replay service. To provide traffic flow confidentiality service, true source and destination information should be hidden. Thus, this service requires that the Encapsulating Security Payload header be used in a tunnel mode.

Figure 10.15 shows the format of the Encapsulating Security Payload header. The Next Header value of 50 in the immediately preceding header indicates that the Encapsulating Security Payload header processing is necessary.

The mandatory Payload Data field contains encrypted data described by the Next Header field. The encryption algorithm used specifies the length and the location of the structure of the data within the Payload Data field. To fulfill the encryption algorithm requirement of the length of the plain text or the 4-octet boundary alignment of the Payload Data field, the use of padding may be necessary.

Figures 10.16 and 10.17 illustrate the sequence of an IPv6 packet with its encrypted portion when Encapsulating Security Payload headers are used in transport mode and tunnel mode, respectively.

Figure 10.15 Encapsulating Security Payload header.

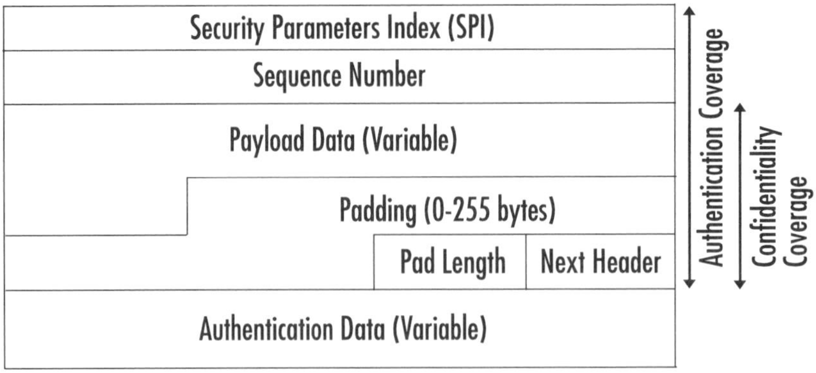

Security Parameters Index	32-bit unsigned integer. Combination of this field, destination address, and Security Protocol (ESP) identifies the Security Association for this packet.
Sequence Number	32-bit unsigned integer. Monotonically increasing counter-value.
Payload Data	Variable-length field containing data described by the Next Header field.
Padding	Variable-length field containing 0 to 255 of 8-bit padding.
Pad Length	8-bit unsigned integer. Indicates the number of pad bytes immediately preceding it.
Next Header	8-bit selector. Identifies the type of data contained in the Payload Data.
Authentication Data	Variable-length field containing an Integrity Check Value (ICV) computed over the ESP packet minus the Authentication Data.

Destination Options Header

A source node may need to convey optional information that needs to be processed by a destination node. For instance, when a mobile node is away from its home network, a home agent (i.e., a router at the home network) may be a proxy forwarding packets to the mobile node. A mobile node away from its home network needs to send control messages to its home agent so that the home agent could set up the proxy service and forwarding packets destined for the mobile node at its current address. An IPv4 network, a packet when containing options in the IPv4 header, will be subject to an examination at every hop on the path.

Figure 10.16 Header order with Encapsulating Security Payload in transport mode.

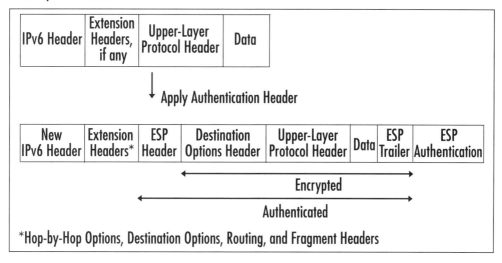

Figure 10.17 Header order with encapsulating security payload in tunnel mode.

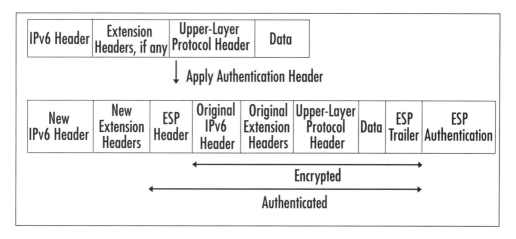

In an IPv6 network, such optional messages can be handled efficiently either using an extension header dedicated for handling specific optional information or using the Destination Options header. Packet fragmentation or authentication information is handled as an extension header as shown previously. The IPv6 Mobility Support

Internet-Draft proposes four Destination Options to support Mobile IPv6.

The optional information may be encoded either in a separate extension header or in the Destination Options header, based on the desired action to be taken at the destination node, when the node does not recognize the option. Optional information that requires a few octets whose desired action is to send an ICMP Unrecognized Type message to the sender only if the destination node is not a multicast address, may be encoded in a separate extension header.

The Destination Options header, identified by a Next Header value of 60 in the immediately preceding header, carries optional information that needs to be examined and processed only by a packet's destination node (nodes, in multicast). The format is shown in Figure 10.18.

Figure 10.18 Destination Options header.

Next Header	Hdr Ext Len	
	Options	

Next Header	8-bit selector. Identifies the type of header immediately following the Hop-by-Hop Options header. Uses the same values as the IPv4 Protocol field [RFC1700].
Hdr Ext Len	8-bit unsigned integer. Length of the Hop-by-Hop Options header in 8-octet units, not including the first 8 octets.
Options	Variable-length field, of lenght such that the complete Destination Options header is an integer multiple of 8 octets long. Contains one or more TLV-encoded options.

Upper-Layer Protocol Issues

The layered architecture in general shields the upper layer protocols from changes in the network layers. However, a couple of issues need to be addressed. For instance, upper-layer protocols that compute checksums over packets must account for changes in IPv6 including use of 128-bit addresses and final destination, not intermediate destinations when the Routing header is used, and so forth.

It has been discussed that the time-to-live field, which behaves differently than its original definition, has been renamed to hop limit. Any upper-layer protocol that relies on the original meaning of the time-to-live may have to make necessary adjustments. The maximum upper layer payload size also needs to be adjusted to reflect that the length of the IPv6 header is 40 bytes long.

Summary

In all aspects of IPv6 design, the limitations imposed upon the design of IPv4 have been resolved or improved, the inefficiency in IPv4 has been eliminated, and the additional capabilities have been added to make IPv6 suitable for next-generation IPs.

IPv6 uses 128-bit addresses, providing a greater number of addressable nodes, better support for stateless autoconfiguration, and a better address hierarchy, which in turn leads to better routing. Embedding optional information in extension heads allows efficient router implementations while being able to handle optional information directed to routers. The use of extension headers to carry optional information fixed the IPv6 header length. Combining with the Fragmentation At Source Only policy simplified the IPv6 header, thus increasing the efficiency of routers. The limit on options has been relaxed, and it is much easier to add new options using extension headers.

Further, the design of IPv6 incorporated the concept of flow, and flow labeling along with the source and the final destination information helps routers maintain the state information of the flow for special handling, if necessary. The security and privacy features are built into the design of IPv6.

FAQs

Q: Where are good resources for obtaining more information on IPv6?

A: There are many sites on the Net. However, these two sites can be a good starting point:

http://www.ietf.org/html.charters/ipngwg-charter.html

http:// playground.sun.com/pub/ipng/html/ipng-main.html

Q: What is the core set of RFCs specifying IPv6 header and extension headers?

A: Most of information in this chapter is based on the following RFCs. Newer RFCs may render these RFCs obsolete:

RFC2460—IPv6, Hop-by-Hop Options, Routing, Fragment, and Destination Options

RFC2402—IP Authentication Header

RFC2406—IP Encapsulating Security Payload Header

Q: What is the implementation status?

A: It is being developed for many host systems and routers, including 3Com, Cisco Systems, Digital, IBM. The http:// playground.sun.com/pub/ipng/html/ipng-main.html site also has information and links providing the details.

References

[RFC2462} "IPv6 Stateless Address Autoconfiguration."
S. Thompson and T. Narten. December, 1998.

[RFC2401] "Security Architecture for the Internet Protocol."
S. Kent and R. Atkinson.

"Route Optimization in Mobile IP." C. Perkins and D. Johnson.
Internet draft, draft-ieft-mobileip-optim-07.txt, November, 1997.
Work in progress.

[RFC2402] "IP Authentication Header." S. Kent and R. Atkinson.

Appendix A

Address Assignment

Solutions in Appendix A:

- Registries
- Provider-Based Assignments
- Cost of an IP Address
- How to Find an IPv4 Address Delegation
- How to Find an IPv6 Address Delegation
- Internet Governance

Introduction

Each host connected to an IP network must have an IP address. For connectivity on the Internet, the address space must be managed to ensure the uniqueness of each address.

In the past, Jon Postel was giving IP addresses to universities connected to the Internet (well, the Arpanet at that time). Then, Internic, an umbrella created by the US government, gave IP addresses to any requesting organization. At that time, Jon Postel was still managing the whole address space, giving ranges of addresses to Internic.

Registries

Now, the Internet Assigned Numbers Authority (IANA) is managing the whole IPv4 address space and the IPv6 address space. IANA gives ranges of addresses to regional registries; those registries give addresses ranges to Internet Service Providers (ISPs) who then give addresses to corporations (or to smaller ISPs). Each level of delega-tion has to prove to the upper level that it has consumed most of its address space before requesting another range of addresses.

The three regional registries are:

- American Registry for Internet Numbers (ARIN): http://www.arin.net

- Réseaux IP Européens-Network Coordination Center (RIPE-NCC): http://www.ripe.net

- Asia-Pacific Network Information Center (APNIC): http://www.apnic.net

ARIN covers North America, South America, the Caribbean, and sub-Saharan Africa. RIPE-NCC covers Europe, the Middle East, and parts of Africa. APNIC covers Asia and the Pacific.

If you are not connected to the Internet and don't want to be, then there is an IP address space reserved for that situation. It is called the private address space and is described in RFC1918 and discussed in the NAT chapter in this book.

On the other hand, if you need addresses for your network, you should ask your upstream Internet provider to give you a range of addresses for your own use. As soon as you move to another provider, you will need to remove the previous range of addresses and renumber to the new range of address.

Provider-Based Assignments

Around 1996, to minimize the routing table explosion, the technical community agreed to enforce Classless Inter-Domain Routing by asking corporations to get their range of IP addresses only from their upstream provider. By doing so, the number of entries in the global routing table will grow at a much lower rate than the number of networks connecting to it, because ISPs aggregate the addresses of their customers. But there are some exceptions to this rule, mainly when you are multihomed.

In IPv6, the addressing architecture is based on provider-based addresses, which means that IPv6 enforces this CIDR at the beginning. As discussed in the IPv6 chapter, IPv6 clearly will be more scalable by this optimized routing and by the address space it has. The drawback of renumbering when using provider-based addresses has been addressed in IPv6 by a specific protocol.

For Managers

Obtaining IP Addresses for the Network

To get IP addresses for your network, ask your upstream provider. Note that when you change providers, you will have to change the IP addresses.

Cost of an IP Address

In theory, an IP address costs nothing. The registries are not-for-profit organizations. They charge a fee to their clients (ISPs) for the registration service, not for the IP address themselves. In some ways, ISPs will include this cost in the prices of their service to their clients, so the effective cost of IP addresses is hidden somewhere.

How to Find an IPv4 Address Delegation

Each regional registry maintains a database of its address assignments. ISPs are mandated to provide the information about their own assignments to customers. All this information is available by using a simple query protocol called whois. From the early days, whois has been available in Unix as a command, but has not been available in the other environments. Now, all registries have a Web interface to the whois database, which makes it accessible to users. The following URLs point to the Web whois interface for all registries:

- ARIN: http://www.arin.net/whois/index.html
- RIPE: http://www.ripe.net/db/whois.html
- APNIC: http://www.apnic.net/apnic-bin/whois.pl
- Network Solutions (Internic):
  http://www.networksolutions.com/cgi-bin/whois/whois
- US Department of Defense: http://nic.mil/cgi-bin/whois

The whois database includes not only IP addresses, but other data, such as the maintenance of those IP addresses, the Autonomous System (AS) numbers, etc.

Here is an example: I want to know who is responsible for the 206.123.31.0 address space. I choose to go to the ARIN whois Web interface (http://www.arin.net/whois/index.html) and ask for the address in Figure A.1.

Figure A.1 ARIN whois web interface.

Whois Database Search

`206.123.31.0`   Submit

The answer given by the ARIN whois database is shown in Figure A.2.

Figure A.2 ARIN whois answer to 206.123.31.0.

```
Canadian Registry (NETBLK-CA-RISQ3) CA-REGISTRY3    206.123.0.0 - 206.123.255.0
ViaGenie Inc. (NET-VIAGENIE)    VIAGENIE                         206.123.31.0
```

The answer in Figure A.2 says that the 206.123.X.X range has been given by ARIN to the Canadian Registry, and the Canadian registry gives the 206.123.31.0/24 range to Viagénie Inc. Then, if I click on NET-VIAGENIE to know more about it, it will show me the information in Figure A.3.

Figure A.3 ARIN whois answer to NET-VIAGENIE.

```
ViaGenie Inc. (NET-VIAGENIE)
    3107 des hotels
    Ste-Foy, Quebec G1W 4W5
    CA

    Netname: VIAGENIE
    Netnumber: 206.123.31.0

    Coordinator:
       Blanchet, Marc   (MB841-ARIN)   Marc.Blanchet@VIAGENIE.QC.CA
       418-656-9254

    Domain System inverse mapping provided by:

    JAZZ.VIAGENIE.QC.CA           206.123.31.2
    SOCRATE.RIQ.QC.CA             199.84.128.1

    Record last updated on 23-Jan-1996.
    Database last updated on 8-Nov-1999 03:49:11 EDT.
```

This answer tells me where Viagénie Inc. is located, who is responsible for it, and what DNS servers are answering for the inverse mapping of those addresses.

The whois databases are all defined with objects (like the NET-VIAGENIE object) that have a maintainer associated with it. In this example, the maintainer ID of the NET-VIAGENIE object is MB841-ARIN. This is the way to keep track of who is responsible for which object. It is the same with the domain names registries.

How to Find an IPv6 Address Delegation

To test IPv6, a test network called 6Bone was built in July 1996. It is still running and alive. Each site has a prefix (address range) delegated from a test prefix allocated by IANA: 3ffe::/16. A registry with a whois interface has been set up to handle the registrations, and is available through the 6Bone Web site: http://www.6bone.net.

The official IPv6 addresses are available from the previous registries (ARIN, RIPE, and APNIC) and these registries have the same Web interface for both the IPv6 and IPv4 addresses.

Internet Governance

For a few years, work has been done in the global community for Internet governance, which covers many domains and issues. The current orientation for IP addresses assignments is to move the IANA functions to the Internet Corporation of Assigned Names and Numbers (ICANN: http:://www.icann.org). But at the time of this writing, many discussions are still pending.

Keep Yourself Informed about the Internet Management Issues

The regulation of the Internet is a hot issue, and it will not be easily resolved, but it will certainly have many consequences for the way the Internet is managed. You should follow the discussions and be up-to-date in this area. The place to begin is at the Internet Society (ISOC) Web site (http://www.isoc.org) or ICANN Web site (http://www.icann.org).

Summary

Address assignments are controlled at the higher level by IANA. It assigns ranges of addresses to regional registries as needed, and those registries assign ranges of addresses to ISPs, which then assign to them to corporations. This enables CIDR, which makes Internet routing efficient. This process is for both IPv4 and IPv6. You can see the assignments by looking at the whois databases at the various registries.

Important discussions are currently being held on Internet governance, mostly around ICANN.

Index

A

ABR. *See* Area Border Router.

ABSR, 261

ACK bit, 167, 173

Active routers, 246

ActiveX, 177

Ad hoc reports, 63

Address Resolution Protocol (ARP). *See* Reverse Address Resolution Protocol.

  cache, 292

  protocol, 322

Addresses. *See* Broadcast; Class A; Class B; Class C; Host; Multicast; Permanent addresses; Private addresses; Reserved addresses; Restricted addresses; Routable addresses; Routers; Supernets.

  administrator, 15, 192

  allocation, 10, 201–205, 220. *See also* Devices.

  assignments, 10–13. *See also* Class A; Dynamic Host Configuration Protocol; Internet Protocol; Internet Service Provider; Manual address assignment; Template-based address assignment.

    examples, 13

    templates, 205

  blocks, 15, 46, 47, 94, 97–98, 214, 234, 378

    assignation, 204

  classes, 3, 226

  conflicts, 162

  conservation strategies, 88–90

  determination. *See* Subnets.

  fields, 365

  hierarchical allocation, 52

  hierarchical organization, 370–375

  information, 126

  management, 286–333

  mapping. *See* Internet; Local net addresses.

  masks, interaction, 27–30

  number, 98

  per interface. *See* Multiple addresses per interface; Single address per interface.

  pools, 310, 312. *See also* Domain Name System.

  quantity, 196–197

  ranges, 55, 57, 207

    determination, subnet usage, 31–32

  scope, 310, 312. *See also* Dynamic Host Configuration Protocol.

  simplification, 396–398

  spaces, 369

    comparison. *See* Public address spaces.

  translation, 98. *See also* Layer 3; Network Address Translation; Port Address Translation.

  usefulness, 196–197

Addressing, 4. *See also* Classful addressing; Classless addressing; Classless Inter-Domain Routing; Multicast addressing; Prefix-based addressing; Private addressing; Secondary addressing.

  basics, 1

  economics, 91–96

  expansion, 415–416

  FAQs, 37–38

  hierarchies, 101

    support, increase, 390–394

461

S

Administering Active Directory

Solutions in this chapter:

- Introduction to Administering Active Directory

- Publishing Objects in Active Directory

- Locating Objects in Active Directory

- Controlling Access to Objects

- Delegating Administrative Control of Objects

- Overview of Active Directory Service Interface (ADSI)

- Best Practices

Introduction to Administering Active Directory

As organizations grow and require more applications, services, and resources, additional management and administration become necessary. Even the smallest companies now seem to require computer networks and their services, including the assistance of an IT professional, as either a full-time employee, a contractor, or a third party. Fulfilling these needs can become expensive very quickly, so it is necessary to find the most effective and efficient methods of reducing total cost of ownership (TCO).

The IT industry has developed many options to ease this burden, including the concept of directory service, which has been used for years to define many different services from one end of the spectrum to the other. For example, Microsoft has called its user accounts database NTDS (NT Directory Service) for some time. Other vendors use other forms of directory services to perform similar functions. Microsoft has incorporated many of the current and new technologies into its new operating system, Windows 2000. Microsoft has also updated and redesigned its previous NTDS into a new form, Active Directory.

Although Active Directory is fairly new, many of the concepts upon which it is based have long been in use throughout the computer industry. The Active Directory namespace is based on current DNS standards that have been in place for years. Other features have been added that are fairly new to Windows; for example, the Encrypting File System (EFS), Kerberos authentication for communications, and Certificate Authorities have been added to provide a more scalable and secure environment. With these features comes a requirement for a robust directory service to support them. This is where Active Directory comes in.

To use and manage Active Directory, you need a good understanding of the components and objects used within it, and you must understand the management interfaces and how to use them. Other features included with Active Directory, such as the search mechanisms and security subsystems, have been enhanced. These can be used to provide advanced administration and a solution that can meet the needs of most organizations.

Active Directory Concepts

You must understand several concepts and components in order to use the services that are available in Active Directory. These concepts define its layout as well as the operational factors that must be considered. Each component of Active Directory is important in making this new directory service work for you.

The components and concepts that make up Active Directory help to form the directory infrastructure, and each must be properly designed and/or maintained to provide a reliable and stable Windows 2000 environment.

Directory

The directory included with Windows 2000 houses the information required to perform many administrative tasks such as user management, printer management, and security information maintenance. Many of the tools included use this directory to integrate their services in order to provide a more comprehensive and cohesive networking environment. The directory information is stored within a data store that is replicated among domain controllers (DC), which are computers that provide services such as authentication, directory replication, and resource location. In other words, if an administrator makes a change to the directory on one domain controller, the change will be copied to all other servers maintaining replicas of the directory. In addition, administrators and users can publish resources within Active Directory.

The directory is stored on domain controllers much as it was in earlier versions of Windows NT. Only one domain controller is required for a domain, and you can have anywhere from one to thousands if necessary. Each domain controller maintains a replica of the directory. These computers are used to provide scalability, redundancy, and efficient resource location by providing users with multiple copies of the directory.

The data that is stored within the Active Directory can be divided into two areas: private and public. The information is stored in a file located on the domain controllers named NTDS.dit and is stored in <system root>\NTDS by default. The location of the database can be specified during the domain controller promotion process. Private data is secured, while public data is freely replicated among domain controllers in a shared system volume.

Three forms of public data are replicated.

- **Configuration information** describes the topology or layout of the directory. Information may include domains, trees, domain controllers, and global catalog servers.

- **Domain information** contains information about the objects located in the directory. This includes the information contained within objects such as user attributes or computer properties.

- **Schema information** defines the attributes and objects that are available within the directory. For example, the schema defines a user object and its available attributes.

Namespace

Active Directory uses namespaces to define its boundaries. A namespace is primarily a boundary that is used to define and resolve names contained in it.

Based on the DNS namespace standards specified in Request for Comments (RFC) 1034 and 1035, the Active Directory namespace is interoperable with the Internet and with any other standard TCP/IP network. These standards are key to the ability of Windows 2000 and Active Directory to provide TCP/IP network services (see Figure 12.1).

Figure 12.1 This is an example of a contiguous namespace.

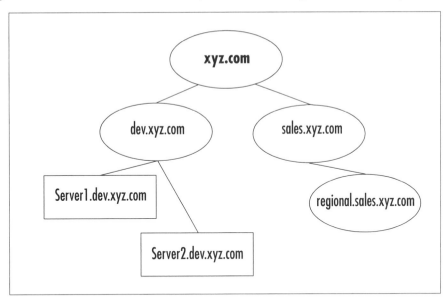

Two types of namespaces can be used: contiguous and disjoint-ed. These also reflect the difference between a Windows 2000 tree and forest. A tree is a contiguous namespace, which consists of a hierarchy of parent and related children domains. A child domain has a direct relationship to its parent. For example, dev.xyz.com is a child domain of xyz.com. Contiguous namespaces define trees in Windows 2000. A forest in Windows 2000 is a disjointed namespace, which is a series of domains that are not directly related. For exam-ple, dev.xyz.com is not directly related to abc.com. These two domains are separate, and a forest must be formed in order to con-nect these two together by setting up bidirectional trust relation-ships. Although mostly a methodology, this concept is one of the most critical concepts in understanding and designing a Windows 2000 Active Directory infrastructure (see Figure 12.2).

Figure 12.2   This is an example of a disjointed namespace.

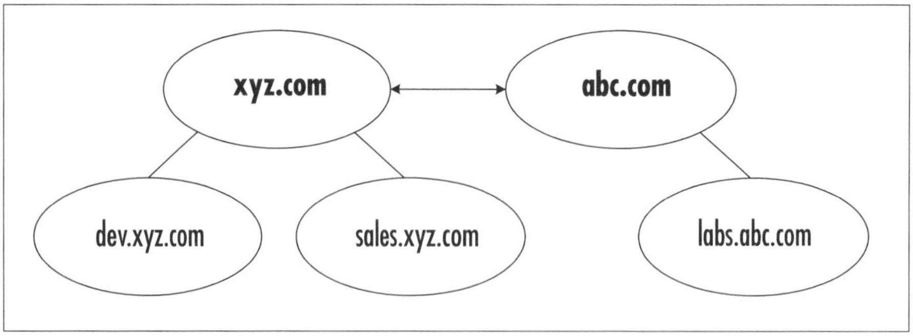

Naming Conventions

Within Windows 2000, every object is identified by a name. Naming conventions have been created to provide a uniform method of identifying a resource. In addition, depending upon the object or its role, a particular item may have more than one name. For example, John Doe may also be known as JohnD. This may be because his full name is John Doe, but his network logon name is JohnD. Several different naming conventions are used within Windows 2000 and Active Directory. To understand each object and how it pertains to other resources, you must understand these naming schemes. The naming schemes are:

- Distinguished Name
- Relative Distinguished Name
- Globally Unique Identifier (GUID)
- User Principal Name

Distinguished Names (DN) is a unique identifier for an object within Active Directory, such as a user or printer. The distinguished name provides the information required to allow a client to request resources. These names include the complete path through Active Directory, including the domain name. Distinguished names must all be unique as well. Because Active Directory uses these names to locate resources within the directory service, no two names can be identical (see Table 12.1).

Table 12.1   Attributes Used in Distinguished Names

Attribute	Description
CN	Common Name
DC	Domain Component
OU	Organizational Unit

Here is an example of distinguished name for John Doe located in the sales OU in the xyz.com domain.

```
CN=John Doe,OU=sales,DC=xyz,DC=com
```

The Relative Distinguished Name (RDN) is used to locate resources based on a particular attribute. For example, you may want to know only whether a JohnD user id exists. This gives you the ability to search throughout the directory for information when the DN is unknown or has been modified. Also, you can have duplicate Relative Unique Identifiers, but only if they do not reside within the same organizational unit. In other words, two JohnD users can exist, but not within the same OU, because if this object is placed within a separate OU, the DN will be different for each object (see Figure 12.3).

Figure 12.3   This illustrates the difference between DN and RDN.

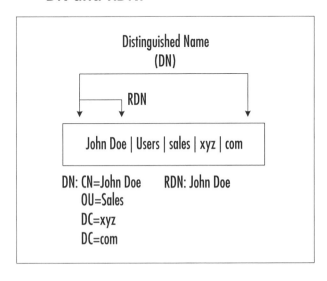

There are two other name types. The first is the Globally Unique Identifier (GUID), which is a 128-bit identifier that is used to identify an object within Active Directory. The GUID is assigned once the object is created and will remain the same if the object is moved or renamed. This allows services to find an object even if its name or attributes are modified. The second type is the User Principal Name (UPN), which is a user-friendly name for an object using the DNS name convention, which is similar to an e-mail address. This makes it easier to find an object located within Active Directory. For example, John Doe may have a UPN of JohnD@xyz.com.

Schema

Within a directory service, rules must be used to define the objects that are available, the attributes of those objects, and how they are applied. This is the job of the schema within Active Directory. The schema contains definitions of the classes, attributes, and their properties, such as the user object with the description attribute. When Active Directory is first installed, a default schema is used. Examples of schema objects included are users, computers, and groups. There are two types of schema objects: attributes and classes. Each is used and defined differently within Active Directory.

An attribute is a field that can contain information about an object such as group name or user e-mail address. These fields can also be applied to multiple classes while being defined only once. Object classes define the objects that can be created with Active Directory. For example, a user account or group account is a class of object. Every object that is created within Active Directory is known as an instance. The attributes for an object are used to define information about them such as name, location, or phone number. Therefore, a class is a collection of multiple attributes. To apply these terms, a user account named JoeS is a single instance of the object class User with attributes including the name JoeS.

The domain controller, acting as the schema master, controls the schema content. By default, this is the first Windows 2000 domain controller installed. A copy of the schema is replicated to all other domain controllers within the forest to maintain consistency. The schema can be modified, but this should only be done after extensive testing. For example, a new class object or attribute for an existing class object can be added. Although Active Directory does not support deleting schema extensions, objects can be marked as deactivated. Extending the schema can have disastrous affects on the Active Directory, as this will modify the rules by which it works. Be sure to perform extensive testing before modifying the schema in any way. Microsoft provides an application-programming interface (API) known as Active Directory Services Interface (ADSI). This tool set is designed to provide an interface with Active Directory that developers can implement without needidng to understand how the interface works technically.

Global Catalog

With any directory, a fast and efficient way to locate resources is required. For example, users who are looking for a printer probably will not want to trudge through the entire network or wait a long time to find what they are looking for. Active Directory uses a global catalog server to provide the ability to index items located within the network. The global catalog is designed to provide information about resources located within the directory as efficiently as possible, which speeds the service to the end user requesting network services. In addition, since a global catalog server maintains information about all domains included within a forest, a server within the domain from which a request originates can answer a query. For example, a user located in domain1 can provide information about a resource located in domain2 without having to cross domain boundaries. Any domain controller can be configured as a global catalog server to fulfill your organization's requirements.

By default, the first domain controller installed in a forest is configured as a global catalog server. The global catalog is created and maintains information on all objects located within its domain and a partial set of information on objects in all other domains. This allows quick and efficient query results for cross-domain lookups. The global catalog is used to provide two main roles:

- Gives the ability to locate objects anywhere within the forest.
- Provides universal group membership to domain controllers for a logon request.

When the logon authentication process begins, the global catalog server provides universal group membership to the domain controller being used, so user authentication can occur anywhere within the forest. If a global catalog server is unavailable, users will not be allowed access to network resources, but will be allowed to log on only locally. The role of global catalog server can be shared with any domain controller, which happens when only one domain controller exists within a domain.

NOTE

Although users are unable to access network resources without a global catalog server, domain administrators are still able to log on the Windows 2000 network. It is also recommended that you place global catalog servers close to users, to provide efficient service.

This is how the global catalog server role is added or removed on a domain controller:

1. Select Start | Programs | Administrative Tools | Active Directory Sites and Services.
2. Expand the site name followed by the Servers container and then the server name to configure.
3. Highlight the NTDS domain controller properties, right-click the object, and select Properties.

4. Figure 12.4 displays the available options. Select or deselect the check box for Global Catalog to determine the domain controller's role.

Figure 12.4   Select this check box to provide another global catalog server.

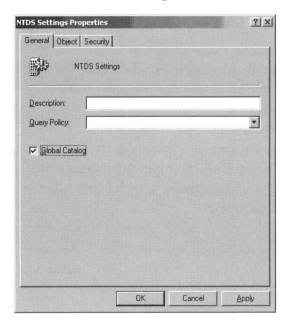

5. Select OK or Apply to approve the modification.

Replication

To enable users to use services such as the directory and global catalog, the directory information must remain consistent throughout all servers that store this data. To accomplish this consistency, a replication strategy has been defined to maintain consistent replicas of directory services data such as the directory store and global catalog. This allows anyone to request a directory resource from anywhere within the network of domains and forests. For example, if User A adds the ability for User B to access a resource, this information must be replicated to the domain controller responding to

User B. Otherwise, User B would not have the ability to access this resource without making the change on both computers.

Although this information must remain consistent, the amount of network traffic required must be monitored as well. If updates occur constantly, an entire network can be consumed quickly. Replication should be monitored closely to control the amount of traffic that is being caused. Windows 2000 uses several techniques to optimize replication traffic. For example, Active Directory evaluates the network connections that are used and selects the most efficient. Also, any available multiple routes are used to provide fault tolerance and redundancy. One of the most effective optimization techniques is the replication of Delta information; in other words, only the changes to an object are replicated. For example, if JoeS changes his password, only that changed attribute is replicated and not the entire object. This can make a dramatic difference for your local and wide-area network.

Two types of site replication can occur. Intrasite communication occurs among all domain controllers located within the same site, and intersite communication occurs between two sites configured with a site link. Two communication methods, IP and SMTP, are available for site links. Intrasite links are automatically generated and maintained, but intersite links must be manually created. Intrasite links are maintained by Active Directory to optimize replication. By default, two links to every domain controller are created to eliminate a single link failure. This replication strategy is continually monitored and updated. For example, when a new domain controller is installed in a site, the replication topology is recalculated to provide the most efficient network replication.

The Global Knowledge Advantage

Global Knowledge has a global delivery system for its products and services. The company has 28 subsidiaries, and offers its programs through a total of 60+ locations. No other vendor can provide consistent services across a geographic area this large. Global Knowledge is the largest independent information technology education provider, offering programs on a variety of platforms. This enables our multi-platform and multi-national customers to obtain all of their programs from a single vendor. The company has developed the unique CompetusTM Framework software tool and methodology which can quickly reconfigure courseware to the proficiency level of a student on an interactive basis. Combined with self-paced and on-line programs, this technology can reduce the time required for training by prescribing content in only the deficient skills areas. The company has fully automated every aspect of the education process, from registration and follow-up, to "just-in-time" production of courseware. Global Knowledge through its Enterprise Services Consultancy, can customize programs and products to suit the needs of an individual customer.

Global Knowledge Classroom Education Programs

The backbone of our delivery options is classroom-based education. Our modern, well-equipped facilities staffed with the finest instructors offer programs in a wide variety of information technology topics, many of which lead to professional certifications.

Custom Learning Solutions

This delivery option has been created for companies and governments that value customized learning solutions. For them, our consultancy-based approach of developing targeted education solutions is most effective at helping them meet specific objectives.

Self-Paced and Multimedia Products

This delivery option offers self-paced program titles in interactive CD-ROM, videotape and audio tape programs. In addition, we offer custom development of interactive multimedia courseware to customers and partners. Call us at 1-888-427-4228.

Electronic Delivery of Training

Our network-based training service delivers efficient competency-based, interactive training via the World Wide Web and organizational intranets. This leading-edge delivery option provides a custom learning path and "just-in-time" training for maximum convenience to students.

Global Knowledge Courses Available

Microsoft
- Windows 2000 Deployment Strategies
- Introduction to Directory Services
- Windows 2000 Client Administration
- Windows 2000 Server
- Windows 2000 Update
- MCSE Bootcamp
- Microsoft Networking Essentials
- Windows NT 4.0 Workstation
- Windows NT 4.0 Server
- Windows NT Troubleshooting
- Windows NT 4.0 Security
- Windows 2000 Security
- Introduction to Microsoft Web Tools

Management Skills
- Project Management for IT Professionals
- Microsoft Project Workshop
- Management Skills for IT Professionals

Network Fundamentals
- Understanding Computer Networks
- Telecommunications Fundamentals I
- Telecommunications Fundamentals II
- Understanding Networking Fundamentals
- Upgrading and Repairing PCs
- DOS/Windows A+ Preparation
- Network Cabling Systems

WAN Networking and Telephony
- Building Broadband Networks
- Frame Relay Internetworking
- Converging Voice and Data Networks
- Introduction to Voice Over IP
- Understanding Digital Subscriber Line (xDSL)

Internetworking
- ATM Essentials
- ATM Internetworking
- ATM Troubleshooting
- Understanding Networking Protocols
- Internetworking Routers and Switches
- Network Troubleshooting
- Internetworking with TCP/IP
- Troubleshooting TCP/IP Networks
- Network Management
- Network Security Administration
- Virtual Private Networks
- Storage Area Networks
- Cisco OSPF Design and Configuration
- Cisco Border Gateway Protocol (BGP) Configuration

Web Site Management and Development
- Advanced Web Site Design
- Introduction to XML
- Building a Web Site
- Introduction to JavaScript
- Web Development Fundamentals
- Introduction to Web Databases

PERL, UNIX, and Linux
- PERL Scripting
- PERL with CGI for the Web
- UNIX Level I
- UNIX Level II
- Introduction to Linux for New Users
- Linux Installation, Configuration, and Maintenance

Authorized Vendor Training
Red Hat
- Introduction to Red Hat Linux
- Red Hat Linux Systems Administration
- Red Hat Linux Network and Security Administration
- RHCE Rapid Track Certification

Cisco Systems
- Interconnecting Cisco Network Devices
- Advanced Cisco Router Configuration
- Installation and Maintenance of Cisco Routers
- Cisco Internetwork Troubleshooting
- Designing Cisco Networks
- Cisco Internetwork Design
- Configuring Cisco Catalyst Switches
- Cisco Campus ATM Solutions
- Cisco Voice Over Frame Relay, ATM, and IP
- Configuring for Selsius IP Phones
- Building Cisco Remote Access Networks
- Managing Cisco Network Security
- Cisco Enterprise Management Solutions

Nortel Networks
- Nortel Networks Accelerated Router Configuration
- Nortel Networks Advanced IP Routing
- Nortel Networks WAN Protocols
- Nortel Networks Frame Switching
- Nortel Networks Accelar 1000
- Comprehensive Configuration
- Nortel Networks Centillion Switching
- Network Management with Optivity for Windows

Oracle Training
- Introduction to Oracle8 and PL/SQL
- Oracle8 Database Administration

Custom Corporate Network Training

Train on Cutting Edge Technology

We can bring the best in skill-based training to your facility to create a real-world hands-on training experience. Global Knowledge has invested millions of dollars in network hardware and software to train our students on the same equipment they will work with on the job. Our relationships with vendors allow us to incorporate the latest equipment and platforms into your on-site labs.

Maximize Your Training Budget

Global Knowledge provides experienced instructors, comprehensive course materials, and all the networking equipment needed to deliver high quality training. You provide the students; we provide the knowledge.

Avoid Travel Expenses

On-site courses allow you to schedule technical training at your convenience, saving time, expense, and the opportunity cost of travel away from the workplace.

Discuss Confidential Topics

Private on-site training permits the open discussion of sensitive issues such as security, access, and network design. We can work with your existing network's proprietary files while demonstrating the latest technologies.

Customize Course Content

Global Knowledge can tailor your courses to include the technologies and the topics which have the greatest impact on your business. We can complement your internal training efforts or provide a total solution to your training needs.

Corporate Pass

The Corporate Pass Discount Program rewards our best network training customers with preferred pricing on public courses, discounts on multimedia training packages, and an array of career planning services.

Global Knowledge Training Lifecycle

Supporting the Dynamic and Specialized Training Requirements of Information Technology Professionals

- Define Profile
- Assess Skills
- Design Training
- Deliver Training
- Test Knowledge
- Update Profile
- Use New Skills

Global Knowledge

Global Knowledge programs are developed and presented by industry professionals with "real-world" experience. Designed to help professionals meet today's interconnectivity and interoperability challenges, most of our programs feature hands-on labs that incorporate state-of-the-art communication components and equipment.

ON-SITE TEAM TRAINING

Bring Global Knowledge's powerful training programs to your company. At Global Knowledge, we will custom design courses to meet your specific network requirements. Call (919)-461-8686 for more information.

YOUR GUARANTEE

Global Knowledge believes its courses offer the best possible training in this field. If during the first day you are not satisfied and wish to withdraw from the course, simply notify the instructor, return all course materials and receive a 100% refund.

REGISTRATION INFORMATION

In the US:
call: (888) 762–4442
fax: (919) 469–7070
visit our website:
www.globalknowledge.com